The Socialist Market Economy in Asia

Arve Hansen · Jo Inge Bekkevold ·
Kristen Nordhaug
Editors

The Socialist Market Economy in Asia

Development in China, Vietnam and Laos

palgrave
macmillan

Editors
Arve Hansen
Centre for Development and the Environment
University of Oslo
Oslo, Norway

Jo Inge Bekkevold
Norwegian Institute for Defence Studies
Oslo, Norway

Kristen Nordhaug
Oslo Metropolitan University
Oslo, Norway

ISBN 978-981-15-6247-1 ISBN 978-981-15-6248-8 (eBook)
https://doi.org/10.1007/978-981-15-6248-8

This Palgrave Macmillan imprint is published by the registered company Springer Nature Singapore Pte Ltd.
The registered company address is: 152 Beach Road, #21-01/04 Gateway East, Singapore 189721, Singapore

Acknowledgments

The idea of this book took shape through the panel "Understanding the Socialist Market Economy: Development, Transformations and Contradictions in China, Vietnam and Laos" at the NORASIA VII conference organized by the Norwegian Network for Asian Studies at the University of Oslo in 2017. We would like to thank Kenneth Bo Nielsen for inviting us to set up a panel at the conference, as well as all the panel presenters and audience for stimulating discussions.

The editors would like to thank all the contributors for excellent work and great cooperation. We would also like to thank the anonymous referees for supporting the project and for providing useful and constructive feedback. And last, a big thank you to Sara Crowley-Vigneau and the excellent staff at Palgrave Macmillan for their support throughout the publishing process.

Oslo
April 2020

Arve Hansen
Jo Inge Bekkevold
Kristen Nordhaug

Contents

Notes on Contributors

Jo Inge Bekkevold is Senior Adviser at the Norwegian Institute for Defence Studies. Bekkevold is a former diplomat, serving in Beijing and Hanoi, and has worked as a trade analyst in China. He has published widely on Chinese politics and foreign policy as well as Asian security issues.

Robert Cole is a Doctoral candidate with the Department of Geography, National University of Singapore, and Research Associate with the Centre for Social Development Studies, Chulalongkorn University. His doctoral research explores interconnections between global agri-food production and agrarian change in Laos' northeast borderlands with Vietnam.

Kristin Dalen is a Researcher at the Fafo Institute for Labour and Social Research in Oslo, Norway. She is also a Ph.D. candidate at the Department for Comparative Politics at the University of Bergen. Her current research focuses on public perceptions of distribution, welfare schemes, and governance in contemporary China.

Thiem Hai Bui is the Director of Research Project Management of the Research Management Board at the Institute for Legislative Studies, National Assembly Standing Committee of Vietnam. His research focuses on civil society, constitutional politics, human rights, and electoral governance in Vietnam.

Arve Hansen is a Postdoctoral Fellow at Centre for Development and the Environment at the University of Oslo and coordinator of the Norwegian Network for Asian Studies. He has a decade of experience working in and on Vietnam and has published widely on development in the country.

Micah L. Ingalls, Ph.D. is a Senior Scientist at the Centre for Development and Environment of the University of Bern, Switzerland. Over the past two decades, he has worked at the interface of research and policy across Asia, focusing on natural resource governance, traditional and non-traditional security, and rural development.

Do Ta Khanh is the Director of the Centre for EU Studies at the Institute for European Studies (under Vietnam Academy of Social Sciences). With background in political economy, his research focuses on industrial policy in Europe and Vietnam, particularly the interaction between policy and the working class.

Hege Merete Knutsen is a Professor in Human Geography, Department of Sociology and Human Geography, University of Oslo. She works in the fields of Economic Geography (political economy), labour and development and has research and fieldwork experiences from a number of countries in the Global South and Global North.

Jonathan D. London is an Associate Professor of Political Economy at Leiden University's Institute for Area Studies. His recent publications include *Welfare and Inequality in Marketizing East Asia* (Palgrave, 2018), as well as numerous book chapters, and journal articles.

Kristen Nordhaug is a Professor of Development Studies at Oslo Metropolitan University. Nordhaug's research has focused on political and economic development in East and Southeast Asia, currently in China and Vietnam. He has previously worked on inter alia Taiwan's development model, the Asian financial crisis, and China's development model.

Stephan Ortmann is an Adjunct Assistant Professor in the Centre for China Studies of Chinese University of Hong Kong. He is the author of *Politics and Change in Singapore and Hong Kong: Containing Contention* (2010) and *Environmental Governance in Vietnam: Institutional Reforms and Failures* (2017).

Boike Rehbein is a full Professor of society and transformation in Asia and Africa at Humboldt University Berlin since 2009. His areas of specialization are social inequality, globalization, and Southeast Asia. He has published 24 books and around 100 articles.

List of Figures

List of Tables

PART I

The Socialist Market Economy: Ideology and Development

CHAPTER 1

Introducing the Socialist Market Economy

Jo Inge Bekkevold, Arve Hansen, and Kristen Nordhaug

China, Vietnam and Laos are three of the few remaining communist regimes in the world. They are also among the fastest growing economies in the world, and indeed have been for some time (IMF 2019a). The fact that three of the best growth performers in global capitalism are authoritarian states led by communist parties with socialism as official development goal is certainly worthy of further study. The three countries indeed claim to have found their own model of development combining a market economy with socialism, what we based on communist party rhetoric summarize here as 'the socialist market economy'. According to official definitions, this is not capitalism, but a more sustainable

J. I. Bekkevold
Norwegian Institute for Defence Studies, Oslo, Norway
e-mail: jib@ifs.mil.no

A. Hansen (✉)
Centre for Development and the Environment, University of Oslo, Oslo, Norway
e-mail: arve.hansen@sum.uio.no

K. Nordhaug
Oslo Metropolitan University, Oslo, Norway
e-mail: Kristen.Nordhaug@oslomet.no

A. Hansen et al. (eds.), *The Socialist Market Economy in Asia*,
https://doi.org/10.1007/978-981-15-6248-8_1

and socially just way of making a market economy work for national development and the improvement of living standards.

China and Vietnam are by now considered major development success stories. China needs little further introduction in this regard, as few countries have received more attention in the development literature over the past decades (Lardy 2014, 2019; Naughton and Tsai 2015; Lin 2011; Steinfeld 2000; Huang 2008; Pei 2006; Yang 2004). Extreme levels of growth over four decades have seen China emerge as a global economic superpower. Vietnam's rapid development has also received significant attention (Earl 2018; Hansen 2015; Hiep 2012; Gainsborough 2010; London 2009; Ohno 2009; Beresford 2008; Masina 2006; Van Arkadie and Mallon 2003; Fforde and de Vylder 1996). Some observers even expect that it will develop into a leading Southeast Asian economic power (World Bank 2020; Beeson and Hung Hung Pham 2012). Laos is in many ways a different story from its communist neighbours. It remains one of the least studied and least understood countries in Asia (Rigg 2012), despite a growing Laos development literature (e.g. Kenney-Lazar 2019; Cole and Rigg 2019; Baird 2018; Friis and Nielsen 2016; Dwyer et al. 2015). Furthermore, few would consider Laos a development success story and its decades of very high levels of economic growth has largely gone under the radar of outside observers.

High GDP growth is just one side of the story, however. Even more impressively, growth in the socialist market economies, particularly China and Vietnam, has been converted into poverty eradication at a speed possibly unprecedented anywhere in the world (Malesky and London 2014). While the rapid development certainly has led to increasingly unequal societies also in the socialist market economies, they do perform better than countries at a similar level of income per capita on a wide range of social and material development indicators. In fact, China, Vietnam and Laos are all among the top ten fastest climbers upwards the UN Human Development Index over the 1990–2015 period (UNDP 2016).

Given these development patterns, it is somewhat puzzling that the three countries have never been subject to thorough comparative analysis. Even China and Vietnam are rarely subject to such comparison (Malesky and London 2014; Womack 2006), although their development models and trajectories obviously share important traits. Laos is usually ignored altogether, and certainly not included in discussions of development in the two other socialist market economies. And, importantly, while many scholars have pointed out the discrepancy between official socialist ideology and developments on the ground (see London, this volume), no study has tried systematically to make sense of the model of the 'socialist market economy' that the three development success stories claim to be following.

This book thus sets out to fill an important lacuna in the literature, providing a comparative look at the development model of these three countries. With Xi Jinping at the 19th Party Congress in 2017 claiming that China is ready to take on the role as a model for other countries, it is now more relevant than ever to take a closer analytical look at the socialist market economy construct. During the global financial crisis in 2007–2009, Beijing refrained from engaging in the debate about whether the so-called *China Model* was a more sustainable and development-friendly model than the market-liberal *Washington Consensus*. The leadership of Xi Jinping is less modest. On several occasions, Xi has suggested that other developing countries can adopt China's growth model. In a world in dire need of new role models, can the Asian 'socialist market economies' provide a realistic alternative for other developing countries? If Beijing is now willing to put money and resources into 'exporting' its development model as part of an expanded south–south dialogue, an in-depth comparative examination of the socialist market economy models of China, Vietnam and Laos carries great significance.

We do not seek to elaborate or examine in depth the reasons for the relative success of the development models of China, Vietnam and Laos. Rather, the main purpose of the authors of this book is to further our understanding of what the socialist market economy construct is, in theory and practice. What features do the development models of China, Vietnam and Laos share and how do they differ? Are the developments in these three countries yet another example of Asian state-led developmentalism or something else completely?

Furthermore, are there any promises of more sustainable development models embedded in their nominally socialist projects? With all three countries increasingly integrated in the capitalist global economy, to what extent are these party states still pursuing a state-driven development? And how much socialism is actually left in these three countries beyond lofty party rhetoric? Finally, how has the state–society relationship developed; in terms of labour, social policies and equality, and what is the role of the emerging middle classes in these countries?

This introductory chapter briefly presents the main developments in China, Vietnam and Laos over the recent decades and their performance on economic and social indicators, and discusses to what extent they are 'development success stories'. It furthermore places these cases in the literature on development as well as in the contemporary world economy. It discusses the socialist market economy in relation to theories on the developmental state and other forms of state-led developmentalism, as well as in relation to regional economic integration and production networks. The chapter ends by outlining how the respective chapters in the book contribute to address the overarching issues in our analysis.

The Socialist Market Economies as Success Stories of Development

Despite significant local variation, China, Vietnam and Laos have overall all seen similar development trajectories, including experiments with planned economies, collectivization of agriculture and a wide range of social policies. Although these pre-reform developments are important to take into account for understanding later achievements, they all also have in common significant bursts in economic growth following market reforms. And although many major changes happened at earlier and later stages, the *Gaige kaifang* ('Reform and opening up') in China (1978/1979), *Doi moi* ('Renovation') in Vietnam (1986) and *Chin Thanakaan Mai* ('New Thinking') or 'New Economic Mechanism' in Laos (1986) represented the official start of transformations with vast consequences for domestic economies and the everyday lives of people.

During the three decades of 1989–2018 China had an average annual GDP per capita growth of 8.4%. This was the third fastest growth of the countries listed by the World Bank. Vietnam ranked as number five with 5.4% average growth, and Laos ranked as number six with 5.1% average growth.[1] With sustained very high growth rates over a period of three decades, coupled with rapid growth of industrial productivity, China has become the world's second largest economy and the largest manufacturer (Naughton 2018). Vietnam and Laos had somewhat lower,

[1] Calculated based on data.worldbank.org.

Fig. 1.1 Annual GDP per capita growth: China 1978–2017, Laos/Vietnam: 1985–2017 (*Source* data.worldbank.org)

but still impressive growth rates (Fig. 1.1). Vietnam has been transformed from one of Asia's poorest countries to an 'emerging economy' (Hansen 2015). Vietnam and Laos are now both classified as lower middle-income countries, according to the World Bank classification, although Laos is still also on the UN's list of the world's least developed countries. China is classified as an upper middle-income country (World Bank 2018a).[2] It took South Korea and Taiwan, widely regarded as the two most impressive success stories in terms of economic development, 19 years to grow from lower middle income to upper middle income. It took China only 17 years to achieve the same, in 2009.

Although growth somewhat slowed down in the 2010s, they maintained comparatively high growth levels (IMF 2019a). According to the International Monetary Fund (IMF), China's GDP will continue growing

[2] For the 2019 fiscal year, low-income economies are defined as those with a GNI per capita of $995 or less in 2017; lower middle-income economies are those with a GNI per capita between $996 and $3895; upper middle-income economies are those with a GNI per capita between $3896 and $12,055; high-income economies are those with a GNI per capita of $12,056 or more.

at an annual rate of 5–6% over the 2020–2024 period, for Vietnam annual GDP growth is estimated to be 6.5%, for Laos 6–7% (IMF 2019a).

While the three countries have seen relatively similar growth trends, however, they differ significantly on other development indicators. Take poverty reduction, where China and Vietnam represent a kind of uncrowned world champions (Banik and Hansen 2016). China's success story is now estimated to have lifted 800 million people out of absolute poverty since the market reforms began (World Bank 2018b), while Vietnam's development has seen more than 45 million people escape absolute poverty in the first two decades of the 2000s alone (World Bank 2020). Laos, on the other hand, has seen significant poverty reduction, but nothing resembling its neighbours. All three countries have achieved impressive results on a wide range of development indicators (Table 1.1). Inequality has increased in all three countries during the reform period. China's average Gini coefficient for the 2010–2015 period at 42.2 was slightly higher than that of the United States, which has the highest inequality of the OECD countries. Inequality was lower in Vietnam and

Table 1.1 Measuring development in the socialist market economy

	China 1990	*China 2017*	*Vietnam 1990*	*Vietnam 2017*	*Laos 1990*	*Laos 2017*
GDP/capita/PPP (current international $)	987	16,807	939	6775	1103	7023
Absolute poverty (% of pop below 1.90 USD)	66.6	0.7 (2015)	52.9 (1992)	2 (2016)	32.2 (1992)	22.7 (2012)
Human development index	0.502	0.752	0.475	0.694	0.400	0.601
Infant mortality (per 1000 live births)	42.1	8	37	16.7	106.1	48.6
Maternal mortality (per 100,000 live births) 2015 numbers	97	27	139	54	905	197
Literacy (adult total, ages 15 and above)	77.8	95 (2010)	87.6 (1989)	93.5 (2009)	60 (1995)	58 (2011)
Access to electricity (% of pop, 2016)	92.2	100	74.1	100	15.3	87.1

Source World Development Indicators and Human Development Index

Laos in the same 2010–2015 period, however, at about the same levels as the two EU countries Spain and Portugal (UNDP 2016: 206–207).

China and Vietnam represent development success stories to a large extent, Laos does to some extent. As is discussed in subsequent chapters, two significant exceptions in all three cases are political freedom and environmental sustainability. The next section discusses what a socialist market economy is, and how it has developed in these three countries.

What Is a Socialist Market Economy?

Even if Hsu (2011: 16) might be right in claiming that 'Economic-success-oriented pragmatism' trumps ideology in the socialist market economy, we should still take notice of the claim forwarded by the communist parties in China, Vietnam and Laos that they are adopting a form of socialist orientation in their policies. Let us first look at how the socialist market economy model is presented in the official rhetoric in the three countries.

The regimes in all three countries in different ways refer to a combination of socialism and market economy, but often using different terms. In China it is usually referred to 'socialism with Chinese characteristics', in Vietnam a 'market economy with socialist orientation' or 'socialist-oriented market economy'. In China and Laos the term 'socialist market economy' is also used, something that is less common in Vietnam.

Party leader Jiang Zemin's report to the 14th National Congress of the Communist Party of China (CPC) in October 1992 was the first time the Chinese leadership publicly declared that the target of China's economic restructuring was a 'socialist market economy'. Jiang, however, clearly positioned the term 'socialist market economy' within the larger framework of 'building socialism with Chinese characteristics' introduced by Deng Xiaoping at the 12th Party Congress in 1982, and the purpose all along was to adopt elements of market economy to foster economic growth (Miller 2018; Gilley 1998). The content and interpretation of these two interlinked terms—'socialist market economy' and 'socialism with Chinese characteristics', have gradually evolved. In a speech at the 80th anniversary of the founding of the Chinese Communist Party (CCP) in 2001, Jiang Zemin added his 'Three Represents' doctrine, calling for private entrepreneurs to be admitted into the Party (Fewsmith 2003).

The latest political theory of 'Xi Jinping Thought on Socialism with Chinese Characteristics for a New Era' adopted at the 19th Party

Congress in 2017, incorporated into the Constitution of the Communist Party of China, is a continuation of Deng's legacy of 'building socialism with Chinese characteristics'. In his speech to the 19th Party Congress, Xi introduced a set of cardinal principles, among which were strengthening party authority and discipline, and to practice socialist core values, including Marxism. Nonetheless, in the same speech, Xi also emphasized the importance for China to develop the public and the non-public sector, to move Chinese industries up the global value chain, foster new growth areas, inspire and protect entrepreneurship, and to make China a country of innovators (Xinhua 2017). Important yardsticks within the Chinese socialist market economy construct are the two centenary goals of building a 'moderately well-off society' by 2021 (the anniversary of the founding of the CCP), and a 'modern socialist country' by the time of the People's Republic of China's 100th anniversary in 2049 (Miller 2018).

Vietnam officially adopted the socialist-oriented market economy at the 9th Party congress in 2001. In the 2013 amended constitution, this was inscribed in the following manner: 'The Vietnamese economy is a socialist-oriented market economy with multi-forms of ownership and multi-sectors of economic structure; the state economic sector plays the leading role'. The socialist market economy is something new, official rhetoric has it. This is not capitalism, the story goes, but rather the application of the market economy as a tool for development rather than a social system. In Vietnam, the model is seen as socialist because of ownership, organization of management and distribution. To quote the government-run Vietnam Law & Legal Forum (2015):

> The socialist-oriented market economy in Vietnam is a type of organization of the economy based on not only the principles and rules of a market economy but also the principles and characteristics of socialism shown in three aspects: ownership, organization of management and distribution.

The embrace of the market has all along been framed as a strategy to support national development. And while market reforms have deepened and also cadres often are involved in private businesses, and amid reports of party decay (Vu 2014), the leading role of the party remains unchallenged. This role was reaffirmed at the 12th Party Congress in Vietnam, when a new and ostensibly simpler, definition of the socialist-oriented market economy was used:

> an economy operating fully and synchronously according to the rule of a market economy while ensuring the socialist orientation suitable to each period of national development. It is a modern and internationally integrated market economy which is administered by a law-ruled socialist state and led by the Communist Party of Vietnam toward the goal of a rich people and a developed, democratic, equal and civilized society. (Vietnam Law & Legal Forum 2015)

The regime has in many ways grown 'business-friendly' (Reed 2019). For example, it has opened up for party membership for private entrepreneurs, and has a strong focus on stimulating investments from domestic and foreign private capital. At the same time, however, and as a useful reminder to anyone expecting political reforms in Vietnam, the regime also recently decided that private businesses need stronger party presence in the form of party cells (Vietnam News 2019). The constitutional ideology of Vietnam remains Marxism–Leninism combined with 'Ho Chi Minh Thought', and Vietnam is officially simultaneously both a socialist country and developing towards socialism.

In Laos there is less direct reference to a particular development model and what it might entail. But the most recent 'Five-year national socio-economic development plan' states as a goal that the country by 2030 'systematically follows a socialist market economy' (Ministry of Planning and Investment 2016: 86). Furthermore, the plan summarizes one of the main lessons learnt from macroeconomic management so far: '[s]ocio-economic development based on a market economy mechanism that is managed and regulated by the Government with a comprehensive system is a key for the development of socialist orientation' (Ministry of Planning and Investment 2016: 77).

Simultaneously, while noting the importance of socialism in practice, socialism is also the goal of development in Laos as well. As put in the five-year plan 2011–2015: 'For Lao PDR, the shift to industrialisation and modernisation is a way forward, and part of the development process and the only way to lift the country out its least developed country status and enter a socialist era' (Lao PDR, five-year plan 2011–2015). Similar statements are found in Chinese and Vietnamese state documents. Now, we turn from local conceptualizations of the 'socialist market economy' to trying to make sense of this particular development model in the development literature.

What Kind of Development Model?

There have been many attempts at defining China's development model, whether it is 'State Capitalism' (Naughton and Tsai 2015), 'Crony Capitalism' (Pei 2016), 'Sino-capitalism' (McNally 2012), 'capitalism with Chinese characteristics' (Huang 2008) or 'Beijing Consensus' (Ramo 2004), the latter representing an alternative to the more neoliberal 'Washington Consensus'. Arrighi (2007) has argued that China may soon be the kind of non-capitalist market economy that Adam Smith once described. Blank (2015) notes that the People's Republic of China may be a non-capitalist market alternative, albeit one that is hardly edifying for socialists. Others have observed that market reforms in China are leading towards a capitalist and foreign-dominated development path, with enormous social and political costs, both domestically in China as well as internationally (Hart-Landsberg and Burkett 2005). Vietnam's development model has been labelled as 'market-Leninism' (London 2017, this volume), 'state capitalism with a Leninist orientation' (Hansen 2015) and as yet another example of an Asian state developmentalism (Beeson and Pham 2012). At the same time, despite their stated socialist orientations, all three countries are frequently portrayed as both 'post-socialist' and neoliberal. The reason behind these quite different and often opposing labels may be the complexity and the many contradictions embedded in the socialist market economy.

While many developments in China, as well as in Vietnam and Laos, can be labelled as neoliberal (see for example Kenney-Lazar 2019; Schwenkel and Leshkowich 2012; Nonini 2008), such as for example the privatization of public services, labelling the 'socialist market economy' as neoliberal is in many ways a stretch (Weber 2018). Although all three countries have clearly moved away from the planned economy and are both decentralizing and deregulating the economy, the states in different ways still have a strong hand in the economy, and the ruling parties are involved in every sector of society. For example, despite the rise of private business in China (Lardy 2014; Tsai 2007), state-owned banks continue to favour state-owned enterprises (SOEs) above private enterprises (IMF 2019b), and even privatized SOE's continue to benefit from government support relative to private enterprises (Harrison et al. 2019). In addition, strategic industries in China remain firmly in the grasp of an 'elite empire of state-owned enterprises' (Naughton and Tsai 2015). Similar trends are obvious in Vietnam.

Many have compared China and Vietnam to the East Asian developmental states, some also refer to them as examples of developmental states (UNDP 2013). Others have argued they are in fact variations of neoliberalism (Harvey 2005), while others again locate them somewhere between developmental states and neoliberalism (Masina 2012; Hsu 2011). However, as Jonathan London discusses more in detail in his chapter in this volume, it is quite clear, that these countries do not represent just another example of the old East Asian success recipe of the developmental state (see Wade 2018 for a recent overview). It is not the strong developmental state as seen in for example South Korea that we see here, although they share some of the traits of long-term planning. In the mid-1990s, a few years after the launch of *doi moi*, it was observed that Vietnamese authorities had to strengthen their capacity to handle market economy reforms (Scholtes and Thanh 1996). Later, Gainsborough (2010) has argued that the Vietnamese state is strong in terms of policing society, but still weak when it comes to implementing economic development plans. Ohno (2009: 35) finds that Vietnam lacks clear strategies and action plans, the 'hallmark of East Asian industrialization', while Pincus (2015: 29) finds that the Vietnamese state 'did not withdraw but rather commercialized itself to take advantage of the opportunities associated with expanding markets', in the process leading to the breaking down of vertical authority relations and horizontal coordination. Hsu (2011) makes similar observations in China, finding that the 'central government's institutional capacity has been simply too weak to pursue the East Asian style of industrial policy' (5) and argues that 'The state's ultimate role [...] is to be comprehended as to nurture and accelerate marketization, liberalization, and privatization, rather than to replace them' (4). Thus, rather than a developmental state, he argues, China is a 'market-enhancing state' (Hsu 2011: 7).

Rather than industrial policy for developing home-grown manufacturing, the reliance on FDI is much higher in China and Vietnam than it was in the developmental states (Masina 2015; Hsu 2011), especially when it comes to exports. For instance, eight out of the top ten exporting firms in China in 2015 were foreign owned (Starrs 2018: 189). Vietnam's manufacturing sector is mainly driven by foreign direct investment (FDI), which accounts for close to 90% of the country's manufacturing exports (Eckardt et al. 2018). While state capacities may be lower than within the developmental states, and reliance on foreign direct investment is higher, the socialist market economies have to a considerable extent retained their control of 'the commanding heights of the economy'. In all three countries, the financial system is dominated by state-owned banks, and in spite of past and present privatization programmes, state-owned enterprises are still major players in their economies.

The introduction of market elements into the three communist states of China, Vietnam and Laos have been gradual, in contrast to the 'shock therapy' of market reforms unleashed in Russia and the Eastern European countries after the collapse of the Soviet Union (Naughton 2018; Pei 2006; Tompson 2002; Gerber and Hout 1998). It is argued that the evolutionary approach in general holds the better prospect of generating economic progress that will be sustained over the long term (Murrell 1992).[3] China's gradual approach to economic reforms is well-known (Naughton 2018; Vogel 2013), but the transition towards market economies have been gradual also in Laos and Vietnam (Chheang and Wong 2014; Guo 2006). Vietnam shifted towards a more market-based economy using a trial-and-error approach, with a gradual recognition of the important contribution of private initiative to economic development (Vandemoortele and Bird 2011), and it is argued that Vietnam's 'cautious and sequenced adoption of market institutions has brought more than two decades of impressive economic performance' (Busch 2017: 1).

Nevertheless, it is important to note that the gradual and evolutionary introduction of market reforms in China, Vietnam and Laos have not been linear. Instead of marching steadily towards more market and less state intervention, each country has faced crossroads where they have halted, turned or even reversed the process. For instance, the political turmoil in China in 1989 almost put an end to the economic reform process (Vogel 2013). The rapid liberalization and globalization of the world financial industry in the 1990s contributed to the Asian financial crisis in the late 1990s in unprepared emerging markets, leading to a growing degree of scepticism and debate about further market reforms in all the socialist' market economies (Wade 2004; Stiglitz and Yusuf 2001). Huang Yasheng (2008) has argued that policies facilitating an

[3] Alternative explanations have been presented, that the 'weighted combination' of macroeconomic and microeconomic reforms in China can be regarded as true 'shock therapy', while the Russian reforms despite initial macro-financial shock have been slow and inconsistent and, for that reason, less successful than in China (See Kazakevitch, Gennadi and Russell Smyth 2005. Gradualism Versus Shock Therapy: (Re)Interpreting the Chinese and Russian Experiences. *Asia Pacific Business Review* 11 (1): 69–81).

entrepreneurial spirit in rural China in the 1980s were reversed and overtaken by more urban-centred and state-controlled reforms in the 1990s. Private businesses have since flourished in China, and play a major role in China's economic growth (Lardy 2014). Still, it seems the state is striking back once more, as Xi Jinping lately has championed state-owned enterprises at the expense of private entrepreneurs (Lardy 2019). Throughout the reform process in China, decentralization has often been followed by new forms of state interventions, in the market as well as in the society at large (Fewsmith 2016; Zheng and Weng 2016). Similar developments have been seen in Vietnam. While new and very powerful private corporations have emerged, these are in complex ways connected to the party state (see Reed 2019). Furthermore, despite the 'equitisation' of a large number of state-owned enterprises, they still dominate all sectors seen as strategic by the state. The party anyways often remains influential also in 'equitised' enterprises and, as pointed out above, the party is now seeking to strengthen its presence in the private sector. In other words, the 'socialist market economy' construct is not constant, or heading uninterrupted in one specific direction, but it is rather in constant flux, between more or less market, state and society, shaped by domestic and international events and trends.

Varieties of Socialist Market Economies

The aim of this book is not to argue that the 'socialist market economy' in China, Vietnam and Laos should be understood as one coherent model for development. We acknowledge the fundamental differences between these three countries, in terms of culture, history, the level of development, and certainly in terms of wealth and power. There is a vast literature discussing the role of culture on development (Woolcock 2014), and its impact on political systems and strategy (Schwartz 1996; Johnston 1995) as well as on economy and business systems (Whitley 1992). One of the most debated cultural legacies in terms of its potential impact on business and development is that of Confucianism (Hahm and Paik 2003; Kim 1997), and while China and Vietnam belong to the 'Confucian cultural sphere', Laos does not. Put simply, even though both Vietnam and Laos are considered Southeast Asian countries, Vietnam has culturally more in common with Northeast Asia, particularly China.

Moreover, the starting point of the comprehensive market reforms in China in the late 1970s differed from that of Laos and Vietnam, normally dated to 1986. When China launched the reform process, it already had a large, state-owned heavy industry sector, and it had developed local industry in rural centres in the 1970s (Naughton 2018). In contrast, the market reforms of Vietnam emerged from economic crisis. Vietnam was reunified in 1975–1976 after independence wars with France, a long period of North–South separation and what is known in Vietnam as 'the American War'. Vietnam did not have any significant manufacturing base prior to the market reforms. Heavy-handed efforts to integrate the previous non-communist South into the planned economy failed. Diplomatic isolation, economic sanctions, declining foreign aid and the high costs of Vietnam's occupation of Cambodia made the situation worse (Fforde and de Vylder 1996; Fforde 1999). Laos faced an even graver economic crisis than Vietnam in 1987–1988. Like in Vietnam, the economy was weakened by war before the communist Pathet Lao seized power in 1975. The new socialist economy struggled with failed efforts at Soviet-style economic planning and economic socialization along with diplomatic isolation, sanctions and declining aid (Rosser 2006).

Vietnam and China were integrated into the regional 'Flying Geese' order of regional export-oriented manufacturing production. Foreign investors from previous 'generations' of industrializing countries in the region, such as Japan and the 'East Asian NICs' (Taiwan, South Korea, Hong Kong and Singapore) invested in labour-intensive manufacturing in new generations, mainly for exports to Western markets. The initial positions of China and Vietnam in this regional order were relatively similar, but China was to a larger extent than Vietnam able to improve its position in the regional production hierarchy through economic upgrading of its export-manufacturing industry (Naughton 2018; Masina 2015; Masina and Cerimele 2018). Unlike China, Vietnam also relied on foreign earnings from agricultural exports and tourism.

In contrast, the small population and landlocked position of Laos were major impediments to industrialisation by import substitution as well as by export orientation. Its integration into the regional economy from the 1990s on was characterized by resource-based exports, including hydropower energy to neighbour countries, coffee and wood products. The tourist industry of Laos is also on the rise (Asian Development Bank 2017).

In result, there are significant differences in the current structures of their economies. China and Vietnam have maintained a focus on industry with export manufacturing sectors that are strongly integrated into the international economy. Laos diverted from that path, and has instead developed a highly extractivist economy based on natural resources. In addition, there are also great variations in development and economic structures within each of the three countries. China's export manufacturing has mainly been located in the southern coastal provinces, while its western interior has lagged behind in terms of economic growth. In Vietnam, the Mekong Delta region has been more entrepreneurial and private enterprise-based than the more state-controlled Red River Delta in the north. Nonetheless, despite these national and local variations within the 'socialist market economy' we find that a comparative look at these three countries and their development model can provide us with useful insight.

Making Sense of the Socialist Market Economy: Outline of the Book

The book consists of four main parts. Part I considers the socialist market economy as a development model, and includes this introductory chapter. In the following chapter, Jo Inge Bekkevold puts our cases into an international context, considering how the international level has shaped economic governance and development in China, Vietnam and Laos. Following that, Jonathan London argues China and Vietnam can be understood as varieties of 'Market Leninism'. The two countries, he argues, exhibit social relational and institutional attributes that are distinctive in relation to all other actually existing varieties of capitalism, and can be understood as distinctive kinds of social formations defined by political settlements founded on the wedding of globally linked markets with Leninist political institutions.

Part II of the book zooms in on state and market relations in the socialist market economies and implications for economic and environmental governance. China, Vietnam and Laos have within the frame of 2–3 decades gone through rapid shifts in their respective economic models. This comprehensive and rapid transformation of their respective economies—although to different degrees—challenges the regulatory apparatus in each country to adapt to new requirements, and raises important questions with regard to the role of the state and the market in developmental states. Bui Hai Thiem analyses the party state from a governance perspective and how the concept of the socialist market economy creates tensions and contradictions. First providing an overview of the development of the party state in China and Vietnam, the chapter proceeds to consider some of its key institutional features and challenges, as well as its prospects for future survival. In their chapter, Hege Merete Knutsen and Do Ta Khanh consider the reforms of state-owned enterprises in Vietnam. Shedding light on contradictions between the Vietnamese socialist ideology and the market imperative and international pressure the Vietnamese economy is subject to as a global player, the chapter focuses mainly on the new phase of SOE reforms starting around 2016. Robert Cole and Micah L. Ingalls then take us to the countryside. Rural development is deeply rooted in the revolutionary origins of the socialist market economies. This chapter considers the cases of Vietnam and Laos, and analyses how rural development fares in the new market economy and the regimes' focus on 'green growth'. Focusing on social and environmental sustainability, the chapter explores the new rural development dynamics in the context of a socialist alliance ideologically founded on bringing about equality of life opportunity to the many, but more often in practice skewed towards opportunistic gain for the few. In his chapter, Stephan Ortmann investigates the Vietnamese party state's attempts to handle mounting environmental problems. Vietnam's authorities have cooperated with international organizations and NGOs to develop environmental political programmes and legislation. However, implementation of policies and legislation is poor as the government's capacity is limited and the authoritarian party state pursues an ineffective top-down approach to environmental governance.

Part III focuses on state and society relations, investigating the social changes and continuations within the processes of rapid economic development in China, Vietnam and Laos. If, as the official story goes, the aim is to construct a socialist society using the market economy as a tool, questions of class, inequality and welfare are obviously fundamental to the socialist market economy. But while the three countries tend to outperform countries at similar income levels on social and material development indicators, social polarization, labour conflicts and dramatic inequalities in income, welfare and access to services are also a central part of contemporary development in these three countries. These trends raise crucial questions concerning both the credibility and the sustainability of the socialist market economy.

Arve Hansen focuses on the rapidly expanding middle classes in China and Vietnam. The chapter launches the term 'consumer socialism' to capture developments in these two countries, and studies the socialist middle classes through the particular political-economic contexts that have fostered them as well as the consumption patterns that define them. In doing so, it seeks to understand what consumer socialism is, how it fits into the visions of the socialist market economy, and whether consumer socialism is something different from the capitalist consumer society. Kristen Nordhaug looks at labour conflicts in China and Vietnam, focusing especially on export-manufacturing centres located in the south of the two countries. While sharing many similarities, such as high prevalence of unskilled labour and party-state-controlled labour unions, Nordhaug finds that strike frequency is significantly higher in Vietnam than in China. The chapter considers the possible explanations for this difference, looking at work organization, living arrangements, labour legislation and governance responses to collective labour demands. In the subsequent chapter, Kristin Dalen zooms in on Chinese social policy and the attempts to build a new welfare state. Approaching these changes in the context of Xi Jinping's 'core socialist values', Dalen considers systems of insurance, pensions and basic education, locating both achievements and challenges. The chapter then provides possible lessons for the development of welfare states in the two other socialist market economies. All the chapters to some extent touch on the contradictions involved in introducing capitalist logics to achieve socialism. Boike Rehbein argues that in Laos only a small part of the elite has truly embraced capitalism while a somewhat larger share still conforms with old socialist values. The majority of the population, however, adheres to lifestyles and livelihood strategies preceding the introduction of both socialism and capitalism to the country. Rehbein studies how the rapid spread of the spirit of capitalism, also within the party leadership itself, is beginning to weaken the control by the party and what the consequences of this might be.

The fourth and last part of the book draws on the many different perspectives presented in the different chapters to assess the development model of the socialist market economy. More than a mere summary, the chapter aims to answer some of the fundamental questions and issues raised by developments in China, Vietnam and Laos over the past three or four decades. Quite simply, yet ambitiously, it tries to make sense of the socialist market economy.

References

Arrighi, Giovanni. 2007. *Adam Smith in Beijing: Lineages of the Twenty-First Century*. London and New York: Verson Press.

Asian Development Bank. 2017. *Lao PDR: Accelerating Structural Transformation for Inclusive Growth*. Manila: Asian Development Bank.

Baird, Ian G. 2018. Secrecy, Falsification and Information Management and Control: The Party and State of the Lao People's Democratic Republic. *Journal of Contemporary Asia* 8 (5): 739–760.

Banik, Dan, and Arve Hansen. 2016. The Frontiers of Poverty Reduction in Emerging Asia. *Forum for Development Studies* 43 (1): 47–68. https://doi.org/10.1080/08039410.2015.1134646.

Beeson, M., and Hung Hung Pham. 2012. Developmentalism with Vietnamese Characteristics: The Persistence of State-led Development in East Asia. *Journal of Contemporary Asia* 42 (4): 539–559.

Beresford, M. 2008. Doi Moi in Review: The Challenges of Building Market Socialism in Vietnam. *Journal of Contemporary Asia* 38 (2): 221–243.

Blank, Gary. 2015. *Is the East Still Red? Socialism and the Market in China*. Alresford: Zero Books.

Busch, Matthew. 2017. The Missing Middle: A Political Economy of Economic Restructuring in Vietnam. Analysis, December, Lowy Institute, Sydney.

Chheang, Vannarith, and Yushan Wong. 2014. Cambodia-Laos-Vietnam: Economic Reforms and Sub-regional Integration. *Kyoto Sangyo University of Economic Review* No. 1 (March): 225–254.

Cole, Robert, and Jonathan Rigg. 2019. Lao Peasants on the Move: Pathways of Agrarian Change in Laos. *The Australian Journal of Anthropology* 30 (2): 160–180.

Dwyer, Michael B., Micah L. Ingalls, and Ian G. Baird. 2015. The Security Exception: Development and Militarization Laos's Protected Areas. *Geoforum* 69: 207–217.

Earl, Catherine (ed.). 2018. *Mythbusting Vietnam: Facts, Fictions, Fantasies*. Copenhagen: NIAS Press.

Eckardt, Sebastian, Deepak Mishra, and Viet Tuan Dinh. 2018. Vietnam's Manufacturing Miracle: Lessons for Developing Countries, April 17, Brookings Institution. https://www.brookings.edu/blog/future-development/2018/04/17/vietnams-manufacturing-miracle-lessons-for-developing-countries/.

Fewsmith, Joseph. 2003. Studying the Three Represents. *China Leadership Monitor*, Issue 8, Fall, Hoover Institution.

Fewsmith, Joseph. 2016. The Challenges of Stability and Legitimacy. In *China in the Era of Xi Jinping: Domestic and Foreign Policy Challenges*, ed. Robert S. Ross and Jo Inge Bekkevold. Washington, DC: Georgetown University Press.

Fforde, Adam. 1999. From Plan to Market: The Economic Transition in Vietnam and China Compared. In *Transforming Asian Socialism: China and Vietnam Compared*, ed. Anita Chan et al., 43–72. Landham, Boulder and New York: Rowman & Littlefield.

Fforde, Adam, and Stefan de Vylder. 1996. *From Plan to Market: The Economic Transition in Vietnam*. Boulder, CO: Westview Press.

Friis, Cecilie, and Jonas Østergaard Nielsen. 2016. Small-Scale Land Acquisitions, Large-Scale Implications: Exploring the Case of Chinese Banana Investments in Northern Laos. *Land Use Policy* 57: 117–129. https://doi.org/10.1016/j.landusepol.2016.05.028.

Gainsborough, M. 2010. *Vietnam: Rethinking the State*. London: Zed Books.

Gerber, Theodore P., and Michael Hout. 1998. More Shock Than Therapy: Market Transition, Employment, and Income in Russia, 1991–1995. *American Journal of Sociology* 104 (1) (July): 1–50.

Gilley, Bruce. 1998. *Tiger on the Brink: Jiang Zemin and China's New Elite*. Berkeley: University of California Press.

Guo, Sujian. 2006. *The Political Economy of Asian Transition from Communism*. Aldershot: Ashgate.

Hahm, C., and W. Paik. 2003. Legalistic Confucianism and Economic Development in East Asia. *Journal of East Asian Studies* 3 (3): 461–491.

Hansen, Arve. 2015. The Best of Both Worlds? The Power and Pitfalls of Vietnam's Development Model. In *Emerging Economies and Challenges to Sustainability: Theories, Strategies, Local Realities*, ed. Arve Hansen and Ulrikke Bryn Wethal. Oxon: Routledge.

Harrison, Ann, Marshall Meyer, Peichun Wang, Linda Zhao, and Minyuan Zhao. 2019. Can a Tiger Change Its Stripes? Reform of Chinese State-Owned Enterprises in the Penumbra of the State. NBER Working Papers 25475, National Bureau of Economic Research, Inc.

Hart-Landsberg, Martin, and Paul Burkett. 2005. *China and Socialism: Market Reforms and Class Struggle*. New York: Monthly Review Press.

Harvey, David. 2005. *A Brief History of Neoliberalism*. Oxford: Oxford University Press.

Hiep, Le Hong. 2012. Performance-Based Legitimacy: The Case of the Communist Party of Vietnam and Doi Moi. *Contemporary Southeast Asia* 34 (2): 145–172.

Hsu, S. Philip. 2011. In Search of China's Development Model: Beyond the Beijing Consensus. In *In Search of China's Development Model: Beyond the Beijing Consensus*, ed. S. Philip Hsu, Yu-Shan Wu, and Suisheng Zhao, Oxon: Routledge.

Huang, Yasheng. 2008. *Capitalism with Chinese Characteristics: Entrepreneurship and the State*. Cambridge: Cambridge University Press.

IMF. 2019a. *IMF World Economic Outlook*. Database October 2019, International Monetary Fund. www.imf.org.

IMF. 2019b. *People's Republic of China 2019 Article IV Consultation*, IMF Country Report No. 19/266, August. https://www.imf.org.

Johnston, Alastair Ian. 1995. *Cultural Realism: Strategic Culture and Grand Strategy in Chinese History*. Princeton: Princeton University Press.

Kenney-Lazar, M. 2019. Neoliberalizing Authoritarian Environmental Governance in (Post)Socialist Laos. *Annals of the American Association of Geographers* 109 (2): 338–348.

Kim, Kyong-Dong. 1997. Confucianism, Economic Growth and Democracy. *Asian Perspective* 21 (2), Special Issue on APEC (Fall), 77–97.

Lardy, Nicholas R. 2014. *Markets Over Mao: The Rise of Private Business in China*. Washington, DC: Peterson Institute for International Economics.

Lardy, Nicholas R. 2019. *The State Strikes Back: The End of Economic Reform in China?* Washington, DC: Peterson Institute for International Economics.

Lin, Justin Yify. 2011. *Demystifying the Chinese Economy*. Cambridge: Cambridge University Press.

London, J. 2009. Viet Nam and the Making of Market-Leninism. *The Pacific Review* 22 (3): 375–399.

London, J.D. 2017. Varieties of States, Varieties of Political Economy: China, Vietnam and the Making of Market-leninism. In *Asia After the Developmental State*, ed. Toby Carroll and Darryl S.L. Jarvis, 388–428. Cambridge: Cambridge University Press.

McNally, Christopher A. 2012. Sino-Capitalism: China's Reemergence and the International Political Economy. *World Politics* 64(4): 741–776. https://doi.org/10.1017/S0043887112000202.

Malesky, Edmund, and Jonathan London. 2014. The Political Economy of Development in China and Vietnam. *Annual Review of Political Science* 17: 395–419.

Masina, P. 2006. *Vietnam's Development Strategies*. Oxon, UK and New York: Routledge.

Masina, Pietro. 2012. Vietnam Between Developmental State and Neoliberalism: The Case of the Industrial Sector. In *Developmental Politics in Transition: The Neoliberal Era and Beyond*, ed. Kyung-Sup Chang, Ben Fine, and Linda Weiss, 188–210. London: Palgrave Macmillan.

Masina, Pietro. 2015. Miracles or Uneven Development? Asia in the Contemporary World Economy. In *Emerging Economies and Challenges to Sustainability: Theories, Strategies, Local Realities*, ed. A. Hansen and U. Wethal. London: Routledge.

Masina, Pietro, and Michela Cerimele. 2018. Patterns of Industrialisation and the State of Industrial Labour in Post-WTO Accession Vietnam. *European Journal of East Asian Studies* 17 (2): 289–323.

Miller, Alice L. 2018. Only Socialism Can Save China: Only Xi Jinping Can Save Socialism. *China Leadership Monitor*, Issue 56, Spring, Hoover Institution.

Ministry of Planning and Investment. 2016. 8th Five-Year National Socio-Economic Development Plan (2016–2020). Vientiane: Ministry of Planning and Investment.

Murrell, P. 1992. Evolutionary and Radical Approaches to Economic Reform. *Economics of Planning* 25: 79–95. https://urldefense.proofpoint.com/v2/url?u=https-3A__doi.org_10.1007_BF00366291&d=DwIFAg&c=vh6FgFnduejNhPPD0fl_yRaSfZy8CWbWnIf4XJhSqx8&r=2NyvwAEuxYghjumEQNU7rXHCfynvo0sefLW8zUC85RDHSERDFBIJtVZc_j5F8pcl&m=2S5YR6a8-m5wdQYGpqdPpd5e-U0BJ4qwIN363Lh5zps&s=JBI7cFDnX6y3jjMa6Pn3FvXw1BZr_QOFgc9Ca-NcaKA&e.

Naughton, Barry. 2018. *The Chinese Economy: Adaptation and Growth*. Cambridge, MA: MIT Press.

Naughton, Barry, and Kellee S. Tsai. 2015. *State Capitalism, Institutional Adaptation, and the Chinese Miracle*. Cambridge: Cambridge University Press.

Nonini, Donald. 2008. Is China Becoming Neoliberal? *Critique of Anthropology* 28 (2): 145–176.

Ohno, K. 2009. Avoiding the Middle-Income Trap: Renovating Industrial Policy Formation in Vietnam. *ASEAN Economic Bulletin* 26 (1): 25–43.

Pei, Minxin. 2006. *China's Trapped Transition: The Limits of Developmental Autocracy*. Cambridge: Harvard University Press.

Pei, Minxin. 2016. *China's Crony Capitalism: The Dynamics of Regime Decay*. Cambridge: Harvard University Press.

Pincus, Jonathan. 2015. Why Doesn't Vietnam Grow Faster? State Fragmentation and the Limits of Vent For Surplus Growth. *Journal of Southeast Asian Economies*, 32 (1): 26–51.

Ramo, Joshua Cooper. 2004. *The Beijing Consensus*. London: Foreign Affairs Policy Centre.

Reed, John. 2019. The Rise and Rise of a Vietnamese Corporate Empire. *Financial Times*, June 27. https://www.ft.com/content/84323c32-9799-11e9-9573-ee5cbb98ed36.

Rigg, Jonathan. 2012. *Living With Transition in Laos*. New York: Routledge. Northamption, MA, USA: Edward Elgar.

Rosser, Andrew. 2006. Lao People's Democratic Republic. *IDS Bulletin* 37 (2): 27–39.

Scholtes, Philippe R., and Hai Nguyen Thanh. 1996. Prospects for Industrial Development in the Red River Delta (Viet Nam): A Case-Study. In *Industrial Economics for Countries in Transition: Evidence from Eastern Europe and Asia Pacific*, ed. Philippe R. Scholtes. Cheltenham: Edward Elgar.

Schwartz, Benjamin I. 1996. *China and Other Matters*. Cambridge: Harvard University Press.

Schwenkel, C., and A.M. Leshkowich. 2012. How Is Neoliberalism Good to Think Vietnam? How Is Vietnam Good to Think Neoliberalism? *Positions: East Asia Cultures Critique* 20 (2): 379–401.
Starrs, Sean Kenji. 2018. Can China Unmake the American Making of Global Capitalism. *Socialist Register 2019*, 173–200. London: Merlin Press.
Steinfeld, Edward S. 2000. *Forging Reform in China: The Fate of State-Owned Industry*. Cambridge: Cambridge University Press.
Stiglitz, Joseph E., and Shahid Yusuf (eds.). 2001. *Rethinking the East Asian Miracle*. New York: Oxford University Press.
Tompson, William. 2002. Was Gaidar Really Necessary? Russian 'Shock Therapy' Reconsidered. *Problems of Post-Communism* 49 (4): 12–21.
Tsai, Kellee S. 2007. *Capitalism Without Democracy: The Private Sector in Contemporary China*. Ithaca: Cornell University Press.
UNDP. 2013. *Human Development Report 2013: The Rise of the South: Human Progress in a Diverse World*. New York, NY: United Nations Development Programme.
UNDP. 2016. *Human Development Report 2016: Human Development for Everyone*. New York, NY: United Nations Development Programme.
Van Arkadie, B., and R. Mallon. 2003. *Viet Nam: A Transition Tiger?* The Australian National University: Asia Pacific Press.
Vandemoortele, Milo, and Kate Bird. 2011. *Viet Nam's Progress on Economic Growth and Poverty Reduction*. London: Overseas Development Institute.
Vietnam Law & Legal Forum. 2015. New Concept of Socialist Market Economy Introduced, August 5. http://vietnamlawmagazine.vn/new-concept-of-socialist-oriented-market-economy-introduced-4582.html.
Vietnam News. 2019. More Party Cells Needed in VN's Private Businesses, March 28. https://vietnamnews.vn/politics-laws/507929/more-party-cells-needed-in-vns-private-businesses.html#HPKAYaU0mMs5HRfC.97.
Vogel, Ezra F. 2013. *Deng Xiaoping and the Transformation of China*. Cambridge: Harvard University Press.
Vu, Tuong. 2014. Persistance Amid Decay: The Communist Party of Vietnam at 83. In *Politics in Contemporary Vietnam: Party, State, and Authority Relations*, ed. Jonathan London. New York: Palgrave.
Wade, Robert. 2004. *Governing the Market. Economic Theory and the Role of Government in East Asia's Industrialization*, 2nd paperback ed. Princeton, NJ: Princeton University Press.
Wade, Robert. 2018. The Developmental State: Dead or Alive? *Development and Change* 49 (2): 518–546. https://doi.org/10.1111/dech.12381.
Weber, I.M. 2018. China and Neoliberalism: Moving Beyond the China Is/Is Not Neoliberal Dichotomy. In *SAGE Handbook of Neoliberalism*, ed. Cahill et al., 219–233. London: Sage.

Whitley, Richard. 1992. *Business Systems in East Asia: Firms, Markets and Societies*. London: Sage.
Womack, Brantly. 2006. *China and Vietnam: The Politics of Asymmetry*. New York: Cambridge University Press.
World Bank. 2018a. *World Bank Country and Lending Groups: Country Classification*. Retrieved 21 November 2018 from https://datahelpdesk.worldbank.org/knowledgebase/articles/906519.
World Bank. 2018b. The World Bank in China. https://www.worldbank.org/en/country/china/overview.
World Bank. 2020. *The World Bank in Vietnam: Overview*. Retrieved 6 April 2020 from https://www.worldbank.org/en/country/vietnam/overview.
Woolcock, Michael. 2014. Culture, Politics, and Development. Policy Research Working Paper 6939. Washington: The World Bank.
Xinhua. 2017. Full Text of Xi Jinping's Report at 19th CPC National Congress, November 3. Retrieved 20 November 2018 from http://www.xinhuanet.com/english/special/2017-11/03/c_136725942.htm.
Yang, Dali L. 2004. *Remaking the Chinese Leviathan: Market Transition and the Politics of Governance in China*. Stanford: Stanford University Press.
Zheng, Yongnian, and Weng Cuifen. 2016. The Development of China's Formal Political Structures. In *China in the Era of Xi Jinping: Domestic and Foreign Policy Challenges*, ed. Robert S. Ross and Jo Inge Bekkevold. Washington, DC: Georgetown University Press.

CHAPTER 2

The International Politics of Economic Reforms in China, Vietnam, and Laos

Jo Inge Bekkevold

Introduction

This chapter shows how the "socialist market economy" of China, Vietnam and Laos is shaped and formed in its unique way through influence from three fundamental premises in the study of international political economy. First, although the economic and political domains cannot be separated in any meaningful way, economic structures and processes are mostly the result of political interactions (Stubbs and Underhill 1994). The "socialist market economy" model confirms this premise. Despite great strides toward market economy, China, Vietnam, and Laos are governed by one-party systems with strong tool-kits regulating their respective economies, including with regard to managing trade and foreign capital.

The second premise is that the international and domestic levels of analysis are closely connected. Ultimately, decisions on economic policy rest with the institutions and agencies of respective states, but the international system shapes domestic policy-making in important ways (Waltz

J. I. Bekkevold (✉)
Norwegian Institute for Defence Studies, Oslo, Norway
e-mail: jib@ifs.mil.no

A. Hansen et al. (eds.), *The Socialist Market Economy in Asia*,
https://doi.org/10.1007/978-981-15-6248-8_2

1959; Spero 1990; Stubbs and Underhill 1994; Kirshner 2008). The East Asian economic success stories are usually explained within two main schools, the neoliberal school emphasizing the role of the market and those emphasizing the role of the state (Evans et al. 1985; World Bank 1993; Amsden 1994; Wade 2004). Nevertheless, the explanatory power of these two schools has ebbed and flowed depending on the international context. The neoliberal era emerging in the United States and the United Kingdom in the 1980s peaked as a model on a global scale in the 1990s, helped by the collapse of the Soviet Union (Perkins 2001; Wade 2004), and it was into this context that China, Vietnam and Laos entered the world economy. Indeed, the impressive economic growth of China, Vietnam, and Laos has taken place in an era of unprecedented globalization, and their economies have grown in tandem with expanded global value chains and increased international flow of trade and capital.

The development path of China, Vietnam, and Laos also confirms the third premise, that wealth and power in the international system are highly intertwined, and that the structure and operation of the international economic system is often shaped and determined by changes and developments in the international political system (Gilpin 1975; Spero 1990; Stubbs and Underhill 1994). This was very much the case during the Cold War, when the US–Soviet Union superpower rivalry divided the world economy into two economic blocs, a division that strongly shaped the early reform periods of China, Vietnam and Laos. When the Soviet economic bloc was dismantled at the end of the Cold War, free trade and globalization thrived under US unipolarity (Ikenberry et al. 2009). China has in a sense emerged as the "winner" of the era of globalization, and the economies of Vietnam and Laos have also prospered. Nevertheless, throughout this period, it has been a debate in the United States about how to balance three interests in its China policy; security, economy, and human rights (Swaine 2011). Despite a few security issue incidents, criticism of the Chinese human rights record, and episodic trade disputes,[1] the overarching US policy has been economic engagement and

[1] The United States has enforced economic sanctions on China, or threatened to do so, on several occassions in the post-Cold War era, both related to China's human rights record, foreign exchange regime (labeling China a "currency manipulator") and security issues. During the two presidential terms of Clinton (1993–2000) and the first term of Bush (2001–2004), the US government sanctioned Chinese entities a total of 70 times, and mostly related to Chinese companies engaged in Weapons of Mass Destruction proliferation or in commercial transactions with Iran (Swaine 2011: 228).

encourage China to be a "responsible stakeholder" in international affairs (ibid.; Zoellick 2005). Japan and the European Union have followed the same approach of engaging China through economic cooperation.[2] However, China's rise has lately reached such a level that strategic rivalry and security concerns begin to trump economic interests in the Sino-US relationship, and the security–economy nexus in their rivalry is now threatening to halt and even reverse globalization, and potentially reshape the international economy in unprecedented ways (Foot and King 2019). The European Union is also increasingly vocal with regard to possible negative effects of China's rise. The return of great power rivalry with China as one of the dominant forces will bring significant consequences for the "socialist market economy."

This chapter examines how these three premises of international political economy—state–market interaction, national and international level dynamics, and wealth and power, have shaped and formed the development path of China, Vietnam, and Laos over three periods; the Cold War, the era of globalization, and under the current shift toward great power rivalry. In each period, I explore two sub-questions; the level of integration into the world economy, and the level of coherence within the "socialist market economy."

With level of integration I refer to how exposed the economies of China, Vietnam, and Laos are to the world economy, both with regard to the importance of foreign trade and capital in their development, and how the state manages to govern trade and capital. The economies of Japan, South Korea and Taiwan, during their classical "East Asian Developmental State" era and later, as well as other selected countries in the region, function as important reference points throughout the analysis. The main argument presented is that China and Vietnam to an even larger degree than the East Asian Developmental States have opted for an export-led development strategy, facilitating for foreign investment in their export manufacturing (Nguyen and Ta 2019; Zhang 2015; Vu 2015; Xing 2014; Breslin 1999). Laos, however, with a more predominantly natural resources and agricultural-based economy, has taken a slightly different path (Sayavong 2015; Menon and Warr 2013; Rigg 1995). In recent years, whereas Vietnam continues on the path of export-led growth,

[2] Japan and the European Union have rarely enforced economic sanctions on China. One notable exception is Japan's development aid sanction on China as a response to China's nuclear tests in the mid-1990s (Kent 2007: 81).

China is moving away from this strategy toward more priority given to domestic consumption, technology, and innovation (Zhang 2015; Xing 2014), and acquiring technology, industrial upgrade, and expertise through outward FDI (Wang 2012).

Despite growing integration into the world economy, Beijing, Hanoi, and Vientiane have throughout the reform period, from the 1970s/1980s until today, balanced between embracing globalization and at the same time shielding their system from it. For instance, they all looked with skepticism at the "shock therapy" type of capital market liberalization pushed by the IMF and other advisors in Russia in the early 1990s, and later during the East Asian financial crisis in 1997–1998.[3] Just like China has balanced embracing and shielding itself from the world economy, the international community, and the United States in particular, has throughout the reform period simultaneously welcomed China into multilateral structures while pressuring Beijing to embrace the spirit of global economic norms on issues ranging from intellectual property rights to climate change to macroeconomic surveillance (Drezner 2015; Kent 2007). Assessing China's entry into the global economy in the early 1990s, Susan Shirk observed that China had been successful facilitating for shallow integration into world trade through reducing tariffs and quotas. However, she predicted that China would find it much more challenging to adjust to a deeper integration into the global economy that entails adjustments to "behind the border" domestic policies and practices as these could diminish national autonomy and even potentially challenge political sovereignty (1994).[4] China has embraced some issues, but resisted others, and Shirks distinction between shallow and deep integration continues to be a useful tool examining the level of integration, for China as well as for Vietnam and Laos.

I examine coherence between China, Vietnam, and Laos through two indicators; similarity in development profile, and the depth of economic cooperation between these three countries. All three countries share a similar approach with regard to the state–market balance and twin policy

[3] In retrospect, the "Washington Consensus" inspired package of advice given during the Asian financial crisis has been criticized for propelling reforms in the wrong direction (Stiglitz 2006; Feldstein 1998).

[4] With "behind the border" issues, Shirk referred to intellectual property rights, environmental standards, labor market policies, worker safety, competition and antitrust laws, tax codes, or regulation and supervision of financial institutions (1994).

of embracing and shielding globalization, but they differ in terms of the direction of their economic growth, with China using FDI inflow, manufacturing and export to gradually climb the value-added ladder, while the economy of Laos largely remains natural resources based. Vietnam's path resembles that of China, but with a considerable time lag in terms of its development. The level of economic cooperation between China, Vietnam, and Laos was nearly nonexistent during the Cold War, and this legacy continued well into the 1990s. China is today a major player and largest investor in Laos, whereas Vietnam still has reservations toward a strong economic cooperation with China. However, the recent rise of China and growing China–US strategic rivalry in the Indo-Pacific region might move the region toward two more distinct spheres of influence, with both Vietnam and Laos placed within China's sphere of influence.

The chapter is divided into four parts. It starts with an elaboration of how the Cold War in significant ways shaped the direction of developments in China, Vietnam, and Laos from the very beginning of their respective economic reforms. In the next part, I assess the interaction of China, Vietnam, and Laos with trade and foreign capital in the era of deep globalization, from the early 1990s through the global financial crisis. I look at how they have managed to balance embracing globalization and shielding their system with regard to foreign trade, foreign direct investments, and portfolio investments, and how successful they have been to make use of their engagement in the world economy to move up the value-added ladder. In the third part, I explore the effects of the recent return of great power rivalry in international affairs on the socialist market economy. The chapter ends with a brief conclusion.

Launching Reforms in the Cold War Era

In East Asia, the Cold War concentrated the minds of political elites on the pressing needs for national survival, resulting in the East Asian Developmental States building state capacity to mobilize resources and facilitate for economic growth, in order to confront the communist threat (Stubbs 2005). The proximity of external security threats during the early phase of the Cold War in East Asia contributed to the "hardening" of the developmental state in Korea and Taiwan and created strong incentives for growth-oriented policies (Haggard 2018). Moreover, US foreign policy during the early Cold War prioritized the cultivation of strong anti-communist allies, and in particular Japan, but also South Korea and

Taiwan. The United States extended massive aid to Japan, South Korea, and Taiwan in the early postwar period (Stallings 1990). Japan still might have developed without American patronage, but it is unlikely that it would have developed as quickly or thoroughly (Beckley et al. 2018; Pempel 1999). The alliance relationships Japan, South Korea, and Taiwan enjoyed with the United States during the Cold War created incentives on both sides of the Pacific to deepen their economic ties. Due to the tense international environment in this period, even though the United States was leading a major multilateral liberalization effort through the GATT (General Agreement on Trade and Tariffs), enabling these economies access to Western markets, the United States still tolerated that its Asian allies pursued relatively inward-looking and closed economic development strategies (Haggard 2018).

During the Cold War, China, Vietnam, and Laos were all situated on the other side of the fence from the East Asian Developmental States. China also launched economic reforms for national survival, but the international context in the early years of reforms in China, Vietnam and Laos differed greatly from that of other East Asian Developmental States. By the time they became fully integrated with the global economy in the late 1990s, the United States and Europe had turned less accepting of "free-riding," resulting in a larger international pressure on China, Vietnam, and Laos to liberalize their markets at an earlier stage in their development than Japan and Asia's newly industrialized countries (NICs) (Haggard 2018). The late entry of China, Vietnam and Laos into the World Trade Organization (see Table 2.1) is just one indicator of the disadvantage

Table 2.1 Membership in the World Trade Organization[a]

Japan + NICs		*2nd and 3rd tier economies*		*Socialist market economies*	
Japan	1955	Myanmar	1948	China	2001
South Korea	1967	Indonesia	1950	Vietnam	2007
Singapore	1973	Malaysia	1957	Laos	2013
Hong Kong	1986	Philippines	1979		
Taiwan[b]	2002	Thailand	1982		

[a]Membership before the establishment of the WTO in 1995 refers to GATT (General Agreement on Trade and Tariffs). [b]Taiwan joined the WTO in 2002 as Chinese Taipei
Source WTO website; www.wto.org

China, and in particular Vietnam and Laos, had in comparison to their other neighboring countries.

Moreover, China, Vietnam, and Laos all had three unique and different international environments to navigate in their early reform periods. In the US–Soviet–China strategic triangle that emerged in world politics in the early 1970s, the improved relationship between China and the United States was an important enabling reason for Beijing launching economic reforms. China was accepted as a member of the IMF and the World Bank in early 1980, and although China was now able to access Western markets, capital, technology, and economic advise (Kent 2007; Jacobson and Oksenberg 1990), it did this at a lower level than what had been the case with US alliance partners in the region (Tong 1991). China, however, had one advantage that neither of the other countries in the region possessed, and that was in particular Hong Kong as a gateway, but also the role that Taiwan and the larger overseas Chinese community played in the early phase of China's opening up and reform period (Perkins 2001; Yahuda 1996; Womack and Zhao 1994). When the Cold War ended and economic globalization deepened in the early 1990s, China had through a decade of reforms put itself in a position to tap into the fruits of the global economy. Vietnam and Laos were both less prepared for this global shift.

Vietnam was reliant on the Soviet Union in the latter half of the Cold War, and when the Soviet Union collapsed, the Vietnamese economy to a certain extent collapsed with it. Moreover, the economic reform package Hanoi launched in 1986 was not only hit by the communist breakdown in Moscow, but rising unemployment as their soldiers occupying Cambodia was demobilized, and above all, Vietnam still faced an international trade embargo (Duiker 1995). The United States lifted its trade embargo on Vietnam only in 1994, and established diplomatic relations with Vietnam the following year, 16 years later than with China. The European Union followed suit, and formalized diplomatic relations with Vietnam in 1996. In November 2000, Clinton became the first US president to visit Vietnam since Nixon had visited South Vietnam in 1969 during the Vietnam War (Gottschang 2001). The United States and Vietnam signed a bilateral trade agreement the same year, which went into force in 2001. As part of the trade agreement, the United States extended to Vietnam conditional most favored nation (MFN) trade status, now known as normal trade relations (NTR), which were made permanent as part of Vietnam's accession to the WTO in 2007 (Martin 2009). When

Laos started its own economic reform process in 1986, it found itself in an even more isolated situation than Vietnam. Mainly due to the legacy of the Vietnam War, Laos had to wait until 2004 before the United States extended normal trade relations to the country, and the first US Presidential visit to Laos took place in September 2016. Another legacy of the Cold War for Vietnam and Laos was their late entry into the Association of South East Asian Nations (ASEAN), with Vietnam joining in 1995 and Laos in 1997. With their membership in ASEAN followed access to the ASEAN Free Trade Area (AFTA).

Even though China, Vietnam, and Laos shared the same political system, and they all moved toward a model of "socialist market economy," the different context of their early reform period was important for their future development and success rate. China's GDP per capita was in the early and mid-1980s lower than in Vietnam and Laos, but China had a number of initial advantages attracting foreign investments for an export-led growth. As mentioned above, China started its reform process one decade ahead of Vietnam and Laos, and it enjoyed access to the world economy through the overseas Chinese and already from the late 1970s through diplomatic relations with the Western developed world. Vietnam and Laos had to wait another 15–20 years to achieve similar access, both to the region through ASEAN and globally. In addition, China had abundant cheap labor and a huge potential market, and it developed a very effective export and FDI attraction strategy (Zhang 2015). Laos was in a very different position from both China and Vietnam. Above all, whereas China and Vietnam have long coastlines, the land-locked geographic position of Laos—as the only country in South East Asia—is a huge disadvantage in terms of export, and Laos was essentially an agrarian society (Rigg 1995). In 1986, agriculture, forestry, and fishing accounted for 48% of value-added in the GDP of Laos, in comparison to 27 and 38% in China and Vietnam respectively, and 86% of the population in Laos classified as rural population (World Bank 2020a).

Moreover, relations between China, Vietnam, and Laos were highly constrained well into the 1990s. The Vietnamese have historically had a skeptical view of Chinese policies and intentions, and China's invasion in January 1979 only strengthened this worldview (Stuart-Fox 2003). China's punitive invasion was of course a direct response to Vietnam invading Cambodia a few weeks earlier, but it was above all motivated by China's Cold War fear of Soviet encirclement (Ross 1988). Beijing and Hanoi normalized diplomatic relations one decade later, in 1990, and signed a bilateral trade agreement the following year (Chau 2000). Cross-border rail links between China and Vietnam reopened in 1996. The border between China and Laos closed in 1979, and it was only when these two countries signed a border agreement in 1992 that trade and traffic across the border increased (Cohen 2000).

Economic Reforms in the Era of Deep Globalization

As China, Vietnam, and Laos entered the global economy in the 1990s, they had to contemplate five international developments that influenced their economic policies in different ways from that of the first and second generation East Asian Developmental States (Haggard 2018). First, as already alluded to, the United States and Europe had by now become less accepting of the "free-riding" of Japan and the Asian NICs, pushing emerging economies to liberalize their trade regimes. Second, the significant deepening of global production networks (GPNs) that took place through the 1980s and 1990s made foreign direct investment a more crucial aspect of any country's development strategy. The East Asian newly industrialized countries included government policies specifically designed to attract foreign investment to a much larger degree than Latin-American countries (Hein 1992). Even so, Japan and South Korea also sought to limit foreign investment in favor of national champions in their early reform period, and actually made this a core element of their reform model (Amsden 2001). China, Vietnam, and Laos on the other hand faced an international context where foreign direct investment had become central to rapid export growth. Third, because dominant interpretations of the Asian financial crisis of 1997–1998 attributed it to misguided state intervention, the crisis generated strong pressures from the United States and multilateral institutions for emerging economies to undertake further market-oriented reforms. In sum, forming their development policies, China, Vietnam, and Laos faced an international context that gave them less room for selective protection and controls on FDI, trade and investment policies, and their exchange rate policies was scrutinized, as did the activities of their state-owned enterprises.

Moreover, a fourth international development would also soon influence the policies in Beijing, Hanoi, and Vientiane; the rapid globalization in the financial industry in the 1990s and 2000s with steep increases in cross-border capital flows as money market instruments, forwards, swaps, and other derivatives were created (World Bank 2013; Hveem and Pempel 2016). This development of course allowed developing countries to connect with the global financial system, but the growing amount of financial capital pouring into unprepared emerging markets in the 1990s contributed to the Asian crisis (Wade 2004; Yusuf 2001), a development that was met with skepticism in the socialist market economies.

In addition, the communist status of China, Vietnam, and Laos continued to inform the policy of the United States also after the Cold War (Swaine 2011). Under the Jackson–Vanik amendment in the US Trade Act of 1974, China was designated, alongside the Soviet Union and other socialist states, a nonmarket economy. As such, it could only be granted most favored nation (MFN) trade status under certain preconditions. In 1980, as relations between the two countries thawed, the United States conditionally granted China MFN status. That status, however, had to be renewed annually, which gave China's critics in Congress an annual opportunity to question the wisdom of doing so. In the aftermath of the 1989 Tiananmen crackdown, China faced harsh criticism, but most of the economic sanctions put in place were lifted already in 1990, although the arms embargo continued to be enforced (Foot 2000). Still, in the five years after the Tiananmen incident, twelve bills were introduced in the US Congress to either revoke or condition China's Most Favored Nation (MFN) trade status to China's human rights record, but every year the MFN status was renewed (Li 2014; Hufbauer et al. 2007). The threats to revoke or condition China's MFN status spanned the administrations of George H. W. Bush and Bill Clinton. In 2004, the United States designated Vietnam as a Country of Particular Concern (CPC) under its Religious Freedom Act, which specifies possible penalties for human rights violations. The CPC was lifted in 2007 as Vietnam entered the WTO. US concerns about the human rights record in Laos contributed to delay normal trade relations (Thayer 2010). In May 2008, Vietnam formally requested to be added to the US Generalized System of Preferences (GSP) program as a "beneficiary developing country." Although Vietnam has already been accepted into the GSP programs of Canada, the European Union (EU) and Japan, the United States has indicated that the Vietnamese government must improve its labor standards in order to qualify for the GSP program (Martin 2016).

The ending of the Cold War resulted in a wider incorporation of human rights into policy-making and global discourse (Christie and Roy 2001; Foot 2000). Many developed countries included rights issues in their economic relations with developing countries and nondemocratic states, and international agencies like the World Bank and others included governance benchmarks in their ODA guidelines (Kent 2007). Trade and foreign investments into the socialist market economies have flourished despite criticism toward their human rights regimes, but the issue has delayed market access and created a certain level of uncertainty at government level as well as among investors that was not present with regard to the East Asian Developmental States in similar ways.

Faced with globalization, China, Vietnam, and Laos opened their economies at an earlier stage in their development than other East Asian states. However, ruled by one-party systems emphasizing stability and security, with distrust toward foreign interference in domestic matters running deep through their political systems (Yahuda 1997), they tried to develop policies that both embraced the global economy and at the same time shielded the system from too much exposure and pressures for reform. In the following, I will look at how China, Vietnam, and Laos managed this balancing act through the three waves of trade, foreign direct investments, and portfolio investments.

Foreign Trade

Opening up for foreign trade in the early 1980s, China did so in a gradual manner controlling the flows of both goods and money through a centrally controlled foreign trade monopoly and a rigid foreign exchange system (Naughton 2007; Shirk 1994). In order to access world markets and sustain an export-driven development strategy, China in 1986 applied to rejoin the GATT, the forerunner of the World Trade Organization (WTO), and undertook several market reforms preparing for negotiations. What at the outset seemed to be a relatively painless process entering GATT turned into 15 years of protracted negotiations. The shift can partly be explained by Western reactions to the Chinese governments' crackdown on demonstrations in 1989. However, the realization in many countries that China was growing into a major economy and exporter shaped the negotiation process, as did the fundamental changes in the world trading institutions in the 1990s with new requirements on trade in services and investments that were more challenging for China to accommodate (Naughton 2007).

When China finally became a member of the WTO in 2001, it entailed exposing its own market for imports and investments. However, by entering the WTO with developing country status, China, and later Vietnam, managed to shield their markets to some degree by being granted longer transition periods implementing the agreement. Laos joined the WTO as a least developed economy. Vietnam's foreign trade regime was at the outset of reforms very similar to China's, but Hanoi had to change its trade regime at an even faster pace than Beijing (Van Arkadie and Mallon 2003). In 1995, just as Vietnam was reestablishing full diplomatic ties with the United States and the European Union, it became a member of the ASEAN and the ASEAN Free Trade Area (AFTA), it began negotiations for membership in the WTO, and for a bilateral trade agreement with the United States. By 2000, Vietnam had completed 57 bilateral trade agreements and 72 most favored nation (MFN) agreements, including the bilateral agreement with the United States. As part of AFTA, Vietnam was given until 2006 to normalize its tariffs and trading system in line with the rest of the ASEAN countries. Vietnam finally joined the WTO in 2007 (Abbot and Tarp 2012; Vo 2005). Laos joined AFTA in 1998, and was given until 2008 to meet tariff reduction requirements.

The foreign trade of Japan and the Asian NICs grew rapidly through the 1970s and the 1980s, and it was an essential part of their growth success (Lee and Naya 1988). However, the foreign trade/GDP ratios presented in Tables 2.2 and 2.3 indicate that foreign trade is an essential part also of the reform model of China, Vietnam, and Laos. Vietnam's trade/GDP ratio has grown continously since the late 1980s and is now at its highest ever, and is comparable to the figures of Thailand and Malaysia. Although regional trade with North East Asia, ASEAN and South Asia still dominates Vietnamese exports, it has an increasingly global export market. The late access to the American market has been a disadvantage

Table 2.2 Foreign trade as percent of GDP, comparative figures 1970–2015

	Japan	*S-Korea*		*China*	*Vietnam*	*Laos*	*Thailand*	*Malaysia*
1970	19.6	32.6	1995	34.3	74.7	60.6	89.7	192.1
1975	24.6	54.1	2000	39.4	111.4	68.8	121.3	220.4
1980	27.2	65.6	2005	62.2	130.7	71.8	137.8	203.9
1985	24.6	53.2	2010	50.7	152.2	84.7	129.2	157.9
1990	19.6	51.3	2015	39.6	178.8	85.8	125.9	131.4

Source World Bank (2020a)

Table 2.3 Foreign trade as percent of GDP, 2018 figures

Selected economies in Asia		*Selected economies*		*Socialist market economies*	
Japan[b]	34.6	United States	26.6	China	38.2
South Korea	83.0	United Kingdom	62.5	Vietnam	208.3
Singapore	326.2	Germany	86.9	Laos[a]	75.1
Indonesia	43.0	India	40.6		
Thailand	123.3	Brazil	24.1		

Source World Bank (2020a). [a]2016 figures; [b]2017 figures

for Vietnam. In 2000, when the United States extended normal trade relations to Vietnam, exports to the United States accounted for only five percent of Vietnam's total exports, whereas in 2018 it accounted for 19.3% (World Bank 2020a). The export of Laos continues to be almost exclusively regional, with 85% of its exports in 2016 going to three markets; China, Thailand, and Vietnam (ibid.).

China's trade/GDP ratio, on the other hand, is declining. In 2018, the combined value of exports and imports equaled 38.2% of GDP, down from its peak of 64.5% in 2006. An important reason for the decline in China's trade/GDP ratio is the global financial crisis in 2008–2010 exposing weaknesses and limitations in an export-led growth strategy, and growing unwillingness and even inability in the United States, Europe, and Japan to run large trade deficits with China (Palley 2012; Rodrik 2010). Beijing responded with devoting stronger efforts to increasing domestic demand. China's trade/GDP ratio is now similar to that of the United States and Japan. Due to its growing trade deficit with China, the United States has throughout most of China's reform period criticized its foreign exchange regime, and occasionally threatened to label China a "currency manipulator," potentially leading to coercive economic measures.[5] China has on a few occassions accordingly made minor adjustments to its currency, but not altered its exchange regime (Swaine 2011). The United States has only on two occasions formally labeled China a

[5]The Omnibus Trade and Competitiveness Act of 1988 requires the US Secretary of the Treasury to analyze the exchange rate policies of other countries to assess if they manipulate the rate of exchange between their currency and the US dollar for the purposes of effective balance of payments adjustments or gaining unfair competitive advantage in international trade.

"currency manipulator," in the early 1990s, and from August 2019 to January 2020 (US Department of the Treasury 2019).

Although the trade/GDP ratio is a useful indicator informing us about the importance of trade to any economy, it is not necessarily a very precise indicator of a country's degree of openness to trade and foreign capital. With global value chains (GVCs) and tariff reductions through both bilateral and multilateral trade agreements being the norm for years, tariffs now have more limited value as an indicator of openness toward trade and foreign capital. China has since the early 1990s made notable progress on a number of the "behind the border" issues, but the distinction between shallow and deep integration outlined by Shirk is still valid. For instance, China has largely complied with the rules working with the World Bank and the International Monetary Fund, but both institutions have been frustrated by lack of implementation and transparency in China, in particular on financial policy issues (Kent 2007). The main criticism toward China in the context of the WTO today is related to its lack of progress in protecting intellectual property, its use of subsidy regimes, and China is urged to open its procurement market to foreign companies, rather than simply give preference to domestic companies (World Trade Organization 2018). According to the latest WTO Trade Policy Reviews of China (in 2018), Vietnam (2013), and Laos (accession report 2013), Shirk's prediction about deep integration challenges still has some truth to it for all three socialist market economies (World Trade Organization 2019).

Moreover, trade in services has for a number of years represented the most dynamic segment of international trade (Matthews et al. 2018), and is also growing fast in China, Vietnam, and Laos (see Table 2.4). The services trade is growing particularly fast in Vietnam as a result of

Table 2.4 Trade in services as percent of GDP, 2017 figures

Selected economies in Asia		*Selected economies*		*Socialist market economies*	
Japan	7.8	United States	6.8	China	5.5
South Korea	13.7	United Kingdom	22.2	Vietnam	13.4
Singapore	103.6	Germany	17.3	Laos	9.2
Indonesia	5.6	India	11.3		
Thailand	26.7	Brazil	5.0		

Source World Bank (2019a)

WTO membership and the government recognizing that services linkages in global production value chains are critical for strengthening the economy (Nguyen and Ta 2019). Still, China, Vietnam, and Laos are not part of the negotiations on a plurilateral Trade in Services Agreement (TiSA) launched in 2013 to deal with regulatory barriers that interfere with services trade. China has expressed interest in joining TiSA, but reportedly, the United States has voiced concerns about China's readiness to undertake the commitments that TiSA would require (Fefer 2017).

Foreign Direct Investments

As with its trading system, when China opened up for FDI it did so only step-by-step through inviting foreign companies to establish production into a gradually increasing number of designated special economic zones, and by limitations on foreign ownership (Shirk 1994). Contractual joint ventures were introduced as an ownership form in the early 1980s as an initial entry method designed to allow foreign participation in the economy while limiting foreign control of enterprises. Wholly foreign-owned enterprises (WFOEs) gradually became the dominant form of FDI in China, rising from 47.3% of total realized FDI value in 2000 to 78.3% in 2008 (Davies 2013). China has also controlled the inward FDI flows through a catalogue of encouraged, restricted, and prohibited industries for investments. From 1992 onward, when Deng Xiaoping confirmed China's adherence to market reforms, FDIs into China boomed and only the United States has received more FDI than China (see Table 2.5).

Table 2.5 Foreign direct investment inward stock, 2017 (USD millions)[a]

Selected economies in Asia		*Selected economies*		*Socialist market economies*	
South Korea	230,597	United States	7,807,032	China	3,828,193
Indonesia	248,510	United Kingdom	1,563,285	Vietnam	129,491
Malaysia	139,540	Germany	931,285	Laos	6560
Philippines	78,788	India	377,683		
Thailand	219,368	Brazil	778,287		

[a]Foreign direct investment inward stock is the level of accumulated FDI in a country
Source UNCTAD World Investment Report (2018)

There is a fundamental difference between China, Vietnam, and Laos in terms of inward foreign investments. While FDI have accounted for the all-dominant part of inward foreign investments into China throughout the reform period, Vietnam and Laos received large amounts of official development assistance (ODA). Through the 1990s and into the early 2000s, Laos was among the world's top ten aid-dependent countries (Action Aid 2011). With a large amount of ODA also comes the influence of bilateral and multilateral donors on domestic economic policies, in contrast to what is the case with FDI. At its most extreme, in 1998, during the Asian crisis, the net ODA[6] Laos received accounted for as much as 22.2 percentage of its Gross National Income (GNI) (World Bank 2018). The same year net ODA to Vietnam accounted for 4.4% of its GNI. As late as in 2003, net ODA to Laos accounted for as much as 15.8% of GNI, but it has since dropped continously, down to 2.6% in 2016, which was only slightly higher than Vietnam's ODA/GNI ratio of 1.5% (World Bank 2018). In other words, over the course of the last decade, inward FDI has replaced ODA as the leading source of foreign investments for both Vietnam and Laos.

Vietnam and Laos attempted to increase the amount of inward FDI in the mid-1990s, and Laos issued the Law on Promotion and Management of Foreign Investment in July 1994 (Menon and Warr 2013). However, investors lost confidence in these two markets in the aftermath of the Asian financial crisis, resulting in a sharp drop in inward FDI (Beresford 2003; Okonjo-Iweala et al. 1999). From the mid-2000s, however, FDI flows picked up again (see Fig. 2.1). In fact, using FDI net inflows as percentage of GDP as indicator, we find that FDI has been more important for Vietnam than for China, and that China, Vietnam, and Laos all received a relatively large amount of FDI in comparison to other countries in East Asia. Incoming FDI was always lower than one percent of the GDP in Japan and South Korea during their periods of most rapid growth, and only slightly higher in Taiwan (Naughton 2007: 4040), while the ratio has been considerably higher in China, Vietnam, and Laos (Fig. 2.1).

[6] Net official development assistance (ODA) consists of disbursements of loans made on concessional terms and grants by official agencies of the members of the Development Assistance Committee (DAC), by multilateral institutions, and by non-DAC countries. It includes loans with a grant element of at least 25% (calculated at a rate of discount of 10%).

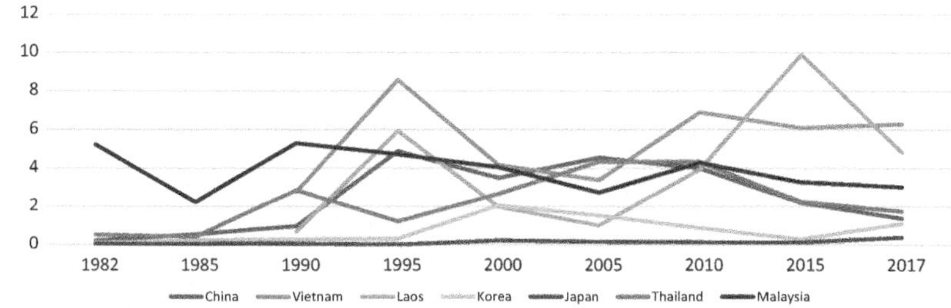

Source: World Bank (2019b).

	1982	1985	1990	1995	2000	2005	2010	2015	2017
China	0,21	0,54	0,97	4,88	3,48	4,55	3,99	2,19	1,38
Vietnam			2,78	8,59	4,16	3,39	6,9	6,1	6,3
Laos			0,69	5,93	1,96	1,01	3,91	9,88	4,82
Korea	0,09	0,23	0,28	0,32	2,05	1,52	0,87	0,29	1,11
Japan	0,04	0,05	0,06	0,01	0,22	0,16	0,13	0,12	0,39
Thailand	0,52	0,42	2,86	1,22	2,66	4,34	4,32	2,24	1,75
Malaysia	5,21	2,23	5,3	4,71	4,04	2,73	4,27	3,26	3,02

Fig. 2.1 FDI net inflows as percentage of GDP, 1982–2017 (*Source* World Bank [2019b])

Chinese authorities preferred FDI above loans, aid, and portfolio investments because through direct investments, China could access technology and commercial expertise as well as capital and at the same time govern the flow (Naughton 2007). With an FDI inflow strategy and the proliferation of global value chains (GVCs), the ratio of foreign value-added to a country's total exports is an important indicator informing us about foreign influence and industrial upgrading in an economy (Xing 2014).[7] The foreign value-added share of China's gross exports used to be rather high at around 35% through the 1990s and 2000s, but has in recent years begun to fall, suggesting that China gradually produces a higher ratio of the technologically advanced and higher-quality materials in its exports, reducing its dependence on foreign high-value goods in domestic production (CSIS 2016). The ratio of foreign value-added in

[7] Foreign value-added to a country's total exports is the percentage of value-added to a country's economy assembled or manufactured in a foreign-invested enterprise in the export country, serving foreign demand (Xing 2014).

Vietnam's exports has been higher than China's for the last decade, and the ratio is increasing (ibid.).

FDI inflows into manufacturing have been much higher in China than in the rest of the world (Naughton 2007), and the large FDI inflow has been helped by China's effective export and FDI attraction strategy (Zhang 2015). FDI continues to play a large role in promoting China's trade, investment, and tax revenue generation, albeit not as large as before. Factors like rising labor costs, shortages of skilled labor, greater competition from Chinese companies, and fears that an investment protectionist trend may be emerging in China, all contribute to this trend (Davies 2013). Moreover, the Chinese government has taken a number of measures to streamline inward FDI flows, aligning them more closely with national priorities on industrial upgrading, supporting innovation, and setting up outsourcing industries (Zhang 2015; Davies 2013). It is argued that China's manufacturing has been most successful in terms of aggregate capacity and intensity, but not yet in quality (Zhang 2015). In fact, Chinese hesitance to implement some "behind the border" regulations, like stronger protection of intellectual property rights, has contributed to overseas capital often flowing into China unaccompanied by new and advanced foreign technologies. The governments of many industrial countries restrict the transfer of new and advanced technologies, and many transnational corporations investing in China often refuse to establish research and development programs. As a result, the ability of Chinese firms to develop technologies in conjunction with foreign enterprises in joint ventures is weakened (Zhou 2012).

Nonetheless, China has for a number of years been seeking to upgrade its production frontier toward more capital and technology-intensive industries, and transition to an innovative knowledge-driven economy (Zhou 2013). For instance, between 2005 and 2016, the operational stock of industrial robots in China increased at an annual average rate of 38%. In 2016 alone, sales of industrial robots in China reached 87,000 units, accounting for around 30% of the global market, and the same year, the total robot sales in all of Europe and the Americas reached 97,300 units (Cheng et al. 2019). Moreover, China has also emerged as a major player in outward FDI, and investing abroad is not only about access to resources, but it is an essential part of the strategy acquiring technology and expertise (Scissors 2020; Wang 2012).

It has been a considerable disparity in growth between China and Vietnam, and especially in the first decade of the 2000s, as China exceeded Vietnam in mobilizing resources to shift from lower to higher productivity firms, activity, and industries (Vu 2015). The figures in Table 2.6, however, tells us that Vietnam as well as China is climbing in the value-added ladder. Whereas the composition of China's export today resembles that of Japan and South Korea, Vietnam's is more similar to Malaysia and Thailand. Laos is the odd man out in this picture, with an economic profile dominated by raw materials and intermediate goods. The state of manufacturing in Vietnam today parallels that of China in the mid-2000s, when low-wage, low-tech, low-added value manufacturing acted as a magnet for FDI into the country. As China moves further up the value chain, many investors have moved their manufacturing south to Vietnam, a trend that was strengthened during China's trade war with the United States (Jennings 2018). However, while the sources of China's inward FDI today are highly global, the sources for inward FDI in Vietnam are still regional. By the end of 2016, the aggregated investments from the four largest sources—South Korea, Japan, Singapore, and Taiwan accounted for 50% of total FDI into Vietnam. In comparison, FDI from the United States accounted for as little as four percent (Ngo et al. 2017).

Even though trade and inward FDI account for important parts of their economies, and China, Vietnam, and Laos are highly integrated into global value chains, institutions such as the Heritage Foundation

Table 2.6 Composition of exports, in percent (2018 figures)

	Raw materials	*Intermediate goods*[a]	*Consumer goods*	*Capital goods*[b]
China (2017)	1.7	16.7	35.6	46.0
Vietnam (2017)	10.3	12.7	38.8	40.2
Laos (2016)	43.4	26.1	22.1	8.4
Japan	1.4	19.7	25.3	47.4
South Korea	0.6	23.4	22.9	53.1
Malaysia	6.2	19.8	29.7	43.7
Thailand	5.8	21.6	34.3	38.3

[a]Intermediate goods is the classification of producer goods or semi-finished products used as inputs in the production of other goods. Examples include car engines, steel, silver and gold, wood, glass, paint, salt, and sugar
[b]Capital goods is the classification of durable goods used in the production of goods or services. Examples are hand tools, machine tools, data centers, oil rigs, or semiconductor fabrication plants
Source World Bank (2020b)

and the Fraser Institute both rank China, Vietnam, and Laos very low on their respective economic freedom indexes (see Table 2.7). According to the Heritage Foundation, China's trade and monetary freedom are both relatively high, but investment freedom and financial freedom are both categorized as repressed. It is further argued that bureaucratic hurdles, weak rule of law and the prevalence of state-owned enterprises in basic industries limits foreign investment, and that the state uses control of the financial system to manage the economy (Heritage Foundation 2018). The Fraser Institute report points to size of government and capital market regulations as the greatest hurdles for economic freedom in China (Fraser Institute 2018). Both reports assess the situation in Vietnam and Laos to be quite similar to China, with under-developed legal systems and strong government control of the banking and financial sectors.

The World Economic Forum's Competitiveness Report also largely corresponds with these findings. In its 2018 Report, the World Economic Forum ranks China's competitiveness relatively high, at 28th of 140 economies, but identifies China together with India, Russia, and Italy as the G20 economies with specific vulnerabilities in their financial systems (Schwab 2018). According to an assessment of Vietnam's financial sector undertaken by the Asian Development Bank in 2014, "Viet Nam will need to fundamentally reshape its financial sector to support long-term

Table 2.7 Economic Freedom Index, selected economies

Heritage Foundation Economic Freedom Index 2018							
Free		*Mostly free*		*Moderately free*		*Mostly unfree*	
1	Hong Kong	13	Taiwan	53	Thailand	110	China
2	Singapore	18	United States	61	Philippines	130	India
3	New Zealand	22	Malaysia	69	Indonesia	138	Laos
4	Switzerland	27	South Korea	71	France	141	Vietnam
5	Australia	30	Japan	79	Italy	153	Brazil
Fraser Institute Economic Freedom of the World Report 2018							
Most free		*2nd Quartile*		*3rd Quartile*		*Least free*	
1	Hong Kong	49	Philippines	84	Thailand	123	Belarus
2	Singapore	54	Italy	87	Russia	132	Pakistan
3	New Zealand	65	Indonesia	95	India	144	Brazil
4	Switzerland	79	Malaysia	107	China	151	Myanmar
5	Ireland	81	Laos	112	Vietnam	160	Argentina

Source Heritage Foundation (2018) and Fraser Institute (2018)

socioeconomic goals" (Asian Development Bank 2014: 2). On a similar note, one of the main recommendations in the International Monetary Fund's 2017 Article IV Consultation with the Lao government was to improve regulation and supervision of the banking system (IMF 2018). In other words, China, Vietnam, and Laos continue to have reservations toward deep integration into the global economy, and in particular with regard to capital market liberalization and the rapid globalization in the financial industry.

Capital Market Liberalization and Portfolio Investments

China, Vietnam, and Laos were all less prepared for and less willing to embrace the globalization in the financial industry and steep increases in cross-border capital flows than the earlier waves of trade in goods and FDIs. The governments in all three countries have reaped the benefits of integrating in global value chains through trade and FDIs in manufacturing, and have viewed this as necessary tools for growth and modernization without losing too much control of their respective economic policies, whereas foreign portfolio investments through purchasing stocks and bonds, that can be bought and sold very quickly, have been looked at with a larger degree of reservations.

When the Asian financial crisis hit in the fall of 1997, China, Vietnam, and Laos were insulated from the sharp credit crunches and rapid flight of portfolio investment observed elsewhere in the region simply because they were not well integrated into global financial markets. They had by then received virtually no short-term capital inflows, they had relatively little short-term foreign debt, and the Chinese renminbi as well as the Vietnamese dong was not convertible on the capital account (Perkins 2001; Gottschang 2001). The Lao kip, given its close link to the Thai baht, took a more severe blow (Okonjo-Iweala et al. 1999). However, there was a substantial capital flow from China during the Asian financial crisis despite restrictions on the capital account, indicating loopholes in the capital controls. Hence, it was to a larger degree China's low exposure to portfolio investments that kept it relatively insulated from the crisis than control of its capital account (Naughton 2007).

Although the international dominant interpretations of the Asian financial crisis attributed it to Asian countries' misguided state intervention, in Asia it was traced to be the result of deregulation, capital account, and financial market liberalization (Sheng 2009). This view was also shared by several international observers (Wade and Veneroso 1998; Stiglitz 2002). The Asian crisis put in question the desirability of free movements of short-term capital (Stiglitz 2010), and led to a renewed discussion about the effects of trade liberalization with or without capital account liberalization (Wade and Veneroso 1998) as well as a debate about the effects of different types of capital flows (FDI versus portfolio and equity investment) on economic growth and development (Soto 2000; Aizenman et al. 2011; Reinhardt et al. 2013).

The governments in Beijing, Hanoi, and Vientiane also took note of the political turmoil unfolding in the countries hit by the financial crisis, with Thailand's Prime Minister Chavalit resigning from office in November 1997 amidst street protests, Kim Dae-jung being elected President in South Korea in December as the first-ever democratically elected opposition victor in Korean history, and in May 1998 Indonesia's President Suharto resigned after 32 years in power (Sheng 2009).

The severe economic and political consequences of the Asian financial crisis convinced China, Vietnam, and Laos to strengthen their banking and financial systems (Gottschang 2001; Okonjo-Iweala et al. 1999). They all knew that their own banks and financial institutions had many of the same faults undermining the financial systems of countries at the epicenter of the Asian crisis, and they recognized the inevitability of moving its own system toward financial globalization. Responding to the Asian crisis, the Chinese government reformed its financial system, it tightened control over foreign exchange, and it imposed stricter control of foreign debt (Leung 2009; Wang 1999). In fact, economic globalization created opportunities for the Chinese leadership to rebuild state institutions and strengthen its ability to govern an increasingly market-oriented economy, while at the same time holding on to its political institutions (Zheng 2004).

However, the strict regime for portfolio investments has contributed to China's stock market not matching the performance of China's real economy (Li and Zhou 2016). It is even argued that the Chinese stock market is merely a fund-raising vehicle for failing state-owned enterprises, and that the regulation of stock markets is subject to the principle of maintaining political stability and the one-party ruling (ibid.). In fact, in the aftermath of the Asian financial crisis, China framed financial stability as an issue of national security (Wang 1999). In Vietnam, as well, the post-Asian crisis financial market reforms were balanced against the government's supreme priority to social and political stability (Leung 2009).

Unlike in manufacturing where foreign investment is pronounced in China and Vietnam, the capital markets have been funded almost entirely by domestic money. Whereas Chinese financial institutions are "going global," the development of foreign banks in China has been relatively slow. For instance, in the 2004–2016 period, the assets of foreign-owned banks in China actually fell behind as a percentage of total bank assets. In 2016, foreign bank assets accounted for only 1.26% of total bank assets in China (Min et al. 2020). Foreign participation in China's stock and bond markets has risen in recent years, but it remains relatively low compared with international peers. Foreign equity holdings are about 2.4% (2017 figures) of the total Chinese equity market capitalization. For instance, the Chinese state retains a majority share in all but one of the 100 largest publicly listed companies (World Trade Organization 2018). In contrast, foreign participation in the stock markets of the United States (about 35% in 2017), South Korea (33%), and Japan (17%) is much higher than in China. Foreign participation in Chinese bond markets is even smaller, at just about 1.6% (Cerutti and Obstfeld 2018: 4–5).

The stock markets in all three countries are comparatively new phenomena, with China establishing stock markets in Shanghai and Shenzhen in 1990, the Ho Chi Minh City Securities Trading Center opened in 2000, followed by the Hanoi Securities Trading Center in 2006 (both has later changed name to stock exchanges), and the Lao Securities Exchange in 2011. The Shanghai and Shenzhen stock exchanges are now among the largest in the world in terms of market capitalization (Caproasia 2017), and in 2017 the Ho Chi Minh Stock Exchange was crowned Asia's best-performing stock exchange and named among the world's top 10 highest-gaining exchanges (World Finance 2018). Such a fast growth of newly established stock exchanges with immature regulatory agencies, human resources, auditing, and reporting would cause growing pains in any country. The manner in which the Chinese government intervened to manipulate the market during the 2015–2016 stock market turbulence (Osnos 2015; Bloomberg 2016), could also be replicated by the governments in Vietnam and Laos. Even though Vietnam is relaxing its stance on foreign ownership in many listed companies (World Finance 2018; Vietnam News 2018), and recent reforms in China's stock market also points toward loosening controls on two-way capital flows (Craik and He

2018), the transition from plan to market economy is slowest in the bank and finance industry.

Closer Cooperation

The end of the Cold War set in motion an unprecedented wave of economic integration, and according to the Asian Development Bank's annual Asian Economic Integration Report, intraregional trade in Asia has been growing continously, and Asia is increasingly part of global value chains and capital flows (Asian Development Bank 2018). The economic integration has been followed hand in hand by diplomatic thaw in the Asia-Pacific, and to such an extent that the period from the late 1980s up to now has been framed as the era of "East Asian Peace" (Tønnesson 2017). This not only enabled China, Vietnam, and Laos to connect with the global economy, as outlined above, but also facilitated closer economic cooperation between them. Improving relations with Southeast Asian countries was an important part of Chinese diplomacy throughout the 1990s, including with Vietnam and Laos (Leifer 1997), which responded largely in positive terms to the Chinese overture. Hanoi and Vientiane soon joined the Association of Southeast Asian Nations (ASEAN), that would go on to play an important role as a platform for dialogue and integration between China and Southeast Asian countries, through the China–ASEAN Free Trade Area and more security-policy-related platforms such as the ASEAN Regional Forum (ARF) (Acharya 2001).

Vietnam and China successively concluded a land border treaty in 1999, and an agreement on maritime rights in the Tonkin Gulf as well as a fishing cooperation agreement in 2000 (Do 2009). This was followed by China and ASEAN settling for a nonbinding Declaration on the Conduct of Parties in the South China Sea (DOC) in 2002. These were all landmark events improving relations and economic cooperation. China–Vietnam bilateral trade increased by almost one thousand percent from 1995 to 2006, and China's trade with Laos by a little more than three hundred percent (Hao 2008).

In recent years, China has continued to increase its economic footprint in both Vietnam and Laos, but more so in Laos than in Vietnam. China is the largest trading partner to Vietnam, and the second largest to Laos (see Table 2.8), but in terms of investments, China has a more prominent position in Laos. Vientiane attempts to balance relations with

Table 2.8 Top trading partners of Vietnam and Laos, in percent of total trade, 2017

	Vietnam		*Laos*	
	Import origin	*Export destination*	*Import origin*	*Export destination*
1st	China 31%	USA 21%	Thailand 65%	Thailand 39%
2nd	South Korea 17%	China 13%	China 17%	China 29%
3rd	Japan 6.3%	Japan 7.7%	Vietnam 6.5%	Vietnam 11%

Source OEC (2020)

its three neighbors Vietnam (closest political partner), Thailand (largest trading partner), and China (largest investor), but China's position in Laos is increasingly dominant. China is the biggest contributor of foreign investments, totalling USD six billion in accumulated investments for the 1989–2016 period, ahead of Thailand and Vietnam (Pang 2017; Lowe 2016). China is now also the largest donor (ODA) to Laos (Pang 2017). China's position in Laos has been growing gradually for the last two decades (Stuart-Fox 2009), and is expected to be further enhanced through investments and infrastructure projects linked to the Belt and Road Initiative (BRI), with Laos and Cambodia as key nodes of China's "Indochina Peninsular Corridor" into Southeast Asia (Pang 2017).

Vietnam does not share the same level of accommodation as Laos toward Chinese interests. As of mid-2017, China was only the fifth largest provider of inward FDI into Vietnam, accounting for less than four percent of total accumulated inward FDI in Vietnam (Vietnam Trade promotion Agency 2017). The largest providers of FDI to Vietnam are South Korea (18%), Japan (15), Singapore (13), and Taiwan (10). This can partly be explained by China emerging as a significant overseas investor later than the other economies, but it is also an outcome of Vietnamese reservations toward Chinese investments, resulting from a troublesome history between these two countries and ongoing maritime disputes. Throughout history, Vietnam has attempted to balance "struggle and cooperation" in its relationship with the more powerful neighbor China (Womack 2006; Thayer 2011). Despite China serving as a model in Vietnam's economic reform process, and trade relations growing, unresolved maritime issues have remained an irritant in their relations (Tønnesson 2003). The South China Sea tensions in the Sino-Vietnamese relationship lingered throughout the 2000s, and since

2009–2010 escalated in tandem with the China-US rivalry (Fravel 2017; Ross and Li 2016). Moreover, in contrast to Laos and most other countries in South East Asia, Vietnam is not part of China's BRI. A recent perception survey among Asian opinion leaders found that there is a relatively high degree of skepticism in Vietnam toward the BRI (Rana 2019).

A New Era of Strategic Rivalry and Mercantilism

China is now one of the main drivers of the global economy. In fact, its economic growth has reached a level where it is a competitor to the United States, Europe, and Japan, resulting in them confronting China with concerns about its restrictive investment practices, pressures for technology transfer, and intellectual property theft (Huang 2017). The criticism toward China is not new (Autor et al. 2013), and developed countries have for years criticized China's exchange rate and huge trade surpluses, leading to the loss of jobs at home and the hollowing out of their middle class (Huang 2017). However, the criticism has gained salience in recent years with the rise of China as an economic powerhouse and peer competitor. For instance, China entering the WTO as a developing country in 2001 was not particularly contested at the time, but the fact that China as the world's second largest economy still has status as developing country is now increasingly being criticized, including by the current Trump administration in the United States (Lester and Zhu 2018).

The recent trade war between China and the United States cannot be explained by the large US trade deficit with China, as the United States almost from the start of China's economic reforms in the late 1970s has suffered from a bilateral trade deficit with China (Dollar and Petri 2018). The trade deficit was not a great concern as long as China was the world factory for labor-intensive products like textiles and footwear. However, with China fast climbing the value-added ladder into high-end industries and technologies, the same type of concerns about industrial decline in the United States and Europe that was directed at Japan and the Asian NIC-states in the 1980s and 1990s (Bluestone and Harrison 1982; Wood 1994) are now being directed at China (Huang 2017). China is now also a major overseas investor, and outward FDI has become a central part of its growth strategy. There are consequently increased calls in the United States for reciprocity, and that American companies should have equal access to the Chinese market as Chinese enterprises have in the United States (Harris 2017; Scissors 2016). The US trade war on China is caused by a mix of populist, isolationist, and protectionist sentiments in the United States, and the rise of China as peer competitor (Lau 2018).

However, the more restrictive view on China as an economic partner is not limited to the United States. In January 2019, the Federation of German Industries (BDI), the leading lobby group for German manufacturers, published a policy paper identifying China's state-dominated economy as a systemic competitor that challenges Europe's liberal and open system, and encourages increased cooperation within Europe and with like-minded countries (BDI 2019). The paper in a way buried the earlier dominating notion in Germany that China's model is destined to converge with the open market economies of the West (Barkin 2019). However, it remains to be seen whether a tougher policy from the United States and Europe will result in more market or more state in China's economic model.

Nonetheless, China has not only emerged as an economic powerhouse but also as a significant military power. Its defense expenditure is now larger than that of Japan, India, and Russia combined (SIPRI 2020), and the modernization of the Chinese PLA Navy challenges the traditional US maritime dominance in Asia (Ross 2018). The 2017 US National Security Strategy describes China as a competitor willing to undermine US interests (White House 2017), and the rhetoric used by US Vice President Mike Pence in his remarks on the administration's China policy at the Hudson Institute in October 2018 are probably the harshest comments on China coming out of the White House since the Cold War era (Pence 2018).

Keohane and Nye reminded us that also in an era of "complex interdependence," "security still outranks other issues in foreign policy" (1998: 84), but three decades of deep economic globalization have to some extent seduced us into thinking that security and force matter less. However, the intensified strategic rivalry between China and the United States, resulting from China's new military prowess, has started to feed into the economic domain. In fact, in the 2017 National Security Strategy, protecting intellectual property and reducing illicit appropriation of US technical knowledge by hostile foreign competitors is identified as a core task. The growing perception of China's rise as a threat to US national security was reiterated in the 2018 industrial base review (DoD 2018). Commenting on the review, Peter Navarro, director of the White

House Office of Trade and Manufacturing Policy, argued that China is strategically targeting US supply chains (CSIS 2018).

In addition to China's rise as an economic competitor and military-strategic rival of the United States, there is a third development unfolding now that enforces the complexity of the security–economy nexus related to China, and that is the arrival of the so-called fourth industrial revolution (4IR) with rapid advances in robotics, artificial intelligence (AI), digitalized manufacturing, and other smart technologies (Schwab 2017; Ezell 2018). The outcome of this "revolution" is still unclear. It might improve living standards, or disrupt societies by redefining the way we work, live, and interact with each other. It might offer countries the potential to leapfrog stages of development, but it could also make the pathway to development less certain for emerging economies betting on industrialization and the demographic dividend as robotics make light manufacturing less labor-intensive. Moreover, it might enable an even faster transfer of ideas, technologies, and innovations across borders, stimulating another round of deep globalization that convinces China and the socialist market economies to embrace deep and complex global interdependence. However, with an international system increasingly shaped by economic competition and strategic rivalry between China and the United States and its allies, it actually seems just as likely that this new industrial revolution will be characterized by China and the United States competing for technological dominance in the world.

Including China in global production networks and value chains on labor-intensive products, cars, and mobile phones has been viewed as win–win, but with regard to robotics, AI, and other smart technologies, with closer links between civilian and military use of the technologies, the United States is more likely to attempt excluding China from these value chains than including China. If so, we are now entering a new era where national security concerns trump economic integration and globalization. Indeed, the United States has already embarked on a global campaign trying to convince allies and partner countries preventing Huawei and other Chinese firms access to build the next fifth-generation (5G) mobile network (Sanger et al. 2019). It is too early to conclude on a worldwide embargo directed at Chinese firms like Huawei, but in 2018 the European Union also hammered out new rules to prevent foreign investments from threatening national security, and the perceived threat from China is seemingly motivating this move (Stearns 2018). The combination of great power rivalry and economic competition as we are on the doorsteps of a new industrial revolution might lead us toward economic mercantilism instead of deeper globalization.

The Future of the Socialist Market Economy

The military-strategic rivalry between the United States and China informs the socialist market economies in two ways. First, as security concerns become more prominent, it is likely to strengthen the Chinese government's incentive to pursue a state-dominated economic model and avoid deep integration with the global economy, at least in certain business sectors. As national security concerns related to new industries grows, it increases the probability of the Chinese party-state retaining the dominant role of state-owned enterprises in strategic sectors to avoid its industrial base diminishing. China has over the last decade or so gradually put in place a formal national security review regime on foreign investments (Liu 2018; Li and Cheng 2016), and it seems that Beijing, like Washington, is now more willing to refer to national security justifying barriers to trade and investment (Tabeta 2018).

Second, with growing rivalry and higher economic barriers between China on the one side and the United States with its European and Asian allies on the other, Vietnam and Laos might soon find themselves in a precarious situation, forced to choose between closer cooperation with China, or with the United States. Some countries in Southeast Asia has for a number of years managed to balance closer economic cooperation with China with leaning on the United States for security (Jackson 2014; Roy 2005).

Sharing a land border with China, and without any tradition of security cooperation with the United States, apart from their anti-communist regimes during the Vietnam War, it will be more challenging for Vietnam and Laos to pursue a hedging strategy. Vietnam is more willing and able than Laos to withstand growing Chinese influence. Hanoi is courting a close relationship with Japan (Grønning 2018), India (Pant 2018), and Russia (Mankoff 2015), both in terms of economic and security cooperation, and Hanoi is to various degree importing weapon platforms from all three countries, In fact, during the period 2012–2016, Vietnam was the tenth largest importer of arms globally (Thayer 2018). Vietnam is also building a closer relationship with the United States, but neither Hanoi nor Washington would want to be too close to each other, in order to manage their respective relationship with Beijing.

China is in a stronger position today than during the Cold War, both vis-a-vis Vietnam as well as compared to the United States, and as China continues building seapower capabilities, the United States might find it increasingly challenging to keep its strategic presence in the South China Sea. Hence, there is a higher likelihood of both Vietnam and Laos drifting into China's sphere of influence today or in the near future, than what was the case during the Cold War. It is not "carved in stone" how Vietnam and Laos' respective relationship with China will unfold, but it is certain that the great power rivalry between China and the United States will shape the future of Vietnam and Laos, and both Hanoi and Vientiane need to take the Sino-US rivalry into account debating their own further development.

Conclusion

This chapter has examined the development path of the socialist market economies through the lenses of the three fundamental premises in international political economy, the interactions between state and market, between the national and international level, and between wealth and power in the international system. The chapter demonstrates that China, Vietnam, and Laos has adopted a twin policy of embracing globalization and at the same time shielding their system from it, and they still find it challenging to open for deep integration with the world economy on so-called "behind the border" issues that requires streamlining their system more fundamentally to international norms and rules.

They have pursued export-led growth, facilitating for trade and inward FDI into their manufacturing industries, although Laos to a much lesser extent than the other two. China has over the last decade gradually moved away from an export-led growth strategy, and shifted toward domestic consumption, innovation, and technology upgrade, and acquiring technology and expertise through outward FDI. All three countries have taken a careful approach with regard to capital market deregulation and inward portfolio investments.

China, Vietnam, and Laos were able to take advantage of being latecomers into the world economy, but China more so than Vietnam and Laos, as the latter two had greater disadvantages to overcome related to their Cold War legacies. There is a huge and growing discrepancy in their respective level of development, with the Chinese economy moving into high-end technology, Vietnam still engaged in foreign-invested labor-intensive manufacturing, and the economy of Laos dominated by natural resources and the agrarian sector. However, this discrepancy in development and industrial upgrading should be looked upon more as a natural variation within the socialist market economy model than a fundamental or ideologically motivated difference in their economic policies.

In the post-Cold War era of globalization, the United States, Japan, and European countries have largely pursued a policy of economic engagement toward China, Vietnam, and Laos, and the level of economic cooperation among the socialist market economies has grown as well. Nevertheless, the emerging great power rivalry between China and the United States brings serious challenges not only to China, but to Vietnam and Laos as well. The rivalry will influence China's economic model, and in a tougher international environment shaped more by security concerns, Beijing will find it difficult and risky to loosen its grip on the Chinese economy. It is too early to conclude if growing barriers between China and the United States will push Vietnam and Laos closer to China or the United States, although it seems more likely that Indochina will gravitate closer to China's sphere of influence. What is beyond doubt is that changes in international politics will shape the future of the socialist market economy model.

Literature

Abbot, Philip B., and Finn Tarp. 2012. Globalization Crisis, Trade and Development in Vietnam. *Journal of International Commerce, Economics and Policy* 3 (1): 23.

Acharya, Amitav. 2001. *Constructing a Security Community in Southeast Asia*. Routledge, London and New York: ASEAN and the Problem of Regional Order.

Action Aid. 2011. *Real Aid: Ending aid Dependency*. London. Accessed 7 January 2017 at http://www.actionaid.org/sites/files/actionaid/real_aid_3.pdf.

Aizenman, Joshua, Yothin Jinjarak, and Donghyun Park. 2011. Capital Flows and Economic Growth in the Era of Financial Integration and Crisis, 1990–2010. *CEPR Policy Portal*, 28 October. Accessed 10 January 2019 at https://voxeu.org/article/capital-flows-and-growth-1990-2010.

Amsden, Alice H. 1994. Why Isn't the Whole World Experimenting with the East Asian Model to Develop? Review of the East Asian Miracle. *World Development* 22 (4): 627–633.

Amsden, Alice H. 2001. *The Rise of "The Rest": Challenges to the West from Late-Industrializing Economies*. Oxford: Oxford University Press.
Asian Development Bank. 2014. *Vietnam: Financial Sector Assessment, Strategy and Road Map*, Manila, July. Accessed 8 January 2019 at https://www.adb.org/sites/default/files/institutional-document/42848/files/viet-nam-financial-sector-assessment-strategy-and-road-map.pdf.
Asian Development Bank. 2018. Asian Economic Integration Reports, Various Years. Accessed 30 January 2019 at https://www.adb.org/publications/.
Autor, David H., David Dorn, and Gordon H. Hanson. 2013. The China Syndrome: Local Labor Market Effects of Import Competition in the United States. *American Economic Review* 103 (6): 2121–2168.
Barkin, Noah. 2019. German Industry Comes Clean on China, Berlin Observer, January 15. https://berlinpolicyjournal.com/german-industry-comes-clean-on-china/.
BDI. 2019. *Partner and Systemic Competitor—How Do We Deal with China's State-Controlled Economy?* Policy Paper, China, January, Federation of German Industries. https://www.wita.org/wp-content/uploads/2019/01/201901_Policy_Paper_BDI_China.pdf.
Beckley, Michael, Yusaku Horiuchi, and Jennifer M. Miller. 2018. America's Role in the Making of Japan's Economic Miracle. *Journal of East Asian Studies* 18 (1): 1–21.
Beresford, Melanie. 2003. Economic Transition, Uneven Development, and the Impact of Reform on Regional Inequality. In *Postwar Vietnam, Dynamics of a Transforming Society*, ed. Hy V. Luong. Singapore: Rowman & Littlefield.
Bloomberg. 2016. The Chinese Investors Who Matter Most Are Losing Faith in Stocks. *Bloomberg News*, January 8. Accessed 9 January 2019 at https://www.bloomberg.com/news/articles/2016-01-08/the-chinese-investors-who-matter-most-are-losing-faith-in-stocks.
Bluestone, Barry, and Bennett Harrison. 1982. *The Deindustrialization of America: Plant Closings, Community Abandonment, and the Dismantling of Basic Industry*. New York: Basic Books.
Breslin, Shaun. 1999. The Politics of Chinese Trade and the Asian Financial Crises: Questioning the Wisdom of Export-Led Growth. *Third World Quarterly* 20 (6): 1179–1199.
Caproasia. 2017. 2016 Stock Exchange Market Capitalization. January 27. Accessed 9 January 2019 at https://www.caproasia.com/2017/01/27/2016-stock-exchange-market-capitalization/.
Cerutti, Eugenio, and Maurice Obstfeld. 2018. China's Bond Market and Global Financial Markets. IMF Working Paper WP/18/253, International Monetary Fund Research Department.
Chau, Thi Hai. 2000. Trade Activities of the Hoa Along the Sino-Vietnamese Border. In *Where China Meets Southeast Asia: Social & Cultural Change in*

the Border Regions, ed. Grant Evans, Christopher Hutton, and Kuah Khun Eng. Bangkok: ISEAS Singapore/White Lotus.

Cheng, Hong, Ruixue Jia, Dandan Li, and Hongbin Li. 2019. The Rise of Robots in China. *The Journal of Economic Perspectives* 33 (2): 71–88.

Christie, Kenneth, and Denny Roy. 2001. *The Politics of Human Rights in East Asia*. London: Pluto Press.

Cohen, Paul T. 2000. Lue Across Borders: Pilgrimage and the Muang Sing Reliquary in Northern Laos. In *Where China Meets Southeast Asia: Social & Cultural Change in the Border Regions*, ed. Grant Evans, Christopher Hutton, and Kuah Khun Eng. Bangkok: ISEAS Singapore/White Lotus.

Craik, Laura, and Laura He. 2018. China Approves Proposal to Allow Foreign Individual Investors to Trade A Shares Through Domestic Brokerages. *South China Morning Post*, July 9. Accessed 9 January 2019 at https://www.scmp.com/business/markets/article/2154324/china-green-lights-proposal-allow-foreign-individual-investors.

CSIS. 2016. Is China the World's Top Trader? *China Power*. China Power Team. Center for Strategic and International Studies, Washington, DC, January 25, updated August 9, 2017. Accessed 8 January 2019 at https://chinapower.csis.org/trade-partner/.

CSIS. 2018. Economic Security as National Security: A Discussion with Dr. Peter Navarro. November 13, Center for Strategic & International Studies. Accessed 28 January 2019 at https://www.csis.org/analysis/economic-security-national-security-discussion-dr-peter-navarro.

Davies, K. 2013. China Investment Policy: An Update. OECD Working Papers on International Investment, 2013/01, OECD Publishing. http://dx.doi.org/10.1787/5k469l1hmvbt-en.

Do, Thi Thuy. 2009. The Implementation of Vietnam-China Land Border Treaty: Bilateral and Regional Implications. RSIS Working Paper, No. 173, IDSS, March 5.

DoD. 2018. *Assessing and Strengthening the Manufacturing and Defense Industrial Base and Supply Chain Resiliency of the United States*, Report to President Donald J. Trump by the Interagency Task Force in Fulfillment of Executive Order 13806, Department of Defense and Department of Defense Industrial Policy, September, Washington, DC.

Dollar, David, and Peter A. Petri. 2018. Order from Chaos: Why It's Time to End the Tit-for-Tat Tariffs in the U.S.-China Trade War, *Brookings Institute Blog*, October 5. Accessed 28 January 2019 at https://www.brookings.edu/blog/order-from-chaos/2018/10/05/why-its-time-to-end-the-tit-for-tat-tariffs-in-the-u-s-china-trade-war/.

Drezner, Daniel W. 2015. Is There an Exceptional American Approach to Global Economic Governance? In *America, China, and the Struggle for World Order:*

Asia Today, ed. G.J. Ikenberry, Wang Jisi, and Zhou Feng. New York: Palgrave Macmillan.

Duiker, William J. 1995. *Vietnam: Revolution in Transition*, 2nd ed. San Francisco: Westview Press.

Evans, Peter B., Dietrich Rueschemeyer, and Theda Skocpol (eds.). 1985. *Bringing the State Back In*. Cambridge: Cambridge University Press.

Ezell, Stephen. 2018. Why Manufacturing Digitalization Matters and How Countries Are Supporting It. *Information Technology & Innovation Foundation*, April. Accessed 25 January 2019 at http://www2.itif.org/2018-manufacturing-digitalization.pdf.

Fefer, Rachel F. 2017. Trade in Services Agreement (TiSA) Negotiations: Overview and Issues for Congress. Congressional Research Service Report, January 3. Accessed 17 January 2019 at https://fas.org/sgp/crs/misc/R44354.pdf.

Feldstein, Martin. 1998. Refocusing the IMF, *Foreign Affairs*, March/April, 20–33.

Foot, Rosemary. 2000. *Rights Beyond Borders: The Global Community and the Struggle Over Human Rights in China*. Oxford: Oxford University Press.

Foot, Rosemary, and A. King. 2019. Assessing the Deterioration in China–U.S. Relations: U.S. Governmental Perspectives on the Economic-Security Nexus. *China International Strategy Review* 1: 39–50.

Fraser Institute. 2018. *Economic Freedom of the World: 2018 Annual Report*. Vancouver. Accessed 8 January 2019 at https://www.fraserinstitute.org/sites/default/files/economic-freedom-of-the-world-2018.pdf.

Fravel, M. Taylor. 2017. Threading the Needle: The South China Sea Disputes and U.S.-China Relations. In *Strategic Adjustment and the Rise of China: Power and Politics in East Asia*, ed. Robert S. Ross and Øystein Tunsjø, 233–260. Ithaca: Cornell University Press.

Gilpin, Robert. 1975. *U.S. Power and the Multinational Corporation: The Political Economy of Foreign Direct Investment*. New York: Basic Books.

Gottschang, Thomas R. 2001. The Asian Financial Crisis and Banking Reform in China and Vietnam. Paper presented at the 2nd International Convention of Asian Scholars, 9–12 August, Berlin.

Grønning, Bjørn Elias Mikalsen. 2018. Japan's Security Cooperation with the Philippines and Vietnam. *The Pacific Review* 31 (4): 533–552.

Haggard, Stephen. 2018. *Developmental States*. Cambridge: Cambridge University Press. https://www.cambridge.org/core/elements/developmental-states/1C537B3DBDDA2F1674C4C6F34E90B600.

Hao, Hongmei. 2008. China's Trade and Economic Relations with CLMV. In *Development Strategy for CLMV in the Age of Economic Integration*, ed. C. Sotharith, 171–208. ERIA Research Project Report 2007-4, Chiba: IDE-JETRO.

Harris, Jennifer M. 2017. Writing New Rules for the U.S.-China Investment Relationship. *Council on Foreign Relations*, December 12. Accessed 7 April 2020 at https://www.cfr.org/report/writing-new-rules-us-china-investment-relationship.

Hein, Simeon. 1992. Trade Strategy and the Dependency Hypothesis: A Comparison of Policy, Foreign Investment, and Economic Growth in Latin America and East Asia. *Economic Development and Cultural Change* 40 (3) (April): 495–521.

Heritage Foundation. 2018. *Economic Freedom Index, 2018*. Accessed 17 December 2018 at https://www.heritage.org/index/ranking.

Huang, Yukon. 2017. *Cracking the China Conundrum: Why Conventional Economic Wisdom Is Wrong*. New York: Oxford University Press.

Hufbauer, Gary Clyde, Jeffrey J. Schott, Kimberly Ann Elliott, and Barbara Oegg. 2007. *Economic Sanctions Reconsidered*, 3rd ed. Washington, DC: Peterson Institute for International Economics.

Hveem, Helge, and T.J. Pempel. 2016. China's Rise and Economic Interdependence. In *China in the Era of Xi Jinping: Domestic and Foreign Policy Challenges*, ed. Robert S. Ross and Jo Inge Bekkevold. Washington, DC, Georgetown University Press.

Ikenberry, G. John, Michael Mastanduno, and William C. Wohlforth. 2009. Introduction: Unipolarity, State Behavior, and Systemic Consequences. *World Politics* 61 (1): 1–27.

International Monetary Fund. 2018. Lao People's Democratic Republic 2017 Article IV Consultation. IMF Country Report, No. 18/84, March. Available at www.imf.org.

Jackson, Van. 2014. Power, Trust, and Network Complexity: Three Logics of Hedging in Asian Security. *International Relations of the Asia-Pacific* 14 (3): 331–356.

Jacobson, Harold K., and Michel Oksenberg. 1990. *China's Participation in the IMF, the World Bank, and GATT: Toward a Global Economic Order*. Ann Arbor: University of Michigan Press.

Jennings, Ralph. 2018. Chinese Get Chances to Invest in Vietnam Despite Political Rifts. *Voice of America*, December 17. Accessed 29 January 2019 at https://www.voanews.com/a/vietnam-and-chinese-investments/4703661.html.

Kent, Ann. 2007. *Beyond Compliance: China, International Organizations, and Global Security*. Stanford: Stanford University Press.

Keohane, Robert O., and Joseph S. Nye Jr. 1998. Power and Interdependence in the Information Age. *Foreign Affairs* 77 (5): 81–94.

Kirshner, Jonathan. 2008. Globalization, American Power, and International Security. *Political Science Quarterly* 123 (3): 363–389.

Lau, Lawrence J. 2018. Behind the US-China Trade War Lies a Competition for Dominance and a Rising Tide of Protectionism. *South China Morning Post*, August 17. Accessed 28 January 2019 at https://www.scmp.com/comment/insight-opinion/united-states/article/2160041/behind-us-china-trade-war-lies-competition.

Lee, Chung H., and Seiji Naya. 1988. Trade in East Asian Development with Comparative Reference to Southeast Asian Experiences. *Economic Development and Cultural Change* 36 (3): 123–152.

Leifer, Michael. 1997. China in Southeast Asia: Interdependence and Accommodation. In *China Rising: Nationalism and Interdependence*, ed. David S.G. Goodman and Gerald Segal. London: Routledge.

Lester, Simon, and Huan Zhu. 2018. The WTO Still Considers China a 'Developing Nation.' Here's the Big Problem with That. *CNBC Markets*, April 25. Accessed 7 January 2019 at https://www.cnbc.com/2018/04/25/what-trump-gets-right-about-china-and-trade.html.

Leung, Suiwah. 2009. Banking and Financial Sector Reforms in Vietnam. *ASEAN Economic Bulletin* 26 (1): 44–57.

Li, Guoping, and Hong Zhou. 2016. The Systematic Politicization of China's Stock Markets. *Journal of Contemporary China* 25 (99): 422–437.

Li, Yitan. 2014. US Economic Sanctions Against China: A Cultural Explanation of Sanction Effectiveness. *Asian Perspective* 38 (2): 311–335.

Li, Yuwen, and Bian Cheng. 2016. A New Dimension of Foreign Investment Law in China—Evolution and Impacts of the National Security Review System. *Asia Pacific Law Review* 24 (2): 149–175.

Liu, Meichen. 2018. The New Chinese Foreign Investment Law and Its Implication on Foreign Investors. *Northwestern Journal of International Business & Law* 38 (2) (Winter): 285–306.

Lowe, Sanda. 2016. Out of Obscurity. *Asia Times*, December 10, Accessed 28 January 2019 at http://www.atimes.com/article/china-top-foreign-investor-behind-laos-fast-growth/.

Mankoff, Jeffrey. 2015. Russia's Asia Pivot: Confrontation or Cooperation? *Asia Policy* 19: 65–88.

Martin, Michael F. 2009. U.S.-Vietnam Economic and Trade Relations: Issues for the 111th Congress. Congressional Research Service, October 29, Washington, DC.

Martin, Michael F. 2016. U.S.-Vietnam Economic and Trade Relations: Issues for the 114th Congress. Congressional Research Service, May 20, Washington, DC.

Matthews, Barbara C., Earl Anthony Wayne, and Cecilia Pan. 2018. Trade in Services Agreement: A Way Out of the Trade War? *Atlantic Council*, July 23. Accessed 17 January 2019 at https://www.atlanticcouncil.org/blogs/new-atlanticist/trade-in-services-agreement-a-way-out-of-the-trade-war.

Menon, Jayant, and Peter Warr. 2013. The Lao Economy: Capitalizing on Natural Resource Exports. ADB Economics Working Paper Series, No. 330, January, Asian Development Bank, Manila, Philippines.

Min, Zhu, et al. 2020. China's Financial Development: A Global Perspective. In *The Jingshan Report: Opening China's Financial Sector*, ed. Hu Bing, 51–108. Canberra, ACT, Australia: ANU Press.

Naughton, Barry. 2007. *The Chinese Economy: Transitions and Growth*. Cambridge and London: The MIT Press.

Ngo, Hanh, Hùng Đao, Hoat Ngyuen, and Dao Trang. 2017. Improving Quality of Foreign Direct Investment Attraction in Vietnam. *International Journal of Quality Innovation*, Issue 3. https://doi.org/10.1186/s40887-017-0016-7.

Nguyen, Dinh Chuc, and Ta Phuc Duong. 2019. Trade, Structural Adjustments and Productivity Growth in Vietnam. Special Issue: Services, Trade and Global Value Chains, *Journal of Southeast Asian Economies* 36 (2) (August): 256–273.

OEC. 2020. Various Figures for Vietnam and Laos. The Observatory of Economic Complexity, MIT. Accessed 23 March 2020 at https://atlas.media.mit.edu/en/profile/country/.

Okonjo-Iweala, Ngozi, Victoria Kwakwa, Andrea Beckwith, and Zafar Ahmed. 1999. Impact of Asia's Financial Crisis on Cambodia and the Lao PDR. *Finance & Development* 36 (3) (September), International Monetary Fund. Available at https://www.imf.org/external/pubs/ft/fandd/1999/09/okonjo.htm#author.

Osnos, Evan. 2015. The Real Risk Behind China's Stock-Market Drama. *The New Yorker*, July 15. Accessed 8 January 2019 at https://www.newyorker.com/news/daily-comment/the-real-risk-behind-chinas-stock-market-drama.

Palley, Thomas I. 2012. The Rise and Fall of Export-Led Growth. *Investigación Económica* 71 (280): 141–161.

Pang, Edgar. 2017. "Same-Same But Different": Laos and Cambodia's Political Embrace of China. ISEAS Perspective Issue No. 66, September 5, 1–7.

Pant, Harsh V. 2018. *India and Vietnam: A "Strategic Partnership" in the Making*. Research Report, S. Rajaratnam School of International Studies, 20 pp.

Pempel, T.J. 1999. The Developmental Regime in a Changing World Economy. In *The Developmental State*, ed. Meredith Woo-Cumings. Ithaca: Cornell University Press.

Pence, Mike. 2018. Vice President Mike Pence's Remarks on the Administration's Policy Towards China, October 4, Hudson Institute. Accessed 28 January 2019 at https://www.hudson.org/events/1610-vice-president-mike-pence-s-remarks-on-the-administration-s-policy-towards-china102018.

Perkins, Dwight H. 2001. Industrial and Financial Policy in China and Vietnam: A New Model or a Replay of the East Asian Experience? In *Rethinking the East Asian Miracle*, ed. Joseph E. Stiglitz and Shahid Yusuf. New York: Oxford University Press.

Rana, Pradumna B., et al. 2019. *China's Belt and Road Initiative: A Perception Survey of Asian Opinion Leaders*. RSIS Working Paper, November 25, S. Rajaratnam School of International Studies, Singapore.

Reinhardt, Dennis, Luca Antonio Ricci, and Thierry Tressel. 2013. International Capital Flows and Development: Financial Openness Matters. Bank of England Working Paper No. 472, Accessed 10 January 2019 at http://siteresources.worldbank.org/INTFR/Resources/InternationalCapitalFlowsandDevelopment_2013march19.pdf.

Rigg, Jonathan. 1995. Managing Dependency in a Reforming Economy: The Lao PDR. *Contemporary Southeast Asia* 17 (2): 147–172.

Rodrik, Dani. 2010. Making Room for China in the World Economy. *The American Economic Review* 100 (2): 89–93.

Ross, Robert S. 1988. *The Indochina Trangle: China's Vietnam Policy, 1975–1979*. New York: Columbia University Press.

Ross, Robert S. 2018. Keeping Up with China's PLAN. *The National Interest*, April 15. https://nationalinterest.org/feature/keeping-chinas-plan-25383.

Ross, Robert S., and Mingjiang Li. 2016. Xi Jinping and the Challenges to Chinese Security. In *China in the Era of Xi Jinping: Domestic and Foreign Policy Challenges*, ed. Robert S. Ross and Jo Inge Bekkevold, 233–265. Washington, DC. Georgetown University Press.

Roy, Denny. 2005. Southeast Asia and China: Balancing or Bandwagoning? *Contemporary Southeast Asia* 27 (2): 305–322.

Sanger, David E., Julian E. Barnes, Raymond Zhong, and Marc Santory. 2019. In 5G Race With China, U.S. Pushes Allies to Fight Huawei. *New York Times*, January 26. Accessed 28 January 2019 at https://www.nytimes.com/2019/01/26/us/politics/huawei-china-us-5g-technology.html.

Sayavong, Vanxay. 2015. Export Growth, Export Potential and Export Resistance: A Case Study of Laos. *Journal of Southeast Asian Economies* 32 (3) (December): 340–357.

Schwab, Klaus. 2017. *The Fourth Industrial Revolution*. New York: Crown Publishing.

Schwab, Klaus (ed.). 2018. *The World Economic Forum's Competitiveness Report 2018*. Geneva: World Economic Forum.

Scissors, Derek. 2016. Fixing US-China Trade and Investment. American Enterprise Institute, April.

Scissors, Derek. 2020. China's Global Investment in 2019: Going Global Goes Small. American Enterprise Institute, January. https://www.aei.org/wp-content/uploads/2020/01/Chinas-global-investment-in-2019-1.pdf.

Sheng, Andrew. 2009. *From Asian to Global Financial Crisis: An Asian Regulator's View of Unfettered Finance in the 1990s and 2000s*. Cambridge: Cambridge University Press.

Shirk, Susan L. 1994. *How China Opened Its Door: The Political Success of the PRCs Foreign Trade and Investment Reforms*. Washington, DC: The Brookings Institution.

SIPRI. 2020. *Military Expenditure Database*, Stockholm International Peace Research Institute. https://www.sipri.org/databases/milex.

Soto, Marcelo. 2000. Capital Flows and Growth in Developing Countries: Recent Empirical Evidence. Working Paper No. 160 (Formerly Technical Paper No. 160), July, OECD Development Centre. Accessed 10 January 2019 at https://www.oecd-ilibrary.org/docserver/633871307443.pdf?expires=1547210413&id=id&accname=guest&checksum=6A324213846E0FE77027BFACF55C8168.

Spero, Joan Edelman. 1990. *The Politics of International Economic Relations*, 4th ed. London: Unwin/Hyman.

Stallings, Barbara. 1990. The Role of Foreign Capital in Economic Development. In *Manufacturing Miracles: Paths of Industrialization in Latin America and East Asia*, ed. Gary Gereffi and Donald L. Wyman. Princeton, NJ: Princeton University Press.

Stearns, Jonathan. 2018. EU Set to Tighten Rules on Foreign Investment to Fend Off China. *Bloomberg*, November 18. Accessed 28 January 2018 at https://www.bloomberg.com/news/articles/2018-11-18/eu-set-to-tighten-rules-on-foreign-investment-to-fend-off-china.

Stiglitz, Joseph E. 2002. *Globalization and Its Discontents*. New York: W. W. Norton & Company.

Stiglitz, Joseph E. 2006. *Making Globalization Work*. London: Penguin Books.

Stiglitz, Joseph E. 2010. Risk and Global Economic Architecture: Why Full Financial Integration May Be Undesirable. NBER Working Paper, 15718, National Bureau of Economic Research, Cambridge, MA.

Stuart-Fox, Martin. 2003. *A Short History of China and Southeast Asia: Tribute, Trade and Influence*. Crows Nest: Allen & Unwin.

Stuart-Fox, Martin. 2009. LAOS: The Chinese Connection. *Southeast Asian Affairs*, 141–169.

Stubbs, Richard. 2005. *Rethinking Asia's Economic Miracle: The Political Economy of War, Prosperity and Crisis*. Basingstoke: Palgrave Macmillan.

Stubbs, R., and Geoffrey R. D. Underhill (eds.). 1994. *Political Economy and the Changing Global Order*. London: Macmillan.

Swaine, Michael D. 2011. *America's Challenge: Engaging a Rising China in the Twenty-First Century*. Washington, DC: Carnegie Endowment for International Peace.

Tabeta, Shunsuke. 2018. China to Toughen Scrutiny of Foreign Investments. *Nikkei Asian Review*, July 31. Accessed 28 January 2019 at https://asia.nikkei.com/Economy/Trade-War/China-to-toughen-scrutiny-of-foreign-investments.

Thayer, Carlyle A. 2010. US Rapprochement with Laos and Cambodia. *Contemporary Southeast Asia* 32 (3): 442–459.

Thayer, Carlyle A. 2011. The Tyranny of Geography: Vietnamese Strategies to Constrain China in the South China Sea. *Contemporary Southeast Asia* 33 (3): 348–369.

Thayer, Carlyle A. 2018. Force Modernization: Vietnam. *Southeast Asian Affairs*, 429–444.

Tong Shuxing. 1991. Sino-American Technology Transfer Since 1972. In *Sino-American Relations Since 1900*, ed. Priscilla Roberts. University of Hong Kong: Centre of Asian Studies.

Tønnesson, Stein. 2003. Sino-Vietnamese Rapprochement and the South China Sea Irritant. *Security Dialogue* 34 (1): 55–70.

Tønnesson, Stein. 2017. *Explaining the East Asian Peace: A Research Story*. Copenhagen: Nordic Institute of Asian Studies (NIAS) Press.

UNCTAD. 2018. *World Investment Report 2018*. worldinvestmentreport.org.

U.S. Department of the Treasury. 2019. Treasury Designates China as a Currency Manipulator, Press release, August 5. Accessed 7 April 2020 at https://home.treasury.gov/news/press-releases/sm751.

Van Arkadie, Brian, and Raymond Mallon. 2003. *Vietnam: A Transition Tiger?* The Australian National University: Asia Pacific Press.

Vietnam News. 2018. Limited Results After Relaxation of Foreign Ownership Cap, September 17. Accessed 25 January 2019 at http://vietnamnews.vn/economy/465823/limited-results-after-relaxation-of-foreign-ownership-cap.html#1i4P0Pf2tqWJ0Bzj.99.

Vietnam Trade promotion Agency. 2017. Vietnam's Nine-Month FDI Hits Record of Nearly US$25.5 Billion, October 24. Accessed 25 January 2019 at http://en.vietrade.gov.vn/index.php?option=com_content&view=article&id=2609:vietnams-nine-month-fdi-hits-record-of-nearly-us255-billion-&catid=270:vietnam-industry-news&Itemid=363.

Vo, Tri Thanh. 2005. Vietnam's Trade Liberalization and International Economic Integration: Evolution, Problems and Challenges. CIRD Report, March, China Institute for Reform and Development. Accessed 14 January 2019 at http://www.chinareform.org/publications/reports/200504/t20050416_111302.htm.

Vu, Minh Khuong. 2015. Can Vietnam Achieve More Robust Economic Growth? Insights from a Comparative Analysis of Economic Reforms in Vietnam and China. *Journal of Southeast Asian Economies* 32 (1) (April): 52–83.

Wade, Robert. 2004. *Governing the Market: Economic Theory and the Role of Government in East Asia's Industrialization*, 2nd paperback ed. Princeton, NJ: Princeton University Press.

Wade, Robert, and Frank Veneroso. 1998. The Asian Crisis: The High Debt Model Versus the Wall Street-Treasury-IMF Complex. *New Left Review* 228 March 1, 3–22.

Waltz, Kenneth N. 1959. *Man, the State and War: A Theoretical Analysis*. New York: Columbia University Press.

Wang, Bijun. 2012. Upgrading China's Economy Through Outward Foreign Direct Investment. In *Rebalancing and Sustaining Growth in China*, ed. Huw McKay and Ligang Song, 149–174. Canberra: ANU Press.

Wang, Hongying. 1999. The Asian Financial Crisis and Financial Reforms in China. *The Pacific Review* 12 (4): 537–556.

White House. 2017. *National Security Strategy of the United States of America*, December, Washington, DC. Accessed 28 January 2019 at https://www.whitehouse.gov/wp-content/uploads/2017/12/NSS-Final-12-18-2017-0905-2.pdf.

Womack, Brantly. 2006. *China and Vietnam: The Politics of Asymmetry*. New York: Cambridge University Press.

Womack, Brantley, and Guangzhi Zhao. 1994. The Many Worlds of China's Provinces: Foreign Trade and Diversification. In *China Deconstructs: Politics, Trade and Regionalism*, ed. David S. Goodman and Gerald Segal. London and New York: Routledge.

Wood, Adrian. 1994. *North-South Trade, Employment and Inequality: Changing Fortunes in a Skill-Driven World*. New York, NY: Oxford University Press.

World Bank. 1993. *The East Asian Miracle: Economic Growth and Public Policy*. New York: Oxford University Press.

World Bank. 2013. *Global Development Horizons. Capital for the Future: Saving and Investment in an Interdependent World*. Washington, DC: International Bank for Reconstruction and Development/The World Bank.

World Bank. 2018. Net ODA Received (% of GNI), World Bank Data. Accessed 18 January 2019 at https://data.worldbank.org/indicator/DT.ODA.ODAT.GN.ZS?locations=CN-LA-VN.

World Bank. 2019a. Trade in Services, World Bank Data. Accessed 17 January 2019 at https://data.worldbank.org/indicator/BG.GSR.NFSV.GD.ZS.

World Bank. 2019b. Foreign Direct Investment. Net Inflows (% of GDP), World Bank Data. Accessed 7 January 2019 at https://data.worldbank.org/indicator/BX.KLT.DINV.WD.GD.ZS?locations=JP-PH.

World Bank. 2020a. Trade as % of GDP, World Bank Data. Accessed 30 March 2020 at https://data.worldbank.org/indicator/NE.TRD.GNFS.ZS.

World Bank. 2020b. World Integrated Trade Solution. Accessed 30 March 2020 at https://wits.worldbank.org/countrysnapshot/en/VNM.

World Finance. 2018. Vietnam's Burgeoning Stock Market Continues Its Resilient Comeback, October 5. Accessed 8 January 2019 at https://www.worldfinance.com/wealth-management/vietnams-burgeoning-stock-market-maintains-its-stirring-comeback.

World Trade Organization. 2018. Trade Policy Review: China, Executive Summary, WT/TPR/S/375 China. Accessed 17 January 2019 at https://www.wto.org/english/tratop_e/tpr_e/tp475_e.htm.

World Trade Organization. 2019. *Trade Policy Reviews*. Accessed 24 January 2019 at https://www.wto.org/english/tratop_e/tpr_e/tpr_e.htm.

Xing, Yuqing. 2014. Measuring Value Added in the People's Republic of China's Exports: A Direct Approach, ADBI Working Paper 493, Tokyo: Asian Development Bank Institute. Available at http://www.adbi.org/working-paper/2014/08/06/6372.measuring.value.added.prc.exports/.

Yahuda, Michael. 1996. *Hong Kong: China's Challenge*. London and New York: Routledge.

Yahuda, Michael. 1997. How Much Has China Learned About Interdependence? In *China Rising: Nationalism and Interdependence*, ed. David S.G. Goodman and Gerald Segal. London: Routledge.

Yusuf, Shahid. 2001. The East Asian Miracle at the Millennium. In *Rethinking the East Asian Miracle*, ed. Joseph E. Stiglitz and Shahid Yusuf. New York: Oxford University Press.

Zhang, Kevin H. 2015. China's Manufacturing Performance and Industrial Competitiveness Upgrading: International Comparison and Policy reflection. In *China's Domestic Transformation in a Global Context*, ed. Ligang Song, Ross Garnaut, Cai Fang, and Lauren Johnston. Canberra: ANU Press.

Zheng, Yongnian. 2004. *Globalization and State Transformation in China*. Cambridge: Cambridge University Press.

Zhou, Xiaobing. 2012. Impact of Capital Inflows and Technology Transfer on the Chinese Economy. In *APEC and Liberalisation of the Chinese Economy*, ed. Peter Drysdale, Zhang Yunling, and Ligang Song. Canberra: ANU Press.

Zhou, Yixiao. 2013. Growing into an Innovative Economy: Evidence from Chinese Firm-Level Data Analysis. In *China: A New Model for Growth and Development*, ed. Ross Garnaut, Cai Fang, and Ligang Song, 125–146. Canberra: ANU Press.

Zoellick, Robert B. 2005. Whither China: From Membership to Responsibility? Remarks to National Committee on U.S.-China Relations, New York City, September 21, U.S. Department of State website. Accessed 1 April 2020 at https://2001-2009.state.gov/s/d/former/zoellick/rem/53682.htm.

CHAPTER 3

China and Vietnam as Instances of Consolidated Market-Leninism

Jonathan D. London

The rapid growth of China's economy over the last four decades and the prominent role of its state in governing the country's economy has generated an ongoing debate but little consensus as to the nature of China's economy. It seems the world has never seen anything like contemporary China's economy and has little idea of how to characterise or make sense of it in comparative terms.

While the Communist Party of China (CPC) has represented the country's experience as a potential model for other countries, the party's wide adoption of comprehensive surveillance technologies, the party's atrocious records on human rights and pollution, its increasingly expansionary foreign policy stances and, not least, its systemic failures in managing public health call such claims into question. But they do not detract from the importance of key questions about what features of China and its political economy can explain the country's rapid industrialisation, how we can best understand the country's experiences, and its implications for theory and practice.

J. D. London (✉)
Leiden University, Leiden, The Netherlands
e-mail: j.d.london@hum.leidenuniv.nl

A. Hansen et al. (eds.), *The Socialist Market Economy in Asia*,
https://doi.org/10.1007/978-981-15-6248-8_3

Within the field of political economy, three broad sets of perspectives on China's economy or political economy are discernible, each containing insights but all reflecting problematic assumptions and claims and corresponding inadequacies. The first of these include varieties of political economy wedded to assumptions of neo-classical economics. While varying substantially in their analysis and not without value, perspectives within this camp are commonly afflicted by the belief that China's experiences can be best explained in terms of principles of neoclassical economics. In China as elsewhere, neoclassical economics is insufficient or worse because it ignores the fundamental ways in which economies and economic aspects of social life are embedded in their social environments leading to all sorts of erroneous claims. The purchase of neoclassical political economy is correspondingly limited.

The second set of perspectives is chiefly concerned with state capabilities, and asks whether China is helpfully understood as a 'developmental state', along the lines of those observed in the past, in Japan, Korea, Taiwan and Singapore. While pursuing an interesting set of questions, some enthusiasts of this perspective encounter difficulties when they mistake superficial similarities (e.g. location, cultural features and rapid industrialisation) for analysis of patterns of state development, or confuse Communist Party propaganda (e.g. the Beijing consensus) for actual practices, or fail to attend to continuity and change in features of the world market and the ways these shape the character and opportunities and constraints China has faced.

However useful, state-focused comparative political economy accounts that seek to identify or place China as a variety of capitalism suffer similar drawbacks. Analysts who address China and Vietnam within the developmental state and VoC literatures often argue along the right lines—these countries' states are developmentalist in their orientation and increasingly capitalist with respect to their social relations. Yet understanding and explaining these political economies' development requires analysis of continuity and change in the power relations and ideas that have underpinned these political economies' development deeper and sociologically thicker than these literatures often provide.

A final set of perspectives, which might be best labelled critical political economy (for its association with classical and contemporary Marxist and non-Marxist critiques of capitalism) avers that China's political economy and developmental arc are substantively capitalist or (by some accounts) neoliberal, in that the country's social relational features reflect a real subsumption of labour by capital. While providing vital insights, the fundamental limits of critical political economy perspectives in general and with respect to China is their poor state of development with respect to contemporary policy debates or activism. While analytically instructive, purely theoretical articles on China are a poor substitute for those seeking links between theory and practice. At a minimum, analysis must attend to practical and policy questions about economic performance and responses to increasingly virulent mixes of capitalist social relations and authoritarianism.

Each of the aforementioned political economy perspectives, then, has basic flaws. China may not be wholly understood in terms of neoclassical political economy because that disembedded perspective offers no credible theory of the relation between state and market, despite institutional economists attempts to address the state through economistic models of 'political settlements'. China is not a developmental state—at least not along the lines of Japan, Korea, Taiwan and Singapore—as the organisation of its economy and the relation between state and capital within it differs fundamentally from that observed in those countries. Nor is it always useful to understand China and capitalist or neoliberal. While the country's political economy is certainly founded on capitalist exploitation, capitalists do not dominate its class structure in ways comparable to political economies elsewhere.

We may ask, then, if China is not usefully mainly understood as a market economy or a developmental state or a capitalist economy, how else are we understand it other than it is different or unique? The response provides here is that China's economy is not best understood as a market economy or a developmental state or a capitalist economy at all. And nor is China unique.

Specifically, I contend that China together with the widely neglected case of Vietnam represent a distinctive variety of society or *social order* that, at the present historical moment, is best characterised as a *consolidated market-Leninist order*. This chapter establishes essential features of market-Leninist orders and develops a comparative analysis of China and Vietnam's experiences to illustrate and explain the value and limitations of this concept.

My arguments are organised as follows. I begin by addressing perspectives from economics, political settlements, developmental states and varieties of capitalism in that order. With respect to all, I warn against accounts that treat institutional forms and patterns as causes in favour of an approach that understands institutions as proximate causes of deeper sociological processes. Following such an approach, I locate the distinctiveness of China and Vietnam's social orders in the particularities of their social histories, including the social dynamics of the two countries' paths to and from state-socialism. I show how these histories generated modes of social coordination, conflict and competition specific to them.

I demonstrate that China and Vietnam's specific combination of market economic institutions and Leninist power relations produce social logics that are not captured by the ideal-typical notion of the developmental state or recognisably 'Asian varieties of capitalism'. Finally, I consider the value and limits of the market-Leninism concept as a heuristic for situating and theorising the Chinese and Vietnamese political economies among historical varieties of political economy and its implications for theory and practice.

As descriptive analysis of institutional forms is not an explanation, through a comparison of Vietnam and China, I explain how differences in the countries' politics and underlying social relations have generated distinctive developmental trajectories or instantiations of market-Leninism in the context of the twenty-first-century world market.

At a general level, China and Vietnam's social orders are best understood with reference to their particular and historically emergent and preponderant combination of Leninist political institutions and market-based strategies of accumulation. As such, they are best understood as unique instances of a distinctive market-Leninist form of social order whose institutional features differ from ideal-typical developmental states and from known varieties of capitalism.

The Value and Limits of Contemporary Political Economy

Over the last four decades the economies of China and Vietnam have been among the fastest-growing in the world. Unlike other all other transitional countries, rapid economic growth in China and Vietnam was sustained over these countries' entire reform periods. This is impressive even when we acknowledge China and Vietnam's low income starting points.

Growth has permitted very significant if highly uneven improvements in living standards. In both countries, poverty has declined precipitously and living standards have improved very substantially. While some inequalities have intensified amid rapid industrialisation and uneven development others have moderated. Both countries have become richer and more unequal.

A consideration of summary statistics is indicative if not explanatory. Between 1990 and 2018, average annual GDP growth in China was estimated at between 9 and 10%, while average annual growth in Vietnam neared 7% (World Bank). A widely cited statistic for China stated that, since introducing reforms in 1978, more than 500 million have been lifted out of poverty (World Bank and DRCSC 2012). Using the 2011 metric of US$1.90 per day per capita, incidence of poverty in China in 2015 was put at less than one percent and 7% for the US$3.20 benchmark. Official figures indicate poverty in Vietnam declined even more sharply. In 1993, 59% of Vietnamese were estimated to be living on less than a dollar a day, but just 6% were by 2010 (World Bank 2012) and less than six percent by 2018 (Rama 2021). While China is vastly wealthier than Vietnam, in 2016 just 2% of Vietnam's population falls below the 2011 metric of US$1.90 per day per capita, while 8.4% fell below the US$3.20 poverty line.

The intensity of interest in China's growth experience in particular occasioned the development of a massive literature, leading one prominent scholar to declare a state of 'Sinomania' (Anderson 2010). By 2020 attention to China's rise had hardly abated, even as the Corona pandemic posed unanswerable questions about the world economy and China's ascendant role within it. By 2016 the pace of China's growth had (somewhat inevitably) slowed. Still, the country's economy has vastly increased in its size and sophistication. Vietnam's rapid growth has also attracted considerable if considerably less attention. In recent years significant FDI has been redirected from China to Vietnam to take advantage of relative costs and in 2018 Vietnam's smaller economy grew at a faster rate than China. On the whole, Vietnam and its state in particular has failed to replicate China's success in moving into the production of higher value goods and services.

The trajectory of both countries' growth in the context of market reforms is particularly striking when viewed in historical and geopolitical terms. Both countries have transitioned from the ranks of Asia's poorest and most isolated to its most upwardly mobile within the span of two decades. In both countries, communist party-state regimes that were once regarded as bulwarks against global capitalism and imperialism have hitched their party-dictatorships to dynamic market-led growth (see

Bui Hai Thiem, this volume). Today, China is using its capital and market power in an imperialist fashion, backed by its growing military power and its ability to shape global public opinion through strategic communication and other means. It's success in so doing has not been harmed by the bumbling corruption that has characterised the US political economy since 2016.

Still, while China's and Vietnam's economic performances have attracted great attention, explaining their performance has posed challenges to leading theoretical accounts of development, particularly those that trace their roots to principles and assumptions drawn from neoclassical economics, its emergent subfield of 'new institutional economics', and such other forms of neo-institutionalism as the literature on 'varieties of capitalism (VOC)". The two country's growth experiences also pose problems for accounts that suggest China and Vietnam to be actual or aspiring developmental states and for critical political economy literature on 'variegated neoliberalism'.

The value and limits of neoclassical and new-institutional economics

In key respects, China and Vietnam's growth experiences contradict the expectations of the principles of neoclassical economics that have prevailed in disciplinary economics approaches to development and development policy since the 1980s. According to this perspective, the more market based on economy is the more efficient and dynamic a growth engine it will become. And yet, in both China and Vietnam, states led by communist parties have presided over rapid economic growth while remaining pervasively involved in economic affairs. But not only this, economic growth has been sustained while under policies that have frequently and intentionally gotten prices 'wrong', have been anti-competitive, and have locked in fuzzy property rights. In both countries, the rule of law is absent, and the economies are pervasively corrupt. In key respects, China and Vietnam have resolutely ignored 'market-friendly' policy prescriptions that neoclassical economists have advocated for and which have been more effectively imposed in economies and societies worldwide.

This does not mean neoclassical economics has nothing useful to say about China and Vietnam. For example, the massive uptick in agricultural productivity observed in the 1980s (in China) and 1990s (in Vietnam) did indeed have a great deal to do with improved incentives that came with marketising reforms, setting the stage for massive increases in agricultural output and rural savings. Furthermore, both China and Vietnam have benefited substantially from trade and China's role in the world economy has almost single handedly propelled processes of global wage compression that neo-Ricardian models of factor-price-equalisation have predicted.

When questions about the relevance of their ideas arise, neoclassical and new institutionalist economists have responded with claims that China and Vietnam would have grown (or will in the future grow) even faster with more 'market friendly' institutions and policies that conform to features of more established or more 'competitive' varieties of capitalism—that is, 'real market economies'. These preferred models are invariably defined by a smaller role for the state, more 'good governance', and more competitive practices. In one of the stronger analyses along these lines, Huang (2008) contends that China's party-state's prominent economic role is broadly destructive of entrepreneurialism. There is truth to this and a similar dynamic has been observed in Vietnam (Vu 2020). There is, furthermore, ample empirical support for the claim that China and Vietnam's state sectors are inefficient and sometimes 'crowd out' the private sector through by way of their preferential access to factor inputs. In neoclassical economics accounts of China and Vietnam's development, improved incentives, low-cost labour and vent for surplus play the heroes against the villains of rent seeking, market imperfections and 'state intervention' (Malesky and London 2014).

Like other approaches to political economy, neoclassical economics can be used to generate parsimonious, empirically grounded explanations of China's and Vietnam's performance. But as guides to understanding or explaining China and Vietnam or as policy prescriptions, these accounts have numerous limits. Furthermore, facts of China and Vietnam's development consistent with certain expectations of neoclassical economics theory do not alone explain observed patterns let alone validate calls for never-ending liberalisation.

Put different, neoclassical 'economic laws' or even 'rules of thumb' are a poor guide for understanding how any economy works. In China and Vietnam, neoclassical economics' sociological thinness severely limits its purchase and, indeed, often makes it a hazardous practice. Absent an account of the politics and social histories that generated the Chinese market and its constituent institutions, such narratives are inadequate to the task of understanding or explaining how the Chinese and Vietnamese economies actually work because they rest on context-free accounts of unreality.

Douglas North's identification of the non-market origins of market economies was among the driving forces of new-institutional economics (NIE), and branch of economics that seeks to explain economic performance in terms of formal and informal rules that shape economic behaviour across countries. Drawing on the insights of North and others and after scores of academic papers, Robison and Acemogulu (e.g. 2012) developed a best-selling account of the institutional sources of countries' economic performance authoritatively titled *Why Nations Fail*.

Advancing the literature on institutions North, Walis and Weingast, together with Mushtaq Khan have pursued their interest in institutions through a theory of political settlements at whose core is the proposition that social orders vary in the extent to which their institutional arrangements are able to control violence. Khan and Sundaram (2000), Khan (2010, 2017) establishes the importance of political settlements in determining conditions economic development, where political settlements are defined as 'a combination of power and institutions that is mutually compatible and also sustainable in terms of economic and political viability'. Khan's conception of political settlements is useful, if suspect in its treatment of power and institutions as separate.

In an argument broadly consistent with Robison and Acemogulu and Khan, North, Webb, Walis and Weingast Et al (ibid.) identify countries' economic performance with the relative openness and long-term viability of their 'access orders'. In countries with unstable political settlements, such as the Philippines, institutional change, political instability and sporadic violence undermine economic performance over the long term. Stable political settlements are those that exhibit stable institutional arrangements around power sharing.

While Robinson and Acemogulu demonstrate that institutions matter, their analysis nonetheless remains mainly faithful to principles of economics and precepts of methodological individualism and thus an undersocialised view of reality. Their account of China has been criticised for characterising the country's economy as fragile, despite decades of sustained growth, and for offering a sort of neo-modernisation account that says good institutions (like the US constitution) are essential. As Ljunggren (2019) has pointed out, from the perspective of delivering sustained economic growth and prosperity, China and Vietnam have 'failed to fail'. We will return to these points later.

Looking beyond neoclassical economics and the emerging political settlements variant of new-institutional economics, the literatures on developmental states and VoC have taken up the question of how to explain states' and political economies' economic performance over time. In contrast to economists, theorists of developmental states have expressed enthusiasm for the idea that, under certain conditions, states can and should govern markets, rather than be governed by them—and, indeed, that the most promising paths to development lie with an approach that, while not denying the centrality of markets, does not leave economic growth to the whims of the market. In what follows, I consider the value and limits of these perspectives in turn.

Developmental States?

The voluminous literature on developmental states has contributed to the construction of an ideal type reflecting institutional, ideational and social relational features said to be characteristic of the experiences of a small number of high-performing economies in East Asia. Beginning with Japan and extending their analysis to Korea, Taiwan and Singapore, developmental state theorists located sources of effective industrial promotion in the combination of these states' historically emergent and unusually high levels of bureaucratic and technocratic capacities on the one hand and their 'embedded autonomy' (Evans 1995); where the latter refers to states ability to forge and maintain relations with non-state economic actors (e.g. firms, rural landlords) that facilitated productive use of resources, capital accumulation and market-oriented technological innovation without being 'captured' by these non-state economic actors (Johnson 1982; Amsden 1989; Woo 1991; Evans 1995; Leftwich 1995; Woo-Cumings 1999; Stubbs 2009, 2017).

Tracing the agrarian roots of Korea's development experience, Shin (1998) shows how state authorities essentially evicted landed capital from the countryside and regulated Korea industrialists over the course of decades. A similar dynamic was observed in Taiwan (Wade 1990).

What were these states' features? As Stubbs notes, most treatments have isolated an 'institutional element'—which refers to a cohesive set of state institutions with sufficient technical capacity and bureaucratic autonomy to design and implement a strategy for capitalist growth and industrialisation—and a 'relational element'—which refers to a tight-knit and even 'seamless web of political bureaucratic, and moneyed influences that structure economic life in capitalist Northeast Asia' (Stubbs 2009:

6). Many conceptualisations have emphasised an ideational component—which refers to states' emphasis on 'nationalism, (neo-)mercantilism, economic transformation, rapid industrialisation, performance legitimacy or some amalgam of a number of these ideas' (ibid.).

Leftwich (1995: 405) distilled six features of developmental states, including (1) a determined developmental elite; (2) relative autonomy of the state from society; (3) a powerful, competent and insulated bureaucracy; (4) a weak and subordinated civil society; (5) the effective management of non-state economic interests and (6) repression, legitimacy and performance. This combination of institutional properties, combined with the 'favourable' circumstances of post-war United States hegemony, permitted rapid and sustained industrialisation (see Berger 2003). Some contend the vulnerable domestic and geopolitical circumstances these states' faced elicited robust state institutions, an element lacking in Southeast Asia, for example (Cumings 1984; Friedman 1996; Doner et al. 2005; Stubbs 2005; see also Bekkevold, this volume).

The developmental states literature has made important contributions to understandings and explanations of East Asian development experiences (prior to China's rise) and the lessons that might be drawn from it. Most importantly, it discredited know-nothing 'free-market' accounts of East Asian development favoured by the likes of the World Bank and other market enthusiasts that circulated in the 1980s, who suggested that the sources of East Asia's dynamism lay principally in their embrace of markets, macroeconomic stability and export orientation, and that developing country governments ought to stay with this prescription and not be lured by anything resembling protectionism or constructed comparative advantage.

Efforts to shield policy advice from inconvenient features of East Asian growth were particularly apparent in the World Bank's 1993 'East Asian Miracle' report, an ill-fated effort to suppress evidence that state industrial promotion and pervasive intervention contributed to those countries' sustained growth (Wade 1996) and which led to the emergence of Joseph Stiglitz as a leading critic of hyper-globalisation.

For the most part, however, mainstream economists have stuck to their favoured account, effectively claiming either that 'there was protectionism, but its contributions to total factor productivity are unclear, and therefore do what we say' (World Bank 1993) or that massive investments in infrastructure, good human capital, rural savings and so on explain these countries' success (Krugman 1994; Lall 1996; Young 1994.)

As indicated above, this position—i.e. that so-called developmental states' experiences are entirely consistent with precepts of neoclassical economics—is seen in contemporary accounts of China and Vietnam, in which improved incentives, together with massive savings and investment, and outward orientation explain these countries' performance, rather than state intervention or industrial policy (e.g. Rama 2021). According to such a perspective, state 'intervention' in China and Vietnam remains a hindrance to faster growth (Huang 2011).

For their part, Marxian critiques have cast the developmental states' experience as instances of 'ceded autonomy', in which captains of industry permitted states to shape policies to a degree in so far as state policies permitted rapid capital accumulation and facilitated access to the US market (Chibber 2005; Gray 2011). More broadly, Marxist analysts have also chided neo-Weberian efforts to 'bring the state back in', insisting states have always been present in structuring, maintaining and expanding capitalism (Cammack 1989; Jessop 2001)

The developmental state literature's second contribution was its fine-grained historical analyses of state formation and industrialisation. Johnson's (1982) initial notion of the developmental state reflected a nuanced analysis of a thicket of institutions and relations that defined Japan's experience. Similarly, Jung-en Woo's (1991) analysis of Korea's experience captured the social, political and world historical context with Geertzian levels of thickness.

Finally, the developmental state literature has done the service of calling into question the institutional mono-cropping impulse that has emerged from normative neoliberal theorists of development, in which getting the 'right' (market friendly) institutions is critical for promoting sustained and 'inclusive' economic growth (Evans 2004). Indeed, for Marxist critics, the good governance literature reflects a broader hegemonic project of domination intent on instituting capitalist social relations on a world scale (Cammack 2014).

Recent theoretical literature on 'effective states' that draws substantially on the developmental state literature, is sceptical of both good governance and Marxist accounts, suggesting possibilities for selectively counterhegemonic form of governance whereby states can navigate the perils and maximise the opportunities to be had under global capitalism, to maximise the capabilities of 'their' citizenry, while achieving these not necessarily at the price of democracy (see, for example, Evans 2005, 2014;

Evans and Heller 2015). In these and other accounts, China and Vietnam are seen to be following their own distinctive path.

Developmental State Variants?

There has been a wide discussion of whether China and Vietnam represent developmental states (for a review see Beeson 2017). At a minimum, the rapid economic growth and industrialisation under authoritarian rule that has occurred in China and Vietnam is consistent with the historical experience of the developmental states of Korea, Taiwan and Singapore, which 'successfully' combined authoritarian politics with rapid economic growth.

China and Vietnam appear to share additional features with the ideal-typical developmental state. And nor is this particularly new. Since the 1980s, scholars (e.g. Johnson 1982; White 1984; Rodan 1989) have called attention to institutional attributes present in both state socialist regimes (i.e. pre-reform) and the developmental states of East Asia. These include, most crucially, an ideology of developmentalism—characterised by a belief in the necessity of explicit state guidance and planning in the pursuit of economic development and modernisation, the use of Leninist or Leninist-inspired organisational tactics (see Friedman 2011; for the case of Taiwan, see Winckler 1999), and the suppression of civil society and political opposition.

Arguing along these lines, White (1984) contends state socialist states together with 'state capitalist' and 'intermediate' states all represent developmental state variants. By state capitalist, White refers to countries 'in which the relationship between state and private capital involves both control and collaboration and where the state itself acts as an economic entrepreneur and exercises a wide range of direct and indirect controls over economic actors', whereas 'intermediate regimes' refers to those 'which, often using "socialist" labels, severely circumscribe the power of private industrial capital and base industrialisation on a massive expansion of state ownership and management, the state class emerging as a crucially independent interest to dominate those of civil society' (White 1984: 102–103). Nearly three decades and a global crisis of socialism later, *The Economist* (2012) declared 'state capitalism' to be an ascendant variety of capitalism, more about which I discuss below.

In light of these similarities it is reasonable to ask whether China and Vietnam have, in the transition from planned to market-based economies, migrated closer to the ideal-typical qualities of developmental states and whether such transitions, if they have occurred, make China and Vietnam developmental states in their own right, or the more qualified claim that China and Vietnam are states with developmentalist attributes and/or aspirations (e.g. Beeson 2004, 2009, 2017).

To explore this question, we can assess the Chinese and Vietnamese cases according to the ensemble of institutional features reflected in the ideal-typical developmental state concept (e.g. Beeson and Pham 2012). These include, most crucially, the presence of a highly capable and determined developmental elite that maintains close relations with capital but manages to maintain autonomy from capital. It is arguable that China and Vietnam possess what Leftwich (1995: 401) terms a 'determined developmental elite'. Like the ideal-typical developmental state, the political elite in both China and Vietnam appear determined in their pursuit of industrial promotion. And yet a closer examination of the 'developmental elite' in both countries paints a picture at odds with the ideal-typical developmental elites of East Asian developmental states as will be seen when we delve deeper into the China and Vietnam contexts.

The status of putatively 'developmentalist' mainland China and Vietnamese elites' 'autonomy' is similarly more complicated given the deeply interpenetrated features of state and society in these countries. In both countries the party and state are pervasively involved in economic governance, though not only state-owned enterprises (SOEs), but also administration, and the countless non-state enterprises that are linked to party and state elements. Johnson's famous distinction of plan-rational and plan-ideological regimes is worth recalling, as it spoke directly to a fundamental difference between state socialist (or 'communist') states and states such as Japan—namely their different orientation with respect to the market (Johnson 1982). As will be seen, while China and Vietnam have pursued development through the market, their orientation to the market and relations with firms differs from ideal-typical developmental states.

Others have been more comfortable with conferring China (if not Vietnam) developmental state status. Writing in 2004 Deans, labelled China a 'post socialist developmental state', noting at the time that while China's state lacked autonomy and capacity, it nonetheless exhibited three institutional criteria identified as characteristic of developmental states, namely 'transformative goals, a relatively insulated pilot agency, and institutionalised government–business cooperation' (Weiss 2000, cited in Deans 2004: 133–134). Writing around the same time, Alvin So (2002) similar claimed that China, like Korea and Taiwan, exhibited a relatively autonomous state, while noting that authoritarian policies that have effectively crushed civil society and political opposition have not damaged legitimacy owing to high growth and nationalism.

With respect to the lesser-known case of Vietnam, Beeson and Pham (2012: 540) have traced features of 'developmentalism with Vietnamese characteristics', noting that 'Even though Vietnam lacks the sort of state capacity and ability to penetrate society that is generally thought to distinguish the ideal-typical developmental state, Vietnamese policy makers have demonstrated a surprising ability to influence the direction and style of economic development'. While I am not sure I see any surprise, their characterisation of Vietnam as an 'aspirant developmental state' is reasonable only to the extent that it reflects a 'general orientation or vision about the appropriate role of government in shaping economic outcomes' (ibid). The CPV's most ardent critics question whether such a vision exists.

The question as to whether China and Vietnam possess powerful, competent and insulated pilot agencies akin to Japan's famed Ministry of International Trade and Industry (now the Ministry of Economy, Trade and Industry) draws a mixed response. In 1998, China announced the formation of the National Development and Reform Commission (NDRC) as a successor to the State Planning Commission. The NDRC plays a key macroeconomic coordination role, and remains a powerful force, dubbed by some as a mini-state council. Those comparable to MITI in respects, it's powers are hardly absolute (more about which, below) and shares power with such other ministries as the Ministry of Industry and Informational Technology. In Vietnam the Ministry of Planning and Investment (MPI), successor to the State Planning Commission of the state socialist period, was meant to develop into a kind of 'super ministry' but today performs a somewhat loose coordinating, policy formation, and advisory role agency alongside other functional ministries.

China in particular exhibits highly influential and capable central agencies in a number of fields, staffed by a corps of elite technocrats, but their powers have been and remain uneven and limited within the country's decentralised political system. Vietnam's central coordinating capacities, by comparison, appear limited to a narrower band of fields, such as disaster mitigation, security and surveillance, but decidedly not (so far) industrial promotion. Notably, the development of higher education in Vietnam is two or three decades behind that of China and the country's stock of skilled technocrats is more limited (London 2011, 2020; Masina 2012).

While the Chinese and Vietnamese central states are 'powerful' in formal terms and with respect to their ability to maintain 'order', their ability to shape the behaviour of local agents (e.g. subnational authorities and firms) is mixed. Both countries (especially China) have seen substantial improvement in the technical capacities of elite bureaucrats and agencies, even as Vietnam's state's technical capacities are comparatively much weaker.

And then there is the matter of decentralisation. In both countries, the size of the central state bureaucracy is limited and sometimes so is its power. In both countries local planners often wield greater power. To suggest that China and Vietnam's developmental bureaucracy at local levels is 'insulated' again begs the question: insulated from whom? The concept of relative autonomy has typically referred to fractions of capital within capitalist economies (Block 1981). With their Leninist political organisation, high degree of decentralisation, and deeply interpenetrated and opaque pattern of public and private ownership, use of the term 'state autonomy' with respect to industrial promotion in China and Vietnam is hardly straightforward. But it is worth attending to. Some observers find that the Chinese central state's practice of rotating officials across provinces and linking officials' promotions to economic performance has both promoted growth and enhanced the power of the central state relative to local officialdom. This perspective has been criticised on the grounds that such accounts do not sufficiently account for localities' growth trajectories or local officials' central ties prior to their arrival (Shih et al. 2012). Malesky and London (2014) and Vu (2020) note that the development of a clientelist pattern in Vietnam, where by national and local officials policy priorities are shaped by interest groups.

As for the 'effective management of non-state economic interests', the very notion of 'non-state economic interests' in both countries is fraught, even in the face growing 'private' sectors. If there is any agreement as to the features China and Vietnam have in common with the idealised developmental state, it is probably their combination of rapid economic growth and state repression backed by comparatively well-functioning if not wholly Weberian bureaucracies. In comparative terms, China's state agencies appear substantially more capable with respect to industrial promotion, as will be discussed in subsequent sections of this chapter.

Are China and Vietnam Usefully Construed as Varieties of Capitalism (VOC)?

Drawing on strands of theoretical institutionalism distant from literature on the developmental state, theorists of VoC have embraced similar claim that attributes political economies' institutional make-up—rather than their conformity to idealised principles of economics—are what best explains their economic performance. In contrast to the developmental state literature, the VoC literature developed through analysis of North Atlantic political economies plus Japan, with much later reference to other East Asian contexts. In recent years, analysts have extended ideas from both the developmental state and VoC literatures to analysis of China and Vietnam. Numerous analysts have construed China as a 'unique' 'variety of capitalism' whose performance is explained by its unique institutional features. In the section below, I review the claims of the developmental state and VoC literature before turning attention to the cases of China and Vietnam

The 'varieties of capitalism' literature traces its roots to the early 1990s, when analysts sought to distinguish capitalist political economies on the basis of their institutional traits and industrial organisation, both to account for perceived patterns of divergence and convergence and to link these to patterns of economic performance, competitiveness and welfare (Albert 1993; Lindeberg et al. 1991). Albert's seminal distinction between Anglo-American and Rhinish models spurred nuanced accounts of capitalist variety across countries, industries, sectors and policymaking fields, down to the level of the firm. Literature along these lines saw steady growth during the 1990s (e.g. Hollingsworth and Boyer 1997) and especially after the publication of several works by Hall and Soskice (e.g. Hall and Soskice 2001).

Beyond their basic distinction between coordinated market economies and liberal market economies, Hall and Soskice and other VoC theorists have explored sources of institutional and organisational change across and within varieties of capitalism, teased out the notion of 'institutional complementarity', the notion that institutional arrangements within any given political economy form a holistic institutional formation consisting of interacting institutional domains which, by some accounts, evolve because of their contributions to economic performance, efficiency, welfare and the like. As Lane and Wood (2011) observed, more functionalist variants of institutional complementarity view it as a result of strategic decision-making and institutional design carried out by elites within a given capitalism with the explicit aims of achieving institutional coherence by use of selective incentives and other means. From the perspective of this more functionalist variant of IC, more or less effective institutional performance (whether with respect to economic performance, skilling and labour markets, or welfare) may be attributed to the relative presence or absence of such coherence, or IC. From this perspective, institutional heterogeneity within specific countries is likely to be the exception rather than the rule (ibid.) Within this strand of the literature, coordinated market economies are deemed more likely to exhibit greater degrees of IC (e.g. Whitley 1999; Aoki 2001).

This approach can be contrasted with the more indeterminate, bottom-up account adumbrated by the likes of Crouch (2005, 2009), Streeck and Thelen (2005) and Boyer (2012), who are open to the possibility that economies with contradictory elements can be structurally stable, and who view institutions as flexible and constantly evolving. This is a more dynamic and open-ended conception of IC. According to this approach, heterogeneity may be expected, insofar as institutions are the product of social competition and conflict. Coherence, according to this perspective, is not stable, but must be constantly worded out and shored up, and is rarely the result of some 'grand design' (Lane and Wood 2011: 11). One example of this that is particularly germane to the concerns of this chapter has been dubbed 'institutional conversion', a situation in which actors adapt an existing institutional set-up to a new purpose and by doing so contribute to the maintenance and/or restitution of complementarity within the broader system (Streeck and Thelen 2005).

There is, then, a tension among those analysts of VoC who see 'a method in the madness' and those who attribute the presence of institutional mechanisms and practices to historical holdovers (whether ideological, organisational or institutional) from previous periods, and not their being the product of some grand design. Within this latter camp of VoC, heterogeneity and internal variation, which might in the past have been seen as evincing 'incoherence', are seen as having the potential to contribute to opportunities for innovation. In such cases, institutional diversity may be seen itself as the grand design. Let a hundred flowers bloom. To what extent, then, are features of capitalism the product of the intentional design of something profoundly indeterminate? The answer to this question is likely to vary across specific contexts depending on balances of power among competing interests and their effectiveness in imposing their will, sabotaging plans that adversely affect them, or simply muddling through. In other words, the question of design or indeterminacy is probably sterile. The questions of interests concern precisely the mechanisms underlying processes of institutional change. The manner in which this occurs varies across countries and even within them, particularly in the world's continental-sized economies.

Proceeding from the VOC literature, analysts have asked whether the world is migrating towards a single (presumably more 'neoliberal') variety of capitalism. According to some observers, financial globalisation, however powerful in the eyes of VoC theorists, has not resulted in the homogenisation of institutional set-ups. Such a claim stands in tension with the assumption of theorists of 'neoliberal globalisation', who insist that, cross-national variation in the details notwithstanding, a process of marketisation is expanding, transforming institutions and deepening capitalist social relations on a world scale, often by working 'through and around' states to this end (Carroll 2017). Either way, there has been increased interest in the determinants and consequences of hybridity and internal diversity across and within national configurations of capitalism (e.g. Boyer 2005; Lane and Wood 2011). This latter aspect is visible on both ends of the spectrum, with analyses bearing titles such as 'variegated neoliberalism' (Brenner et al. 2010) and 'institutional diversity in business systems' (Jackson and Deeg 2008). The 'so what?' question in this debate concerns effects on diversity of outcomes.

Seeking to extend VoC ideas to new terrain, analysts have sought to establish causal links between features of economic governance in East Asia and patterns of economic performance. Along these same lines, scholars have sought to distinguish key features of East Asian 'business systems' with particular attention to the role of the state, financial systems, industrial organisation, industrial relations, skilling and inter-firm relations (Witt and Redding 2014).

Still others have trained their attention to variegation across and within East Asian capitalist economies and various sectors (Carney et al. 2009; Peck and Theodore 2007; Ebner 2015). In these accounts, Hall and Soskice's (2001) distinction between 'liberal market economies' (LMEs) and 'coordinated market economies' (CMEs) proves far too narrow and static to capture features and dynamics of institutions in lower- and middle-income, late-industrialising or formerly state socialist economies, where states vary enormously in attributes, interests and power (Boyer

2005; Schmitter and Todor 2014; Szelenyi 2015) and where institutions are in flux.

Which brings us back to the cases of China and Vietnam. A number of analysts have extended VoC ideas and analytic frames to the Chinese case and Boyer's many analyses show the promise in doing so (see, for example, Boyer 2012). Starting with the familiar question of 'just what kind of economy is it?' Boyer avers that, substantively and structurally, China is indeed a variety of capitalism. China does not appear capitalist, in formal terms, owing to the close relation between politics and the economy, the fuzziness of property relations and other features. In a structural sense, however, Boyer (2012) maintains that China is indeed a variety of capitalism on the grounds that competitive markets play a preponderant role in the allocation of resources, that capital–labour relations are prevailing in the organisation of social and economic relations, and that market competition and labour–capital induced an imperative for capital (ibid.: 34).

Boyer's (2012), Lane's (2007), and Wilson's (2007) arguments are convincing for their adeptness in illustrating the path-dependent nature of China's institutional development, the presence of institutional layering and institutional residues, processes of institutional conversion, the salience of internal diversity, and, most generally, a (largely unintended) outcome of a complex history of institution building. London's (2009) analysis of Vietnam broadly shares these emphases.

Peck and Zhang (2014) offer a useful critique of the VoC perspective from the standpoint of critical geography that emphasises the significance of space and regional variation, leading them to propose an agenda of research on variegated capitalism in China, 'Chinese-style', rather than seeking to force China into a VoC box of Anglo-European origins. In their words, the two seek to develop an analysis of uneven development in China through an account of 'polymorphic capitalism (s)' that accounts for 'meaningful variegation and spatial/scalar fixes positioned in the context of shifting macro-ecologies of accumulation and regulation' across 'space/time' that is 'embedded within international divisions of labour and transitional regulatory relations' and which unfolds according to social processes of 'contradictory disequilibria' featuring '(co)evolving forms of combined and uneven development' (Peck and Zhang 2014: 56).

Though excessively dense at times, their analysis provides ways and means of pursuing research on what they term 'sub-models' of capitalism (hence the talk of 'polymorphism') within what they see as China's formidably heterogeneous economy. In this way Peck and Zhang do the service of identifying 'varieties within varieties', or 'multi-scalar variegation in space/time (ibid.)' as they put it.

Viewed more broadly, many of the conceptual problems observed in attempts to extend VoC analysis to China stem from the question of just what kind of political economy China is and how it compares with the known varieties of capitalism; that is, of the difficulty of meaningfully placing China within identified varieties of capitalism without arriving at well-reasoned but unsatisfactorily and unconvincingly general characterisations, such as 'quasi LME' (Witt 2010; Fligstein and Zhang 2011). Peck and Zhang's main response to this has been to place programmatic emphasis on the presumptive need to move away from national political economies and to accept the 'fragmented, multi-scalar, and "polymorphous" styles of governance' that may be found within any large country, which for them calls attention to the numerous limitations of analyses that feature a 'near-exclusive focus on nationally scaled formal institutions and economic dynamics' (Peck and Zhang 2013: 361–362).

Eschewing the question of whether China is or is not neoliberal, Weber (2018) explores the way in which neoliberalism has been relevant for China both ideationally and as a multi-dimensional force shaping the country's development. She finds that logics of China's 'mixed economy' are distinct from that of neoliberalism even as it has been in numerous respects shaped by neoliberalism and can and should be the subject of a critique of neoliberalism. This resonates with Masina's (2009: 204) analysis of Vietnam as an instance of 'liberalization without liberalism'. Overall, these accounts of China and Vietnam are on the right track: they reflect elements of neoliberalism but their political economies are not usefully understood as neoliberal. Indeed, I believe it useful to characterise essential features of 'national political economies' in a more encompassing and sociological way.

Towards a More Sociological Perspective

The most informative analyses of developmental states and varieties of capitalism are precisely those that delve deeply into the social and political relationships underpinning institutions. Absent such an approach, we are left with varieties of 'institutional fetishism' that mistake institutional forms as causes themselves rather than the products of historically emergent social relations. Extensions of developmental state ideas to the Chinese and Vietnamese contexts can avoid this trap by not ticking boxes of where institutional attributes of developmentalism appear, but looking at political economies' social constitution. With such an approach one observes that, despite significant similarities, China and Vietnam differ from both ideal-typical and the real developmental states of Korea, Taiwan and Singapore during their decades of developmentalism.

But nor is there a need to jettison macro-sociological analysis. Recent critiques of VoC from the field of critical geography have rightly underscored the diversity and dynamism within capitalism and the perceived need to move beyond the alleged 'institutional fetishism' and 'geographical reductionism' of earlier VoC literature (Peck and Theodor 2007). Such thinking has informed a sub-stream of literature focused on variegated capitalism (ibid.; Jessop 2011) or variegated neoliberalisation (Brenner, Peck and Theodore, 2010) that have sought to explain how the expansion of world markets has registered across 'uneven institutional landscapes' (ibid.). A key contribution of debates around VoC has been precisely the recognition that states are neither 'hermetically sealed' nor defined by national borders (Crouch 2009: 91). National political economies are today interpenetrated with agencies and institutions of the global political economy to a greater extent than in the past.

These are vital points. But I do not believe they recommend a rejection of nationally scaled macro-sociological analysis, particularly if our aim is to understand political economies comparatively. Indeed, in the section that follows I will argue that the features that distinguish China and Vietnam from other varieties of state and other varieties of political economy and which have conditioned their development lie precisely with the form and content of the power and class relations that have animated the development of their national states from the revolutionary periods, through state socialism, to the present.

From National Political Economies to Social Orders

China and Vietnam are best understood not as developmental states or varieties of capitalism but as instances of a distinctive variety of political economy or social order, i.e. a nationally scaled, globally embedded, territorially delimited and stably dynamic socio-spatial network of power defined by social relational and institutional attributes specific to them and their historical path to the present.

Construing China and Vietnam's political economies or social orders in this way facilitates analysis of their distinctive social constitution and historical development across multiple institutional fields (Brachet-Marquez 2017; London 2018). For the purposes of the present chapter, we focus on China and Vietnam's path from state socialism and their development across three key dimensions, including politics (domination), economy (accumulation) and reproduction (welfare)

China and Vietnam on the Path from State Socialism

The social orders in China and Vietnam have developed through path-dependent processes of institutional development that are specific to them, in terms of both their internal properties and their external links. The two countries reflect distinctive combinations of political, economic and welfare institutions that have mediated economic development and patterns of welfare and stratification. In both countries, thick and active legacies of state socialism continue to shape social life across the full spectrum of institutional fields. As will be demonstrated, however, China and Vietnam's paths from past to present differ, and these differences are traceable to differing local circumstances, political choices and institutions, and the particular ways in which the countries have become embedded in the broader world market. Despite these differences, China and Vietnam as social orders differ from ideal-typical accounts of developmental states and established varieties of capitalism. Instead, they are most usefully understood as unique instances of a single market-Leninist variety of social order.

The historical development of the Chinese and Vietnamese political economies has differed fundamentally from that of other countries in East Asia. The two countries have taken a distinctive but shared path from the past to the present, transitioning through decades of revolutionary socialism and state socialist central planning under conditions of semi-autarchy, violence, chaos and trauma before undergoing processes of social reconstitution in the transition to market-based political economies that have become progressively enmeshed in the institutions and processes of a single world market. These experiences have shaped the development of political and economic institutions in both countries, generating distinctive states, markets and modalities of political and economic integration. The distinctive institutional features that China and Vietnam display are manifest in the character of their politics and underlying patterns of domination, in the manner in which market institutions have been emplaced, and the latter's effects on welfare and stratification. Hence, while states in contemporary China and Vietnam may be safely regarded as developmentalist and perhaps even capitalist, the character of their developmentalism and capitalist social relations are distinctive from those observed in other countries.

The discussion here is specifically concerned with the formation of market economies within the crumbling foundations of the planned economies and, indeed, the reconfiguration or reconstitution of social relations by ruling interests. This was achieved through the piecemeal adaptation of existing institutions to the pursuit of market-based strategies of capital accumulation within the framework of Leninist political institutions. This last point bears emphasis: while over the last two decades or more, capitalist social relations have come to pervade both countries, the emplacement of market relations has taken place within relations of domination of a specifically Leninist character. And it is this relationship of domination, its historically emergent features and its amalgamated and often contradictory ideational features, that makes the Chinese and Vietnamese states behave differently from other states and which recommends against characterising the countries as garden varieties of East Asian capitalism.

Within the literatures of market transitions, the work of Ivan Szelényi is particularly useful to the explanation of the Chinese and Vietnamese political economies and how their paths from state socialism are distinctive. Specifically, Szelényi and King (2005) and Szelényi (2010) have distinguished three ideal-typical paths of transition from state socialism. Where the transition occurred through a 'revolution from above', state elites orchestrated change according to a 'blueprint' designed by neoliberal economists, resulting in the nomenklatura (and its clients) being transformed into a 'grand bourgeoisie'. Such was the path taken in Russia. The case of other Eastern European societies such as Hungary resembled a 'revolution from without'. An alliance of technocrats and elites adopted neoliberal blueprints but blocked attempts at appropriation by the old nomenklatura, in addition to forging economic alliances with foreign investors and multinational capital (Szelényi 2010: 3). Still, Communist Party rule ended in both ideal-typical Eastern European experiences, even as subsequent political configurations varied considerably, a phenomenon that Szelényi and King (2005) contrast with a singular third approach termed the 'Chinese' or 'East Asian' path. Here, the transition was said to involve a process of 'transformation from below' or from the bottom up, which was then developmental statism.

Political Institutions and Domination

In China and Vietnam, communist parties have overseen the consolidation of market-Leninist regimes, where Leninist political institutions remain the vital integrative force supplying the formal and informal rules that govern politics, regulate economic activity and shape patterns of social stratification. China and Vietnam did not experience the demise or comprehensive decay of state socialist political institutions, but rather their reconstitution.

States are integral to the constitution of market-based economies and the communist parties in both China and Vietnam effectively refashioned relations between state and economy, adjusting the rights and responsibilities of the state and citizens to establish new regimes of accumulation within a market-based institutional framework. The forging of a qualitatively distinctive 'market-Leninist' political economy thus entailed both the development and subordination of market institutions. Analyses such as Shirk's *The Political Logic of Economic Reform in China* (1993) and Yang's *Remaking the Chinese Leviathan* (2004) have provided an overview how this occurred in the Chinese context. Standing in tension with these accounts are studies that insist that the power and authority of both countries' communist parties have been and remain in a process of decay and or decline (e.g. Pei 2016; Vu 2010; Fforde and Homotova 2017). While there is no sense in exaggerating the powers of resilience communist parties in China and Vietnam or their legitimacy, their resilience—some 30 to 40 years into their governance of markets—is manifestly obvious (Shambaugh 2017, London 2021).

A more useful exercise is to appreciate both communist parties' powers and their limits, to observe qualitative features of political institutions in the two countries, to understand and explain what the two countries share, the ways in which they diverge, and its implications for theory and practice. Yes, compared with the past, market economic institutions play a more determinative role in all aspects of social life in both countries (Pieke 2017, Markussen and Ngo 2019). Yes, both countries exercise limited if quite different levels of influence in the international arena. But it is equally the case that in both countries parties, along with their Leninist institutions and ideational components, have been remain interpenetrated with state, market, welfare, and coercive institutions and shape social life across all institutional spheres. To suggest otherwise is not profound but inaccurate.

Core institutions of Leninist political organisation have been maintained in China and Vietnam, notably the Communist Party's structures and institutions, as well as the vast array of administrative and representative institutions, mass organisations, police and public security agencies (McGregor 2010, 2019; Gillen 2011, London 2021). Despite the widely hyped inclusion of private entrepreneurs, market-Leninist regimes, party actors and institutions continued to dominate and guide non-party institutions. Between 1923 and 1989 and, in China and Vietnam to the present, Marxism–Leninism served as a malleable straitjacket (Wallerstein and Gao 2012), custom-fitted to the needs of communist parties at different historical junctures. But it is more than this. Leninism today is not only a set of ideas or formal institutions, it is a set of historical experiences, institutionalised residues and discourses, and contemporary manifestations that show signs of decay, resilience and renewal in both countries.

Economic Institutions and Accumulation Regimes

Although all the formerly state socialist regimes in Eastern Europe passed through a period of state retrenchment, the differences in the path-dependent effects of the transition between Russia and Central and Eastern Europe have been unmistakable (Szelényi 2008: 170). Russia's economy, having recovered from the lost decade of the 1990s where GDP fell by 50%, has had its market institutions developed and become more entrenched. The commanding heights of its political economy are contested by a neo-patrimonial elite and business 'oligarchs'—remnants of the nomenklatura of the state socialist regime. Contrastingly, Eastern European countries such as Poland and Hungary have continued to adopt formal market institutions that are in many respects more liberal than those of the United States and the United Kingdom. The engine behind economic growth has moved from initial massive foreign investment to one propelled by a developing domestic bourgeoisie that partly comprises a large contingent of former state managers.

Similarly, market transitions in China and Vietnam have also had path-dependent—albeit non-deterministic—effects on configurations of class power. The Chinese political logic of economic reform, which evolved in the 1980s and 1990s, reflected its decentralised fiscal and enterprise structure. Piecemeal economic reforms transformed enterprise managers into enterprise owners while the 'eat in separate kitchens' fiscal model meant that provinces maintained a degree of financial autonomy from the centre (Shirk 1993), resulting in provinces pursuing (successful) developmentalist economic policies in a way largely unseen in Vietnam. China today, as Szelényi (2008) notes, resembles 'capitalism' from above, more than it did during the early stages of its transition. Particularly, SOEs have been appropriated by well-placed officials and their clients, all of whom have benefited disproportionately from multinational capital (ibid.: 171). The privatisation of SOEs further suggests movement towards capitalism, alongside Walder's (1995) observation of the rise of an economic elite separate from the state.

The case of Vietnam is one where its economic policies have appealed to various constituencies within the state rather than conforming to a coherent developmentalist plan. Malesky et al. (2010) have attributed this to Vietnam's more fragmented and pluralistic political leadership as compared to China's. The main thrust of Vietnamese state policies is securing state control over the commanding heights of the economy, from which a state business class has emerged, with its favourable position within or on the borders of state power enabling it to exploit market opportunities for personal gain (Cheshier 2010). The development of an independent bourgeoisie is simultaneously suppressed (London 2009). Formal decentralisation in the 2000–10 decade created similar incentives for province-level developmentalism as in China, but, in the context of a less sophisticated economy and flimsy industrial base, tended to fuel speculative over productive investments, economic redundancy and pernicious forms of corruption (London et al. 2010). In an extended and ultimately costly bout of 'chaebol dreaming', Vietnamese leaders undertook swift efforts to transform ailing SOEs into dominant businesses and then into chaebols overnight.

In pursuit of this goal, state leaders exhibited an unhealthy confidence in their ability to build dynamic, world-beating enterprises while lacking the felicitous conditions of the Korean case, such as national systems of innovation, managerial expertise, infrastructure, technology transfer and capital. The resultant multi-billion-dollar bankruptcies have added significantly to Vietnam's debt load while doing nothing to build the industrial base its leaders envisioned. One key difference in this context is the near complete absence of a private or even quasi-private enterprise sector and the relative absence of forward and backward linkages across various sectors of Vietnam's economy. This situation has yet to change.

Welfare Institutions and Reproduction Regimes

Preponderant modes of political and economic integration directly and indirectly determine welfare regimes (Esping-Andersen 1990) and their attendant social inequalities (Szelényi and Manchin 1987). Under state socialist regimes, institutional responsibility for welfare lay predominantly within the sphere of the planned economy, with economic institutions designed to ensure security through administrative and redistributive allocation of capital, full employment and welfare-producing goods. Social inequality arose from unequal relations to bureaucratic–allocative institutions (Szelényi and Manchin 1987), while households and black markets played secondary roles in welfare allocation, possibly counteracting the former's effects. Beyond these, access to employment and state-financed social services helped provide for social welfare. However, fiscal malaise followed soon after state socialist economic institutions faltered.

The development and eventual predominance of markets means that market-based inequalities became the major mechanism of stratification and social inequality in market-Leninist regimes. As Szelényi and Manchin (1987) delineated—drawing upon and extending Polanyi's (1957) distinction among reciprocal, formal and redistributive forms of market coordination—the transition to a market-Leninist regime promised to flatten the state socialist opportunity structure by providing greater economic freedoms to those previously subject to administrative exclusion. While the state retains a dominant role in providing many forms of welfare, private (i.e. market-based) provision also occurs, sometimes within the shell of state—nominally 'public'—institutions. In the context of markets, both markets and administrative principles operate as levers of inequality. In practical terms, the income and resources flowing through official redistributive and administrative channels represents only a fraction of the financial sums involved. In the pursuit of operational stability, 'public'-service delivery units make use of a wide array of practices to boost revenues, including a litany of informal charges. In this context, political inequalities associated with party membership remain as mechanisms of social stratification, mediating market-based inequalities, access to services and life chances.

Countries undergoing market transition have faced the problems of (1) the significant time gap of a generation between the collapse of the state socialist welfare regime and recovery of regular economic growth, and (2) the adoption of new formal institutions governing welfare that were strangely more liberal than the most capitalist of welfare states. The resulting minimalist approach to social welfare has been observed across formerly state socialist countries. This combination has proved capable of supporting rapid economic growth, but many essential social services promised (if not delivered or delivered equally) under state socialism have been subjected to market-based principles, as outlined above. As failing to provide public goods to large segments of the population potentially undermines regime legitimacy, states in China and Vietnam has sought to address tensions through a combination of communist corporatism (extending privileges to those with relations to the state), populist rhetoric and targeted support.

The welfare regimes in China and Vietnam are a particularly interesting angle from which to explore market-Leninism. Within the eroded shell of state socialism, both countries have experienced the commodification of most essential services under the authority of regimes that profess a commitment to achieving 'socialist-oriented' market economies. In both countries, economic development policies and corresponding patterns of production have intensified social inequalities. In both countries the shifting of responsibility for payment onto households has occasioned the development of market-based social inequalities of access to essential services.

In both countries, emerging social inequalities have generated pressure on the state to respond with ameliorative policies and programmes of varying magnitudes. And in both countries, leaders have professed a long-term commitment to universalist principles and programmes but the stratification outcomes have a dual and overlapping character: the resilience of Leninist political organisation continues to generate inequalities through the exercise of arbitrary power and the political allocation of economic resources, whereas markets generate their own inequalities (London 2014). In more recent years, both countries have seen significant expansions in the scale and scope of social policies, reflecting the emergence of distinctively market-Leninist forms of welfare states and citizenship (London and Pincus 2021).

China and Vietnam as Instances of Consolidated Market-Leninism

In China and Vietnam, Leninist parties that have dominated politics in their respective countries for decades have instituted market-based methods of economic accumulation to support political, economic and social imperatives. These specific and consolidated institutional attributes are what distinguish contemporary China and Vietnam from other (including other former socialist) forms of political economy. While the term 'market-Leninism' is not new,[1] my use of the term differs as it sheds light on the consolidated form of political economy that has evolved under the leadership of communist parties who have developed its institutional and ideological underpinnings over more than thirty years. While its future is indeterminate, construing it as a fifty or 100-year transitional phase distracts from understanding its properties and significance.

Conceptual Foundations of Market-Leninism

The American sociologist Erik Wright often counseled that good social-science concepts summarise essential features of social phenomena. Efforts to conceptualise the essences of the political economies of China and Vietnam have not resulted in a consensus choice. Analysts have put forward numerous alternatives, but there have been no winners of what Baum and Schevenko (1999) have playfully termed the 'conceptual sweepstakes'. Without seeking to win a prize, the case made here is that, among alternatives, market-Leninism offers the most concise summary of these political economies' institutional attributes. While concepts are not theories, identifying political economies' core institutional attributes

[1] The term was coined, it seems, by the New York Times columnist Nicolas Kristof (1993): 'China sees "Market-Leninism" as way to future'. Kristof wrote, 'After Deng Xiaoping, China's current paramount leader, was purged in 1976, the People's Daily quoted Mao Zedong as saying that Mr. Deng "knows nothing of Marxism-Leninism." Mao may have been half-right, for the 89-year-old Mr. Deng has even advised visitors from developing countries not to bother with Marxism. At the same time, Mr. Deng and other Chinese leaders retain a fondness for Leninism, in the sense of highly disciplined one-party rule with centralised decision-making. Their aim, in other words, is Market-Leninism'.

is crucial to their explanation. Market-Leninism meets these conceptual and facilitative aims in ways other prominent typological characterisations do not.

To see why it is useful to consider the alternatives, let us start with the popular but problematic label of 'market socialism'. China's Communist Party has described the country's system as a 'socialist market economy' while Vietnam has embraced the label of 'a market economy with a socialist orientation' (see Bekkevold, Hansen and Nordhaug, this volume). References to market socialism are found throughout the literature (see Chan et al. 1999; Lin 1995). 'If the Chinese and Vietnamese leadership ultimately insist on calling their regime "socialist"', write Kornai and Qian (2009: 22), 'no one can deny them'.

Their account is consistent with the earlier analysis of Zbignew Brzezinski and his (1989) notion of 'commercial communism', which views China as an instance of 'post-communist' authoritarianism that will similarly be characterised by the fading significance of Marxist–Leninist doctrine (Brzezinski 1989: 254) their right to do so'. But this still raises the question of what meaning, if any, should be attached to the term 'market socialist' or, for that matter, socialism. Kornai and Qian (ibid.: 21) insist that China and Vietnam are not socialist according to standard definitions of Marxism, Walrassian market socialism, Leninism or social democracy. Leaving social democracy aside, we may consider this argument.

Marx's definition of socialism entails the elimination of private property and capitalist social relations and brings with it the implication of planning. A situation in which quasi-private ownership and recognisably capitalist social relations are preponderant and in which the market is the chief mode of economic governance is not socialist, at least by Karl Marx's standards. For Walras, socialism means public ownership, full stop. As for the 'Leninist' conception of socialism, Kornai and Qian are referring to 'classical socialism'—viz. those institutional arrangements that actually prevailed in state socialist countries in the period between communist seizure and consolidation of their power but before things unravelled—its institutional hallmarks are: (1) dictatorship of the party in the name of the proletariat, (2) public ownership and the elimination of private property, (3) the predominance of central planning and (4) the sacrosanct status of Marxist–Leninist (together with Mao Zedong or Ho Chi Minh) thought. While Kornai and Qian accept that in organisational terms China and Vietnam have maintained an 'extremely important attribute of the

Leninist kind of socialism' (Kornai and Qian 2009: 21), they rightly note that central planning is not the preponderant mode of economic coordination.

Kornai and Qian's claim that the state no longer plays a 'leading role' in the two countries is debatable, regardless of one's normative view of the state in the economy. According to data from 2013, China's public sector accounts for 'only 30 per cent of total firms but roughly 55 per cent of assets, 45 per cent of revenue and 40 per cent of profits' (Scissors 2016) and, at any rate, it does not include the uncountable legions of firms closely tied to the state. By the Vietnamese state's own estimates, it accounts for 30–40% of GDP, not including innumerable 'equitised' firms owned and controlled by members of the Communist Party and their kin. What is clear is that in both countries Leninist ideology has undergone drastic changes. Perhaps most strikingly, communist parties have become 'friendly' to the presence of private-property arrangements and indeed often appear 'pro-capitalist' in their views and principles. Indeed, some party members have become capitalists, as will be discussed further later. 'Today's communist parties in these two countries', Kornai and Qian (ibid.: 21) conclude, 'are parties friendly to capitalism disguised by Marxist–Leninist slogans and by faithful references to the thoughts of Mao and Ho Chi Minh'. They are a new breed of political-business state (Gomez 2002) and, by virtue of their capitalist-hugging tendencies and interests, China and Vietnam are not Marxist–Leninist in the classical sense.

In political economy terms, the value of such conceptions as 'resilient Leninism' (Chen 2007), 'consultative Leninism' (Baum 2007; Tsang 2009) and 'late Leninism' (Gallagher 2004) are uncertain as they are without reference to economy. The same applies to various 'post-' formulations, and the literature on China and Vietnam has no shortage of these, including 'post-totalitarian communism' (Linz 2000), 'post-socialism' (Ho 2010), 'postcommunism' (Ding 1994; Szelényi 2010), 'post-Leninism' (Winckler 1999: 3; Chen 2010), post-state capitalism (Witt and Redding 2014) and so on. The 'post' labels are useful in so far as they highlight the path dependency of the communist/socialist/Leninist roots of these regimes but do not positively designate what these political economies' current features are.

Most observers are comfortable in characterising China and Vietnam as market economies, if hyphenated in some way, but there has been less agreement on whether the countries ought to be characterised as 'capitalist'. The view trending now is that China (and Vietnam) exhibits capitalist or functionally capitalist social relations with some element of political or state management. Indeed, characterisations such as 'managed capitalism' (Putterman 2008) and 'state capitalism' (*The Economist* 2012) have the merit of directing attention to the nexus of politics and economy. Yet the presence of 'management' or of 'the state' does not tell us enough about exactly what kind of state and exactly what kind of management they are. These formulations provide few hints of the essentially Leninist character and organisation of that nexus that so pervasively and deeply mediates relations between politics and economy in both countries.

Why the Leninism in Market-Leninist Orders Still Matters

Leninism here is construed as a set of ideologies and dispositions that inform governance. While Leninist ideals are rooted in Marxism, Lenin's canon and variants of it contain important deviations from Marxism. The ideologies of socialism, socialist internationalism and communist teleology are—whatever their precise meanings at different times—essential to Leninism. Without these deviations, Leninism loses much of its ideological coherence. But a no less-essential feature of Leninism and Leninist ideology is the indispensable role of the Vanguard Party and its apparatuses of power. Leninism in this sense refers to a set of more or less formal principles and ideologies governing the organisation and activities of communist parties, serving as a central integrative force coordinating politics, rightly labelled by Selznick (1951) an 'organisational weapon to eliminate autonomous social action and achieve a stable totalitarian social order'. No doubt, Leninist ideologies have been used flexibly, in the past as in the present. And the premium on flexibility was raised to new heights with the involution and eventual dismantlement of planned economies.

What, then, might be the significance of Leninism in the wake of state socialism? The first observation is that Leninism today is not a set of dead ideas, but rather a set of historical experiences, institutionalised residues and discourses that retain significance as they inform practices in the present and expectations about the future. One does not have to embrace Leninism to recognise that its presence in China and Vietnam is not necessarily as ossified as its critics claim. There are plenty of people in power in China and Vietnam who continue to take Leninist ideology seriously. Political anthropologists have shown, for example, how dominant agents in China and Vietnam have simultaneously taken advantage of markets and Leninist heritage to consolidate new forms of domination (Nguyen-Vo 2009; Anagnost 1997; Gillen 2011). Recent decisions in China to promote 'red culture' or in Vietnam to 'build socialism' and 'criticise and self-criticise' capture a significant difference between these cases and the accepted 'Asian developmental states'. As such, they only reinforce the call for an understanding of the historical and contemporary political bases of Leninism.

With reference back to Jayasuriya's (2005: 384) proposed 'focus on state transformation, state building and the processes through which new notions of stateness are created', therefore, I identify as critical the decisions of the Chinese and Vietnamese states to embark on a process of market/capitalist development in a Cold War context, and with the avowed intention that the process should be led not merely by Leninist organisations, but by a Leninist Communist Party that insists upon a monopoly of power and a hegemonic position intellectually. With this distinction in mind, I return to the definition of 'developmental state' offered by Leftwich (1995): (1) a determined developmental elite; (2) relative autonomy of the state from society; (3) a powerful, competent and insulated bureaucracy; (4) a weak and subordinated civil society; (5) the effective management of non-state economic interests and (6) repression, legitimacy and performance. I suggest that at a broad level, these six points sufficiently capture the characteristics of the Chinese and Vietnamese regimes to make assimilation of those cases to the model plausible. But, equally important, I suggest that they do so in a critically distinctive manner, arising from the starting point set out above.

Specifically, the market-Leninist variant of developmental state is characterised by (1) a determined Leninist elite, (2) relative autonomy of the monopoly-party-controlled state from society, (3) a powerful bureaucracy subordinated to the monopoly party, (4) a controlled and mobilised civil society, (5) a subordination of non-state economic interests to state economic interests as the engine of accumulation and (6) maintenance of the monopoly-party state through repression, and its legitimisation through performance, and in particular through defence of sovereignty against a hostile 'West'. In every case, there is a significant inflection that can be traced back to the timing, character and context of the original project. This is fleshed out further below.

However indeterminate the future of Leninism in the Vietnamese and Chinese contexts may be, it cannot be denied that Leninist political institutions remain the distinguishing feature of the two countries' politics, even as these countries' economies have marketised. In both countries, Leninist political institutions dominate the political field and play a preponderant role in defining and regulating the relation between state and economy.

The recent analysis of Richard McGregor (2010) has strongly affirmed the Leninist essence of China's current political economy. Still, the use of term 'market-Leninism' has tended to carry theological assumptions and connotations of transience and instability. This tendency emanates from three faulty assumptions.

The first of these is that market-based growth is intrinsically incompatible with Leninism over the long term. This premise is rooted in textbook political economy and Cold War ideology that associate certain types of polity with certain types of economy. Markets go with liberties, and command economies with tyranny. Or so we are told. But political theorists sought to dispel this myth long ago. Writing in 1966, Barrington Moore questioned this presupposition on historical grounds, as did Samuel Huntington in 1968. More recent history lends further credence to both authors' view. Indeed, if the so-called 'East Asian miracle' taught us anything, it is that one-party rule and market-based strategies of accumulation can generate rapid and sustained economic growth and industrialisation under certain conditions. As the case of Singapore shows us, such regimes can indeed survive over the longue durée.

A second assumption—that the 'hollowing out' of Leninist ideology means that Leninist political institutions will collapse—is also suspect. The most fundamental precept of Leninist ideology is that the Communist Party is and will remain indispensable in perpetuity. This aspect of socialism is not trivial. It helps distinguish Leninist regimes from other sorts, yet it also causes confusion for foreign observers. Set against the backdrop of dynamic market economies, socialist rhetoric often rings anachronistic, incoherent and even absurd. But this in no way reduces the force of Leninist institutions, much less nullifies the significance of ideological activities. While the elaborate ideological frameworks that once encompassed every facet of social life in China and Vietnam have faded from view, party operations in both countries are by no means a sideshow. These parties still rule and their ideological activities retain force.

The final assumption is that the coercive capacities of the state will be pushed to a brink and implode. Communist parties in China and Vietnam have proved adept at refashioning the bases of their political rule thus far. Coercive collectivisation has given way to economic liberalism and political repression, of which the latter feature can be succinctly encapsulated in the sentence 'socialism is whatever we say it is and precisely what it is doesn't matter' (Wallerstein and Gao 2012). Such a combination is attractive not only to those in power, but also to the many millions who have benefited materially from rapid growth. There is freedom in consumption, even if that freedom is often illusory (see Hansen, this volume). Inequalities and corruption may present dangers but do not mean that Leninist political institutions will wither in the short-, medium or long-term future.

Thompson's (2002) taxonomy of varieties of post-totalitarian regimes in the wake of 'communism' furnishes a characterisation fully consistent with the analysis presented in this chapter. There, he labels China and Vietnam, along with Hungary of the Kádár era and pre-1989 Yugoslavia, as instances of 'consolidated hybrid' regimes. Following Thompson, it is entirely reasonable to assert that post-totalitarian regimes constitute a real category distinct from other forms of political economy. It is also likely, as Thompson contends, that sustained economic growth and significant—if uneven—increases in living standards in China and Vietnam may 'immunise' these countries from political challenges (ibid.: 92). Yet at some point the prefix 'post-' and the label 'consolidated hybrid regime' do not tell us enough. China and Vietnam are best understood as consolidated market-Leninist regimes.

Making Sense of Market-Leninism

Werner Bonefeld (2012) reminds us that in any country an economy and its institutions do not exist independent of politics and, as such, capitalism or indeed any form of market economy is ultimately a political practice. Along these lines, China and Vietnam may be understood as social orders exhibiting a specific variant of developmentalist state with distinctive political institutions bearing specific consequences for the development of economic institutions and the goals, conduct and outcomes of state policies. I have sought to show how attention to the social and institutional constitution of China and Vietnam helps to delineate their distinctiveness as political economies or social orders, not only in relation to recognised developmental states but also with respect to varieties of capitalism in Asia. I have argued that for varieties of capitalism to have any meaning, there is a need to specify the social and political foundations of market economies or the way market economies or capitalist economies are embedded in specific social environments. For it is through socially embedded politics and power relations that varieties of capitalism and their distinctive institutions take from.

The political economies of contemporary China and Vietnam are led by long-ruling communist parties who approach economic governance with uncommon developmentalist zeal. While it is fashionable to dismiss the significance of Leninism, it is precisely the combination of Leninism and markets that distinguishes China and Vietnam's political economies from others in East Asia. The development and character of Leninist political institutions—organisational, ideological and cultural—in a world-political and economic context distinguish China and Vietnam from other varieties of developmentalism.

China and Vietnam, then, are best understood to represent two instances of a distinctive form of political economy or social order that is most appropriately understood as market-Leninist. The principal conceptual advantage of market-Leninism is that it captures essential features of these regimes in a way that alternative labels do not. In market-Leninist regimes, market-based economic institutions develop in subordination to Leninist principles of political organisation. Party members mediate political and market opportunities, and maintain power through a variety of compliance procedures. A heritage of left-wing political culture and lore remains intact, and is invoked relentlessly in the defence of eternal one-party rule. This specific combination of institutional attributes and its attendant patterns of stratification distinguishes market-Leninist regimes from other forms of political economy and from other varieties of developmentalist states in particular.

Where, then, do contemporary China and Vietnam fit within the historical universe of political economies? I conclude that China and Vietnam are not appropriately construed as developmental states, at least in the conventional sense of that term. More importantly, I have argued that the reified institutional attributes by which developmentalism is defined distracts us from more important aims of understanding how the Chinese and Vietnamese political economies have been socially and politically constituted. The dynamic interplay of markets and Leninist political institutions in these countries, and its attendant effects on welfare, stratification and political consciousness, have generated outcomes absent in other Asian capitalisms.

As this book came to press the world economy was beset by a global economic and public health calamity of a scale not seen since 1918. Within the span of a few weeks, basic questions about the appropriate role of the state in the economy were back on the table as states invested massively to protect and sustain national political economies. While questions about the role of the state in China and Vietnam's economies remain, these can be set within a wide discussion of the social and political constitution of economies. In this context, approaches that view countries principally as economies need to be rejected in favour of approaches that view countries as societies or social orders.

While mainstream economics provide certain insights into China and Vietnam's political economies, the value of these insights are limited by their inattention to the power relations that have define and animate countries' economies over time. By contrast, an analysis of China and Vietnam as instances of consolidated market-Leninism trains our attention squarely on power relations and how their logics have shaped these countries' political, economic and social development from past to present.

References

Albert, M. 1993. *Capitalism vs. Capitalism*, vol. 52, 488–506. New York: Four Walls Eight Windows.

Amsden, A.H. 1989. *Asia's Next Giant: South Korea and Late Industrialisation.* Oxford: Oxford University Press.

Anderson, P. 2010. Sinomania. *London Review of Books* 32 (2): 3–6.

Anagnost, A. 1997. *National Past-Times: Narrative, Representation, and Power in Modern China.* Durham, NC: Duke University Press.

Aoki, M. 2001. *Toward a Comparative Institutional Analysis.* Cambridge, MA: MIT Press.

Baum, R. 2007. Limits of Authoritarian Resilience. Paper presented at the French Centre for the International Studies and Research (CERI).

Baum, R., and A. Shevchenko. 1999. The 'State of the State'. In *The Paradox of China's Post-Mao Reforms*, ed. M. Goldman and R. MacFarquhar, pp. 333–360. Cambridge, MA: Harvard University Press.

Beeson, M. 2004. The Rise and Fall (?) of the Developmental State: The Vicissitudes and Implications of East Asian Interventionism. In *Developmental States: Relevancy, Redundancy or Reconfiguration*, ed. L. Low, pp. 29–40. New York: Nova Science Publishers.

Beeson, M. 2009. Developmental States in East Asia: A Comparison of the Japanese and Chinese Experiences. *Asian Perspective* 33 (2): 5–39.
Beeson, M. 2017. What does China's Rise Mean for the Developmental State Paradigm? In Asia after the Developmental State. *Cambridge University Press*, 174–198.
Beeson, M., and H.H. Pham. 2012. Developmentalism with Vietnamese Characteristics: The Persistence of State-Led Development in East Asia. *Journal of Contemporary Asia* 42 (4): 539–559.
Berger, M. T. 2003. *The Battle for Asia: From Decolonization to Globalization*. London: Routledge.
Block, F. 1981. Beyond Relative Autonomy: State Managers as Historical Subjects. *New Political Science* 2 (3): 33–49.
Bonefeld, W. 2012. Adam Smith and Ordoliberalism: On the Political form of Market Liberty. *Review of International Studies* 39 (2): 233–250.
Boyer, R. 2005. How and Why Capitalisms Differ. *Economy and Society* 34 (4): 509–557.
Boyer, R. 2012. The Chinese Growth Regime and the World Economy. In *Diversity and Transformations of Asian Capitalisms*, ed. R. Boyer, H. Uemura, and A. Isogai, 184–207. London and New York: Routledge.
Brachet-Márquez, V. 2017. Mi interinato en la dirección de Estudios Sociológicos. *Estudios sociológicos*, Vol. 34. Mexico City, Mexico. January 18.
Brenner, N., J. Peck, and N. Theodore. 2010. Variegated Neoliberalization: Geographies, Modalities, Pathways. *Global Networks* 10 (2): 182–222.
Brzezinski, Z. 1989. Post-Communist Nationalism. *Foreign Affairs* 68 (5): 1–25.
Cammack, P. 2014. World Development Report 2015: Programming the Poor. The Multilateral Development Banks and the Global Financial Crisis Working Papers Series, 7.
Carney, M., E. Gedajlovic, and Yang, X. (2009). Varieties of Asian capitalism: toward an institutional theory of Asian enterprise. *Asia Pacific Journal of Management* 26 (3): 361–380.
Carroll, T., and Jarvis, D. (ed.). (2017). Disembedding Autonomy. In Asia after the Developmental State: Disembedding Autonomy. *Cambridge Studies in Comparative Public Policy*, 3–48 Cambridge: Cambridge University Press. https://doi.org/10.1017/9781316480502.002.
Chan, A., B.J.T. Kerkvliet, and J. Unger (eds.). 1999. *Transforming Asian Socialism: China and Vietnam Compared*. Boulder, CO and Sydney: Rowman & Littlefield and Allen & Unwin.
Cammack, P. 1989. Bringing the State Back In? *British Journal of Political Science* 19 (2): 261–290.
Chen, C. 2007. *The Prospects for Liberal Nationalism in Post-Leninist States*. University Park: Pennsylvania State University Press.

Chen, C. 2010. *The Prospects for Liberal Nationalism in Post-Leninist States*. University Park: Pennsylvania State University Press.
Cheshier, S. 2010. The New Class in Vietnam. PhD dissertation, School of Business and Management, Queen Mary University of London.
Chibber, V. 2005. Reviving the Developmental State? The Myth of the 'National Bourgeoisie'. *Socialist Register* 41: 44–165.
Crouch, C. 2005. Models of Capitalism. *New Political Economy* 10 (4): 439–456.
Crouch, C. 2009. Typologies of Capitalism. In *Debating Varieties of Capitalism: A Reader*, ed. B. Hancke, pp. 75–94. Oxford: Oxford University Press.
Cumings, B. 1984. The Origins and Development of the Northeast Asian Political Economy: Industrial Sectors, Product Cycles, and Political Consequences. *International Organization* 38 (1): 1–40.
Deans, P. 2004. The People's Republic of China: The Post-Socialist Developmental State. In *Developmental States: Relevancy, Redundancy or Reconfiguration*, ed. L. Low, 133–147. New York: Nova Science.
Deng, X. 1994. Build Socialism with Chinese Characteristics. In *Selected Works of Deng Xiaoping*, vol. 3, 1982–1992. Beijing: Foreign Languages Press.
Ding, X. 1994. *Post-Communism and China*. Oxford: Oxford University Press.
Doner, R.F., B.K. Ritchie, and D. Slater. 2005. Systemic Vulnerability and the Origins of Developmental States: Northeast and Southeast Asia in Comparative Perspective. *International Organization* 59 (2): 327–361.
Ebner, A. 2015. Editorial: Exploring Regional Varieties of Capitalism. *Regional Studies* 50 (1): 3–6.
The Economist. 2012. The Rise of State Capitalism, January 21.
Evans, P.B. 1995. *Embedded Autonomy: States and Industrial Transformation*. Princeton, NJ: Princeton University Press.
Evans, P. 2004. Development as Institutional change: The Pitfalls of Monocropping and the Potentials of Deliberation. *Studies in Comparative International Development* 38 (4): 30–52.
Evans, P.B. 2005. Counterhegemonic Globalization: Transnational Social Movements in the Contemporary Global Political Economy. In *The Handbook of Political Sociology: States, Civil Societies, and Globalization*, ed. T. Janoski, R. Alford, A. Hicks, and M. A. Schwartz, 655–670. Singapore and New York: Cambridge University Press.
Evans, P.B. 2014. The Capability Enhancing Developmental State: Concepts and National Trajectories. In *The South Korean Development Experience: Beyond Aid*, ed. E. M. Kim and P. H. Kim, 83–110. Basingstoke and New York: Palgrave Macmillan.
Evans, P.B., and P. Heller. 2015. Human Development, State Transformation and the Politics of the Developmental State. In *The Oxford Handbook of Transformations of the State*, ed. S. Leibfried, E. Huber, M. Lange, J.D. Levy, F. Nullmeier, and J. D. Stephens, 691–713. Oxford: Oxford University Press.

Esping-Andersen, G. 1990. *Three Worlds of Welfare Capitalism*. Cambridge: Polity.
Fforde, A., and L. Homutova. 2017. Political Authority in Vietnam: Is the Vietnamese Communist Party a Paper Leviathan? *Journal of Current Southeast Asian Affairs* 36 (3): 91–118.
Fligstein, N., and J. Zhang. 2011. A New Agenda for Research on the Trajectory of Chinese Capitalism. *Management and Organization Review* 7 (1): 39–62.
Friedman, E. 1996. A Democratic Chinese Nationalism? In *Chinese Nationalism*, ed. J. Unger, 169–182. Armonk, NY: M. E. Sharpe.
Friedman, E. 2011. China's Future in an Asian Authoritarian Context. Paper presented at conference on Authoritarianism in East Asia: Vietnam, China, North Korea, City University of Hong Kong, 30 June–2 July, Hong Kong.
Gallagher, M. 2004. The Limits of Civil Society in a Late Leninist State. In *Civil Society and Political Change in Asia: Expanding and Contracting Democratic Space*, ed. M. Alagappa, 419–452. Stanford, CA: Stanford University Press.
Gillen, J. 2011. A Battle Worth Winning: The Service of Culture to the Communist Party of Vietnam in the Contemporary Era. *Political Geography* 30 (5): 272–281.
Gomez, E. 2002. *Political Business in East Asia*. London and New York: Routledge.
Gray, K. 2011. The Social and Geopolitical Origins of State Transformation: The Case of South Korea. *New Political Economy* 16 (3): 303–322.
Hall, P. A., and D. Soskice (eds.). 2001. *Varieties of Capitalism: The Institutional Foundations of Comparative Advantage*. Oxford: Oxford University Press.
Ho, W.C. 2010. *The Transition Study of Postsocialist China: An Ethnographic Study of a Model Community*. Singapore: World Scientific Press.
Hollingsworth, J.R., and R. Boyer (eds.). 1997. *Contemporary Capitalism: The Embeddedness of Institutions*. New York. Cambridge University Press.
Huang, Y. 2008. Capitalism with Chinese Characteristics. In *Capitalism with Chinese Characteristics: Entrepreneurship and the State*, 233–298. Cambridge: Cambridge University Press.
Huang, Y. 2011. Rethinking the Beijing Consensus. *Asia Policy* 11 (1): 1–26.
Huntington, S.P. 1968. *Political Order in Changing Societies*. Hew Haven, CT: Yale University Press.
Jackson, G., and R. Deeg. 2008. Comparing Capitalisms: Understanding Institutional Diversity and Its Implications for International Business. *Journal of International Business Studies* 39 (4): 540–561.
Jayasuriya, K. 2005. Beyond Institutional Fetishism: From the Developmental to the Regulatory State. *New Political Economy* 10 (3): 381–387.
Jessop, B., 2001. Bringing the State Back in (Yet Again): Reviews, Revisions, Rejections, and Redirections. *International Review of Sociology/Revue internationale de sociologie* 11 (2): 149–173.

Jessop, B. 2011. Rethinking the Diversity and Variability of Capitalism. In *Capitalist Diversity and Diversity Within Capitalism*, ed. G. Wood and C. Lane, 209–237. London: Routledge.

Johnson, C.A. 1982. MITI and the Japanese Miracle: The Growth of Industrial Policy: 1925–1975. Stanford, CA: Stanford University Press.

Khan, M. 2010. Political Settlements and the Governance of Growth-Enhancing Institutions. Unpublished Working Paper. School of Oriental and African Studies, University of London. https://eprints.soas.ac.uk/9968/1/Political_Settlements_internet.pdf.

Khan, Mushtaq. 2017. Introduction: Political Settlements and the Analysis of Institutions. African Affairs, 1–20.

Khan, Mushtaq H., and J.K, Sundaram. 2000. Rents, Rent-Seeking and Economic Development: Theory and Evidence in Asia. Cambridge: Cambridge University Press.

Kornai, J., and Qian, Y. (eds.). 2009. *Market and Socialism: In the Light of the Experiences of China and Vietnam*. Basingstoke. Palgrave Macmillan.

Kristof, N.D. 1993. China Sees 'Market-Leninism' as Way to Future. *New York Times*, September 6.

Kristof, N.D., and S. WuDunn. 1994. *China Wakes: The Struggle for the Soul of a Rising China*. New York: Vintage Books.

Krugman, P. 1994. The Myth of Asia's Miracle. *Foreign Affairs* 73 (6): 62–78.

Lall, S. 1996. *Learning from the Asian Tigers: Studies in Technology and Industrial Policy*. Basingstoke and New York: Palgrave Macmillan.

Lane, D. 2007. Post-State Socialism: A Diversity of Capitalisms? In *Varieties of Capitalism in Post-Communist Countries*, ed. D. Lane and M. Myant, 13–39. Basingstoke and New York: Palgrave Macmillan.

Lane, C., and G. Wood. 2011. Institutions, Change and Diversity. In *Capitalist Diversity and Diversity within Capitalism*, ed. G. Wood and C. Lane, 1–31. London: Routledge.

Leftwich, A. 1995. Bringing Politics Back In: Towards a Model of the Developmental State. *Journal of Development Studies* 31 (3): 400–427.

Lin, J.Y. 1995. The Needham Puzzle: Why the Industrial Revolution Did Not Originate in China. *Economic Development and Cultural Change* 43 (2): 269–292.

Lindberg, L.N., J.L. Campbell, and J.R. Hollingsworth. 1991. Economic Governance and the Analysis of Structural Change in the American Economy. In *Governance of the American Economy*, ed. J.L. Campbell, J.R. Hollingsworth, and L.N. Lindberg, 3–34. Cambridge: Cambridge University Press.

Linz, J. 2000. *Totalitarian and Authoritarian Regimes*. Boulder, CO: Lynne Reiner Press.

Ljunggren. Börje. Vietnam's Communist Party Takes an Unorthodox Path to a Market Economy, But May Need to Move Beyond the Party-State for Full

Potential. Thursday, March 14, 2019. https://yaleglobal.yale.edu/content/vietnam-globalized-party-state.

London, J.D. 2009. Vietnam and the Making of Market Leninism. *Pacific Review* 22 (3): 373–397.

London, J.D. 2011. *Education in Vietnam*. Singapore. ISEAS Press.

London, J.D. 2014. Welfare Regimes in China and Vietnam. *Journal of Contemporary Asia* 44 (1): 84–107.

London, J.D., 2018. *Welfare and Inequality in Marketizing East Asia*. London, UK: Palgrave Macmillan.

London, J.D. 2020. Vietnam in 2019: The Politics of Growth, Progress, and Pollution. *Asian Survey* 60 (1): 93–99.

London, J.D. 2021. Vietnam: Consolidating Market-Leninism. In *The Routledge Handbook of Contemporary Vietnam*, ed. Jonathan London.

London, J.D and J. Pincus. 2021. Welfare and Inequality in Contemporary Vietnam. In *The Routledge Handbook of Contemporary Vietnam*, ed. Jonathan London.

London, J.D., B. van Arkadie, T.L.H. Pham, T.H. Tran, and T.H.O. Khuat. 2010. Joint Country Analysis: Development Challenges in a Middle-Income Vietnam. Working Paper Development Program, United Nations, Hanoi.

Malesky, E., and J.D. London. 2014. The Political Economy of Development in China and Vietnam. *Annual Review of Political Science* 17: 395–419.

Malesky, E., J. Regina, M. Abrami, and Y. Zheng. 2010. Institutions and Inequality in Single-Party Regimes: A Comparative Analysis of Vietnam and China. Online publication, available at http://papers.ssrn.com/sol3/papers.cfm?abstract_id=1669708.

Markussen, T., and Q.-T. Ngo. 2019. Economic and Non-Economic Returns to Communist Party Membership in Vietnam. *World Development* 122: 370–384.

Masina, P. 2012. Vietnam Between Developmental State and Neoliberalism: The Case of the Industrial Sector. In *Developmental Politics in Transition*, 188–210. London: Palgrave Macmillan .

McGregor, R. 2010. *The Party*. New York: Harper.

McGregor, R. 2019. Xi Jinping's Quest to Dominate China. *Foreign Affairs 98*: 18.

Moore, B. 1966. *Social Origins of Democracy and Dictatorship*. Boston: Beacon.

Nguyen-Vo, T.H. 2009. *The Ironies of Freedom: Sex, Culture, and Neoliberal Governance in Vietnam*. Seattle: University of Washington Press.

Peck, J., and N. Theodore. 2007. Variegated Capitalism. *Progress in Human Geography* 31 (6): 731–772.

Peck, J., and J. Zhang. 2013. A Variety of Capitalism … with Chinese Characteristics? *Journal of Economic Geography* 13: 357–396.

Peck, J., and J. Zhang. 2014. Variegated Capitalism, Chinese Style: Regional Models, Multi-Scalar Constructions. *Regional Studies* 50 (1): 52–78.

Pei, M. 2009. *China's Trapped Transition: The Limits of Developmental Autocracy*. Cambridge, MA: Harvard University Press.

Pei, Minxin. 2016. China's Crony Capitalism : The Dynamics of Regime Decay. Cambridge, MA : Harvard University Press.

Pieke, F.N. 2017. The Communist Party and Social Management in China. In *Critical Readings on Communist Party of China*, 998–1018. Leiden and Boston: BRILL.

Polanyi, K. 1944. *The Great Transformation: The Political and Economic Origins of Our Times*. Boston: Beacon Press.

Polanyi, K. 1957. The Economy as Instituted Process. In *Trade and Market in the Early Empires: Economies in History and Theory*, ed. K. Polanyi, C. M. Arensberg, and H. W. Pearson, 243–269. Glencoe, IL: The Free Press.

Putterman, L. 2008. China's Encounter with Market Socialism: Approaching Managed Capitalism by Indirect Means. In *Market and Socialism in Light of the Experiences of China and Vietnam*, ed. J. Kornai and Y. Qian, 47–65. Basingstoke: Palgrave Macmillan.

Rama, Martin. 2021. From Poverty to Prosperity: Vietnam's Extraordinary Economic Path. In *The Routledge Handbook of Contemporary Vietnam*, ed. Jonathan London.

Rodan, G. 1989. *The Political Economy of Singapore's Industrialisation: National State and International Capital*. New York: Palgrave Macmillan.

Schmitter, P.C., and A. Todor. 2014. Varieties of Capitalism and Types of Democracy. *Stato e mercato* 34 (1): 87–116.

Scissors, D. 2016. China's SOE Sector Is Bigger Than Some Would Have Us Think. American Enterprise Institute, online publication, available at www.aei.org/publication/chinas-soe-sector-is-bigger-than-some-wouldhave-us-think.

Shin, G.W. 1998. Agrarian Conflict and the Origins of Korean Capitalism. *American Journal of Sociology* 103 (5): 1309–1351.

Shirk, S. 1993. *The Political Logic of Economic Reform in China*. Berkeley: University of California Press.

Selznick, P. 1951. Institutional Vulnerability in Mass Society. *American Journal of Sociology* 56 (4): 320–331.

Selznick, P. 2014. *The Organizational Weapon: A Study of Bolshevik Strategy and Tactics*. New Orleans: Quid Pro Books.

Shambaugh, D. 2017. International Perspectives on the Communist Party of China. In *Critical Readings on Communist Party of China*, 1529–1545. Leiden and Boston: BRILL.

Shih, V., C. Adolph, and M.X. Liu. 2012. Explaining the Advancement of Central Committee Members in China. *American Political Science Review* 106: 166–187.

So, A.Y. 2002. Introduction. *Chinese Economy* 35 (3): 3–25.
So, A.Y. 2009. Rethinking the Chinese Developmental Miracle. In *China and the Transformation of Global Capitalism*, ed. H.-F. Hung, 50–64. Baltimore: Johns Hopkins University Press.
Streeck, W., and K. Thelen. 2005. *Beyond Continuity: Institutional Change in Advanced Political Economies*. Oxford: Oxford University Press.
Stubbs, R. 2005. *Rethinking Asia's Economic Miracle: The Political Economy of War, Prosperity and Crisis*. Basingstoke: Palgrave Macmillan.
Stubbs, R. 2009. What Ever Happened to the East Asian Developmental State? The Unfolding Debate. *Pacific Review* 22 (1): 1–22.
Stubbs, R., 2017. The Origins of East Asia's Developmental States and the Pressures for Change. In *Asia after the Developmental State*, 51–71. Cambridge University Press.
Szelényi, I. 1978. Social Inequalities in State Socialist Redistributive Economies: Dilemmas for Social Policy in Contemporary Socialist Societies of Eastern Europe. *International Journal of Comparative Sociology* 19 (1–2): 63–106.
Szelényi, I. 2008. A Theory of Transitions. *Modern China* 34 (1): 165–175.
Szelényi, I. 2010. Capitalism in China? Comparative Perspectives. In *Chinese Capitalisms*, ed. Y.W. Chu, 199–223. Hong Kong: Palgrave Macmillan.
Szelényi, I. 2015. Weber's Theory of Domination and Post-Communist Capitalisms. *Theory and Society* 45 (1): 1–24.
Szelényi, I., and L. King. 2005. The New Capitalism of Eastern Europe: Towards a Comparative Political Economy of Post-Communism. In *Handbook of Economic Sociology*, ed. N. Smelser and R. Swedberg, 205–229. Princeton: Princeton University Press.
Szelényi, I., and R. Manchin. 1987. Social Policy Under State Socialism: Market, Redistribution, and Social Inequalities in East European Socialist Societies. In *Stagnation and Renewal in Social Policy: The Rise and Fall of Policy Regimes*, ed. G. Esping-Andersen, M. Rein, and L. Rainwater, 102–139. Armonk, NY: M. E. Sharpe.
Thompson, M.R. 2002. Totalitarian and Post-Totalitarian Regimes in Transitions and Non-Transitions from Communism. *Totalitarian Movements and Political Religions* 3 (1): 79–106.
Tsang, S. 2009. Consultative Leninism: China's New Political Framework. *Journal of Contemporary China* 18 (62): 865–880.
Tu Anh, Vu Thanh. 2020. The Political Economy of Private Sector Development in Vietnam Since Đổi Mới. In *The Routledge Handbook of Contemporary Vietnam*, ed. Jonathan London.
Vu, T. 2010. *Paths to Development in Asia*. New York: Cambridge University Press.

Wade, R.H. 1990. *Governing the Market: Economic Theory and the Role of Government in East Asian Industrialization*. Princeton, NJ: Princeton University Press.

Wade, R.H. 1996. Japan, the World Bank, and the Art of Paradigm Maintenance: The East Asia Miracle in Political Perspective. *New Left Review* 217 (May–June): 3–36.

Walder, A. 1995. The Quiet Revolution from Within: Economic Reform as a Source of Political Decline. In *The Waning of the Communist State: Economic Origins of Political Decline in China and Hungary*, ed. A. Walder, 1–24. Berkeley: University of California Press.

Wallerstein, I., and J. Gao. 2012. Lenin and Leninism Today: An Interview with Immanuel Wallerstein. *International Critical Thought* 2 (1): 107–112.

Weber, I. 2018. China and Neoliberalism: Moving Beyond the China Is/Is Not Neoliberal Dichotomy. The SAGE Handbook of Neoliberalism, 219–233.

Weiss, L. 2000. Developmental States in Transition: Adapting, Dismantling, Innovating, Not 'Normalizing'. *Pacific Review* 13 (1): 21–55.

White, G. 1984. Developmental States and Socialist Industrialisation in the Third World. *Journal of Development Studies* 21 (1): 97–120.

Whitley, R. 1999. *Divergent Capitalisms: The Social Structuring and Change of Business Systems*. Oxford: Oxford University Press.

Wilson, J. 2007. China's Transformation Towards Capitalism. In *Varieties of Capitalism in Post-Communist Countries*, ed. D. Lane and M. Myant, 239–257. Basingstoke and New York: Palgrave Macmillan.

Winckler, E. (ed.). 1999. *Transitions from Communism in China: Institutional and Comparative Analyses*. Boulder and London: Lynne Rienner.

Witt, M.A. 2010. China: What Variety of Capitalism? INSEAD Faculty and Research Working Paper No 2010/88/EPS. Available at http://ssrn.com/abstract=1695940.

Witt, M.A., and Redding, G. 2014. China: Authoritarian Capitalism. In *The Oxford Handbook of Asian Business Systems*, ed. M. A. Witt and G. Redding, 11–32. Oxford: Oxford University Press.

Woo, J.E. 1991. *Race to the Swift: State and Finance in Korean Industrialization*. New York: Columbia University Press.

Woo-Cummings, M. 1999. *The Developmental State*. Ithaca, NY: Cornell University Press.

World Bank. 1993. *The East Asian Miracle: Economic Growth and Public Policy*. New York: Oxford University Press for the World Bank.

———. 2012. World Development Indicators. Annual Report of Development Data Group, International Economic Development, Washington, DC.

World Bank and DRCSC (Development Research Center of the State Council). 2012. China 2030: Building a Modern, Harmonious, and Creative High-Income Society. Beijing: World Bank.

Yang, D.L. 2004. *Remaking the Chinese Leviathan: Market Transition and the Politics of Governance in China*. Redwood City: Stanford University Press.
Young, A. 1994. Lessons from the East Asian NICS: A Contrarian View. *European Economic Review* 38 (3–4): 964–973.

PART II

State, Market and the Environment

CHAPTER 4

Governance, the Socialist Market Economy, and the Party-State in Vietnam and China

Thiem Hai Bui

Introduction

Ever since China and Vietnam embarked on a path of market reforms, various aspects of the concept "socialist market economy" have been employed in introducing economic, legal and political reforms in these two countries. This concept has featured prominently alongside the economic success of China and Vietnam. Since 2010, China has become the world's second largest economy and Vietnam has graduated from a low-income status to become a middle-income country according to the World Bank standard. This chapter investigates how the socialist market economy has been working in Vietnam in comparison to China. More specifically, the centrepiece of the investigation is state ownership in the Vietnamese party-state, which extends to public services, land issues and local government. The main argument is that both party-states in Vietnam and China flexibly adjust to neoliberalism, while they continue to retain control over the commanding heights of the economy. The chapter reviews a key theme on the economic governance of the party-state that

T. H. Bui (✉)
Institute for Legislative Studies, National Assembly of Vietnam,
Hanoi, Vietnam

A. Hansen et al. (eds.), *The Socialist Market Economy in Asia*,
https://doi.org/10.1007/978-981-15-6248-8_4

embraces developmentalism and how they are struggling with issues such as accountability and ownership. In doing so, it investigates the negative effects of these processes.

The market-based reforms in both China and Vietnam indicate a search for a new type of socialist developmental state and have recorded undeniable success. The East Asian model of state-led developmentalism had great appeal to the party-state when embarking on the market-based reforms. The activist and interventionist role of the state in directing the course of development corresponds with the desire of the party-state to maintain control as the commander-in-chief. However, the construction of a socialist market economy has faced sustained tensions and contradictions that have complicated the process of governance and the party-state in both countries.

The Introduction of Developmentalism into a Socialist System

The conspicuous departures of China and Vietnam in late 1970s and 1980s, respectively, from the orthodox socialist governance to embrace market-based reforms and elements of global capitalism took slightly different forms. While China was relatively successful in traditional socialist terms, Vietnam was not (Fforde 1999). Thus, in Vietnam, the reforms came as response to acute crises that placed the country on the verge of collapse and gave the socialist state renewed vitality to be resilient. Since then, both China and Vietnam have consistently recorded impressive economic growth for decades[1] and managed to navigate through two economic crises at regional and global level within a decade, i.e. the Asian economic crisis in 1997–1998 and the global economic crisis in 2008–2009. Both countries have been hailed by the international community for lifting a large proportion of the population out of poverty. Economic successes in these countries are highly credited with market-based reforms that unleash tremendous power from inside, which is sometimes dubbed as "market socialism" or "autocratic capitalism." Nevertheless, there remains an important set of questions about how the reforms and transformation have been governed and what are

[1] The average GDP growth rate of China and Vietnam between 1997 and 2011 is 9.8 and 7%, respectively, according to the World Bank (http://data.worldbank.org/indicator/NY.GDP.MKTP.KD.ZG?page=3, accessed 22 May 2013).

the institutions, the ideological forces at work and practical activity that have shaped and reshaped the mode of governance in these countries.

When China and Vietnam embarked on market reforms, they held tight to socialist statism or a Leninist political system with the communist party monopolising political power. Despite strong resistance to political reforms, these party-states have started rationalising their political activity, which implicitly undermines various absolute single truths in the socialist mode of governance beyond the economy. The claims by socialist states about their superiority in providing free and quality healthcare and education, a better environment and welfare system have faded away and have been replaced by new survival strategies. They have been manifested among others as the market-Leninist welfare regime with distinctive patterns of state socialist evolution and involution and of post-socialist development (London 2014).

While sanctioning against political pluralism, the party-states have adopted various programmes as an aspect of governmental rationality that emphasise "diversification" strategies ranging from the economy, foreign affairs and healthcare to education, welfare and the environment. In a way, these programmes can be understood as "explicit, planned attempts to reform or transform regimes of practices by reorienting them to specific ends or investing them with particular purposes" (Dean 2010: 268). Due to exposure to global capitalism where neoliberalism has been riding the waves in various economic and social fields, the programmes are inevitably influenced by neoliberal logic.

In Vietnam, during the 1990s and 2000s, the presence of neoliberalism was felt in a number of programmes across different areas of governance. A number of services traditionally monopolised by socialist states were transferred partly to private control and ownership. Remarkably, the "socialisation" (*xã hội hóa*) programmes by the party-state in healthcare and education have produced a mixed picture of governance in these areas. Despite high investment from the party-state in education and health services, which amounts up to 17% of the GDP, so many epidemic problems seem incurable and the quality remains so poor that it has long been public frustration.[2] Basically, "socialisation" in the Vietnamese context denotes the policy attempts by the party-state to improve the public services for the population by diversifying the resources providers.

[2] Domestic media almost daily reports on different kinds of problems plaguing education and health service.

On the one hand, as the "socialisation" programmes are designed to overcome the constraints of public finance, they have diversified and widened the accessibility of these services, thus contributing to improvements in the living standards of the people. On the other hand, its application over the past two decades has produced a dismal picture painted as "a chaotic and inefficient system which deepens inequalities, slows poverty reduction, and threatens to retard the country's future economic growth" (London 2013). The widespread implementation of these programmes has generated a superficial impression about the retreat of the party-state, as neoliberalism would suggest. However, a closer examination of their implications reveals a more complex and confusing picture.

While being placed under the authoritarian control by the party-state, the programmes, such as in education and healthcare, have, in one way or another, indiscriminately taken on some elements of neoliberalism, which credits free-market capitalism as the most rational and efficient way of social and economic organisation. At face value, it seems to lead to an inevitable crash with socialist ideology claimed by the party-state. However, as argued by Schwenkel and Leshkowich, the ambivalence of the term "neoliberalism" and its ramifications mean "enduring socialist interpretive frameworks, relations of power, and modes of socioeconomic organisation contest and rework neoliberalism and its global techniques and technologies of regulation" (2012: 381). Whatever the results of programmes in various functional areas of governance are, there are significant implications in place. The programmes were initially designed as interventions in "survival strategies" once scoring some successes, albeit limitations and problems accompanied, would manufacture new kind of pressures for rationalised performance upon the regime. Part of neoliberal logics have been in operation and tied in the socialist mode of governance as the practices of the regime are now frequently measured against the neoliberal standards of "good governance." The party-state, at different degrees, has been responsive to the neoliberal logics of accountability, transparency, enumeration and quality in which rationalities are embedded. On a similar note, Masina (2010) claims that Vietnam is somewhere in between the developmental state and neoliberalism. Hence, the co-existence and juxtaposition of both neoliberal and socialist forms of governance is in place, which were once deemed unthinkable.

The introduction of developmentalism in Vietnam has added to a complex web of interests evidenced by the rise of powerful interest groups with rent-seeking activity. This phenomenon had been noted earlier in

China (Ding 1998). It has deepened the inequality and exploitation in development and repression in politics. Meanwhile, inherent structural problems of the economy after a period of euphoria without a carefully thought-out development strategy have now acutely surfaced. The global economic crisis in 2008–2009 marked the downward spiral of economic growth and various governance problems. Economic mismanagement resulting in high inflation, massive bad debts and economic slowdown[3] between 2011 and 2013 had undermined the confidence of the population in the performance-based legitimacy. The economic performance in recent years has been improved, hitting 7.1% growth in GDP in 2018. The improvements following the economic downturn in early 2010s have helped boosted the confidence in the party-state's ability to overcome mistakes in economic management. In fact, the requirements in the practice of neoliberal governmentality have raised insurmountable challenges for the party-state in Vietnam. As it is unlikely for them to return to the past of orthodox socialist mode of governance, the Vietnamese party-state is now facing a dilemma. If they choose to invest more in the rational-legal sources of legitimacy, they have to make bolder steps towards neoliberalism, thus becoming more dependent on the liberal order for survival. This requires immediate political reforms and it is unlikely for the authoritarian one-party state to sustain. Otherwise, they need to search for new approach of governmentality, the one that can release them from the pressure of popular consent where the rationality-based performance prevails. As argued by Vuving (2019: 376), Doi moi "has given rise to a political-business complex that commercialises the state's ownership of land, policy, firms and funds for private interests." The influence of businesspeople on policymaking process has been more easily observable at both local and central government agencies. An investigative article by John Reed (2019) exposed further this kind of connection with the rise of Vingroup as a case in point. Vingroup is a Vietnamese conglomerate focusing on real estate development, retail, and services ranging from healthcare to hospitality, and even car manufacturing.

Evidences in both China and Vietnam point to the combination of a vibrant business environment with a non-democratic single-party state that helps to create the conditions for economic take-off. As Reed (2019) argued, "the absence of the normal checks and balances, such as a free

[3]Economic growth rate of Vietnam in 2011 and 2012 was 5.9 and 5%, respectively, according the World Bank.

press and a citizenry allowed to speak its mind, there is a risk of big companies gaining too much power—even one with Vingroup's mission 'to create a better life for the Vietnamese people'."

In fact, the party-states in both Vietnam and China have quietly shifted the focus of legitimacy to rule from abstract socialist ideals and historical legacies to a more distinct governmental rationality. The traditional mode of governance by a communist party regime is further reinforced to a large extent by coercive forms of rule and surveillance as the main form of political control (Kornai 1992). In the post-reform era, the party-state has been producing and reproducing popular consent over its performance-based legitimacy or the regime's efficacy by pointing to relative successes during the past few decades in bringing about progress and improvements in various areas of governance, particularly impressive successes in economy and poverty reduction but still keeping reference to abstract socialist ideas. The party-state's willingness to govern has now been closely associated with the concern with the "welfare of the population, the improvement of its conditions, the increase of its wealth, longevity, health, etc." (Foucault 1991: 100). Thus, the willingness to govern is no longer an axiomatic absolute truth, but conditional on "the will to improve" by means of applying calculated programmes and techniques based on rational and scientific principles of management (Li 2007: 275). With an explicit aim to follow the developmental state, the party-state has employed a number of such programmes with neoliberal elements in managing and disciplining the population. However, it should be noted that the neoliberal standards of compliance such as assessment, transparency and accountability have been substantially reconfigured and reworked in different ways in China and Vietnam.

Although Vietnam and China maintain the authoritarian control by the communist parties, both have now moved to a post-socialist era. Their path to follow the developmental state model has increased exponentially their dependence on the liberal world order in which neoliberal governmentality has been a distinct feature for the last few decades. It means they have been engaging with "a political project that is justified on philosophical grounds and seeks to extend competitive market forces, consolidate a market-friendly constitution and promote individual freedom" (Jessop 2013: 70). Their exposure to global capitalism in a neoliberal era has left its imprints in various areas of governance with neoliberal logics. Now that a grand rupture in the political vision of the post-socialist states, the party-state needs to think of alternative forms of governance for their own survival. Their post-socialist projects of governance with a recombination with neoliberal elements are likely to offer both distinct and similar characteristics.

Since the 2008–2009 global economic crisis, the critical question about the political legitimacy of the party-state has consistently re-emerged. It has become an imperative to search for a refined mode of economic governance. While the rational-legal source needs overhaul, the traditional source with legitimate claim to nationalism is also seriously challenged. As China becomes more aggressive in its claims over the South China Sea and is widely seen as a threat to Vietnam's territorial integrity, the close ties established between the two party-states of Vietnam and China after the normalisation of relations in 1990s have weakened the former's position to exploit nationalism to its advantage. In summer 2014, there were a series of anti-China protests followed by unrest and riots across Vietnam in May 2014, in response to China deploying an oil rig in a disputed region of the South China Sea.

Furthermore, the lack of a coherent and consistent political vision for a grand governance project has been evidenced by the dominance of a rent-seeking state, indicating an imminent crisis of the party-state (Vuving 2013). Overall, it is now struggling in search of a kind of economic governance that can reverse the downward trend of popular support by reconfiguring the way the consent of the population is understood.

The economic governance by the party-state is being developed in the form of re-combining and rearranging different elements of neoliberalism and statist socialism in a highly complex and fluid context. While the convergent point is to reclaim and revitalise the role of the state, their objectives might be very different. The ultimate goal remains to strengthen and sustain the monopoly of political power of the communist party. It seeks to deliver more social and political inclusion and better welfare policies with an emphasis on the moral responsibility of the state towards its citizenry (Grugel and Riggirozzi 2012: 3–4). It is argued that the economic governance in the form of socialist market economy is not characterised by something totally novel and revolutionary, but rather that there is a great deal of continuities that need to be appreciated despite neoliberal strictures being recognised. Thus, the post-socialist processes taking place in a country like Vietnam are amorphous and ambivalent at this stage. What is more certain is that the party-state must adopt economic governance that can better accommodate the ever increasingly diverse aspirations of the population and more effectively respond to the more widespread resistance from quarters of the society. As a result of state spatialisation in the forms of verticality and encompassment, the claims traditionally monopolised and long depended on by the state have been challenged and undermined (Ferguson and Gupta 2002: 995). By so doing, they are most likely to use a "new bottle, old wine" approach to deal with the governance problematique. Whatever efforts are in place to rebuild and reclaim the party-state, it is highly unlikely that they could abandon the commitment and promise to lead the country to modernisation. This is a critical aspect of the grand new legitimacy (Brocheux 2012: 91) that the party-state's governance can be tenable.

It is demonstrated that the party-state has been trying to apply various techniques and practices based on both "inclusions and exclusions of particular knowledge" (Schwenkel and Leshkowich 2012: 394) to improve its governance capacity and the welfare of the population. At the same time, the party-state starts to take steps towards governing people from a distance more than direct repression so that "people are not necessarily aware of how their conduct is being conducted or why" (Li 2007: 275). This is actually what has been done with the tightening of the cybersecurity with new laws put in place. As argued by Börje Ljunggren (2019), the Vietnamese party-state "has managed its unorthodox path to a market economy, but could soon face tough choices." The "tough choices" are meant as coping with the challenge of "choosing a more open way forward than China."

Reality Check on Socialist Market Economy in Vietnam and China

Embracing developmentalism, the Vietnamese party-state has emphasised a strong role for the state, or more accurately the party-state, over the economy and development. The economic success over the two decades after the market-based reforms in 1986 is arguably attributable to the developmental state model that Vietnam has been following in line with that of East Asian countries. While the developmental state itself is a loosely-defined concept denoting institutional, relational and ideational aspects of an activist and interventionist state in directing the course of development (Stubbs 2009: 5–6), some of these characteristics have been playing out in the case of Vietnam (Beeson and Pham 2012). However, as demonstrated below, the inherent limitations of this model exposed in late 1990s, particularly after the 1997–1998 Asian financial crisis, coupled with acute internal problems and contradictions in Vietnam's governance mode have taken the practices of state-led developmentalism far away from its original form. The benefits from trade liberalisation and an emphasis on export-led growth had turned Vietnam into an economic tiger in Southeast Asian by the mid-2000s. The performance in poverty reduction is also impressive, reducing the rate from 60 to 20% within 20 years between 1993 and 2012 and to as low as 9.8% in 2016 according to the World Bank (Pimhidzai 2018). For almost three decades, Vietnam has been a favourite destination for the flows of foreign direct investment (FDI) and official development assistance (ODA) and international donors have consistently hailed the country as a success story. Overall, the role of such a developmental state is widely recognised as the party-state and its agencies have clearly been proponents or facilitators of certain policies, strategies and knowledge that contribute to such performance. However, the role of the socialist states is being subject to a more critical scrutiny by recent studies. Evaluating the roles of the party-states of China and Vietnam in their developmental successes, Malesky and London (2014) argue that their most robust growth was in periods of state withdrawal from the economy and their current economic difficulties stem from the scale and character of the party-state's role in the economy. Furthermore, the focus on the role of the party-state might come at the expense of obscuring other complex factors and the interplay of different forces at the societal level and global level.

The relative success of Vietnam over the past few decades is significantly attributable to a developmental structure from which capacities of the party-state derive. According to Tuong Vu (2010: 4), a developmental state requires such a structure as "cohesive internal organisations and alliance with capital at the expense of workers and peasants." While the socialist states like Vietnam and China demonstrate certain attributes of the developmental structure like stable and centralised government, cohesive institutions and effective coercive institutions, they differ significantly from capitalist developmental states in the sense that state ownership is overly dominant. It is noteworthy that pre-1979 China was considered "the socialist developmental state" while pre-1986 Vietnam was not (Vu 2010: 100–105). Since their reforms, both China and Vietnam still have not relied on private ownership and market mechanism but to a decreasing extent, "draw power from direct control of productive organisations" (Vu 2010: 6). In Vietnam, this kind of developmental structure embraced by the party-state has borne detrimental effects on the long-term wellbeing of its people. It has placed too much emphasis on economic growth and material prosperity at the expense of political freedoms and social inequality. The resultant problem is that the party-state has accommodated certain influences of neoliberalism in the economic sense for the purpose of increasing material wealth without adequate attention to social justice mechanisms. This problem is even greater in China.

It is also important to factor in the influences of global institutions, including inter-governmental organisations (IGOs), non-governmental organisations (NGOs), multinational corporations (MNCs), domestic social organisations at the grassroots and national levels that "cut across familiar top-down and bottom up spatial imaginings of statehood" (Schwenkel and Leshkowich 2012: 388). Clearly, just like China, Vietnam has benefited greatly from the liberal order outside and has been locked into that order for the foreseeable future (Lee 2012). For the past few decades, Vietnam has integrated into that order so extensively and deeply that they are now bound by the various rules and norms produced within the order. It does not mean that the party-state is strictly and rigidly imposed by these rules and norms, but there exists a certain room for the party-state to swing by reworking them in their local contexts as suggested earlier. However, the agents of neoliberal governance, such as the United Nations Development Program (UNDP), the World Bank (WB), the International Monetary Fund (IMF), the World Trade Organization (WTO) and a number of aid agencies from the capitalist countries, have exerted unfettered pressure on the party-state for neoliberal restructuring of the economy through expansive knowledge systems and expertise as well as capital investments.

The dilemma that Vietnam is facing raises an intriguing question about whether Vietnam will choose to continue increased integration into the liberal rules-based order. For some, this question might be irrelevant because Vietnam has already been so closely tied into that order that it cannot escape and it is inevitable for the country to open up new reforms to follow that line. However, there is also significant merit in the question because it is argued that Vietnam is actually not dependent on such a liberal world outside for survival, but rather on communist China (Vuving 2013: 325–326). This crucial question is still left without a conclusive answer. In terms of economic survival, China is Vietnam's greatest trading partner. However, Vietnam runs a large trade deficit with China. Meanwhile, the US is Vietnam's largest export market where Vietnam runs a large trade surplus. According to Smith (2019), by allowing Vietnam to have trade surplus, the US has boosted investment there, which is "far more powerful of a poverty-reducing force than any foreign aid, development assistance or governmental loans," and Vietnam is apparently benefiting from the Trump trade war with China.

Between 2011 and 2013, Vietnam struggled with an economic downturn and embattled in the task of fundamental economic restructuring. Criticisms were levelled at economic mismanagement by the government and the slow pace of reforms. The economy's high vulnerabilities had been exposed through the indication of depleting foreign exchange reserves, massive bad debts, and a large number of enterprises' closures and liquidations.[4] After dragging debates about the solutions to the economy, the Communist Party of Vietnam (CPV) Central Committee issued a resolution identifying three areas for restructuring, i.e. state-owned enterprises (SOEs), public investment and financial-credit institutions.[5] Although a version of the socialist economy based on "public ownership of main means of production" supported by the CPV General Secretary Nguyen Phu Trong was vetoed at the 11th CPV National Congress in January 2011, the state-owned sector of the economy is still given the pivotal role. Despite notorious scandals of major state conglomerates, i.e. Vinashin (Vietnam Shipbuilding Industry Group) and Vinalines (Vietnam National Shipping Lines),[6] large state-owned corporations continue to be regarded as "red iron fists" of the economy. It is the firm belief of the party-state that restructuring SOEs will make them work more effectively and buttress the new form of economic governance (CPV 2017).

The first important point to note about the reform of SOEs in Vietnam is its contextual origin, which is a key difference from that in China. Vietnam initiated market-based reforms about a decade later than China

[4] In 2012, Vietnam's foreign exchange reserves were sufficient for only 2.3 months of import, public debts in 2011 accounted for 106% of GDP, according to international standards, and the number of closures and liquidations between 2011 and 2012 amounted to 104,000, making up half the total number over the past 20 years (Vuving 2013; Vu 2013).

[5] The resolution of the 3rd Plenum of the 11th Tenure Central Committee of the CPV in October 2011.

[6] Vinashin was on the verge of a bankruptcy with debts totalling US$4 billion in 2010; Vinalines had a debt of US$2 billion and defaulted on five loans worth US$1.1 billion by 2012 due to mismanagement (Vuving 2013: 328).

by first addressing the SOEs to save the economy from a looming collapse, while China's economic reforms started in the rural sector to reinvigorate the stagnating economy (Fforde 1999). The reform on the SOEs in Vietnam was planned as early as the late 1980s with "equitisation" schemes and efforts to reduce the number of 100% SOEs which was about 12,000 in early 1990s. Throughout the next two decades, the pace of reform remained quite slow as there were still more than 3200 SOEs by 2010.[7] Equitisation efforts had been accelerated with a stronger political will between 2016 and 2019 aiming for the number of 100 SOEs by 2020 (see also Knutsen and Do Ta Khanh, this volume). As of the end of 2018, there were 500 enterprises 100% owned by the state. The SOEs still dominate the most important and lucrative sectors of the economy, including banking and finance, insurance, minerals, natural resources, construction, infrastructure, shipping, civil aviation and telecommunications. These are the core sectors of the economy and considered as so politically and strategically sensitive that both foreign investment and private domestic enterprises are either discouraged or disadvantaged in terms of market access, loans and land use. However, at the domestic level, the SOEs' poor performance compared to private and FDI enterprises is striking (Vu 2009: 404–405).

The explicit objectives of the restructuring of SOEs are to strengthen and revitalise the role of the SOEs in the core sectors by gradual divestment in non-core business and to take the commanding heights of the economy. The aim clearly stated is to sharpen the role of SOEs as macroeconomic regulatory tools. It echoes exactly the official attitudes towards SOEs in China focusing on how to maintain control of "the commanding heights of the economy while allowing small-scale enterprises to survive in an increasingly market-driven economic environment" (Beeson 2007: 176). Indeed, the underlying goal behind the restructuring programmes is to maintain Leninist political control over the economy through SOEs as the CPV can continue to command the allegiance of the elites and partly the middle class through the revenues generated by SOEs. As the socialist dogmas have failed to produce and maintain the loyalty of the elites in ideological terms with plenty of evidence throughout the 11th CPV National Congress and recent 6th and 7th Plenum of the CPV Central Committee, the party-state has turned to rationalise a complex

[7] Among them, eight economic groups and 96 corporations have about US$20 billion in capital and hold 75% of national fixed assets.

web of interests where all privileges and opportunities are closely tied to the Party's discretionary power. In this sense, the structure of political economy of Vietnam strikes a similar note to that of China where the Party "remains the dominant dispenser of commercial, business, professional and even social opportunity" (Lee 2012). The Vietnamese party-state's capacity to effectively direct the development course has been seriously compromised by its self-fulfilling and rent-seeking patterns.

The designed political economy of Vietnam has become a fertile ground for clientelism and rent-seeking activities with the ethos "to create barriers and extract rents from society" (Vuving 2013: 325). The patronage system resulting from such a political economy is promoting exclusion, rather than inclusion. In terms of personnel, there is a strong link between SOEs and the CPV. All SOEs executives are CPV members. Most important positions of central economic groups and corporations are nominated and appointed directly by the Prime Minister upon the approval by the CPV Secretariat and Central Organization Commission. However, the near collapse of large corporations like Vinashin and Vinalines, as well as the continuous loss-making by various SOEs, had exposed corruption and poor competence of many SOEs executives. Moreover, investigative reports from the National Assembly of Vietnam revealed the weak and insecure governance structure of the SOEs, especially the large economic groups. All these factors have significantly blunted their competitive edge at the regional and international level despite their great advantages in access to market, capital and land.

While the SOEs reform plans imply exclusive programmes and technical practices to maintain the political control of the party-state, there are certain aspects indicating a trend towards more social inclusion in the governmentality. During the debates for the amendments of the 1992 Constitution, there had been polemical attacks on the idea of the state-owned economic sector as the mainstay of the economy (Nguyen 2010). However, the party-state resolutely sticks to the idea that is strongly entrenched in the new Constitution passed by the National Assembly in November 2013. Article 51 (1) of the 2013 Constitution reads: "The Vietnamese economy is a socialist-oriented market economy with multi-forms of ownership and multi-sectors of economic structure; the state economic sector plays the leading role." Interestingly, the Constitution indicates some ambivalent attitude of the party-state over the treatment with all non-state economic sectors. On the one hand, it clearly prioritises the state-owned economic sector. On the other hand, the Constitution places an emphasis on the equal treatment to all economic sectors, regardless of state-owned, private or foreign-owned sectors. Article 51 (2) of the Constitution reads: "All economic sectors are important constituents of the national economy. Actors of different economic sectors are equal, cooperate, and compete in accordance with the law." This highly ambivalent attitude towards the economic sectors produces a compromising effect. Thus, such a contradiction could be mediated by practical policymaking of the party-state.

The party-state has been making various efforts to restore the confidence of the public and investors in its path for state-led development. The grand plan for economic restructuring, despite all its flaws and criticisms, is designed as intervention programmes to present a more socially-inclusive development and better welfare policies to solicit public consent. Some initial results of stabilisation measures have been produced. For the first time since 1993, there was a foreign trade surplus in 2012 with Vietnam posting a record surplus of 2.7% in the current account balance. And since then, Vietnam has continuously posted a trade surplus, reaching more than US$11 billion in 2019. The government has consistently implemented the roadmap for minimum wage increases and announced plans for wage reform despite resources constraints. The measures taken by the party-state are to demonstrate the commitment to the developmental state, rather than a rent-seeking state. However, there is increasing evidence pointing to an imminent comprehensive crisis that economic restructuring alone is no longer sufficient. The longer political reforms are delayed, the closer such a crisis will approach. As far as the regime resilience concerns, the claim that each regime's ability to maintain checks and balances is the critical element to on-going Communist rule in both places still has its merit (Abrami et al. 2013). In addition to that strategic argument about the performance of the party-state in China and Vietnam, the introduction of different menu sets of good governance and public administration has also been recognised as important factors for sustained economic growth and human development in these countries (Nguyen et al. 2019).

Case Study: Discourses of Land Ownership, State-Owned Economic Sector and Local Governance in Vietnam

Land ownership has great psychological, sentimental, social and economic meanings for Vietnamese people. The majority of Vietnamese people rely on land as either their major property asset or livelihood, or both. Land ownership as a legal right was been politicised in Le Duan's doctrine of entire people's ownership. The norm that all land belongs to entire people's ownership represented and managed by the state was codified in the 1980 Constitution and kept unchanged in the 1992 Constitution and later revisions. The economic and legal reforms since *Doi moi* have "unleashed waves of conflict over property rights and property use" (Gillespie 2011: 241). Land disputes have become a frequent phenomenon and a source of protest politics for the past few decades. According to a government report, more than 70% of complaints and denunciations are related to land disputes, making it one of the most contentious issues for the party-state to tackle on a daily basis. Most concerns are about the potential social unrest related to land disputes. The discourse of land ownership during the process of amending the 1992 Constitution touches on this sensitive nerve.

Most societal groups with interests independent from the party-state provide an account of land disputes which attributes the land ownership to the root cause. Their voices were indeed represented by a group of 72 senior scholars and retired officials who presented a petition to the Constitutional Amendment Drafting Committee in 2013. They request that diverse types of ownership, including the private, collective and community ownership of land, should be recognised in the Constitution to prevent abuse of power and corruption. They challenge the absolute truth about the entire people's ownership of land which annuls all other types of land ownership. Petition 72 and Letter of the Vietnam Episcopal Council on draft constitutional amendments represent the emergence of plural interests in land ownership by offering an alternative narrative of land ownership. The strongest critique is that the current pattern of behaviour by the party-state reflects changing goals in which the goal of a socialist society increasingly gives way to that of acquisition, particularly of land, sundering traditional communities and ties to the society.

The party-state stands firm on the issue of land ownership which is regarded as a critical death spot of the entire regime (Hoang 2013).

Its securitisation of land ownership has ruled out any radical demand of private ownership of land throughout the process of amending the Constitution. However, it is prepared to make some concessions with regard to broadening and strengthening the legal rights of land users. As Gillespie opines, "the socialist idea that land is a special commodity is giving way to state recognised private land markets" (Gillespie 2013). Due to serious contestations over the proposed Article 57 in the January 2013 version on land confiscation for the purpose of economic-social development projects, it has been revised with two options, one with and the other without that ground for land grab.[8] It continues to be subject to heated debate at National Assembly meetings and internal discussions of high-level leaders. The CPV National Congress in 2016 reviewed this debate and agreed on the need to "restructure the agricultural sector towards large-scale commodity production through the intensive deployment of high-technology methods" (CPV 2016). This general policy direction has opened up further discussion in the following years on land accumulation and concentration as a way of transition from small-householder production to large-scale agricultural production by means of better mobilisation of capital, technology and resources held by the private sector. As far as the existing land law concerns, there are certain limits placed on the amount of land area allowed to be transferred among agricultural households and the duration of agricultural land leases (To et al. 2019: 6). The 2013 Land Law has been under consideration for amendments scheduled in 2020 to address the issue of fragmented land holdings and inefficient land use by easing the limits on land use and developing the land use right market. However, due to the complexity and unforeseen impacts of this policy, major changes to the land law might be delayed once again. The Vietnamese party-state has not been prepared to venture into the new waters implicated in land reforms on the verge of the fast-approaching National Congress of the CPV to be held in January 2021.

Another important discourse related to ownership is that of the state-owned sector of the economy. For long, Vietnam has held firm to the socialist idea of the state-owned sector as playing the leading role in the economy in terms of both its disproportionate size and role. However, economic mismanagement and poor performance of major

[8] The version of the draft 1992 Constitutional Amendments dated 26 August 2013.

large conglomerates have given rise to severe criticisms of these sectors and its supposed roles. As a result, the pressure for accelerated restructuring of SOEs had been mounted. The CPV issued Resolution 12 in 2017 and the National Assembly issued Resolution 60/2018/QH14 in 2018 on improving and implementing law and policy on management and use of capital and assets owned by the State at SOEs and equitisation. A new model of governance over SOEs was endorsed with the inception of a super-ministerial committee called the Committee on State Capital Management at Enterprises in 2018. All major state-owned conglomerates are now placed under the purview of this Committee.

Many societal groups and individuals have engaged in efforts to debunk the dominant orthodox narrative about the role and strength of the state-owned economic sector. There have been lively debates at the NA with polemic attacks at the state-owned economic sector as the mainstay of the economy and cogent critiques on the media (Nguyen 2010). There are plural interests from societal groups, including private businesses, with economic incentives in a more equal sharing of resources and access. The contestation of this norm resulted in some shift in the construction of the draft Constitutional amendments. Article 54 (2) of the December 2012 version of the draft Constitution released for public consultation drops the term on the leading role of the state-owned economic sector. It reads "all economic sectors are important components of the national economy for long-term development, cooperation, equality and competition in accordance with laws." Clearly, the newly drafted constitutional rule places a strong emphasis on the equal treatment to all economic sectors, regardless of state-owned, private or foreign-owned sectors. This represents a major compromise by the party-state over the changing character of a special norm.

The force of resistance in the party-state is still strong enough to shore up its position. The core principle of the leading role of the state-owned economic sector was quickly re-introduced to the later version of the Constitutional amendments submitted to the NA Standing Committee in April 2013 (Hoang 2013). Both high-ranking officials from the CAC and party-state leaders stressed that an absolute majority of ideas confirms the leading role of the state-owned economic sector (Vo 2013). The existence of two different options in the later versions of the draft Constitution concerning the role of the state-owned economic sector indicates the harsh struggle and contestation between different forces. Whether this draft constitutional rule will signal some fundamental turn in the economic governance or represents some cosmetic changes to ease public frustration over the state-owned economic sector is now called into question. It is mostly likely that even such a constitutional rule is passed, it can be mediated by practical policymaking of the party-state to continue prioritising the state-owned economic sector.

Last, but not least, the discourse of local governance is an important recurring theme throughout the process of amending the Constitution. This discourse constructs the knowledge and practices in the power relations between the local and central government and among the local government themselves. As earlier discussed, it (re-)emerged in the 2001 process of amending the Constitution and was left unresolved until a first serious effort to tackle it in 2008 by launching a pilot scheme for abolishing the People's Council at district and city ward levels in ten major cities and provinces in April 2009. With the current homogenised structure and organisation of local government across the country in the Constitution, the party-state is struggling with problems arising from highly disparate patterns of governance between the local governments in the metropolitan areas, those in the rural areas, in the islands, and the exclusive economic and administrative zones.[9] Local interest groups are now pressing the central government for "particularistic mechanisms" of governance in the name of development.

In this discourse, local governance involves the People's Council, People Committee and mass organisations at local levels which are stipulated in the 1992 Constitution. The structure and power relations of local governments represent the constancy of the Soviet model comparable to Russian matryoshka dolls referring to a set of government structures of decreasing size with one nested inside the other (Nguyen 2012). The socialist idea of the existing model of local government as a representative body of both the higher level state power body (vertical accountability) and as the people within its territorial boundary (horizontal accountability) has faced with sustained criticisms. As it is entirely dependent on the party's leadership and instructions from the higher levels, they are overshadowed by formalities, passiveness and ineffectiveness in operation (Bui 2012). There have been ample evidences of local governments being self-serving, abusive and corrupt which contribute to widespread discontent among the people (Kerkvliet 2004: 16–17). Thus, there is

[9] Several Exclusive Economic and Administrative Zones are now under construction like Vân Đồn (Quảng Ninh), Vân Phong (Khánh Hòa), and Phú Quốc (Kiên Giang).

a strong emphasis on decentralisation, autonomy and diversification of local governments in the counter-hegemonic narrative penetrating into the process of amending the 1992 Constitution. This idea is gaining increasing influences in the constitutional debates and in the drafts given the strong support of many legal scholars affected by liberal thinking and the powerful interest groups from local governments, especially in major metropolitan areas like Ho Chi Minh city, Hanoi and Da Nang.[10]

The December 2012 version of the draft produced for public comments does not reflect any substantive change from the 1992 Constitution on local governments. The section of the draft on local government soon becomes one of the most contentious issues and faces heavy criticisms. The May 2013 version offers a compromise with two options, reflecting a shift in views towards a more flexible provision allowing plural forms of local governments and their power relations. Option 1 has only two short articles which do not provide for any description of the role or mandate of the local governments but leave them for the laws. Option 2 keeps all 8 articles of the 1992 Constitution unchanged. Both options are controversial because those pressing for changes are seeking a clear principle of local governance and more detailed stipulations about the roles and relations of the local government in the Constitution. The August 2013 version demonstrates more concessions to accommodate dissenting views by three options of which two represent a liberal view and the other reflects a stronghold of socialist idea with some cosmetic changes about the more active role of local government. Remarkably, the two liberal options now stress the principle of local autonomy and self-government and local government is a legal public entity.

The October 2013 draft, as well as the final text of the Constitution adopted in November 2013 rejects the liberal options and continues to assert the central government's formal control over local government. This reflects a strong fear of provincialism rather than a vision for reform of local governance. As a matter of fact, the National Assembly adopted Law on Local Government in 2015 in this spirit. The result of this process is greater pressures from the society on local governments for more accountability and democratic institutions. The National Assembly is now considering amendments to the Law on Local Government to accommodate societal demand.

[10]See, for example, the text of the speech delivered by Tran Du Lich, an NA deputy from Ho Chi Minh city at the NA plenary session in the morning of 16 November 2012.

Conclusion

Economic governance by the party-state in both Vietnam and China under the socialist market economy has been characterised as uneven, exceptional, novel and problematic. It has reflected the development path the countries under the reign of the Leninist state has travelled for the past three decades. Taken at face value, this development path seems to be expressive of a move towards a more violent form of illiberal capitalism. At closer scrutiny, as the chapter has demonstrated, there are inherent limits and contradictions of neoliberal advances in the domestic sphere that it could not go far. Now that both countries stand at a critical juncture with an imminent crisis: Its entrenched socialist political vision needs to move beyond both socialist and neoliberal projects. There is little sign that the post-socialist states in Vietnam and China can embark upon a complete new vision, but instead, they retain various elements of the past in novel recombinations and rearrangements. In the final analysis, the socialist market economy in Vietnam and China involves evolutional continuity more than revolutionary change. By analysing the evolution of the developmental state, the chapter seeks to demonstrate how the double movement of accommodating and resisting neoliberalism is playing out in such a cacophony of ideas and practices. It should also be noted that while the chapter invariably draws on some parallels between Vietnam and China on a number of issues, it does not mean at all to overlook the differences between them. While both countries might face similar problems, they differ substantially in size, scope and origin. While both have to chart a new terrain of governance in a similar transitional direction, they're doing so separately.

Both China and Vietnam are now in search of new forms of economic governance, which aims to strengthen and revitalise the role of the single-party state. In this context, there have been important governmental interventions with different effects. However, the deliberate attempts do not always conform to the initial plans due to the complex interplay of various forces of resistance and co-optation. The processes are neither totalising nor distinct as they embrace both old and new elements recast in an amorphous form. These processes are characterised by uncertainties.

References

Abrami, Regina, Edmund Malesky, and Yu Zheng. 2013. Vietnam through Chinese Eyes. In *Why Communism Did Not Collapse: Understanding Authoritarian Regime Resilience in Asia and Europe*, ed. M. Dimitrov, 237–275. Cambridge: Cambridge University Press.

Beeson, Mark. 2007. *Regionalism and Globalization in East Asia: Politics, Security and Economic Development*. Basingstoke: Palgrave Macmillan.

Beeson, Mark, and Hung Hung Pham. 2012. Developmentalism with Vietnamese Characteristics: The Persistence of State-Led Development in East Asia. *Journal of Contemporary Asia* 42 (4): 539–559.

Brocheux, Pierre. 2012. Reflections on Vietnam. *New Left Review* 73: 73–91.

Bui, Xuan Duc. 2012. Vị trí, tính chất của Hội đồng nhân dân trong cơ cấu tổ chức của cơ quan chính quyền địa phương ở Việt Nam - Những vấn đề đang đặt ra và phương hướng đổi mới [The Position and Character of the People's Council in the Structure of Local Governments in Vietnam—Problems and Orientation for Reform]. Paper presented at the Workshop on 'Improving the Organizational Model and Operational Method of Local Government Towards the Amendment of the 1992 Constitution' organized by the Institution for Legislative Studies, Vũng Tàu, 2–3 August 2012.

Communist Party of Vietnam (CPV). 2016. Văn kiện Đại hội 12 [Party Principle Documents of the 12th National Congress]. Available online at http://tulieuvankien.dangcongsan.vn/ban-chap-hanh-trung-uong-dang/dai-hoi-dang/lan-thu-xii. Accessed 15 March 2020.

Communist Party of Vietnam (CPV). 2017. Resolution No. 12-NQ/TW by the 5th Plenum of the Central Committee on Continued Restructuring, Renovation, and Improvement in Efficiency and Effectiveness of State-Owned Enterprises dated 3 June 2017.

Dean, Mitchell. 2010. *Governmentality: Power and Rule in Modern Society*, 2nd ed. London: Sage.

Ding, Yijiang. 1998. Corporatism and Civil Society in China: An Overview of the Debate in Recent Years. *China Information* 12 (4): 44–67.

Ferguson, James, and Akhil Gupta. 2002. Spatializing States: Toward an Ethnography of Neoliberal Governmentality. *American Ethnologist* 29 (4): 981–1002.

Fforde, Adam. 1999. From Plan to Market: The Economic Transition in Vietnam and China compared. In *Transforming Asian Socialism: China and Vietnam Compared*, ed. Benedict Kerkvliet, Anita Chan, and Jonathan Unger. Canberra: Department of International Relations, RSPAS, ANU.

Foucault, Michel. 1991. Governmentality. In *The Foucault Effect: Studies in Governmentality*, ed. Graham Burchell, Colin Gordon, and Peter Miller, 87–104. Chicago: University of Chicago Press.

Gillespie, John. 2011. Exploring the Limits of the Judicialization of Urban Land Disputes in Vietnam. *Law and Society Review* 45 (2): 241.

Gillespie, John. 2013. Vietnam's Land Law Reforms: Radical Changes or Minor Tinkering? *East Asia Forum*, May 14. http://www.eastasiaforum.org/2013/05/14/vietnams-land-law-reforms-radical-changes-or-minor-tinkering/.

Grugel, Jean, and Pía Riggirozzi. 2012. Post-neoliberalism in Latin America: Rebuilding and Reclaiming the State After Crisis. *Development and Change* 43 (1): 1–21.

Hoang, Xuan Phu. 2013. 'Hai tử huyệt của chế độ' [The Two Death Spots of the Regime]. Blog Hoàng Xuân Phú. Hanoi, January 11. http://hpsc.iwr.uni-heidelberg.de/hxphu/index.php?page=readwriting&w=HaiTuHuyetCuaCheDo-20130111.

Hoang, Tu. 2013. Lại đề xuất kinh tế nhà nước giữ vai trò chủ đạo [Repeated Proposal to Keep the Pivotal Role of the State-Owned Sector]. *Kinh te Sai Gon online*, April 16. http://www.thesaigontimes.vn/Home/xahoi/sukien/94774/.

Jessop, Bob. 2013. Putting Neoliberalism in Its Time and Place: A Response to the Debate. *Social Anthropology* 21 (1): 65–74.

Kerkvliet, Benedict J. Tria. 2004. Surveying Local Government and Authority in Contemporary Vietnam. In *Beyond Hanoi: Local Government in Vietnam*, ed. Benedict J. Tria Kerkvliet and David G. Marr, vol. 359, pp. 16–17. Singapore: Institute of Southeast Asian Studies.

Kornai, Janos. 1992. *The Socialist System: The Political Economy of Communism*. Oxford: Oxford University Press.

Lee, John. 2012. China's Corporate Leninism. *The American Interest*, May–June.

Li, Tania Murray. 2007. Governmentality. *Anthropologica* 49 (2): 275–281.

Ljunggren, Börje. 2019. Vietnam—Globalized Party-State. Yale Global online. https://yaleglobal.yale.edu/content/vietnam-globalized-party-state.

London, Jonathan D. 2013. *The Contributions and Limits of 'Socialization': The Political Economy of Essential Services in Viet Nam*. Hanoi: UNDP Vietnam. Available at: http://blog.jonathanlondon.net/?p=142. Accessed 2 June 2013.

London, Jonathan D. 2014. Welfare Regimes in China and Vietnam. *Journal of Contemporary Asia* 44 (1): 84–107.

Malesky, Edmund, and Jonathan London. 2014. The Political Economy of Development in China and Vietnam. *Annual Review of Political Science* 17: 395–419.

Masina, Pietro. 2010. Vietnam Between Developmental State and Neoliberalism: The Case of the Industrial Sector. Working Papers 1007, c.MET-05.

Nguyen, Quang A. 2010. Kinh tế nhà nước giữ chủ đạo: Sự lẫn lộn trong tư duy [State-Owned Economic Sector Plays the Leading Role: A Confusion in Thinking]. Dien dan Kinh te Viet Nam [Vietnam Economic Forum].

Available at: http://vnr500.vn/2010-09-28-kinh-te-nn-giu-chu-dao-su-lan-lon-trong-tu-duy.Pashigian.

Nguyen, Đăng Dung. 2012. Mô hình tổ chức và phương thức hoạt động của hệ thống chính quyền địa phương từ 1945 đến nay và những kiến nghị đổi mới [Organisational Model and Operational Mode of Local Government System Since 1945 and Proposals for Reform]. Paper presented at the Workshop on 'Improving the Organizational Model and Operational Method of Local Government Towards the Amendment of the 1992 Constitution' organized by the Institution for Legislative Studies, Vũng Tàu, 2–3 August 2012.

Nguyen, Viet Cuong, Thanh Long Giang, Ngoc Anh Tran, and Thanh Huyen Do. 2019. Do Good Governance and Public Administration Improve Economic Growth and Poverty Reduction? The Case of Vietnam. *International Public Management Journal* 1–31. https://doi.org/10.1080/10967494.2019.1592793.

Pimhidzai, Obert. 2018. Climbing the Ladder: Poverty Reduction and Shared Prosperity in Vietnam (English). Washington, DC: World Bank Group.

Reed, John. 2019. The Rise and Rise of a Vietnamese Corporate Empire. *Financial Times*, June 26.

Schwenkel, Christina, and Ann Marie Leshkowich. 2012. How Is Neoliberalism Good to Think Vietnam? How Is Vietnam Good to Think Neoliberalism? *Position* 20 (2): 379–401.

Smith, Noah. 2019. Look Who's Winning the US-China Trade War. *Bloomberg*, 4 June. https://www.bloomberg.com/opinion/articles/2019-06-04/look-who-s-winning-the-u-s-china-trade-war.

Stubbs, Richard. 2009. What Ever Happened to the East Asian Developmental State? The Unfolding Debate. *The Pacific Review* 22 (1): 1–22.

To, Phuc, Sango Mahanty, and Andrew Wells-Dang. 2019. From "Land to the Tiller" to the "New Landlords"? The Debate over Vietnam's Latest Land Reforms. *Land* 120 (8): 1–19.

Vo, Van Thanh. 2013. Hiến pháp còn 4 vấn đề lớn có ý kiến khác nhau [There Remain Four Major Controversial Issues Regarding the Revised Constitution]. *Tuoi tre online*, September 29. https://tuoitre.vn/hien-phap-con-bon-van-de-lon-co-y-kien-khac-nhau-571463.htm.

Vu, Quang Viet. 2009. Vietnam Economic Crisis: Policy Follies and the Role of State-Owned Conglomerates. *Southeast Asian Affairs*.

Vu, Tuong. 2010. *Paths to Development in Asia: South Korea, Vietnam, China, and Indonesia*. Cambridge: Cambridge University Press.

Vu, Quang Viet. 2013. Khủng hoảng và hệ thống tài chính tín dụng: Phân tích ứng dụng với kinh tế Mỹ và Việt Nam [Crisis and Financial-Credit System: Applied Analysis of the US and Vietnam Economies]. *Thoi dai moi*, March 2013 (27).

Vuving, Alexander L. 2013. Vietnam in 2012: A Rent-Seeking State on the Verge of a Crisis. *Southeast Asian Affairs* 2013: 325–347.
Vuving, Alexander L. 2019. Vietnam in 2018: A Rent-Seeking State on Correction Course. *Southeast Asian Affairs* 2019: 375–393.

CHAPTER 5

Reforming State-Owned Enterprises in a Global Economy: The Case of Vietnam

Hege Merete Knutsen and Do Ta Khanh

Introduction

This chapter examines what the latest phase of state-owned enterprise (SOE) reforms in Vietnam starting around 2016 tells us about economic and institutional changes in Vietnam. In doing so we shed light on

This research has received funding from the European Union's Horizon 2020 research and innovation programme under grant agreement N° 770562 (CRISEA).

The original version of this chapter was revised: Chapter 5 is now open access under a CC BY 4.0 license with the copyright holder updated to 'The Author(s)'. The correction to this chapter is available at https://doi.org/10.1007/978-981-15-6248-8_13

H. M. Knutsen (✉)
Department of Sociology and Human Geography, University of Oslo, Oslo, Norway
e-mail: h.m.knutsen@sosgeo.uio.no

D. T. Khanh
Institute for European Studies, Vietnam Academy of Social Sciences, Hanoi, Vietnam

A. Hansen et al. (eds.), *The Socialist Market Economy in Asia*,
https://doi.org/10.1007/978-981-15-6248-8_5

some challenges and contradictions between the socialist ideology and the market imperative, which the Vietnamese economy is subject to as a global player.

In Vietnam, the *doi moi* process for economic renewal and market orientation was launched in 1986 with SOE reforms being an important part of the agenda. The first equitization of SOEs took place in 1992. Equitization—or 'privatization with Vietnamese characteristics'—means that enterprises are turned into joint stock companies in which the state, workers and private investors hold shares. Either the state or the private investors hold the majority shares, usually the state. In Vietnam, the concept of equitization has less negative ideological overtones than privatization because it marks a difference to capitalism (Hiep 2017). With considerable resistance from SOE managers and for fear of job losses, the first phases of equitization went slowly.

Our interest in the new phase of SOE reforms is actualized by the real economy challenges Vietnam faces to become an upper middle-income economy by 2035. We do not claim that studies of SOE reforms are sufficient to understand the breadth of political-economic change and challenges in Vietnam. Having said this, SOE reforms are an interesting entry point to the topic as success and failure of SOEs have been used as an important criteria whether reforming paths of planned economies converge with or diverge from Western market capitalism (Hu 2005: 703–704). 'Socialism', although vaguely defined, is the development goal of Vietnam. SOEs have been designated the leading role in the socialist-oriented market economy, which is a strategy to attain socialism. This role may now be up for change:

As stated at the 9th Party Central Committee 2001:

> ....the state sector plays the decisive role in *holding fast the socialist orientation*'... and *SOEs must be 'the core force*, main contributor for the state economic sector to perform the leading role in the *socialist-oriented market economy*, and the main force in international economic integration. (ref. in Vu-Thanh 2017: 89, our emphasis)

The resolution of the 12th Party Congress in 2016, represents a break with the above statement:

> The socialist-oriented market economy of Viet Nam includes many forms of ownership, many economic sectors, *with the private sector as an important driving force of the economy*; the market plays the major role in mobilizing and effectively allocating resources for development, the state

> plays the role in orientation, building and perfecting the economic institutions for fair, transparent and healthy competition. (World Bank 2017: 12, our emphasis; Communist Party of Vietnam 2016: 261)

In this chapter, we examine what characterizes the latest phase of SOE reforms, what is new about the context that the reforms are implemented in, how the Vietnamese government presents the reforms and how industry and international stakeholders relate to the reforms. More concretely, we examine how three enterprises in the category of SOEs where the Government aims at full divestment perceive and experience the reforms. These enterprises are the two breweries Saigon Beer - Alcohol - Beverage Corporation (Sabeco), Hanoi Beer - Alcohol - Beverage Corporation (Habeco) and the producer of dairy products, Vinamilk. Among the international stakeholders we address the World Bank, UNDP, OECD, the US, the EU through the EU-Vietnam Free Trade Agreement (EVFTA) (awaiting approval by the respective member countries as of August 2019)[1] and the Comprehensive and Progressive Agreement for Trans-Pacific Partnership (CPTPP).[2]

Our data are a combination of resolutions and public reports where the Government addresses the reforms, semi-structured interviews with enterprise managers, information from the web-sites of the enterprises, news reports on how the enterprises are affected by the SOE reforms, and publications and reports of the international stakeholders.

The conceptual framework provides a short review of changing conceptualizations of SOEs as presented in scholarly articles and by international organizations. Then follows a sub-chapter on the Vietnamese context, addressing how the Communist Party of Vietnam (CPV) has conceptualized the socialist market economy from 1986 through 2016. After a brief history of SOE reforms before 2016, we address the reasons, objectives and strategies of the new phase of reform. Then follow two sub-chapters on how the international stakeholders consider the SOE sector in Vietnam and how the selected enterprises have experienced equitization in general

[1] EVFTA, see the text at the end of the negotiation here: http://trade.ec.europa.eu/doclib/press/index.cfm?id=1437 (accessed May 2019).

[2] CPTPP, see the legally verified text here: https://www.mfat.govt.nz/en/trade/free-trade-agreements/free-trade-agreements-in-force/cptpp/comprehensive-and-progressive-agreement-for-trans-pacific-partnership-text-and-resources/ (accessed May 2019). CPTPP is the revised Trans-Pacific Partnership framework after the US withdrew from the negotiations.

and the new phase in particular. We wind up with what might be the implications of the new phase of reforms to the state-socialist market economy.

Conceptualizations of SOE

SOEs are legal entities over which the state exercises control 'through full, majority, or minority ownership' (Kim and Ali 2017: 1). Minority ownership control can be exercised through the shareholder agreement or golden shares with special rights to veto decisions. In addition to the government itself, development banks, pension funds and sovereign wealth funds can hold government minority shares (Musacchio and Lazzarini 2012).

As producers, SOEs can generate profits, contribute to government revenue, keep control over sectors of importance to national security and vital natural resources, and secure public utilities in fields that are too risky or not sufficiently rewarding to the private sector. In countries such as Japan, Taiwan and South Korea, SOEs have been used to attain industrialization and start new industries. SOEs can also have social objectives such as securing reasonably priced consumer goods and employment (Amsden 1989; Wade 1990; Chang 2003; Knutsen and Nguyen 2004).

The main argument against SOEs is that they are not sufficiently efficient producers. Multiple economic and social objectives reduce the focus on profitability and productivity increases. The same applies to limited autonomy and a heavy bureaucracy. When control is dispersed between several state agencies, there is room for opportunistic behaviour. Additionally, SOEs rely on preferential treatment by the state, which may crowd out the private sector and challenge competitive neutrality in the host countries when SOEs go international (Capobianco and Christiansen 2011; IEG 2018). The state can rescue loss-making SOEs not to fail, for instance by soft credits, tax exemptions and subsidies (Kornai 1986).

The neoliberal approach to SOEs that gained a strong foothold in the 1980s and 1990s builds on the notion that privatization of SOEs will expose them to the market mechanism and competitive pressure and force them to develop new and better products. SOEs should thus be restricted to sectors that are important to control over national defence and vital natural resources, and public utilities that are not sufficiently remunerative for the private sector (see Knutsen and Nguyen 2004).

The wave of liberalization and privatization in the 1980s and 1990s stimulated 'a new form of hybrid capitalism where the government influences the investment decisions of private companies largely through minority capital' (Musacchio and Lazzarini 2012: 4). Moreover, the World Bank (2014) points to a continuation and expansion of SOEs in all types of economies in the twenty-first century and that they play a significant role in the world economy. SOEs have internationalized to bail out private enterprises in connection with the financial crises of 2008, to strengthen their presence in specific sectors such as finance, insurance and utilities and for geopolitical purposes (Musacchio et al. 2015; UNCTAD 2017). Actualized among other by the internationalization of Chinese SOEs, international organizations and partners of trade agreements want domestic enterprises to be protected from unfair competition from SOE-TNCs that are subsidized in their country of origin (Kawase and Ambashi 2018).

The fact that state majority ownership and different forms of minority ownership coexist all over the world, questions the conventional polarized view of state versus private ownership (Cuervo-Cazurra et al. 2014; Cuervo-Cazurra 2018). The European Commission (2016) found that with some exceptions there are no systematic difference in productivity and profitability between private enterprises and SOEs in the member states. Where differences occur, such as in the manufacturing sector, they are small. Having said this, negative effects on profitability are less likely in majority-owned and minority-owned SOEs than wholly-owned SOEs due to the checks and balances external investors represent. The same applies to restrained patronage by a technical bureaucracy (Musacchio et al. 2015), although the process of transferring 'public monopolies into private hands may incentivize rent-seeking' (European Commission 2016: 2). The salient point, however, is '[not to] assume that all SOEs will suffer from the liabilities of stateness (and consequently underperform private firms)' (Musacchio et al. 2015: 124). The argument represents a break with the arch-type neoliberal notion of SOEs (above) and calls for more context-sensitive approaches in explaining the role and performance governance of the SOEs where they operate (Hu 2005; Musacchio and Lazzarini 2012; Musacchio et al. 2015; Cuervo-Cazurra et al. 2014).

In the following, we address SOE reforms in the institutional context of Vietnam's socialist market economy. The Vietnamese definition of SOEs has changed over time. Before 2003, it referred to enterprises wholly-owned by the state. In the Enterprise Law of 2003, SOEs comprised both 100% state-owned enterprises of limited liability and enterprises where the state owns 50% or more in form of share holding and capital contribution. In the updated Enterprise Law effective from 2015, SOEs are defined as 100% state-owned enterprises (Taussig et al. 2015). As the new phase of SOE reforms addresses equitization of wholly state-owned enterprises, further divestment in majority-owned SOEs and listing on the stock exchange, we apply the terminology wholly-owned, majority-owned and minority-owned SOEs.

The SOEs sort under different agencies of the state at the central, provincial and district levels. The nineteen largest state economic groups and corporations form the core of the economy, among them are Petrovietnam, Vietnam Electricity, Vietnam Chemical Group, Vietnam Rubber Group, Vietnam Mobile Telecom Services, Vietnam Airlines and Vietnam National Shipping Lines (see Vietnam Investment Review 2018a).

In 2016, the state owned 50% or more in 2662 SOEs, down from 3281 in 2010. The number of workers declined by 0.7 million in the same period (GSO 2017a). The SOE sector accounted for 29% of GDP in 2016,[3] and the share of SOE workers according to enterprise ownership was only 11% in 2015 compared to 62% in 2000 (GSO 2017b). Although the role of the private sector has increased in the economy, SOEs are an important target for economic reform, much due to low productivity and bad debts, and because revenue from divestments of SOEs are called for to finance Vietnam's economic and social development goals (below).

CVPs Notion of a Socialist Market Economy and the Role of SOEs

Doi moi and SOE reforms were initiated to cope with severe economic challenges in the late 1970s and early 1980s after the reunification of North and South Vietnam and move forwards to socialism. The CPV did not use the term 'market economy' in the beginning of *doi moi*. The rationale was that a 'market economy' is a product of capitalism and should be eliminated in a communist country. The term socialist-oriented market economy was first applied at the 9th Party Congress in April 2001. It refers to as a multisector economy with a state sector, private sector, foreign capital and different types of ownership. It is subject to the market

[3] See https://www.gso.gov.vn/default.aspx?tabid=775 (accessed August 2019).

mechanism and at the same time led by the state based on a socialist orientation: Public ownership of the means of production is the target at 'the end of the road' to socialism. In the meantime, the socialist-oriented market economy will be led by the state by strategies, plans and policies that promote the advantages of the market mechanism. The state will protect the interests of the people from the negative impacts of the market economy and there will be a system of social security (Communist Party of Vietnam 2016). Hence, according to Nguyen (2016), the economic model of Vietnam has been a multisector economy led by the state.

The notion of 'socialism', however, is vague, other than referring to a civilized and equitable society in which the state represents the long-term interests of the nation (Beresford 2008; Malesky and London 2014). The same applies to the meaning of 'socialist orientation'. Quantitative and qualitative criteria to distinguish between a socialist-oriented market economy and a market economy have not yet been set. Acknowledging the need for clarification, the Party has just started to discuss the topic at the high level in the political system, with reference to experience in other countries in the world (Communist Review 2018).

Another term that warrants more precision is 'the leading role of the state'. There is an on-going debate over what a 'leading role of the state' actually entails which 'is used by some to justify preserving a dominant state role in commercial business activity' (World Bank 2017: 15; the Communist Party of Vietnam 2016). Whereas the state holds a leading role both in managing the economy by policies and plans and as a producer, it is the understanding of the role of the SOE sector that is considered ambiguous.

The intended role of the SOEs has been to take the lead in the accumulation of wealth and development of the material base for future socialism. It is, however, important to distinguish between the role that the SOEs play in political rhetoric and policies and the outcome of it in the real economy. Having analyzed data from 1991 to 2004, Beresford (2008) argues that although SOEs were designated the dominant role in the economy, they were not able to assume it. She attributes this to the lack of direct investment support from the state budget. Technology had been outdated since before *doi moi*, but the SOEs could only get low interest loans for working capital needs and trade protection against international competition. The state focused on institutional reforms, enterprise autonomy and investment in infrastructure, in line with the Washington

Consensus, rather than a coherent industrial policy of picking and disciplining winners that could have supported upgrading. The policy choice has to be understood in light of donor pressure and the strive for WTO accession and international integration at that time. In practice, it meant that the private sector, and especially the foreign-invested sector, was allowed to take the leading role in the economy.

Based on a review of research on the role of SOEs in the real economy, including the first years after the WTO accession in 2007, Malesky and London (2014: 413) conclude that SOEs are 'remarkably unproductive relative to non-state competition'. They explain the poor performance of SOEs by their access to cheap land and capital, whereby managers can maximize individual revenue and invest in unrelated and low productive business activities.

In 2016, the Party Congress for the first time, after more than three decades of *doi moi*, acknowledged the contribution of the private sector to the economy: 'the state sector plays the leading role while the private sector is an important driving force of the economy' (Communist Party of Vietnam 2016: 103, our translation). The contribution relates to the growing share of the private sector in GDP and employment and the importance of foreign-invested firms for exports. The 5th Plenum of the Party Central Committee (tenure XII), organized in 2017 stated that the private sector shall be treated on par with other sectors of the economy. It is encouraged to hold shares in SOEs when the Government equitizes or divests them and to make joint ventures with SOEs to establish a production network or join a value chain (Communist Party of Vietnam 2017).

SOE Reforms Between 1990 and 2015

The number of wholly-owned SOEs declined from about 12000 in 1989 to about 6000 by the end of 1995 (Riedel and Turley 1999).[4] Most of the decline is attributed to liquidation and merger of small SOEs under local control that suffered chronic deficits and had been tapping the state for resources (Ishizuka 2009).[5]

[4] The figures conform to other sources quoted by UNDP (2006).

[5] Local SOEs refer to SOEs under agencies such as Provincial People's Committees, District People's Committees and local branches of the Communist Party (Ishizuka 2009).

Altogether, some 4000 SOEs equitized between mid-1998 and end-2010 (Hiep 2017). During this period, equitization peaked from mid-1998 to end-2000 resulting from Decree 44/1998/ND-CP. The Decree defined the types of SOE eligible for equitization, and the Government offered many preferences to equitized SOEs, such as tax deduction and credit on favourable terms (Nguyen et al. 2014). Equitization reached another peak 2003–2006 stimulated by the application for WTO membership and establishment of the first stock exchange (Hiep 2017). In terms of international aid, SOE reforms were important for poverty reduction credits from the World Bank resulting in financial support directly to the government budget (UNDP 2006).

Re-arrangement of SOEs into larger groups is another element of the reforms. In line with the Prime Minister's Decision no. 90 and Decision no. 91 in 1994, SOEs were merged into SGCs. The objective was to enhance the scale of operation and increase the influence of the Central Government (Beeson and Pham 2012). The decisions paved the way for the establishment of state economic groups (SEGs) around 2006 (Vu-Thanh 2017). SEGs are conglomerates of large SOEs where the state holds the controlling stake. The objective was to prepare for the global competition that the SOE sector would meet from multinational enterprises as part of the WTO agreement, and prevent erosion of the socialist orientation of the market economy that SOEs were to play a leading role in (above). Supported by the state with capital, land and natural resources, SEGs diversified horizontally and into non-core activities such as real estate, banks and insurance (Vu-Thanh 2017).

The poor performance of the Vietnamese stock exchanges and the long time it takes for large SOEs to prepare equitization and find strategic partners slowed equitization in the 2011–2015 period. Foreign investors lost confidence in the equitization process due to slow listing on the stock exchanges and the fact that the state retained the majority share in most SOEs (Ministry of Planning and Investment [MPI] 2016).

By 2015, some 4500 SOEs had been equitized and 600 remained wholly state-owned (Government of Vietnam 2017a; 2017b ref. in Hiep 2017), but only 8% of the state ownership had been transferred to the private sector (Vietnam Economic Times 2017). Moreover, poor management of the SEGs and negative impacts of the global financial crisis led to bankruptcies in SOEs and private enterprises alike (Viet Nam News 2017). Higher interest rates and high inflation caused difficulties to the economy as a whole.

Over time, equitized SOEs became a source of private accumulation, which gave rise to a new business elite with close ties to the party system. The business elite could be serving or formerly serving officials and children of the party elite (Dixon and Kilgour 2002; Beresford 2008; Gainsborough 2010; Malesky and London 2014). This form of commercialization of the state blur the boundaries between the public and the private sector. It results in weak state co-ordination of the sectoral businesses that could tip Vietnam into cronyism rather than successful state-led development (Beresford 2008). More recently, scholars address how the SOE sector drains the private sector of resources, especially in light of the mismanagement of the SEGs (Malesky and London 2014; Pincus 2015). According to figures from the World Bank and MPI (2016), SOEs accounts for 40% of total investment in Vietnam but only 30% of GDP growth. Labour productivity and productivity measured by land and capital assets have been low between 2001 and 2014, and labour productivity stagnated and even declined in some SOE sub-sectors. They also show 'a steady erosion in the productivity growth of the domestic private sector' and argue that '[this] leaves it just as inefficient as the state sector' (World Bank and MPI 2016: xxii).

The New Phase of SOE Reforms

Legacies of the 2011–2015 period and earlier phases of reform are important to understand the context of the new phase of SOE reform from 2016: Vietnam faced a huge and persistent state budget deficit, sharply increasing public debts, difficulties in handling bad debts and difficulties in controlling inflation at the end of the period (MPI 2016). Restructuring of the SOEs was slow and there were no substantial improvements in productivity, quality and efficiency of industrial production and services. Especially the SEGs with many cross-ownerships and banks internal to the groups were running at a loss and contributed to the development of bad debts (MPI 2016). Equitization and divestment in the new phase are thus a way to mobilize resources from SOEs to finance the government's budget deficit and finance investments in physical and social infrastructure to improve the labour productivity of the SOE sector. This reflects stronger necessity from within for changes in policy and implementation. In addition, further international integration calls for equal terms of competition for all enterprises and transparency in ownership, control and operation of the SOEs.

The plan for SOE reforms 2016–2020 is to accelerate equitization of the remaining SOEs that are not of strategic interests; sell more shares in already equitized SOEs; and list equitized SOEs on the stock exchange (Government of Vietnam 2017a). The aim is to equitize 137 SOEs and divest in 406 joint stock companies and limited liability companies with two or more members (Government of Vietnam 2017b; JonesDay 2017). In terms of ownership, the state is going to hold 100% of the charter capital in 103 enterprises (this includes 11 sectors that make up the most sensitive areas of the economy such as defence, public security, electricity, petroleum and railways); at least 65% in four enterprises (mineral extraction, oil exploration and extraction, finance and banking); more than 50% but less than 65% in 27 enterprises; and less than 50% in 106 enterprises. The actual enterprises have been identified to ensure transparency (Government of Vietnam 2016).

The 2016–2020 five-year plan states that the Government will use the market mechanism to improve the efficiency of the SOEs, both in terms of a level playing field between the economic sectors and a strengthening of state management and owner's management in the SOEs (Socialist Republic of Vietnam 2016). Gradually, political and administrative bodies such as the ministries are not going to manage SOEs (Dang 2016). This is to avoid that a policy-making institution is also a beneficiary of the policy. Registration of the equitized enterprises on the stock exchange is a means to enhance transparency, meet international standards of corporate governance and make the SOEs operate more efficiently.

Despite the number of changes in policy and regulations, the Government lags well behind its goals for the accelerated SOE reforms. The target was to divest 135 SOEs in 2017 and 181 SOEs in 2018. The respective results were 13 and 52. The delay is attributed to the need of careful valuation of the SOEs to avoid losses to the state budget and poor interests of potential investors. Valuation of land-use rights has taken time because the government requires SOEs to complete their land-use plans and get them approved before equitization (Tapchitaichinh 2019; Vitnamplus 2019).

As stated by Pham Duc Trung, Director of the Department of Enterprises' Reform and Development (under Central Institute of Economic Management): 'crony and interest relationship is officially recognized to be a reason for the delay of reform of State-owned enterprises' (Tien 2017, our translation). By maintaining the status of SOEs, the enterprises can also continue to enjoy privileges such as easy access to land or capital with the support of local administrations (ibid.). From this angle, the difficulties of some SOE managers and local administrations in giving up SOEs due to vested personal interests are a root cause of the delay. This is not to obscure that there is also a fear at the provincial and local level of what a demise of SOEs will mean to local revenue and budget allocations.

International Stakeholders

International organizations emphasize underperformance of SOEs, preferential treatment of SOEs cum lack of a level playing field, the burden of heavily indebted SOEs, the challenge of multiple principals and rent seeking and corruption in their reports on SOEs in Vietnam (Vietnam Development Report 2012; World Bank 2014, 2018; UNDP 2016; OECD 2018). More specifically, OECD (2018: 10) calls for a policy agency to guide further equitization to prevent 'anti-competitive legacy issues'… 'in markets where SOEs held significant market power'.

Key trade partners such as the US and the EU do not yet consider Vietnam as a market economy, although Vietnam should be recognized as such after 12 years of WTO-membership. The argument is that '[a]lthough most prices have been deregulated, the Vietnamese government still retains some formal and informal mechanisms to direct and manage the economy' (Congressional Research Service 2018: 11; Vietnam Manufacturing Federation 2018). The 'historic lack of progress in reforming the SOE sector' is of key concern (US Department of State 2017: 13): There has not been much change in the SOEs' capital structure, they still enjoy preferential access to resources and their boards lack political independence. Regarding transparency, the SOEs also have small incentives to disclose the information that they are obliged to disclose.

In January 2019, Vietnam became a member of CPTPP. The agreement contains a separate chapter on SOEs, referred to as 'the first comprehensive and detailed disciplines of SOEs' (Kawase and Ambashi 2018: 1). The chapter bans anti-competitive practices in trade and services and prescribes a level playing field for SOEs, domestic private firms and foreign firms. There are rules for home country subsidies to overseas investments and requirements on transparency concerning ownership, special voting rights, operational data and business results of the SOEs. However, it only applies to enterprises where the Government owns more than 50% of the shares and voting rights, it exempts small SOEs with annual revenue from commercial activities of less than Special Drawing

Rights (SDR)[6] 200 million, and it will not apply to sub-central SOEs (Kawase and Ambashi 2018; WTO Center—VCCI 2019). Moreover, the transparency rules will not fully apply to Vietnam until 5 years after the entry to the agreement (Kawase and Ambashi 2018).

The EVFTA contains a separate chapter on SOEs too. It addresses non-discrimination and transparency, much in line with the provisions and exemptions of the CPTPP. The EU is concerned about weak implementation of labour laws in Vietnam and thereby a cheap manufacturing base for tariff-free exports of goods into the EU. A similar concern was raised by the US when it was part of the TPP-negotiations (Kawase and Abashi 2018; WTO Center—VCCI 2019).

In sum, the international stakeholders hold that successful reform requires more than reduction in the number of SOEs and divestments according to the international organizations and stakeholders. They call for substantial changes to separate the various roles that the Government holds in relation to the SOEs and to improved transparency in the sector. There is nonetheless some slack in the CPTPP.

According to the World Bank and MPI (2016), Vietnam faces several challenges, such as stagnating productivity, inefficient public investment, and uncoordinated and often incoherent investment decisions of a fragmented state structure. They argue that the institutional foundation for an advanced market economy is insufficiently developed, that this undermines private-property rights and competition in product markets and that an unclear mix of allocation by market and fiat governs the factor market. Institutional change allowing for more market is a standard call by the World Bank both concerning SOEs and transition economies more generally (World Bank 2014).

The Party, on its part, recognizes that the socialist-oriented market economy has not lived up to its expectations and that it needs to be completed. Among the shortcomings are lack of conformity between political and economic reforms, conflicts between legal documents, unequal access to resources by economic actors, insufficient attention to the ease of doing business and that the gap between the rich and the poor is increasing. Completion of the socialist market economy is thus decisive to the industrialization and modernization of the country (Communist Party of Vietnam 2017). One of the measures taken is

[6] https://www.imf.org/en/About/Factsheets/Sheets/2016/08/01/14/51/Special-Drawing-Right-SDR (accessed May 2019).

the establishment of the Commission for the Management of Capital in Enterprises (CMCE) in 2018 to separate ownership from the operations of the 19 largest SOEs (Vietnam Investment Review 2018a). It is inspired by Temasek[7] in Singapore and is the type of institution that the OECD (2018) calls for.

Industry Experiences

To supplement data collected from mass media, we have conducted semi-structured interviews in three SOEs with different experiences from both earlier and the current phase of SOE reforms. The main reason for examining equitization and divestment in Saigon Beer - Alcohol - Beverage Corporation (Sabeco), Hanoi Beer - Alcohol - Beverage Corporation and Vinamilk, is that the Government has signalled that it aims at full divestment in beverage and dairy production (Customsnews 2017).

Both breweries originate from breweries founded by French nationals in Vietnam in 1875 and 1890, respectively (interview Habeco and Sabeco 2017). Habeco is based in the North of Vietnam and its main product is Bìa Hanoi. Its predecessor became a SOE already in the late 1950s (http://www.habeco.com.vn). The main product of Sabeco with headquarter in the South of Vietnam is Bìa Saigon. Its predecessor became a SOE in 1977 (http://www.sabeco.com.vn/en-US/home). Sabeco has been subject to a more business-exposed environment than Habeco and is currently tapping into the beer market in the North of Vietnam. Sabeco is the market leader, catering to 40% of the market for beer in Vietnam, followed by Heineken with 24% of the market, Habeco with 16% and Carlsberg with 10% (Zing 2018).

Vinamilk emerged from a SOE established in the South of Vietnam in 1976, based on three dairy factories of the old regime (https://www.vinamilk.com.vn/en/). Unlike Sabeco and Habeco that equitized in 2008, Vinamilk equitized already in 2003 (interviews, Sabeco, Habeco, Vinamilk 2017).

[7] Temasek, see https://www.temasek.com.sg/en/index.html.

Sabeco

In terms of government revenue, Sabeco stands out as a highly successful example of divestment. In December 2017, 53.59% of the enterprise was sold to Thai Beverage for USD 4.84 billion or USD 14.1 per share, 'about 36 times core earnings', [and] more than double the trading multiples for global peers' (Reuters 2017: unnumbered). Despite a 49% foreign ownership cap on state-owned listed companies, Thai Beverage could secure the Sabeco deal through another local beverage company that it holds stocks in, Vietnam Beverage, and further increase its share to 63.35% in December 2018 (Reuters 2017; Nikkei 2018; Vietnam Investment Review 2019a).

The willingness to pay such a high price to secure the deal has to do with Thai Beverage's vision to become a regional player in the beer market (Bloomberg 2017). Vietnam is highly attractive in this respect. In 2016, it ranked the ninth largest beer consuming market of the world and the third largest in Asia after China and Japan. The high and growing consumption of beer has been be attributed to a high share of the population in the working age, rising incomes, a growing middle class and a culture where drinking alcohols 'builds and maintains social networking and business relationships' (Ho Chi Minh University of Education in Vietnam Briefing February 2018: 3; Vietnamnet 2018).

The multibillionaire Chaoren Sirivadhanabhakdi who is a big investor in Thai Beverage also holds investments in grocery retail, Metro Cash and Carry, in Vietnam through TCC Holding and 20% in Vinamilk through Fraser and Neave (Bloomberg 2017). Hence, investments in Sabeco can be a means to strengthen his overall positioning in Vietnam, a market that is attractive for its growing middle class consumption. Sabeco is attractive because it holds the largest market share of the breweries in Vietnam. It has a famous name in Vietnam and sells at 'affordable prices', but does not export much. Despite increasing sales, Sabeco's share of the Vietnamese market does not increase due to competition from imported brands (interview 2017). Hence, from the angle of Sabeco, Thai Beverage's acquisition is promising because it can boost investments in Vietnam. Thai Beverage has also expressed interests in exploring export opportunities for Sabeco. However, both may take time as the profits of Sabeco have declined in the aftermath of the deal (Retail Asia 2018). There is also a question of where the values of further production and expansion are created, enhanced and captured when companies are included in a regional value chain. Before the divestment, Sabeco was the second and third largest contributor to the provincial budgets where their factories are located (interview Sabeco 2018).

At the time of divestment the stake of the Government was reduced from 90 to 36% (The Leader 2017). The Sabeco case illustrates that it can be challenging for SOE managers to let go of control after divestment to new large owners. Although Thai Beverage had become the largest owner, it had to complain to the Ministry of Industry and Trade to be included in the management board (Viet Nam News 2018).

When Sabeco equitized in 2008, Heineken, which has become Sabeco's largest competitor in Vietnam, bought 5% of the enterprise. Equitization did not result in any significant changes in how the enterprise was operated because the Government still held 90% of the enterprise. Contrastingly, the Vietnamese management expects many changes with the large Thai investment. However, the only aspect they could concretize was that it would require workers to become more professional: 'Now workers come and go a little as they want, they can come to work a little late and leave a little early and have a long lunch' (interview Sabeco 2017).

Habeco

The state, through the Ministry of Industry and Trade, owns 81.79% of Habeco followed by Carlsberg with 17.51%. Carlsberg went into a strategic partnership with Habeco just before Habeco equitized in 2008.

Habeco concentrates on the domestic market for 'affordable beer' in the North of Vietnam and exports very little of its total production. In the North of Vietnam, Habeco has lost market shares to Sabeco, which focuses more on marketing of its beers. Habeco also faces competitive challenges from other breweries in the Northern provinces (interview Habeco 2017).

Carlsberg entered Vietnam already in 1993 through a joint venture with another Hanoi-based brewery and expanded its operations to more joint ventures in the mid and the South of Vietnam, even a joint venture with Habeco in the South. Carlsberg is now the only owner and both produces and distributes it its own brands of beer in Vietnam (Journal.Beer October 31, 2016). A higher share in Habeco would be important to a company that ranks number four in the same market as Sabeco/Thai Beverage, Heineken and Habeco.

Divestment in Habeco has been on the agenda since 2016, but takes time. In 2017, Carlsberg flagged that it wanted to increase its share to 61.79% and argued that it holds priority purchase rights for 60% ownership as a strategic partner (Reuters December 13, 2017). Habeco, on the contrary, refers to the 49% cap on foreign investment in SOEs. This happens in a context where the Government claims that it wants to divest its entire share in the brewery sector. It also plans to remove the cap on foreign investment in SOEs by end 2019 (Nikkei October 10, 2018). Currently, Carlsberg expects to buy all of the stakes owned by the Ministry of Industry and Trade, equivalent to 81.79% of the charter capital, when the state divests (Tri 2019).

The Habeco case illustrates the challenges that the valuation of shares entails (above). It cannot sell for a lower price than the Government's floor price. Carlsberg finds Habeco's share price too high compared with Carlsberg's own valuation but has 'promised to offer a competitive price' (Vietnam Investment Review 2018b). The results of the negotiations between Habeco and Carlsberg were submitted to the Ministry of Industry and Trade to be considered for approval in late April 2019 (Hanoi Times May 9, 2019). Since 2017, Habeco's market share and profits have declined (Vietnam Investment Review 2019b), which may increase the leverage of Carlsberg regarding the price of the shares. Moreover, becoming a member of the Carlsberg group, which requires that Carlsberg owns at least 30% of the enterprise, might ease upgrading of Habeco in areas important to the competition with Sabeco/Thai Beverage.

Vinamilk

Vinamilk is in a different position than Sabeco and Habeco. When it equitized in 2003 the state kept 80% ownership, but since then the enterprise has been subject to gradual divestments down to 36% state ownership through the State Capital and Investment Corporation (SCIC) by 2017. In 2006, it was listed on the stock exchange. Foreign investors hold 59% of the stocks, the largest among them are the Singapore-based food and beverage and publishing conglomerate Fraser and de Neave (where Thai Beverage holds shares) and the Singapore listed investment holding company Jardine Cycle & Carriage.

Vinamilk is the biggest dairy company in Vietnam, with 50% market share based on net sales.[8] It bases its production on 70% imported milk powder and 30% fresh milk form Vietnamese farmers that it works with directly. The business strategy is to provide consumers with high quality products at an affordable price by constantly working to bring the costs down. Sales and marketing are important to the strategy, but the focus on cost cutting does not prevent pioneering into new products. Vinamilk presents itself as a successful enterprise. It has taken market shares in Vietnam from the foreign brand, Dutch Lady, and it has expanded production abroad to joint ventures and wholly-owned companies in New Zealand, the US, Cambodia and Poland (interview Vinamilk 2017, https://www.vinamilk.com.vn/en/).

'Vinamilk is not a SOE anymore', the manager we interviewed insisted, because the management only reports to the shareholder meeting and external auditors. However, Vinamilk gets the decisions to sell down by letter from the Government. Equitization and divestment were referred to as highly positive to the enterprise. Before equitization all business decisions had to be approved by the Government, a slow process that resulted in lost opportunities. Moreover, equitization helps to develop the stock market and reduce corruption. Listing on the stock exchange had resulted in transparency and good governance by inputs from the foreign partners. Hence, equitization (and the listing on the stock exchange) 'made it possible to perform much, much better' (interview Vinamilk). Similarly, in the interview at Habeco experiences with equitization were expressed this way: 'performance is better because we have some independence in how we run business and salaries have increased'.

SCIC, the largest owner of Vinamilk, was established in 2005 to enhance the efficiency of state capital utilization and contribute to the 'strengthening of the dominant role of the state sector while respecting the market rules'.[9] To what extent and how the good performance of Vinamilk can be attributed to SCIC as an institution or the actual composition of the board and characteristics of its members require further research. The fact that both of the main foreign investors have attempted to raise their stakes in Vinamilk a few times in 2018 and 2019 reflects the attractiveness of the enterprise and the fast growing market for dairy

[8] See https://biinform.com/Reports/2909-vietnam-dairy-market-2018-3530.html.

[9] See http://www.scic.vn/english/.

products in Vietnam. The reason why they did not succeed in their bids suggests that the state, as in the Habeco case, wants to get more out of the sales than the buyers are ready to offer.

Summary and Concluding Discussion

What distinguishes the new phase of reform from the former is the strong push from within. It comes from the internal difficulties of bad debts, corruption and the need of assuring sufficient capital and technology to upgrade the Vietnamese economy if it is to reach an upper middle-income status by 2035. As access to capital and technology requires international integration this strengthening of internal pressure adds to the external calls for reform.

To the international stakeholders, the contradiction of the socialist market economy is mainly that there is still 'too much state' and no level playing field, as implied by the US and EU (above) that do not recognize Vietnam as a market economy. This also applies to SOE divestment. Having said this, the SOE-specific regulations of the CPTPP contains a number of blanket exceptions and country-specific exceptions, suggesting that several partners have an interest in protecting their SOEs. This situation to some extent eases the pressure on Vietnam for fast changes and may reflect international interests in access to the Vietnamese market.

The new phase of SOE reform is characterized by its many achievements in market-oriented policy change. The Government has made a number of decisions in the form of resolutions and decrees that are in line with external advice and requirements and conform to the World Bank's thinking on SOE reform. Among the most important, are Decision 707QD-TTg/2017 that in detail specifies what SOEs to retain and divest, the requirement of listing on the stock exchange and the establishment of the Commission for the Management of Capital in Enterprises to improve the transparency of the SOEs ownership structure and operations. The Commission for the Management of Capital in Enterprises model is inspired by Temasek in Singapore and is a type of institution that the OECD (2018) calls for. The SOEs that are going to remain wholly-owned operate in sectors such as national defence and vital natural resources and types of public utilities that are generally internationally accepted.

Implementation of the policy changes, especially in terms of equitization and further divestment of SOEs however, is still lagging behind targets. One reason for this is that potential investors think that the Government overvalues the SOEs and that the valuation framework for assets is unreliable (The Economist Intelligence Unit 2018: unnumbered), as indicated by the Habeco case above. The Government on its part wants to raise as much revenue as possible for necessary infrastructure to spur economic and social development and pave the way for socialism.

At another level, the problems in meeting the targets can be explained by the large number of regulations that have to be changed and have to match for an economic transformation to take place. The challenges to implementation are also deeply embedded in the social structure and power constellations that arose with the new politically linked business elite that emerged with the introduction of *doi moi* and their vested interests (Dixon and Kilgour 2002; Beresford 2008; Gainsborough 2010; Malesky and London 2014; Pincus 2015).

Institutional change such as a shift towards greater reliance on the market forces takes time because it requires changes in norms and values. This is also, why we find *the internal push* towards 'more market' in the new phase of SOE reform and clear policy change in this direction of particular interest. In 2016, the Government recognized the role of the private sector as an important driving force of the economy. This recognition together with the programme for equitization and further divestment means that the intended role of SOEs in the economy is changing, but the exact role remains to be defined. A way of seeing it is that the Government has given up the socialist economic model of management inspired by the Soviet Union. The policy of the Government has been to use the SOEs to accumulate wealth for socialism and thereby skip capitalism on the way to socialism. The trade liberalization and policies of the new phase of SOE reform however, suggest that a capitalist economy under the communist regime is about to become an accepted policy for the transition to socialism.

Beresford (2008) regretted that SOE reform was all about institutional reform and enterprise autonomy at the detriment of a coherent industrial policy. The new phase of SOE reform and acceptance of the private sector as a driver of development entail even more such institutional reform. Although equitization may enhance autonomy and enterprise efficiency, as in the case of Vinamilk, it is not given that Vietnam will benefit much from value enhancement and value capture that may arise from large-scale equitization. State-involvement for a coherent industrial policy, however, may increase the odds. Local and national value capture are essential to attain short-term development goals and the future development goal of socialism, but what a coherent industrial policy should consist of and what would be the exact role of the state in it, are outside the scope of this chapter.

References

Amsden, A. 1989. *Asia's Next Giant? South Korea and Late Industrialization.* Oxford: Oxford University Press.

Beeson, M., and H.H. Pham. 2012. Developmentalism with Vietnamese Characteristics: The Persistence of State-Led Development in East Asia. *Journal of Contemporary Asia* 42 (4): 539–559.

Beresford, M. 2008. Doi Moi in Review: The Challenges of Building Market Socialism in Vietnam. *Journal of Contemporary Asia* 38 (2): 221–243.

Bloomberg. 2017. ThaiBev bets big in Vietnam, December 17. https://www.bloombergquint.com/business/thaibev-unit-registers-to-bid-for-4-8-billion-sabeco-shares. Accessed Mai 2019.

Capobianco, A., and H. Christiansen. 2011. Competitive Neutrality and State-Owned Enterprises: Challenges and Policy Options. OECD Corporate Governance Working Papers 1.

Chang, H.-J. 2003. *Globalisation, Economic Development and the Role of the State.* London: Zed Books.

Communist Party of Vietnam. 2016. *Văn kiện Đảng toàn tập* [Collection of Party Documents], volume 60. Hanoi: National Political Publishing House.

Communist Party of Vietnam. 2017. https://baotintuc.vn/chinh-tri/nghi-quyet-hoi-nghi-trung-uong-5-khoa-xii-ve-phat-trien-kinh-te-tu-nhan-20170606120529775.htm (12th Party Congress about the private sector). Accessed May 2019.

Communist Review. 2018, September 19. Tiêu chí nền kinh tế thị trường định hướng xã hội chủ nghĩa ở Việt Nam—Lý luận và thực tiễn [Criteria for Socialist-Oriented Market Economy in Vietnam—Theory and Practice]. http://www.tapchicongsan.org.vn/Home/Quan-triet-thuc-hien-nghi-quyet-dai-hoi-dang-XII/2018/52364/Tieu-chi-nen-kinh-te-thi-truong-dinh-huong-xa-hoi-chu.aspx. Accessed May 2019.

Congressional Research Service. 2018. US-Vietnam Economic and Tade Relations: Ey Issues in 2018. R45174. https://www.everycrsreport.com/files/20180416_R45172_da991d55c12fe09afeb13ad53dde5ce8fb658a86.pdf. Accessed May 2019.

Cuervo-Cazurra, A. 2018. Thank You But No Thanks: State-Multinationals from Emerging Markets and Host Country Policies. *Journal of International Business Policy* 1 (3–4): 128–156.

Cuervo-Cazurra, A., A. Musacchio, and K. Ramaswamy. 2014. Governments as Owners: State-Owned Multinational Companies. *Journal of International Business Studies* 45: 919–942.
Customsnews. 2017, December 27. https://customsnews.vn/strict-management-of-revenue-from-equitisation-5581.html. Accessed May 2019.
Dang, Quyet Tien. 2016. *Cổ phần hóa doanh nghiệp nhà nước: Chặng đường 2011–2015 và định hướng 2016–2020* [Equitization of State-Owned Enterprises: Review of 2011–2015 and Orientation of 2016–2020] http://tapchitaichinh.vn/tai-chinh-kinh-doanh/tai-chinh-doanh-nghiep/co-phan-hoa-doanh-nghiep-nha-nuoc-chang-duong-2011-2015-va-dinh-huong-2016-2020-115513.html. Accessed May 2019.
Dixon, C., and A. Kilgour. 2002. State, Capital and Resistance to Globalisation in the Vietnamese Transitional Economy. *Environment and Planning A* 34 (4): 599–618.
European Commission. 2016. State-Owned Enterprises in the EU: Lessons Learnt and Ways Forward in a Post-Crisis Context. Institutional Paper 031.
Gainsborough, M. 2010. *Vietnam: Rethinking the State*. London: Zed Books.
Government of Vietnam. 2016. Decision No. 58/216/QD-TTG. Criteria Classifying State-Owned Enterprises, Enterprises with State Capital and the List of State-Owned Enterprises to Be Arranged 2016–2020. http://vanban.chinhphu.vn/portal/page/portal/chinhphu/hethongvanban?class_id=1&mode=detail&document_id=187832. Accessed April 2019.
Government of Vietnam. 2017a. Decision No. 707/QD-TTg. Approval of the Plan: Restructuring State-Owned Enterprises, Particularly State Economic Group and Corporations in the State of 2016–2020. http://vanban.chinhphu.vn/portal/page/portal/chinhphu/hethongvanban?class_id=2&_page=1&mode=detail&document_id=189901. Accessed April 2019.
Government of Vietnam. 2017b. Decision No. 1232/QD-TTg017. Approval of the List of Enterprises with State Capital to Be Divested 2017–2020. http://vanban.chinhphu.vn/portal/page/portal/chinhphu/hethongvanban?class_id=2&_page=1&mode=detail&document_id=190826. Accessed April 2019.
GSO. 2017a. *Statistical Yearbook*. Hanoi: General Statistical Office.
GSO. 2017b. *Doanh nghiệp Việt Nam 15 năm đầu thế kỷ XXI (2000–2015)* [Enterprises in Vietnam in the First 15 Years of 21st Century (2000–2015)]. Statistics Publishing House.
Hanoi Times. 2019, May 9. http://www.hanoitimes.vn/investment/news/2018/03/81e0c32a/carlsberg-promises-fair-price-for-habeco/. Accessed May 2019.
Hiep, L.H. 2017. Vietnam's New Wave of SOE Equitization: Drivers and Implications. ISEAS Yusof Ishak Institute. *Perspective* 57: 1–8.

Hu, F.Z.Y. 2005. Deconstructing State-Owned Enterprises in Socialist China Under Reform: A Scalar Examination. *Environment and Planning A* 37: 703–722.

IEG. 2018. *Approach Paper. World Bank Group Support for the Reform of State-Owned Enterprises, 2007–2018: An IEG Evaluation*. Washington, DC: The World Bank Group.

Ishizuka, F. 2009. Vietnamese Local State-Owned Enterprises (SOEs) at the Crossroads: Implications of SOE Restructuring at the Local Level. Institute of Developing Economies, IDE Discussion Paper 193.

JonesDay. 2017. Vietnam Directs Divestment of State-Owned Enterprises. https://www.jonesday.com/files/Publication/5dbc68d6-efcc-42e2-bc37-a09cbc506184/Presentation/PublicationAttachment/704a08d4-14f1-4dc7-90bd-ac303f9db01a/Vietnam%20Directs%20Divestment.pdf. Accessed May 2019.

Journal.Beer. 2016, October 31. https://journal.beer/2016/10/31/vietnam-carlsberg-in-talks-over-additional-habeco-stake/. Accessed May 2019.

Kawase, T., and M. Ambashi. 2018. Disciplines on State-Owned Enterprises Under the Trans-Pacific Partnership Agreement: Overview and Assessment. ERIA Discussion Paper Series. ERIA-DP-2017-13.

Kim, C.J., and Z. Ali. 2017. Efficient Management of State-Owned Enterprises: Challenges and Opportunities. ADB Institute Policy Brief 2017-4.

Knutsen, H.M., and Nguyen Manh Cuong. 2004. Preferential Treatment in a Transition Economy: The Case of the State-Owned Enterprises in the Textile and Garment Industry in Vietnam. *Norwegian Journal of Geography* 58 (4): 125–135.

Kornai, J. 1986. The Soft Budget Constraint. *Kyklos* 39 (1): 3–30.

Malesky, E., and J. London. 2014. The Political Economy of Development in China and Vietnam. *Annual Review of Political Science* 17: 395–419.

MPI. 2016. Summary Report on the Economic Restructuring Plan for the Period 2016–2020. Report No. 460/BC-CP. http://www.mpi.gov.vn/en/Pages/tinbai.aspx?idTin=35701&idcm=273. Accessed May 2019.

Musacchio, A., and S.G. Lazzarini. 2012. Leviathan in Business: Varieties of State Capitalism and Their Implications for Economic Performance. SSRN: https://ssrn.com/abstract=2070942 or http://dx.doi.org/10.2139/ssrn.2070942. Accessed May 2019.

Musacchio, A., S.G. Lazzarini, and R.V. Aguilera. 2015. New Varieties of State Capitalism: Strategic and Governance Implications. *The Academy of Management Perspectives* 29 (1): 115–131.

Nikkei. 2018, October 10. https://asia.nikkei.com/Economy/Vietnam-to-remove-49-foreign-ownership-cap-on-listed-companies. Accessed May 2019.

Nguyen, Thanh Tuan. 2016. Socialist-Oriented Market Economy in Party's Documents in the doi moi State. Communist Review. http://www.tapchicon

gsan.org.vn/Home/xay-dung-dang/2016/37544/Kinh-te-thi-truong-dinh-huong-xa-hoi-chu-nghia-qua-cac.aspx. Accessed September 2018.

Nguyen, Quang Thuan, Cao Duc Nguyen, An Ha Nguyen, Xuan Trung Nguyen. 2014. *Cải cách doanh nghiệp nhà nước ở Việt Nam sau gần 30 năm đổi mới: thực trạng và giải pháp* [The Reform of State-Owned Enterprises After Nearly 30 Years of doi moi: Current Situation and Solutions]. Hanoi: Social Sciences Publishing House.

OECD. 2018. OECD Peer Reviews of Competition Law and Policy Viet Nam. http://oe.cd/vtn. Accessed May 2019.

Pincus, J. 2015. Why Doesn't Vietnam Grow Faster? State Fragmentation and the Limits of Vent for Surplus Growth. *Journal of Southeast Asian Economics* 32 (1): 26–51.

Retail Asia. 2018, May 8. https://www.retailnews.asia/shrinking-profit-for-sabecos-vietnam/. Accessed May 2019.

Reuters. 2017, December 17. Thai Beer Magnate Extends SE Asia Push. https://www.reuters.com/article/us-sabeco-m-a-sale/thai-beer-magnate-extends-se-asia-push-with-4-8-billion-sabeco-deal-idUSKBN1EB0DM. Accessed May 2019.

Riedel, J., and W.S. Turley. 1999. The Politics and Economics of Transition to an Open Market Economy in Vietnam. OECD Development Centre. Working Paper 152.

Socialist Republic of Vietnam. 2016. *The Five-Year Socio-Economic Development Plan 2016–2020*. Hanoi.

Tapchitaichinh. 2019, April 1. Lắm kế trì hoãn cổ phần hóa, thoái vốn [Many Tricks to Avoid Equitization, Divesment] http://tapchitaichinh.vn/su-kien-noi-bat/lam-ke-tri-hoan-co-phan-hoa-thoai-von-304802.html. Accessed May 2019.

Taussig, M., C.H. Nguyen, and T.L. Nguyen. 2015. *From Control to Market: Time for Real SOE Reform in Vietnam?* Chartered Institute of Management Accountants and National University of Singapore Business School.

The Economist Intelligence Unit. 2018. *A Crucial Year for Privatisation*. http://country.eiu.com/article.aspx?articleid=1746456758&Country=Vietnam&topic=Economy&oid=916543875&aid=1. Accessed May 2019.

The Leader. 2017, October 14. https://e.theleader.vn/moit-to-submit-plans-to-sell-sabeco-shares-next-week-20171013232153572.htm. Accessed May 2019.

Tien, Phong. 2017. https://www.tienphong.vn/kinh-te/co-phan-hoa-cham-do-bi-tri-hoan-loi-ich-ca-nhan-1162509.tpo. Accessed April 2019.

Tri, Thức Trẻ. 2019, April 24. Habeco và Calsberg họp bàn thoái vốn 13 lần trong năm 2018, kết quả đã trình Bộ Công thương [Habeco and Carlsberg Had 13 Meetings in 2018 to Discuss the Divestment, the Results Submitted to Ministry of Industry and Trade]. http://ttvn.vn/kinh-doanh/habeco-

va-carlsberg-hop-ban-thoai-von-13-lan-trong-nam-2018-ket-qua-da-trinh-bo-cong-thuong-420192441555516624.htm. Accessed May 2019.
UNCTAD. 2017. *World Investment Report 2017*. Geneva: United Nations.
UNDP. 2006. The State as Investor: Equitisation, Privatization and the Transformation of SOEs in Viet Nam. UNDP Viet Nam Dialogue Paper 2006:3.
UNDP. 2016. Growth works for all. *Viet Nam Human Development Report 2015*. Hanoi: Social Sciences Publishing House.
US Department of State. 2017. *Investment Climate Statements*. Vietnam: Bureau of Economic and Business Affairs. https://www.state.gov./e/eb/rls/othr/ics/2017/eap/269866.htm. Accessed May 2018.
Vietnam Briefing. 2018, February 9. https://www.vietnam-briefing.com/news/industry-spotlight-vietnams-alcoholic-beverage-industry.html/. Accessed May 2019.
Vietnam Development Review. 2012. Market Economy for a Middle-Income Vietnam. Joint Donor Report to the Vietnam Consultative Group Meeting 6 December 2011. The World Bank Group.
Vietnam Economic Times. 2017, September 11. https://www.vneconomictimes.com/article/vietnam-today/little-state-capital-sold-in-soe-equitization. Accessed May 2019.
Vietnam Investment Review. 2018a, October 11. https://www.vir.com.vn/super-commission-to-streamline-soes-63000.html. Accessed May 2019.
Vietnam Investment Review. 2018b, April 18. https://www.vir.com.vn/domestic-brewers-expand-operations-to-fight-back-foreign-competitors-58456.htmlestic. Accessed May 2019.
Vietnam Investment Review. 2019a, April 10. https://www.vir.com.vn/turmoil-at-sabeco-after-historic-ma-66998.html. Accessed August 2019.
Vietnam Investment Review. 2019b, February 12. https://www.vir.com.vn/habeco-reports-lowest-profit-in-four-years-65732.html. Accessed May 2019.
Vietnam Manufacturing Federation. 2018, May 11. http://vmfederation.com/news-events/item/79-economy-status-a-boost-for-growth.html. Accessed May 2019.
Viet Nam News. 2017, August 2. https://vietnamnews.vn/economy/381228/soe-restructuring-must-be-more-efficient-experts.html#c1mlHCg8HXrb7TpZ.97. Accessed May 2019.
Viet Nam News. 2018, April 24. https://vietnamnews.vn/economy/426838/thaibev-joins-sabeco-board-after-govt-steps-in.html. Accessed May 2019.
Vietnamnet. 2018, January 16. https://english.vietnamnet.vn/fms/business/194045/beer-consumption-in-vn-still-rising-rapidly.html. Accessed May 2019.
Vitnamplus. 2019, April 19. https://en.vietnamplus.vn/fiscal-deficit-to-stay-high-in-2019-due-to-delayed-soe-divestment/151288.vnp. Accessed May 2019.

Vu-Thanh, T.-A. 2017. Does WTO Accession Help Domestic Reform? The Political Economy of SOE Reform Backsliding in Vietnam. *World Trade Review* 16 (1): 85–109.
Wade, R. 1990. *Governing the Market*. Princeton: Princeton University Press.
World Bank. 2014. *Corporate Governance of State-Owned Enterprises: A Tool-Kit*. Document 91357. Washington, DC: World Bank.
World Bank. 2017. *The Role of the State in Vietnam's Economic Development: Enhancing the Role of the State in Facilitating a More Competitive and Productive Economy*. The World Bank Group and Australian Government.
World Bank. 2018. *Taking Stock: An Update of Vietnam's Recent Economic Developments*. Washington, DC: World Bank.
World Bank, MPI. 2016. *Vietnam 2035 Toward Prosperity, Creativity, Equity, and Democracy*. Washington, DC: World Bank.
WTO Center VCCI. 2019, February 15. http://www.wtocenter.vn/chuyen-de/13399-cptpp-tariff-cuts-and-soe-monopoly-removal-usher-in-opportunities. Accessed May 2019.
Zing. 2018. https://news.zing.vn/dai-gia-ngoai-chi-phoi-thi-truong-bia-viet-ra-sao-post895657.html. Accessed May 2019.

CHAPTER 6

Rural Revolutions: Socialist, Market and Sustainable Development of the Countryside in Vietnam and Laos

Robert Cole and Micah L. Ingalls

Introduction

Rural development is a core policy concern deeply rooted in the revolutionary origins of both the Socialist Republic of Vietnam and Lao People's Democratic Republic (Lao PDR, or Laos). The peasant support base had been pivotal in the conflict against colonial powers, and garnered through aims and actions to end rural inequality (Evans 1990; Jamieson 1993; Kerkvliet 1998). Since Vietnam's reunification and the establishment of the Lao PDR in 1975, improving and 'modernising' livelihoods and living conditions in the countryside has been a consistent tool

R. Cole (✉)
Department of Geography, National University of Singapore, Singapore, Singapore
e-mail: coler@u.nus.edu

M. L. Ingalls
Centre for Development and Environment, University of Bern, Bern, Switzerland

A. Hansen et al. (eds.), *The Socialist Market Economy in Asia*,
https://doi.org/10.1007/978-981-15-6248-8_6

of state legitimation: from the 'high communist' objective of agricultural collectivisation; through market reforms and trade liberalisation; to contemporary emphases on development and growth; as well as in the management of rural populations and efforts to integrate upland minorities within the mainstream (Evans 1988; Woodside 1989; Kerkvliet 2005; Évrard 2011; Singh 2012; Dang 2018). In parallel, this policy arc has transformed the discursive position of agriculture within the (market-)socialist development model, from Soviet-influenced narratives of mass collective farming as a steppingstone to industrialisation, to market-driven agricultural intensification in pursuit of economic growth. As the two countries courted global re-engagement both in terms of foreign investment and with the international development sector, tensions emerged between the latter growth narrative, increasing exploitation of natural resources, and would-be notions of environmental sustainability (Cole et al. 2017; Ingalls et al. 2018a, b; Kallio et al. 2018). Both governments can be viewed as having pragmatically played to different audiences, on the one hand seeking to maximise possibilities for resource-intensive investments, while on the other incorporating sustainability into the vocabulary of governance. The degree and evenness with which resource revenues filter into grassroots rural development in either country is strongly contested.

This chapter examines the rationales and impacts of rural policies through different phases of the socialist and capitalist development of Laos and Vietnam, how changing rural life has been moulded by the transition from collectivisation and command planning to (post-)socialist market economies, and subsequent regional and global market integration. In each phase, the chapter compares and contrasts how policy ideals have mapped to realities on the ground in Laos and Vietnam, the role of the rural sector within the shifting development models of the two regimes, and ways in which rural populations of the two countries have navigated the great structural changes underway around them. The following section examines the circumstances and processes through which communist planners sought to harness supposed collective modes of living embodied by the predominantly peasant post-war rural societies of Vietnam and Laos, the subsequent abandonment of collectivisation, and return to subsistence and small-scale commercial farming under the market reforms. The third section focuses on the interplay between the ensuing reforms, emerging regionalism and concurrent rural development policies and practices, and how farmers and the environments they depend on have been affected by widening exposure to markets, land-based investments and accelerating agricultural commercialisation and trade. The chapter concludes by reflecting on some of the implications of these trajectories of rural development, which although bearing striking resemblance between the two regimes, have had somewhat different outcomes both for sustainability and for rural populations in Laos and Vietnam, based on contrasting conditions and objectives within the two countries. In comparing the developmental experiences of the two countries, the chapter emphasises the role of rural places and people in the transition to the socialist market economy, and their engagement in wider circuits of capitalist accumulation within an integrating ASEAN region.

Socialist Transformation of the Countryside in Laos and Vietnam

The much earlier establishment of communist North Vietnam (or the Democratic Republic of Vietnam) in 1954 meant that this became a proving ground for efforts towards dismantling rural colonial institutions, in which a large proportion (estimates vary between one third and more than half) of the country's farmland was owned by a small elite (Kerkvliet and Selden 1998; Hirsch et al. 2015). French colonial policy had heavily favoured large landholdings at the expense of traditionally predominant smallholdings, granting tracts of land to colonial settlers and Vietnamese collaborators that resulted in severe land inequality (Dang 2018). The communists fostered the allegiance of the peasantry over decades of conflict against French and American forces through rural policies supporting poor farmers and periodic land redistribution, but ongoing unequal access to land meant that it was also necessary to reallocate holdings from those considered to be land-endowed 'middle peasants' (Raymond 2008). Land reform was consequently among the first rural policies to be enacted by the communist leaders in the mid-1950s, aiming for equal reallocation from landlords to farmers, though the actual process proved fraught with grievances and instances of brutality (Woodside 1989), including against ostensibly 'patriotic' landlords who had supported the revolution (Lentz 2019). An important distinction from Vietnam was Laos' historic land abundance relative to its population, which had been little disturbed or monopolised by elites or the colonial administration (Hirsch and Scurrah 2015). Prior to the revolution, all national territory had been nominally royal property, while the remoteness from state authority of much of Laos' sparse and ethnically diverse rural population meant that land was commonly (re)distributed through a profusion of local customary practices (Ducourtieux et al. 2005). The establishment of the Lao PDR in 1975 therefore took place in the context of relatively even land distribution (Hirsch and Scurrah 2015), largely bypassing the kind of chaotic land reforms undertaken in Vietnam. All Lao territory transferred to the property of the nation under the management of the state, and functionally via cooperatives which, as well as reorganising agricultural production, had a further role in redistributing land access (Vandergeest 2003; Ducourtieux et al. 2005).

In sharp contrast with Laos' relatively low land inequality, the violence that accompanied Vietnam's land reforms ultimately contributed to their abandonment in favour of large-scale, Soviet model agricultural collectivisation, first initiated in North Vietnam in the late 1950s (Jamieson 1993). Drawing heavily on the ideologies and material support of communist Vietnam, the Lao government launched collectivisation soon after its establishment, as a perceived mechanism for the socialist transformation of the countryside (Evans 1990). For both countries, as well as an ideological target, collectivisation represented a means to address pressing, interlinked security concerns: Firstly, in terms of geopolitical security, by re-ordering and managing rural spaces and populations to render them legible to the state; and secondly improving food security and living conditions—a benchmark of the legitimacy of the two regimes—by expanding cultivated area, introducing technology and boosting resource- and labour-efficiency (Evans 1988; Stuart-Fox 1996; Hirsch et al. 2015). Productivity targets proved largely elusive under the collectivisation model, for reasons explored below, though the policies nevertheless set the scene for state aims and rationales towards rural development in Laos and Vietnam over proceeding decades.

Re-ordering Rural Spaces

The similarities between the timings, trajectories and policies that underpinned collectivisation in late 1970s Laos and Vietnam, coupled with the strong political influence and support from Vietnam towards Laos, hint at an underlying relationship of control. Thayer argues, however, that "the Lao-Vietnamese 'special relationship' reveals a pattern of consultation, cooperation, coordination and reciprocal influence in many policy areas", often seeking mutual advantages, and in which Laos frequently operated independently of Vietnamese influence (1982: 246). Amid fragile post-war economic and social conditions, the threat of new regional conflict was significant by 1979, with Vietnamese troops fighting the Khmer Rouge in Cambodia, a Chinese invasion of its northern border, and forces hostile to the communists in Laos, fuelled in some part by Thai and Chinese state interference (Evans 1988; Dwyer et al. 2015). From the perspective of the Lao and Vietnamese governments, rural spaces had to be brought under the control of the state to try to protect the embryonic regimes from these diverse potential threats. With the primarily agrarian Lao economy in an extremely precarious condition due to decades of destructive conflict, successive poor harvests, and concerns of peasant unrest, agricultural modernisation and collectivisation were urgent initial policies of the Lao regime (Thayer 1982; Stuart-Fox 1996). Evans later observed that although "there is no question that Vietnamese communist thinking strongly influences their counterparts in Laos" who "openly acknowledge their ideological indebtedness to the Vietnamese" (1988: 29), Laos' collectivisation was more likely a parallel response to economic and security risks than a directive from Hanoi.

In both Laos and Vietnam, planners considered it imperative that collectivisation should be implemented gradually, accompanied by mass instruction aimed at reassuring and encouraging the envisioned voluntary uptake of the peasantry (Kerkvliet 1998; Evans 1990). The initial step in the campaigns was to foster mutual aid teams who would work together and share the harvest, before moving to a more organised labour exchange unit based on work points, in which each member was intended to contribute and benefit equally (Evans 1990; Kerkvliet 1998; Raymond 2008). Communist leaders enacted further land reforms and collectivisation in the former South Vietnam following reunification in 1975, aiming to steer the southern population away from capitalist modes of production while harnessing the productivity of the Mekong Delta for national development and industrialisation (Woodside 1989). Where collectivisation in the north was initially met with resignation rather than either overt support or resistance (Kerkvliet 1998, see below), in the south, the policy was rolled out among a largely hostile peasant population (Ravallion and De Walle 2008). Southern farmers who had done relatively well under the previous regime resented the constraints placed on their livelihoods through pooling productive assets and earning work points

(Jamieson 1993), which misguidedly sought to mimic putatively time-honoured peasant reciprocity in labour-intensive tasks, such as harvesting and transplanting (Beresford 1990). Beneath socialist ideals were large assumptions over the extent of collective peasant endeavours, which functioned within specific social boundaries (Kervliet 2005; Evans 1990; High 2014). While it had been recognised as early as the mid-1960s by several local state authorities that collectivisation was not working, attempts to introduce household-based work contracts were initially stymied out of reluctance to stray from the heavily Soviet-influenced collective model (personal communication Do Ta Khanh 2019). Together with mismanagement and failure to achieve productivity gains, the imposition of reciprocity created tensions that would eventually undermine the system (Evans 1990; Kerkvliet 1995; Dang 2018).

Managing Rural Populations

Processes of collectivisation and rural restructuring in post-war Laos and Vietnam also involved significant relocation of rural populations according to policy aims for the development of the countryside. Between 1975 and 1990, as many as 5 million Vietnamese resettled, including those displaced by the conflict itself, as well as a large number who relocated in response to national development policies intended to 'tame' Vietnam's remote uplands (De Koninck 1996). Initially, settling these perceived wild and isolated regions was strategically vital in the fight for an independent Vietnam (Hardy 2003), though waves of economic migrants later followed the market reforms, "hoping to get rich in a region recently described in the lowlands as a 'promised land'" (Hardy 2000: 22; see also Lenz 2019 on the discursive construction of Vietnam's 'resource frontier'). The initial movement of lowland (largely ethnic Kinh) people into Vietnam's upland areas historically dominated by ethnic minorities was emblematic of Vietnam's attempts to extend state control into rural areas, as well as to increase agricultural production to achieve national targets. During this period, the total area of agricultural land in Vietnam increased by around 60% (De Koninck 1996). This expansion of agricultural land, as well as intensive logging to fuel Vietnam's growing wood processing industry, reduced Vietnam's forests from more than 11 million ha in 1975 to around 9 million hectares, or 28% of Vietnam's total area, by 1990 (Nguyen 2001). In Laos, resettlement initially focused on restoring bomb damaged and depopulated farmland, which necessitated pooling labour and resources (Evans 1988), while about a quarter of the population had been displaced by the end of the war, many of whom settled in locations other than natal villages (Hirsch and Scurrah 2015).

Laos' collectivisation campaigns were further linked to government aims to bolster control over forest resources and reduce shifting cultivation, or swidden, which has been historically viewed by the lowland population as destructive and backward (Brown and Zasloff 1986; Kenney-Lazar 2013; Castella et al. 2013). Although shifting cultivation—an agricultural practice that relies on periodically clearing and burning fallow land and patches of forest—dominated upland areas and constituted the livelihood basis for the majority of the rural population, it had come into direct conflict with state interests. The export of timber provided much-needed revenue for the nascent Lao state, while shifting cultivation was an ill-fit with objectives of modernisation and an emerging national identity largely imagined by the lowland Lao elite, as well as an obstacle to state control of the rural peripheries (Baird and Shoemaker 2007). In its initial programme of action in December 1975, the government set out the objective "to persuade and assist the peasants of all ethnic groups in the regions where cultivation on burnbeat [swidden] land is practised to gradually put an end to their nomadic life ... [and] to endeavour to renovate the cultivation techniques of burnbeat fields, to expand the area of rice cultivation to dry land terraces and to preserve forests" (Brown and Zasloff 1986: 303).

Starting in the 1970s, the eradication of shifting cultivation in Laos has been continuously attempted through a range of policies and development interventions, including bans, alternative livelihood programmes and mass resettlement of upland communities to lowland areas—the latter a polar opposite to Vietnam's efforts to settle its uplands, though both with the same objective: to extend state control. Because Laos' upland interventions produced a number of negative social outcomes, it was necessary to legitimise shifting cultivation eradication efforts, not only to the rural peasantry but more recently to development and aid agencies. Shifting cultivation was discursively blamed not only for its negative environmental impacts (particularly deforestation, but also soil erosion) but also as a cause of rural poverty (Baird and Shoemaker 2007; Fox et al. 2009; GoL 2004; Hett et al. 2011; Hirsch 2000; Messerli et al. 2009). Policy aims during the high communist period to induce settled rice in the uplands were nevertheless often resisted or simply unrealistic, due to geographical, practical and cultural differences between shifting, terraced and paddy cultivation (Evans 1990). These factors remained true at the time of writing among communities who continue to practise swidden cultivation in remote uplands, whether by preference or necessity, despite decades of policies aimed at its eradication.

Paper Cooperatives and the End of the Collective Ideal

While in the late 1970s, collectivisation had been considered vital to socialist development and the improvement of rural living conditions, and hence the legitimacy of the Lao and Vietnamese regimes, the programme was never fully implemented and stalled in both countries for largely similar reasons. They were inefficient, weakly managed, and founded on state-driven socialist ideals that were out of step with the priorities of the peasantry, who in Vietnam made this increasingly known through acts of everyday resistance, including avoiding collective tasks and sabotage (Evans 1995; Kerkvliet 2005). Vietnamese cooperatives became shells in which members reverted to family-based, subsistence farming on subdivided land, while national grain output from cooperatives declined through the early 1980s (Kerkvliet 2009; Raymond 2008). Falling production brought about widening food shortages, damaging state legitimacy and forcing a rebalance between collective and individual farming through the legalisation of contract production for cooperatives in 1981, under 'Directive 100' (loosely resembling China's 'household responsibility' system), with farmers free to sell surpluses (Pingali and Xuan 1992; Kerkvliet 2005; Raymond 2008).

Although on a much-reduced scale, the collapse of collectivisation in Laos was markedly more precipitous, as "smaller, village-level cooperatives merged into bigger ones and became so bureaucratic that they finally existed more on paper than in reality" (Castella and Bouahom 2014: 186). Officials focused on the expansion of the cooperatives rather than production, while confusion reigned over cooperative management (Evans 1988). Because of a climate of coercion, inability to avoid government orders, and in some cases, fear (High 2014), peasant resistance most commonly took the form of evasion in Laos. This included smuggling, moving to remote areas away from state interference, and the mass exit of refugees across the Mekong River to Thailand (Brown and Zasloff 1986; Bourdet 2000; Scott 2009). Similar to Vietnam, dire harvests in the late 1970s risked the validity of the Lao leadership, and although collectivisation would continue to be advocated in policy for years afterwards as the way to 'liberate' peasants from outmoded practices, it was officially suspended after only one year of operation, in 1979 (Evans 1990; Stuart-Fox 1996). Established cooperatives continued to operate, but lacking inputs, techniques and skilled managers, their dismantlement began as the economic compass shifted towards liberalisation in the mid-1980s (Castella and Bouahom 2014). As was also underway in Vietnam, the Lao government's response to the failings of both collectivisation and the wider economy was "a radical re-thinking of economic policy and a modification of the role of agriculture and the peasantry within it" (Evans 1988: 2).

Reforms, Re-engagement and New Forms of Rural Development

Doubts over the efficacy of central planning in Vietnam were mounting in the late 1970s, as over-optimistic 5-year plans failed to produce intended results, and even the staunchest communists were forced to acknowledge that failing socio-economic policies, not only the impacts of war and geopolitical isolation, were part of the problem (Beresford 2008; Goscha 2016). Collapsing rice harvests occurred alongside withdrawal of food aid, on which Vietnam was among the ten most dependent countries globally in the 1970s (Moore and Stanford 2010). China first withdrew food aid amid rising bilateral tensions, followed by loss of Western aid in the wake of Vietnam's invasion of Cambodia in 1979 (Ravallion and De Walle 2008). From the early 1980s, a changing leadership recognised that market liberalisation and global reintegration were vital to Vietnam's economic survival (Ravallion and De Walle 2008), hence that of the regime. Inflationary pressures that took hold towards the mid-1980s, in tandem with chronic poor conditions of farmers, were enough to drive widespread abandonment of cooperative fields (Raymond 2008). In response, the government more proactively encouraged private production, as had already been gradually introduced via work contracts across a number of sectors and locations (personal communication Do Ta Khanh 2019), feeding into the wider *Doi Moi* ('Renovation') reforms launched in 1986. Despite the partial devolvement of decision-making from cooperatives to households in 1981, production continued to fail and by 1988 famine struck several provinces, followed the same year by large-scale de-collectivisation under 'Resolution 10' (Pingali and Xuan 1992; Fforde and Sénèque 1994; Raymond 2008). As well as ending collective labour commitments, the policy granted long-term land use rights to households (though land remained the property of the state), enabled farmers to sell output both to the state and privately, purchase inputs on open markets and allocate resources and manage crops autonomously (Ravallion and De Walle 2008; Raymond 2008). The agricultural sector responded to the ensuing "functioning market system with a socialist face" with high productivity growth through the 1990s and 2000s (Luibrand 2002: 1), and dramatic falls in poverty over the same period (Tarp 2015). The impacts of agricultural reforms were fundamental to the decline in poverty throughout Vietnam, by supporting development and economic growth at both the national level and in terms of the livelihoods of the rural poor (Banik and Hansen 2016).

In Laos, similar circumstances had brought about a retreat from centrally planned agriculture as cooperatives proved dysfunctional, risking not only national food security but social unrest and further refugee flight, while calling into question "the government's claim to represent, in class terms, the worker-peasant alliance" (Stuart-Fox 1996: 177). Since 1975, critical areas of the Lao economy and government had been kept afloat by financial and technical aid from the communist bloc, following years of strategic aid targeting rival factions during the conflict (Phraxayavong 2009). By mid-1979, the Lao leadership had received high-level policy advice from its main donors in the USSR and Vietnam that cooperatives were better off abandoned (Stuart-Fox 1996). Economic cooperation was a central facet of the Lao–Vietnamese 'special relationship', and the two sides regularly exchanged ministerial delegations for planning purposes. However, although Vietnamese guidance was typically positively received by the Lao leadership, Thayer (1982) notes that this was always with an underlying regard for Laos' independence over its own policies. Thus, although undertaken with periodic consultation from Vietnam and over similar timeframes, Laos' tentative reinstatement of private enterprise and market exchanges was rooted in mounting domestic economic concerns over the late 1970s (Evans 1991; Bourdet 2000). The Lao government began to refer after 1979 with increasing frequency to socialism as a 'transitional' process, in which the 'positive characteristics' of markets could be harnessed, while the state moderated negative aspects "without being afraid that when capitalism is fully developed it will override socialism" (Evans 1988: 52). The gradual shift towards reforms was the subject of vigorous debate within the leadership, with opposing camps believing socialist transformation would either be enabled or demolished by the reintroduction of market structures (Ng 1987). Nevertheless, it was clear by the mid-1980s that remaining state controls over private enterprise, exchange and trade were curtailing growth, modernisation and the improvement of living conditions—all central concerns in the project of national development that formed the basis of state legitimacy. Like *Doi Moi*, Laos' 'New Economic Mechanism' (NEM) was enacted in 1986, and sought to reverse the country's economic isolation by liberalising key aspects of the economy and significant efforts to attract foreign direct investment, integrate with regional markets and expand commodity production for export (Rigg 2005). At this point, "the goal of building socialism receded into some hazy future" (Stuart-Fox 1996: 196). The effects of the NEM were initially most pronounced in urban centres, bypassing sparsely populated mountainous areas which were considered to have little to contribute to the new economic direction (Evans 1988), a view that would later dramatically reverse as Laos became a 'resource frontier' for transnational capital (Barney 2009).

Regional Integration and Agricultural Commercialisation

A further emphasis of the ensuing reforms in Vietnam and Laos was the growing necessity by the late 1980s to re-engage with the global economy. As regional integration, political rapprochement, and liberalisation gathered pace in Southeast Asia, the collapse of the Soviet Union brought an end to the aid that shored up the post-war economies of Vietnam and Laos (Stuart-Fox 1996; Pholsena and Banomyong 2006; Thanh 2015). Studies and consultations led by the Asian Development Bank in the early 1990s resulted in an agenda for regional economic cooperation under the banner of the Greater Mekong Subregion (GMS), identifying priority sectors of trade and investment, transport infrastructure, telecommunications, energy, environmental management and human resource development (Stuart-Fox 1995). These priorities were aimed at nurturing the newly integrating regional market, from which Vietnam benefitted significantly in terms of FDI in technology and manufacturing, later focusing its own outward investments regionally (Nam and Nam 2008), including resource- and land-based investments in Laos. Meanwhile, Laos' economic integration emerged as "a regional collaborative project, supported (financially and politically) by multiple national and international actors" (Pholsena 2005: 184), including Vietnam, China, multilateral donors and development agencies. Since the GMS programme relied on forging new transport connections, Laos found itself in a strong position to benefit from bordering each of the GMS countries of Thailand, Myanmar, Cambodia, Vietnam, and China, with potential for "being propelled along by the dynamism of its neighbours" (1995: 178–179).

This also came with the possibility of widening rural–urban and ethnic disparities, however, as well as heightening political and economic influence over different regions of the country from China, Vietnam and Thailand (Stuart-Fox 1995). The wave of regional integration was further stimulated by Vietnam and Laos gaining ASEAN membership in 1995 and 1997, respectively. In parallel with the GMS programme, Vietnam's first decade of ASEAN membership resulted in rising foreign investment in textiles, electronics and manufacturing, via subsidiaries of transnational companies (Mirza and Giroud 2004). By contrast, foreign investment took time to gain traction within the rural sector, including through acquisition of farmland for urban expansion, industry and infrastructure (later resulting in highly publicised disputes, Hirsch et al. 2015), as well as foreign-owned industrial farming enterprises, such as livestock and feed mills. Comparatively scarce labour but a rich natural resources endowment placed Laos in a rather different position as it joined ASEAN in 1997, favouring investments in primary sectors and gearing the economy to transboundary demands (Bourdet 2000). With the improving ease of transport created by GMS infrastructure and relaxation of trade barriers came greater flows of commodities, capital and people; the Lao government acknowledged in policy that domestic production would remain strongly influenced by the growing Vietnamese, Chinese and Thai economies (Rigg 2005).

Sustainability and 'Green' Growth

Alongside the regional priorities enshrined in the GMS programme, domestic policies in Laos have merged the lingering attachment to market socialism with a 'high modernist' environmental or 'green' (i.e. sustainable) development discourse, which is mutually supported by state and international development organisations (Singh 2014; Cole et al. 2017). Sustainability became increasingly central to mainstream development approaches, thereby funding flows, following the influential Brundtland report (WCED 1987), subsequent Rio Earth Summit and adoption of the Millennium Development Goals (since succeeded by the Sustainable Development Goals). Sustainability is both a material and rhetorical concept, however, and highly fragmented in its implementation among different actors with diverse strategies and interests. Policies and governance structures ostensibly aimed at sustainable development in Laos and Vietnam coexist alongside path dependencies entrenched by the market reforms towards exploiting forests and natural resources, intensive commercial agriculture, and conditions of economic growth that outpace efforts to protect the environment (Cole et al. 2017; Hansen 2015). Recent 'green growth' policy narratives in Vietnam and Laos can be viewed as seeking to bring these concerns together under a development model promising synergies between growth and environmental sustainability, though thus far focusing primarily on limiting environmental harm resulting from economic growth (Kallio et al. 2018; Hansen 2015). The discursive framing of resource-based development as a 'green' pursuit in the GMS countries can be traced to a wider re-imagining of international donors, as the "'green' development partner of states" in managing so-termed environmental trade-offs for economic gains (Wong 2010: 3), with increasing ubiquity in policy, project documents and the media (Kallio et al. 2018).

The risk of the 'greenness' narrative is that potentially irreversible environmental damage is taking place while outwardly masked by perceptions of sustainability. In particular, the zeal and rapidity with which Laos' abundant rivers are being dammed according to the government's target of becoming the 'battery of Asia' are undermining the viability of fisheries, displacing livelihoods and riverine farming and fishing communities (Baird 2011; Delang and Toro 2011; Orr et al. 2012). Meanwhile, recent policy emphasis on 'turning land into capital' (TLIC) has opened the countryside to large-scale agribusiness investments (Dwyer 2011), often resulting in further displacement of marginal populations. Though measures appear to have been taken at central level to strengthen regulation of concession-granting procedures, it remains to be seen how effective these are in response to powerful elite interests, as well as how equitably the profits of such ventures filter to wider rural development. Functioning at the meeting point of external and national policy agendas represented by green development, a long-term focus of rural policies in Laos since the 1990s has been to isolate agricultural land from forests while promoting permanent, commercial agriculture to support economic growth and poverty reduction (Castella et al. 2013). Key policy instruments to further suppress swidden and tighten control over forest land and ethnic minorities since the market reforms of the 1980s, with varying support from international donors, have included zoning and categorisation of forests, land and forest allocation, focal area development and ongoing village resettlement and consolidation within the ambit of the state (Baird and Shoemaker 2007; Kenney-Lazar 2012). While land categorisation and allocation in part feed into the neoliberal logics underpinning the NEM, in terms of privatising state-owned or (nominally) common resources (Barney 2012), this has proven highly discretionary and fragmented in practice, and open to assignment of land according to accessing potential revenues (Dwyer and Ingalls 2015).

The extension of state authority over rural spaces in Vietnam has taken a somewhat different path, initially involving actively populating frontiers for cultivation of commodity crops, and widespread systematic land titling (Markussen 2015). This is reflective of the significantly higher constraints on the land base in Vietnam that necessitated redirecting people from highly populated areas such as the Red River Delta, as well as structural changes under *Doi Moi* around de-collectivisation, tenure reforms that enabled a land market, and the relaxation of household registration that catalysed large-scale internal migration (Adger et al. 2002). De Koninck (1996) observes that an 'anarchic' phase of illegal land transactions was triggered by the 1993 extension of use rights (set at 15 years for annual crops and 50 years for perennial crops), resulting in extensive deforestation, including by military-associated logging operations and land conversion for agriculture which, though largely enacted by in-migrants, was commonly attributed to upland minorities. While the scale of land titling undertaken in Vietnam dwarfs that in Laos, subnational variations persisted, with limited land titling and government expropriation for development purposes in the marginal northern uplands (Markussen 2015). Agricultural commercialisation since the reforms, particularly of rice, commodities and industrial tree crops, has in nevertheless further accelerated declines in rural poverty (McKay et al. 2015). This has come with significant costs. The exploitation of land and natural resources to meet economic priorities have physically transformed rural Vietnam through widespread conversion to commercial agriculture and intensive chemical inputs, ultimately resulting in the degradation of land, forests and other environmental resources (Hansen 2015). The latter scenario has more recently begun to take hold across the border in Laos, pointing to growing environmental and human impacts as intensive commercial agriculture has expanded into marginal rural spaces.

Government efforts to halt deforestation and re-green the uplands in Vietnam have taken the form of logging bans set in policy at the time of the anarchic land market described by de Koninck (1996), initially to stem the loss of forest reserves, and later applied to over 50% of the national forest estate, while slashing logging quotas (Pham et al. 2012). Although Vietnam's recovering forests can to some extent be attributed to the logging bans and agricultural intensification, this has taken place in the context of rapid growth in land- and forest-intensive sectors of the Vietnamese economy (Meyfroidt and Lambin 2008, 2009; Meyfroidt et al. 2010). Considering this puzzling contradiction, Ingalls et al. (2018a) observe that "Vietnam's ability to at once secure and increase its forest estate while achieving unprecedented expansion of land- and forest-risk commodity sectors hinges on its importation of raw and semi-processed materials from abroad, representing a substantial displacement of deforestation and forest degradation to source countries" (p. 257), a large proportion of which came from Laos.

Tensions between forest exploitation and conservation in the context of rural development in Laos and Vietnam have re-emerged in a somewhat new form under climate change mitigation programmes aimed at limiting forest carbon emissions. Reducing Emissions from Deforestation and Forest Degradation (REDD+) initiatives promoted by the World Bank, the Food and Agriculture Organization of the United Nations and civil society organisations such as the World Wide Fund for Nature (WWF) have advanced considerably over the past decade (Dwyer and Ingalls 2015; Ingalls and Dwyer 2016). Similar to other green growth approaches, REDD+ purports to reduce tensions between economic development and environmental conservation by leveraging new environmental values (forest carbon) to generate forest-based revenue. However, the creation of such new economic values has also re-animated long-standing tensions between state forest managers and rural communities. This is perhaps most immediately apparent in Laos, where the commodification of carbon has renewed attention to shifting cultivation. While the secondary forests and regenerating vegetation produced by swiddening had limited timber values, the potential for carbon sequestration and thus carbon-based revenues have pushed shifting cultivation to the forefront of REDD+ programmes. With this in mind, state planners are in the process of launching new and more expansive land use planning and zonation of forests and agricultural areas while tightening forest protection laws (Ingalls et al. 2018a; and see, for example, GoL 2018). This could presage new opportunities for rural development, depending on the degree to which planning approaches are fully participatory and the proportion of carbon-based revenues that devolve to local communities. However, this remains to be seen and, as historic patterns of rural development strongly suggest, should be viewed with caution.

The Emerging Lay of the Land: The AEC, Investments and Transboundary Commodities

A new layer of regional integration took effect with the 2016 enactment of the ASEAN Economic Community (AEC), advocating free movement of goods, services, capital, investment and skilled labour (ASEAN 2008). The AEC is the product of long-term infrastructure and institution-building, including in the GMS, which has enabled both the rapid expansion of ASEAN trade (rising by US$700 billion from 2007 to 2015, almost one quarter of which was intra-ASEAN) and a regional platform for attracting FDI (around US$120 billion in 2015, with intra-regional investment accounting for the largest share, ASEAN 2016). Within these figures are certain disparities, however, both in terms of destination countries and sectors. In particular, more diversified ASEAN economies such as Malaysia, Thailand and Vietnam have favoured FDI in manufacturing but in some cases restricted investments in agriculture and natural resources, while higher rates of investment liberalisation are seen in the latter sectors among the less advanced members, including Laos (Intal 2015). Vietnam has more recently pursued FDI in agriculture as a means of achieving large-scale, technologically advanced production that meets with increasingly stringent quality demands, both domestically and for export (Do Ta Khanh and Hansen 2017). For Laos, transnational investments in commercial agriculture and other land-based sectors are actively targeted by state agencies and elite actors, and considered a shortcut to by now time-honoured objectives of economic development, agricultural modernisation, and to harness marginal land into more productive uses (Scurrah and Hirsch 2015).

Alongside hastening regional integration and courting of transnational capital, the effects of national policies such as TLIC have substantially transformed rural land relations in Laos (Ingalls et al. 2018b). Particularly since 2008, land concessions and land-based investments have grown dramatically, currently encompassing more than 1 million hectares in Laos, including agricultural, plantation, and operational mining and hydropower concessions. Within this investment landscape, China and Vietnam hold the largest per-country shares of land concessions. Landholdings under concession to Vietnamese companies total nearly 135,000 ha, spread across more than 100 investment projects in agriculture, mining, forestry and other primary sectors (Hett et al. 2019). While these land-based investments have generated some revenue for the state treasury, they have also produced significant social and environmental impacts, which have largely accrued to rural communities. The recent collapse of the Xe Pian Xe Nam Noy Hydropower Project in southern Laos was a particularly glaring example, resulting in catastrophic loss of life, property and farmland (*The Diplomat* 2018; *The Guardian* 2018). State planners have become increasingly aware of the costs of land-based investments in Laos, and over the last decade, three moratoria have been issued, though these have largely been ineffective to halt the rapid and typically uncontrolled expansion of investments (Hett et al. 2019), facilitated by political and economic elites. The pace and scale of land-based investments have been mirrored by a rapid growth in the export of land-intensive commodities, primarily to China, Thailand and Vietnam. Lao primary exports to Vietnam have grown considerably over the last decade, particularly with respect to agricultural commodities, which have tripled in total export value, and rubber latex, which has increased a staggering 280-fold since 2009 (Ingalls et al. 2018b).

In the background of soaring transboundary land investments and commodity exports, the AEC's enactment has been accompanied by sector-specific policies designed to respond to the development needs of the member countries and enhance opportunities to benefit from globalisation, while maintaining a focus on sustainability. In terms of food, agriculture, and forestry, the AEC aims to enhance competitiveness concurrently with sustainability and resilience among rural populations who continue rely on these sectors (ASEAN 2015), which remain particularly prominent in Laos and Vietnam. In this regard, the AEC's 'Strategic Plan' recognises that "globalization and regional integration not only open up access to larger regional and global markets, but also expose domestic producers to intensified competition from more technologically sophisticated, better endowed foreign competitors" (ASEAN 2015: 4). This has certainly proven the case in Laos, where meeting transboundary demand for commodities is heightening competition over agricultural and forest land and resources (Rigg 2005; Razal et al. 2015; Ingalls et al. 2018a). While the distribution of agricultural landholdings across farming households in Laos continues to be the most equal in the Mekong region, factoring in landholdings under concession to foreign and domestic companies raises the Gini coefficient from 0.34 to 0.49, meaning that only 12% of rural land holders command more than 40% of all land (Ingalls et al. 2018b). This holds important implications for both food and land security, since transboundary production and investments absorb land that might otherwise provide for local needs, whether through appropriation in the form of concessions or the present proliferation of transboundary contract and land-rental arrangements for agricultural commodities (Vongvisouk et al. 2016; Scurrah and Hirsch 2015).

Although the redistribution of land was seen as the cornerstone of rural development during the socialist reforms of the 1960s and 1970s, the distribution of agricultural land in Vietnam has remained highly unequal. The Gini coefficient of land holdings by agricultural households is 0.54, the highest among the Mekong countries (Ingalls et al. 2018b). Studies of wage migration from rural areas in Vietnam highlight the tendency for migrants to retain plots of land, however marginal, as a familial anchor and safety net (Anh et al. 2012). Despite the perception of increasingly meagre prospects amid substantial structural shifts in the rural economy, farming is nevertheless considered a secure livelihood by comparison to more remunerative, but riskier urban employment. An attempt to bolster rural development in Vietnam is embodied by the New Rural Development (NRD) policy, enacted in 2010 and in its second phase at the time of writing, breaking development down to a range of targets to be met by each given location. In this respect NRD is highly reflective of lingering socialist planning approaches, though incorporating key concerns of contemporary market economy. These include "planning new rural areas; developing socio-economic infrastructure; economic restructuring; enhancing income and reducing poverty; promoting social welfare; promoting innovative production methods; enhancing the quality of the education system; enhancing the quality of the healthcare system; promoting culture, information and communication; assuring water supply and sanitation; enhancing the quality of party and government agencies to maintain the security in rural areas" (Anh et al. 2017; GoV 2010). Anh et al. (2017) observe the positive effects on the rural economy of the NRD targets since 2010, though this must also be understood as a period of general rapid growth in Vietnam, which perhaps had the greater underlying impact on improving rural living standards.

In Laos, it is hoped that strengthening regional integration and the revenues generated by foreign investments will contribute to graduation from the United Nations' list of Least Developed Countries (LDC), long targeted for 2020 though recently pushed back to 2024 (*Asia Times* 2018). Exiting LDC status is a cross-sector policy tenet that provides a common rationale for rural development and investments, with almost continuous media coverage in Laos since the 2000s. As time began to dwindle for the UN criteria to be met within the targeted period, Prime Minister Thongloun Sisoulith issued a Decree in 2017 clarifying the government's own criteria for 'graduation from poverty' and becoming 'developed' at family, village and district scales in reference to the country's ongoing 5-year National Socio-economic Development Plans (GoL 2017). The list of conditions emphasises social order and political stability, physical infrastructure such as housing, schools, water, energy and public health facilities, stable income and access to markets. All three scales include the effective and sustainable management, protection and use of natural resources and the environment. The question remains as to how effectively sustainability can be achieved on the basis of the lingering socialist motif of target setting, in the face of more powerful and impactful targets surrounding resource- and land-based revenues. This question becomes particularly pressing once Laos exits LDC status, losing significant official development aid in the process, with further resource investments a likely way to make up for the loss.

Conclusion

This chapter has traced the trajectories of rural policies through different phases of Laos' and Vietnam's shared socialist, market and professed sustainable development, which has followed an oftentimes uneasy balance between striving for a functional, then developing rural economy, and improving the living conditions of the rural population. This began with the period of 'high communist' transformation through agricultural collectivisation, the collapse of which quickly reinstated household-based and/or subsistence-oriented production and the resurgence of peasant ways of life. This process was driven by the resistance of cooperative members in Vietnam, while in Laos, although peasants fled collectivisation in large numbers, it was ultimately dismantled through economic necessity. As both countries launched reforms, the ongoing transformation of the countryside was increasingly driven by markets, whose influence and impacts spanned wider scales as regional integration gained momentum in the 1990s. Alongside 'high modernist' environmental state-making and sustainability ideals (Singh 2014), policies towards rural areas in both Laos and Vietnam have entailed continual state efforts to cultivate legibility and control over remote or 'non-state' spaces (Scott 1998), echoing earlier high communist collectivisation—albeit this time to foster the integration of marginal territories within the mainstream (De Koninck 1996). Increasing GMS and ASEAN integration and engagement with the international development sector have meanwhile played significant roles in remoulding the concept of rural development in both Laos and Vietnam, though with distinctive lingering socialist logics.

Yet the focus of the two regimes has moved ever farther from fundamental socialist concerns of collective welfare, and towards potentially irreconcilable emphases on exploiting natural resources and agricultural intensification on the one hand and sustainability on the other. Both Laos and Vietnam have aggressively pursued investments in land- and resource-intensive sectors since the market reforms and opening of borders. Where Vietnam has for the most part directed FDI inflows into manufacturing, bolstered by a large labour force and ease of maritime exports; comparative remoteness, low population density and a rich resource endowment contributed to Laos' rise as a frontier for investments in exploitation of land and natural resources—investments coming primarily from Vietnam and China. Laos' contemporary rural development has become increasingly geared towards primary sectors (initially forestry, and subsequently mining, plantation agriculture and hydropower) by leveraging large and sparsely populated land resources to attract commercial investments through concessions. This diverges from Vietnam's approach, not only because of its smaller land base relative to population, but also because the land pressures this created made the possibility of concession-based development politically unfeasible (Ingalls et al. 2018a).

Vietnam and Laos can further be argued to exhibit differentiated and geopolitically informed relations of interdependency with China, which have in turn played a role in steering development priorities in Laos towards meeting the needs of its neighbours for raw materials. The present pattern appears to entail flows of land-intensive, export-oriented investments from China and Vietnam to Laos; and raw commodities from Laos to Vietnam for domestic use, as well as processing and/or re-export to China. This reflects the influence of shifting regional politics over market relations between the so-termed post-socialist neighbours, and seemingly inexorable pivot away from socialist notions of rural development towards regionalised capitalist accumulation. China's equivalent trajectory from a poor agrarian society, via an experiment in command central planning on a vastly larger scale than Vietnam or Laos, to among the world's most powerful capitalist economies is well documented. More recently, the rapid growth that resulted from *Doi Moi* gave cause for bastions of global neoliberal policy to ponder the lessons for the capitalist world from Vietnam's 'market socialist' development model (Hansen 2015). Laos' rural revolutions may outwardly appear fractional compared to those of its neighbours, though perhaps not from the perspectives of the rural Lao population. A key question surrounds the will and ability of policymakers to regain control over the extractive 'frontier capitalism' that threatens to strip Laos' resource- and land-base, to the profit of political and economic elites and largely transnational investors. With significant decision powers held by provincial and district-level actors, it remains unclear whether and how the state may widen the benefits of resource-based growth, and steer Laos' present rural transformation towards some facsimile of the equitable society at the heart of earlier socialist ideals. Vietnam meanwhile takes up ASEAN chairmanship in 2020 in the wake of the wide-ranging 'Partnership for Sustainability' advanced under Thailand's tenure (ASEAN 2019), heavily prioritising regional security, strategic cooperation and growth. Given the environmental pressures mounting on rural places and people throughout the region, the meaning of sustainable development as catch-all ceremonial rhetoric appears more questionable than ever.

References

Adger, W.N., P.M. Kelly, A. Winkels, L.Q. Huy, and C. Locke. 2002. Migration, Remittances, Livelihood Trajectories, and Social Resilience. *Ambio* 31: 358–366.

Anh, N.T., J. Rigg, L.T.T. Huong, and D.T. Dieu. 2012. Becoming and Being Urban in Hanoi: Rural-Urban Migration and Relations in Vietnam. *Journal of Peasant Studies* 39: 1103–1131.

Anh, N.T., V.T.C. Ly, L.T. Hoa, and L.T.M. Trang. 2017. The Environment of Craft and Cottage Industry Villages in the Context of Viet Nam's New

Rural Development Process. *Journal of Social Sciences and Humanities* 3 (2): 187–202.

ASEAN. 2015. *Vision and Strategic Plan for ASEAN Cooperation in Food, Agriculture and Forestry*. ASEAN Ministers of Agriculture: Makati, Philippines.

ASEAN. 2016. *ASEAN Economic Community at a Glance*. Jakarta, Indonesia: ASEAN Secretariat.

ASEAN. 2019. ASEAN Leaders' Vision Statement on Partnership for Sustainability, June 23. Bangkok.

Asia Times. 2018. Laos Will Be a Least Developed Country Till 2024, PM Admits. Accessed online 7 November 2018. http://www.atimes.com/article/laos-will-be-a-least-developed-country-till-2024-pm-admits/.

Association of Southeast Asian Nations (ASEAN). 2008. *ASEAN Economic Community Blueprint*. Jakarta, Indonesia: ASEAN Secretariat.

Baird, I.G. 2011. The Don Sahong Dam: Potential Impacts on Regional Fish Migrations, Livelihoods, and Human Health. *Critical Asian Studies* 43 (2): 211–235.

Baird, I.G., and B. Shoemaker. 2007. Unsettling Experiences: Internal Resettlement and International Aid Agencies in Laos. *Development and Change* 38 (5): 865–888.

Banik, D., and A. Hansen. 2016. The Frontiers of Poverty Reduction in Emerging Asia. *Forum for Development Studies* 43 (1): 47–68.

Barney, K. 2009. Laos and the Making of a 'Relational' Resource Frontier. *The Geographical Journal* 175: 146–159.

Barney, K. 2012. Locating 'Green Neoliberalism,' and Other Forms of Environmental Governance in Southeast Asia. Newsletter 66. Center for Southeast Asian Studies, Kyoto University, 25–28.

Beresford, M. 1990. Vietnam: Socialist Agriculture in Transition. *Journal of Contemporary Asia* 20 (4): 466–486.

Beresford, M. 2008. Doi Moi in Review: The Challenges of Building Market Socialism in Vietnam. *Journal of Contemporary Asia* 38 (2): 221–243.

Bourdet, Y. 2000. *The Economics of Transition in Laos: From Socialism to ASEAN Integration*. Cheltenham: Edward Elgar.

Brown, M., and J.J. Zasloff. 1986. *Apprentice Revolutionaries: The Communist Movement in Laos, 1930–1985*. Standford, CA: Hoover Institution Press.

Castella, J.-C., and B. Bouahom. 2014. Farmer Cooperatives Are the Missing Link to Meet Market Demands in Laos. *Development in Practice* 24 (2): 185–198.

Castella, J.-C., G. Lestrelin, C. Hett, J. Bourgoin, Y.R. Fitriana, A. Heinimann, and J.-L. Pfund. 2013. Effects of Landscape Segregation on Livelihood Vulnerability: Moving from Extensive Shifting Cultivation to Rotational Agriculture and Natural Forests in Northern Laos. *Human Ecology* 41: 63–76.

Cole, R., G. Wong, M. Brockhaus, M. Moeliono, and M. Kallio. 2017. Objectives, Ownership and Engagement in Lao PDR's REDD+ Policy Landscape. *Geoforum* 83: 91–100.

Dang, T. 2018. *Vietnam's Post-1975 Agrarian Reforms: How Local Politics Derailed Socialist Agriculture in Southern Vietnam*. Canberra: ANU Press.

De Koninck, R. 1996. The Peasantry as the Territorial Spearhead of the State in Southeast Asia: The Case of Vietnam. *Sojourn: Journal of Social Issues in Southeast Asia* 11 (2): 231–258.

Delang, C.O., and M. Toro. 2011. Hydropower-Induced Displacement and Resettlement in the Lao PDR. *South East Asia Research* 19 (3): 567–594.

Do Ta Khanh, and A. Hansen. 2017. *Industrialising Agriculture: The Changing Food Production System in Vietnam and the Role of Large-Scale Enterprises*. Conference Paper, EuroSEAS, University of Oxford, August 16–18, 2017.

Dosch, J. 2006. Vietnam's ASEAN Membership Revisited: Golden Opportunity or Golden Cage? *Contemporary Southeast Asia* 28 (2): 234–258.

Ducourtieux, O., J.-R. Laffort, and S. Sacklokham. 2005. Land Policy and Farming Practices in Laos. *Development and Change* 36 (3): 499–526.

Dwyer, M.B. 2011. Building the Politics Machine: Tools for Resolving the Global Land Grab. Paper Presented at the International Conference on Global Land Grabbing, April 6–8, 2011, University of Sussex.

Dwyer, M.B., and M. Ingalls. 2015. *REDD+ at the Crossroads: Choices and Tradeoffs for 2015–2020 in Laos*. Working Paper 179. CIFOR: Bogor, Indonesia.

Dwyer, M.B., M.L. Ingalls and I.G. Baird. 2015. The Security Exception: Development and Militarization in Laos's Protected Areas. *Geoforum* 69: 207–217.

Evans, G. 1988. *Agrarian Change in Communist Laos*. Occasional Paper No. 85. Singapore: Institute of Southeast Asian Studies.

Evans, G. 1990. *Lao Peasants Under Socialism*. Chiang Mai: Silkworm Books.

Evans, G. 1991. Planning Problems in Peripheral Socialism: The Case of Laos. In *Laos: Beyond the Revolution*, ed. J.J. Zasloff and L. Unger. Basingstoke: Macmillan.

Evans, G. 1995. *Lao Peasants Under Socialism and Post-Socialism*. Chiang Mai: Silkworm Books.

Évrard, O. 2011. Oral Histories of Livelihoods and Migration Under Socialism and Post-socialism Among the Khmu of Northern Laos. In *Moving Mountains: Ethnicity and Livelihoods in Highland China, Vietnam and Laos*, ed. J. Michaud and T. Forsyth. Vancouver: UBC Press.

Fforde, A., and S. Sénèque. 1994. *The Economy and the Countryside in Vietnam: The Relevance of Rural Development Policies*. Economics Division Working Paper 94/5. Canberra: Australian National University.

Fox, J., Y. Fujita, D. Ngidang, N. Peluso, L. Potter, N. Sakuntaladewi, J. Sturgeon, and D. Thomas. 2009. Policies, Political-Economy, and Swidden in Southeast Asia. *Human Ecology* 37: 305–322.

Goldman, M. 2001. Constructing an Environmental State: Eco-Governmentality and Other Transnational Practices of a 'Green' World Bank. *Social Problems* 48 (4): 499–523.

Goscha, C. 2016. *Vietnam: A New History*. New York: Basic Books.

Government of Lao PDR (GoL). 2004. *National Growth and Poverty Eradication Strategy*. Poverty Reduction Strategy Paper. International Monetary Fund, Washington, DC.

Government of Lao PDR (GoL). 2017. *Decree on the Criteria for Poverty Graduation and Development*. Decree No. 348/GOL Dated 16 November 2017 (Unofficial translation).

Government of Lao PDR (GoL). 2018. *Emissions Reduction Program Document: Lao PDR*. Ministry of Agriculture and Forestry, Vientiane: Department of Forestry.

Government of Vietnam (GoV). 2010. *Decision Approving the National Target Program on New Rural Development in the Period 2010–2020* (English translation in Anh et al. 2017).

Hansen, A. 2015. The Best of Both Worlds? The Power and Pitfalls of Vietnam's Development Model. In *Emerging Economies and Challenges to Sustainability: Theories, Strategies, Local Realities*, ed. A. Hansen and U.B. Wethal. London: Routledge.

Hardy, A. 2000. Strategies of Migration to Upland Areas in Contemporary Vietnam. *Asia Pacific Viewpoint* 41 (1): 23–34.

Hardy, A. 2003. *Red Hills: Migrants and the State in the Highlands of Vietnam*. Copenhagen: NIAS Press.

Hett, C., J.-C. Castella, A. Heinimann, P. Messerli, and J.-L. Pfund. 2011. A Landscape Mosaics Approach for Characterizing Swidden Systems from a REDD+ Perspective. *Applied Geography* 32: 608–618.

Hett, C., V. Nanhthavong, S. Hanephom, A. Phommachanh, B. Sidavong, K. Phouangphet, M. Epprecht, J. Lu, A. Shattuck, M.L. Ingalls, R. Bernhard, S. Phathitmixay, C. Phomphakdy, and A. Heinimann. 2019. Land Deals in the Lao PDR: A Characterization of Investments in Land and Their Impacts. Centre for Development and Environment (CDE), University of Bern, Switzerland, and Ministry of Natural Resources and Environment (MoNRE), Ministry of Planning and Investment (MPI), Ministry of Agriculture and Forestry (MAF), Ministry of Energy and Mines (MEM) of the Lao PDR, Vientiane, Lao PDR.

High, H. 2014. *Fields of Desire: Poverty and Policy in Laos*. Singapore: NUS Press.

Hirsch, P. 2000. Underlying Causes of Deforestation in the Mekong Region. Report presented at regional workshop on Forest Management Strategies in the Mekong Region. National University of Laos, Vientiane.

Hirsch, P., M. Mellac, and N. Scurrah. 2015. *The Political Economy of Land Governance in Viet Nam*. Vientiane: Mekong Region Land Governance.

Hirsch, P., and N. Scurrah. 2015. *The Political Economy of Land Governance in Lao PDR*. Vientiane: Mekong Region Land Governance.

Ingalls, M.L., and M. Dwyer. 2016. Missing the Forest for the Trees? Navigating the Trade-Offs Between Mitigation and Adaptation Under REDD. *Climatic Change* 2 (136): 353–366.

Ingalls, M.L., P. Meyfroidt, P.X. To, M. Kenney-Lazar, and M. Epprecht. 2018a. The Transboundary Displacement of Deforestation Under REDD+: Problematic Intersections Between the Trade of Forest-Risk Commodities and Land Grabbing in the Mekong Region. *Global Environmental Change* 50: 255–267.

Ingalls, M.L., J.-C. Diepart, N. Truong, D. Hayward, T. Neil, C. Phomphakdy, R. Bernhard, S. Fogarizzu, M. Epprecht, V. Nanhthavong, D.H. Vo, D. Nguyen, P.A. Nguyen, T. Saphangthong, C. Inthavong, C. Hett, and N. Tagliarino. 2018b. *State of Land in the Mekong Region*. Centre for Development and Environment, University of Bern and Mekong Region Land Governance. Bern, Switzerland and Vientiane, Lao PDR, with Bern Open Publishing.

Intal, P. Jr. 2015. *AEC Blueprint Implementation Performance and Challenges: Investment Liberalization*. ERIA Discussion Paper Series 32. Economic Research Institute for ASEAN and East Asia (ERIA), Jakarta.

Jamieson, N.L. 1993. *Understanding Vietnam*. Berkeley: University of California Press.

Kallio, M.H., N.J. Hogarth, M. Moeliono, M. Brockhaus, R. Cole, I.W. Bong, and G.Y. Wong. 2018. The Colour of Maize: Visions of Green Growth and Farmers' Perceptions in Northern Laos. *Land Use Policy* 80: 185–194.

Kenney-Lazar, M. 2012. Plantation Rubber, Land Grabbing and Social-Property Transformation in Southern Laos. *Journal of Peasant Studies* 39 (3–4): 1017–1037.

Kenney-Lazar, M. 2013. Shifting Cultivation in Laos: Transitions in Policy and Perspective. Report Commissioned by the Secretariat of the Sector Working Group for Agriculture and Rural Development of Lao PDR, Vientiane.

Kerkvliet, B.J.T. 1995. Village-State Relations in Vietnam: The Effect of Everyday Politics on Decollectivization. *The Journal of Asian Studies* 54 (2): 396–418.

Kerkvliet, B.J.T. 1998. Wobbly Foundations: Building Co-operatives in Rural Vietnam, 1955–61. *South East Asia Research* 6 (3): 193–251.

Kerkvliet, B.J.T. 2005. *The Power of Everyday Politics: How Vietnamese Peasants Transformed National Policy*. Singapore: Institute of Southeast Asian Studies.
Kerkvliet, B.J.T. 2009. Everyday Politics in Peasant Societies (and Ours). *The Journal of Peasant Studies* 36 (1): 227–243.
Kerkvliet, B.J.T., and M. Selden. 1998. Agrarian Transformations in China and Vietnam. *The China Journal* 40: 37–58.
Lentz, Christian C. 2019. *Contested Territory—Dien Bien Phu and the Making of Northwest Vietnam*. New Haven and London: Yale University Press.
Luibrand, A. 2002. *Transition in Vietnam: Impact of the Rural Reform Process on an Ethnic Minority*. Development Economics and Policy series no. 31. Various locations, Peter Lang.
Markussen, T. 2015. *Land Issues in Vietnam 2006–14: Markets, Property Rights, and Investment*. Working Paper 2015/088. United Nations University World Institute for Development Economics Research.
McKay, A., C. Cazzuffi, and E. Perge. 2015. Commercialization in Agriculture in Rural Viet Nam, 2006–14. Wider Working Paper 2015/096. United Nations University World Institute for Development Economics Research.
Meyfroidt, P., and E.F. Lambin. 2008. The Causes of Reforestation in Vietnam. *Land Use Policy* 25: 182–197.
Meyfroidt, P., and E.F. Lambin. 2009. Forest Transition in Vietnam and Displacement of Deforestation Abroad. *Proceedings of the National Academy of Sciences of the United States of America* 106 (38): 16139–16144.
Meyfroidt, P., T.K. Rudel, and E.F. Lambin. 2010. Forest Transitions, Trade, and the Global Displacement of Land Use. *Proceedings of the National Academy of Sciences of the United States of America* 107 (49): 20917–20922.
Messerli, P., A. Heinimann, and M. Epprecht. 2009. Finding Homogeneity in Heterogeneity—A New Approach to Quantifying Landscape Mosaics Developed for the Lao PDR. *Human Ecology* 37: 291–304.
Moore, W., and S. Stanford. 2010. Why Do Some Countries Have a Long-Term Dependence on Food Aid? *Journal of Economic Studies* 37 (4): 438–454.
Mirza, H., and A. Giroud. 2004. Regionalization, Foreign Direct Investment and Poverty Reduction: Lessons from Vietnam in ASEAN. *Journal of the Asia Pacific Economy* 9 (2): 223–248.
Nam, C.W., and K.Y. Nam. 2008. Economic Factors Shaping Private Sector Development in the Greater Mekong Subregion. *Internationales Asien Forum* 39 (304): 325–341.
Ng, S.M. 1987. Laos in 1986: Into the Second Decade of Reconstruction. *Southeast Asian Affairs*. Singapore: Institute of Southeast Asian Studies.
Nguyen, Van Dang. 2001. *Lam Nghiep Vietnam* [Vietnam Forestry Sector]. Agricultural Publishing House, Hanoi.

Orr, S., J. Pittock, A. Chapagain, and D. Dumaresq. 2012. Dams on the Mekong River: Lost Fish Protein and the Implications for Land and Water Resources. *Global Environmental Change* 22: 925–932.

Pham, T.T., M. Moeliono, T.H. Nguyen, H.T. Nguyen, T.H. Vu. 2012. *The Context of REDD+ in Vietnam: Drivers, Agents and Institutions*. Occasional Paper No. 75. Bogor, Indonesia: Center for International Forestry Research (CIFOR).

Pholsena, V. 2005. Laos in 2004: Towards Subregional Integration: 10 years on. *Southeast Asian Affairs*, 173–188.

Pholsena, V., and R. Banomyong. 2006. *Laos: From Buffer State to Crossroads?*. Chiang Mai, Thailand: Mekong Press.

Phraxayavong, V. 2009. *History of Aid to Laos: Motivations and Impacts*. Chiang Mai: Mekong Press.

Pingali, P.L., and V.-T. Xuan. 1992. Vietnam: Decollectivization and Rice Productivity Growth. *Economic Development and Cultural Change* 40 (4): 697–718.

Ravallion, M., and D. van de Walle. 2008. *Land in Transition: Reform and Poverty in Rural Vietnam*. Washington, DC: World Bank.

Raymond, C. 2008. 'No Responsibility and No Rice': The Rise and Fall of Agricultural Collectivisation in Vietnam. *Agricultural History* 82 (1): 43–61.

Razal, A.R., A.F.F. Firmalino, and M.C.S. Guerrero. 2015. *Impact of the ASEAN Economic Community (AEC) on Social Forestry and Forestry Products Trade*. Jakarta: ASEAN Social Forestry Network Non-Timber Forest Products Exchange Programme.

Rigg, J. 2005. *Living with Transition in Laos: Market Integration in Southeast Asia*. London and New York: Routledge.

Rigg, J. 2007. *An Everyday Geography of the Global South*. Oxford: Routledge.

Scott, J.C. 1976. *The Moral Economy of the Peasant: Rebellion and Subsistence in Southeast Asia*. New Haven: Yale University Press.

Scott, J.C. 1985. *Weapons of the Weak: Everyday Forms of Peasant Resistance*. New Haven: Yale University Press.

Scott, J.C. 1998. *Seeing Like a State: How Certain Schemes to Improve the Human Condition have Failed*. Newhaven: Yale Agrarian Studies.

Scott, J.C. 2009. *The Art of Not Being Governed: An Anarchist History of Upland Southeast Asia*. Newhaven: Yale University Press.

Scurrah, N., and P. Hirsch. 2015. *Foreign Direct Investment and Land Access: Extended Synopsis*. The Regional Centre for Social Science and Sustainable Development: Chiang Mai University.

Singh, S. 2012. *Natural Potency and Political Power: Forests and State Authority in Contemporary Laos*. Honolulu: University of Hawai'i Press.

Singh, S. 2014. Developing Bureaucracies for Environmental Governance: State Authority and World Bank Conditionality in Laos. *Journal of Contemporary Asia* 44 (2): 322–341.

Stuart-Fox, M. 1995. Laos: Towards Subregional Integration. *Southeast Asian Affairs*, 177–195.

Stuart-Fox, M. 1996. *Buddhist Kingdom, Marxist State: The Making of Modern Laos*. Bangkok: White Lotus.

Tarp, F., ed. 2015. *Growth, Structural Transformation, and Rural Change in Viet Nam*. UNU-WIDER Studies in Development Economics. Oxford University Press.

Thanh, V.T. 2015. Managing Domestic Consensus for ASEAN Community Building in Vietnam. *Journal of Southeast Asian Economics* 32 (2): 275–288.

Thayer, C.A. 1982. Laos and Vietnam: The Anatomy of a 'Special Relationship'. In *Contemporary Laos. Studies in the Politics and Society of the Lao People's Democratic Republic*, ed. M. Stuart-Fox. St Lucia: University of Queensland Press.

The Diplomat. 2018. Laos Dam Collapse Brings Flood of Questions. Accessed online 7 November 2018. https://thediplomat.com/2018/07/laos-dam-collapse-brings-flood-of-questions/.

The Guardian. 2018. Laos Dam Collapse: Work Continues on Huge Projects Despite Promised Halt. Accessed online 7 November 2018. https://www.theguardian.com/world/2018/aug/21/laos-dam-collapse-work-continues-on-huge-projects-despite-promised-halt.

Tran, V.C. 2006. Migration and Tropical Forests in the Central Highlands of Vietnam. In *The Social Ecology of Tropical Forests—Migration*, ed. W. De Jong, L. Tuck-Po, and A. Ken-Ichi. Populations and Frontiers: Kyoto University Press.

Vandergeest, P. 2003. Land to Some Tillers: Development-Induced Displacement in Laos. *International Social Science Journal* 55 (175): 47–56.

Vongvisouk, T., R.B. Broegaard, O. Mertz, and S. Thongmanivong. 2016. Rush for Cash Crops and Forest Protection: Neither Land Sparing Nor Land Sharing. *Land Use Policy* 55: 182–192.

Woodside, A. 1989. History, Structure and Revolution in Vietnam. *International Political Science Review* 10 (2): 143–157.

Wong, T. 2010. *Making the Mekong: Nature, Region, Postcoloniality*. PhD thesis. Department of Geography, Ohio State University.

World Commission on Environment and Development (WCED). 1987. *Our Common Future*. New York: United Nations.

CHAPTER 7

Evolving Environmental Governance Structures in a Market Socialist State: The Case of Vietnam

Stephan Ortmann

Introduction

Environmental protection has become a pressing concern in Vietnamese politics in recent years because most people are faced daily with many apparent environmental problems which have been the consequence of rapid economic development under a weak environmental state. Similar to other developing countries like China, which has also prioritized economic growth in the past, air pollution clogs the cities, often smells badly, and causes unknown numbers of deaths and other health-related issues. Many of the rivers are seriously polluted as large amounts of wastewater are discharged directly into the waterways without any treatment. The growing amount of waste fills unsanitary landfills and is ruining the drinking water and causing serious smells. These downsides of the rapid economic development of the past decades are compounded

S. Ortmann (✉)
Centre of China Studies, Chinese University of Hong Kong,
Sha Tin, Hong Kong
e-mail: stephan.ortmann@cuhk.edu.hk

A. Hansen et al. (eds.), *The Socialist Market Economy in Asia*,
https://doi.org/10.1007/978-981-15-6248-8_7

by increasingly violent weather as a result of climate change, an issue which is especially pertinent for Vietnam's low-lying areas. The threats include flooding of coastal areas, salt water destroying farm land, and extreme droughts. The World Bank has declared the country as one of the five most affected countries when it comes to climate change (World Bank 2013). In addition to the increasing visibility of the problem, international pressure and support have also increased significantly. As a consequence, the government has allowed new forms of governance to emerge that reflect changes in the interaction between the state, the market, and the society, which are the focus of this chapter.

As Vietnam has abandoned the planned economy in 1986 under Doi Moi (Reformation) and has since shifted toward a more plural market-oriented economy, this has necessitated a transformation of the governmental institutions, which has resulted in more professional, less hierarchical, and more transparent governance structures. There have been efforts to strengthen the capacity of the central as well as local governments. Another outcome has been a rapid increase of NGOs, networks between different actors, and a growing involvement of increasingly powerful industries. Slowly, the hierarchical structures of the government are being opened for greater participation by new political actors, such as local and international non-governmental organizations, who have carved out political space to influence government decisions.

Even though environmental policy-making and institution building have made significant progress, the most important part of environmental politics, the implementation of environmental legislation, is still severely lacking. This is due to the fact that the Vietnamese government lacks the capacity to enforce environmental regulations, while at the same time it is reluctant to abandon its top-down approach, preferring "environmental management" over "environmental governance." Enhancing participatory mechanisms, the development of an independent legal system, and other attempts to increase transparency and accountability entail that the ruling Vietnamese Communist Party would have to share more power, which it has publicly rejected. Instead of allowing greater checks-and-balances, the Market-Leninist regime relies primarily on economic growth as the basis for its legitimacy, which complicates the efforts of environmental protection.

Nevertheless, there has been a slow transformation from a purely hierarchical system to a hybrid system which, even though it is still dominated by top-down mechanisms, allows a certain degree of pluralism that can best be described as "evolving environmental governance." In order to develop an understanding of this process, I employ an integrated multiple-actor network approach which includes the linkages between key actors in the policy field and is based partially on in-depth interviews with some of the most important players within these networks. In addition, I also analyzed a range of other sources including newspaper reports in the Vietnamese press, official government documents, and websites of environmental organizations.

Evolving Environmental Governance

While traditionally, most attention has been focused on governments dealing with environmental problems, scholars as well as practitioners are increasingly focusing on what has become known as "environmental governance" (Lemos and Agrawal 2006). Proponents of this concept argue that complex environmental problems require more than just the government's top-down implementation of environmental policies but also the involvement of society and business (Rozzaque 2013). For developmental aid organizations, this has meant the need to find local nongovernmental partners in addition to working with the government. From an academic perspective, it has entailed research on the kind of interactions and mechanisms that exist between the government, societal actors, businesses, and international actors. Cooperation and partnerships between the different groups of actors are seen as beneficial to the development of more effective sustainable development. Clearly, none of these relationships is free of conflict and by focusing only on successful examples, the governance perspective tends to underestimate the inherent contradictions that can arise between the various players. Nevertheless, greater collaborations do lead to a degree of trust between the players that has overall led to more positive results. As Michael Mann (1986) has observed, the despotic power of the state is not sufficient to achieve the goal of policy-makers in a modern state. Instead, infrastructural power is needed to overcome resistance from society, which includes industries and individuals. Put in simple terms, punishments alone are rarely effective in achieving the cultural change necessary to develop an environmental consciousness.

As a consequence of the growing interaction between state and non-state actors, the boundaries between them have become less distinct and the latter often take on responsibilities previously the sole domain of the state. Implicit in this description is that new power dependencies emerge between those institutions. As Benz et. al. (2007) argue governance describes the patterns of interaction between the state and societal actors. Instead of a pure control situation in which the state both regulates and mandates other actors, the state itself becomes dependent on non-state actors for both cooperation and compliance, which occurs in networks of actors that govern themselves autonomously. In this process, the government often takes the role of steering and guiding other actors toward goals of the national agenda (Stoker 1998). In general, most scholars arguing for a "governance perspective" have stressed a general trend away from strong hierarchies toward more mutually cooperative arrangements.

Traditionally, the basic elements of governance seem to completely contradict the role of the state in authoritarian regimes, which are thought to be governed mainly through top-down processes. According to Sigley (2006), socialist one-party states prefer a "technoscientific" approach to deal with any administrative problems. This is based on the belief that a technical solution to any problem can be found, which then necessitates a strong party-state to deal with. Despite its potential for rapid response, authoritarian regimes have, however, a far worse track record in regard to the environment. This is not only due to the fact that most lack the power to implement environmental legislation or that the countries have low environmental awareness due to weak societal involvement (Gilley 2012) but more importantly because authoritarian regimes are governed by a small group of people that profit disproportionately from the exploitation of the environment. In addition they depend on economic growth for providing spoils to specific elite groups in order to quell possible discontent and maintain power.

The only time environmental problems actually become important for the authoritarian leader is when the situation is so serious that it threatens the social stability, which essentially forces the government to become more inclusive. In order to avoid potential threats to its power, hierarchically organized one-party states have introduced new governance mechanisms, which has been analyzed extensively in China (Howell 2004; Shi and Zhang 2006; Economy 2006). This includes the strengthening of environmental institutions, the development and improvement of regulatory networks, the emergence and involvement of non-governmental organizations, the decentralization and strengthening of local environmental capacity, the development of market mechanisms to create incentives for environmental protection. These are just some examples that demonstrate that environmental politics in market Leninist regimes have been transformed.

The key problem, however, is the fact that historically state socialist countries lack the separation between the three spheres of the governance perspective. The state is basically still the main owner of key industries and thus more intimately linked with those interests. While even in the best democracies, lobby groups have gained significant influence over the state, the functional separation has allowed state institutions some degree of independence in implementing environmental legislation, sometimes with the help of courts. Moreover, in a market socialist system, industry is still subordinate to the state, which reduces the possibility of partnerships. While some have argued that this theoretically enhances the state's capacity to implement environmental technologies, in reality this is stifled by the competing interest with economic development. Similar problems exist for the role of civil society, which is far less independent than in Western countries. Non-governmental organizations, for instance, are required to register with government institutions and follow very restrictive rules. The state rarely is willing to grant these actors enough power to fulfill functions usually part of the state. In general, the government prefers a hierarchical top-down process which makes true partnerships highly unlikely.

In order to develop an understanding of the ongoing transformations, it is necessary to modify the predominantly static concept of governance and make it useful for the analysis of what are essentially constantly changing interactions between different actors. The goal is to capture both the emerging complexities of the new patterns of politics while also directing our attention to the processes that enable and obstruct their emergence. I thus adopt the concept of "evolving governance" to analyze the changes which occur as a result of the political adaptation to the economic transformation in Vietnam. In particular, the rising significance of environmental concerns, both in terms of increasingly becoming a challenge as the economy has become much more advanced and in terms of perception as political actors have become more aware of the negative consequences of unfettered economic growth.

This chapter thus argues that the concept of evolving governance captures the reality of Vietnamese state-society interaction better than the concept of state-corporatism. While Vietnam fulfills many aspects of corporatism, such as the attempt to closely control societal players by tying them to the state (Jeong 1997), the approach fails to recognize the growing influence of independent-minded NGOs and unregistered networks of activists (as opposed to coopted traditional NGOs), volunteering beyond the state (Wells-Dang 2010). It also ignores the involvement of international actors, which at times even participate in the policy-making process (McCarty 2001). Similarly, however, the still dominant role of the state also precludes the usefulness of a society-centric perspective in countries ruled by a Communist Party (Gilley 2011). Societal actors have grown in importance but their power is still heavily curtailed by a dominant state. Ignoring this fact potentially gets a biased understanding of the significance of (civil) society in Vietnam.

The approach used here is twofold: first, I want to create a broad perspective of environmental politics by including all the actors and not just the state. Secondly, I will trace the emerging governance patterns which involve various different types of networks as well as the adoption of market-based approaches. In other words, the analysis will demonstrate that despite all of the shortcomings in implementing environmental policies, there have been significant steps toward developing and adapting new approaches to dealing with environmental problems.

The Party-State

An analysis of Vietnam's environmental state is crucial for our understanding of how environmental politics works in the market socialist regime. In addition to sketching the existing institutions, both formal and informal, it is the necessary to add a historical dimension to the analysis because environmental politics is still very much a work in progress. It is necessary to recognize that the government is not a monolith but instead a heterogeneous edifice which has undergone significant market-oriented reforms that have replaced the planned economy of the Communist era. In the following, I will concentrate on the most important changes: There have been a number of institutional reforms meant to consolidate environmental policy-making and enhance the power of environmental concerns within the government. Part of this has been an increasing professionalization of the environmental state. As a consequence, there have also been a number of legal reforms that have strengthened Vietnam's environmental state. To more effectively implement the rules but also to increase the leverage of the environmental officials, there has been a push for greater transparency. Finally, there have also been attempts to improve the implementation of environmental regulations which, many government officials acknowledge, has so far been the least successful aspect of the reform process.

Before it is possible to evaluate these changes, it is important to understand some basic institutional aspects of the Vietnamese state. The dominant force is the Communist Party which in theory represents the people as a whole and which may not be questioned. Most of the members of Vietnam's legislature, constitutionally the highest organ of the state, are also members of the Communist Party. Next to the party is the state apparatus which has mainly administrative tasks but is also deeply involved in the policy-making process. It too is closely linked to the Party through membership. The state consists of many ministries which are given certain areas of responsibility, which overlap to some degree, and which have different positions within an informal internal hierarchy. Due to the size of the state and the lack of transparency, few if any are able to fully understand the workings of the government. Last but not least, there are many local governments in its 58 provinces and five municipalities. The central government does not have direct control over local governments, which often "interpret central policies any way they like, ignore central policy with impunity, or comply only when subsidies are provided" (Vu 2014: 32). The lack of unity within the government has made it necessary for respective administrators, who are interested in making some difference, to become advocates in a heterogeneous network of actors and use various mechanisms to achieve some change.

Environmental politics is very new in Vietnam. In the 1990s, most of the Vietnamese government focused almost solely on economic development at the expense of natural resources and the environment. The National Development Strategy until 2020 passed at the Eighth Party Congress of the VCP in 1996 did not even mention the environment (Bach 2004). Since then Vietnam's government has made great progress. The Law of Environmental Protection was first enacted in 1994, revised in 2004 and 2014, and is presently being revised yet again. Many other laws and legal documents related to environmental issues were also passed. Three environmental strategies were conceived and environmental goals have eventually become an integral part of the country's sustainable development strategy. On August 12, 2012, Vietnam's Prime Minister Nguyen Tan Dung approved the Viet Nam Sustainable Development Strategy for 2011–2020, which incorporated environmental protection as a key cornerstone of national development.

One of the most important processes in recent years has been the rapid pace of professionalization of environmental politics. A crucial part in this process has been the establishment of a number of think tanks within the ministry, which enable "evidence based policy making" (Stone 2005: 9). This not only enhances the quality of environmental policy but also increases the power of the ministry within the informal power structure which consequently can raise pressure on the rest of the government. Traditionally, the environmental ministry has been one of the weaker institutions within the government. Through the use of hard evidence, the ministry tries to create a consensus on environmental policy that is hard to ignore. The professionalization is most visible in the publication of the environmental strategy, which happens once in a decade. The 2003 strategy is still very broad and rather superficial in its approach. It states that environmental protection is "the task of the whole society" which is achieved under the "leadership of the Party" and the "management of the State" (Government of Vietnam 2003: 10). Overall, the document lays out a perhaps overly ambitious program, which could not have been met. While in the 2003 strategy document, there are still references to the party and its organizations, this is no longer the case in the 2012 strategy. In addition, the document's presentation has become much more professional. Instead of the simple, black and white layout of the 2003 strategy, the 2012 document was printed on glossy paper with colorful images in solid book format. The book includes both a Vietnamese and English version which is helpful for the many international organizations active in Vietnam. The international cooperation, moreover, also extended to the development of the document from the support of international experts who provided advice to the eventual printing of the document, which was facilitated by the Hanns Seidel Foundation.

Secondly, there is an increasing consolidation of environmental matters within a single environmental ministry. In 1993, the National Environmental Agency was established under the newly created Ministry of Science, Technology and Environment (MOSTE) together with environmental management divisions at local levels. Environmental concerns were further strengthened in 2002 when the Ministry of Natural Resources and Environment (MONRE) was created and NEA became the Vietnam Environment Administration (VEA). Presently, there are discussions on forming an independent Ministry of the Environment. This process meant to reduce the conflicts of interest between different ministries and streamline policy-making. The goal of this consolidation is also to increase the influence of the ministry within the government and thus put greater pressure on environmental concerns. Officials within the environmental ministry are aware that much of the government is concerned with other issues such as economic development and awareness for environmental concerns still remains low. However, while increasing the power of the environmental ministry is the key concern of the administrative reorganization, it is also necessary to mainstream environmental concerns in the Vietnamese government. To achieve this, a number of ministries have established a department related to the environment. For instance, the Ministry of Transport now includes its own Department of Environment, which is not linked directly to MONRE. In addition, the National Assembly, the legislature, has also established a permanent committee which includes environmental issues.

Despite the consolidation into an increasingly powerful environmental ministry, environmental officials have been adamant about maintaining a consensus orientation for policy-making. Developing the environmental strategy, for instance, is a long drawn out process with multiple stages in which the different ministries and local governments participate. The purpose of these discussions is to attain greater support for environmental concerns from other ministries, which still often lack interest or knowledge about environmental concerns. Other stakeholders including businesses and communities may also be heard but are not accorded a central role in the process. Essentially, their input is only sought at the beginning of the process. Still, Vietnam's environmental strategy has become an ambitious document that has far reaching targets.

In order to improve the environmental management, the government has not only aimed toward strengthening its capacity but also heavily relied on the cooperation of international actors, which will be discussed later. It is, however, noteworthy at this point to highlight the growing willingness to engage in formal networks set up in cooperation with these foreign institutions. They allow the government to become more effective in both policy-making and implementation. The former can be seen in the Technical Working Group on the Environment (TWGE) which meets twice a year and provides a common forum to link international donors such as the Asian Development Bank (ADB), World Bank, the Japanese International Cooperation Agency (JICA), the Danish International Development Agency (DANIDA), and others with the Vietnamese government. A goal has been to improve the environmental impact assessment process, which still has many shortcomings. Donor organizations such as the ADB demand that impact assessments, with its involvement of all stakeholders, should be conducted at a very early stage of a new project as well as have a decisive influence on both the planning and implementation phase of a project, which is not yet the case in Vietnam (Clausen et.al. 2011).

In contrast to formulating new laws and ambitious strategies, their implementation is often much less successful. Instead, local governments are often incapable of effectively translating environmental policy into outcomes. The government is deeply aware of this problem as manifested in their environmental strategy (MONRE 2011). The lack of environmental state capacity is reflected in the lack of sufficient qualified staff and the lack of environmental awareness among many officials. On the one hand, this is due to the lack of sufficient resources as the government spends only one percent of its budget on the environment. On the other hand, however, local officials are also not skilled enough to even make use of the meager environmental funds available to them.

Particularly important for the success of the implementation of environmental policies (as well as other policies) are informal networks and relationships. Similar to China and other East Asian societies, relationships play a particularly important role in daily life. In particular, family bonds are strong and burden individuals with extra responsibilities. Moreover, while they potentially have a great impact on any attempts to enhance policy implementation and may be more important than institutional structures, they are often difficult to detect, especially to uninitiated outside observers. They are thus not only difficult for any rational bureaucratic implementation but also frustrating to foreign organizations which are supporting the Vietnamese state to enhance its capacity.

Part of the informal structures is corruption, which has a direct impact on environmental protection efforts. In 2018, Vietnam ranked 117th in the 2018 Transparency International Corruption Perception Index, which covers 180 countries in the world. This is much worse than China, which ranked 87th. Moreover, Transparency International has indicated that corruption is getting worse and the Vietnamese are least likely to expose corruption in Southeast Asia (An 2013). As corruption is widespread, powerful corporations, especially state-owned corporations, are likely able to resort to extralegal methods to avoid stringent environmental protection efforts. This problem could be overcome with institutions that can effectively monitor the government, such as an independent judiciary.

However, a system of checks-and-balances would weaken the dominance of the Communist Party and is thus unlikely to be implemented.

The Society

The emergence and rapid growth of new societal actors is the clearest indicator of the evolving governance structures. Compared to the past, these groups are starting to play an unprecedented role in policy-making and implementation. This is particularly evident in the rapid increase of so-called Vietnamese non-governmental organizations (VNGOs). For instance, in his study of Vietnam's civil society, Wischermann (2010) identified an increase of civic associations from 709 in 2003 to 1453 in 2009 in Hanoi and Ho Chi Minh City combined. A growing number of organizations are focusing on environmental issues, a sphere where activism outside of the state apparatus has been tolerated and even sometimes encouraged. According to the leader of one of the most prominent Vietnamese NGOs, PanNature, there are around 20–30 active nature NGOs in Vietnam. This, however, excludes the hundreds of technical research centers which many also consider as environmental NGOs. Even the government has helped in the formation of "NGOs" which are headed by former influential government officials and which are reminiscent of government organized non-governmental organizations (GONGOs) in China.

In addition to growing numbers of NGOs, there has also been an increase in environmental protests in local communities. Faced with a deteriorating living environment, many people have tried to pressure local governments and businesses to comply with environmental regulations and in some cases they have been successful. O'Rourke (2004) has called this community-driven regulation. However, the fact that this only works in some instances and depends on several factors including whether the community is unified, can get the support of local officials, and the strategies of the activists, clearly demonstrates that this cannot be called "regulation" but is rather selective compliance. Even in some successful cases, companies only comply to the minimum extent necessary or revert to their old behavior after the pressure has subsided. In addition, few of the newly emerging organizations have created linkages with communities and build on cases of successful resistance. Only environmental journalists, which are also growing in number and influence, have helped community activists in drawing attention to their plight. The emergence of social media has also helped activists to mobilize communities for environmental causes. For instance, in Hanoi, citizens used Facebook to successfully prevent the cutting of old trees along the city's roads (Vu 2017). The government has, however, not always been tolerant toward bottom-up activism. Most prominently, is the 2016 crackdown on protests against the massive pollution by the Taiwanese Formasa Ha Tinh Steel corporation that had affected three provinces. The movement had become a national issue with protests in major cities and was thus viewed as a threat to the one-party regime (Ortmann 2017).

Traditional socialist mass organizations under the Fatherland Front, which are the traditional form of social organization in Vietnam and thus encompass a large section of the society, also play a limited role in environmental politics. For instance, a study on an environmental rehabilitation program in Than Xuan showed that the women's union was the most active organization in the project. The union members participated in waste collection activities and raised awareness among citizens for proper waste management. In addition, the women's union also oversaw the involvement of the youth union. However, these organizations are mostly controlled by the hierarchical organizational structure of the Party and state, for instance the president of the women's union is being paid by the city of Hanoi, and thus rarely act independently except for some minor projects (Parenteau and Ngyuen 2005).

A growing number of networks have emerged linking different NGOs and allowing them to combine resources. The advantages for small NGOs is to collaborate on different projects and to exchange information. Moreover, the networks also enable some of the NGOs to cooperate with international actors because they create credibility and trust. However, such networks are not useful for everyone. PanNature does not see networks as helpful for its activities because they create competition for the scarce project funding. Moreover, NGO networks are separate from networks that link international NGOs as well as the government. This entails that local NGO networks have it difficult to play a more important role in forming an effective movement.

Most of the research dealing with this rise of societal activism and network formation has concentrated on the question whether there is a civil society in the making. The key issue of contention rests with the definition of the term civil society because Vietnam's authoritarian regime has allowed very little space for truly independent activism (Norlund 2007; Thayer 2009; Wells-Dang 2010). A number of scholars working on Vietnam have argued for identifying action that resembles civil society activities (Hannah 2007; Wischermann 2010). While this reveals that politics in Vietnam exists beyond the narrow confides of the state, it does not help in understanding either the magnitude of such activity nor influence. Vietnam's party-state has not fully embraced the idea of civil society, which is considered by many as problematic in regard to Communist ideology and thus never publicly included in any statements. Instead, it has sought to include the newly emerging organizations within a corporatist system. The strong inclination toward centralized control has made it very difficult for societal players, which are forced to be registered with the government, to truly reflect societal demands. In particular, it has made them wary of political conflicts even when it runs counter to their own perspectives.

Non-governmental organizations have remained very weak, with few members and very few financial resources (Taylor et. al. 2012). The fact that they are registered with the government and many actually work for and are funded by the government as well as donor organizations has raised questions over whether they should actually be called non-governmental organizations (Aschhoff 2008). The majority focuses solely on technical solutions and has very limited influence in the political system. Because the government remains suspicious of any organization outside of government control, it has been reluctant to reduce its control. The legal framework governing the registration and management of civil society organizations is very restrictive. In particular, the process of registering a membership organization is especially tedious (Nguyen 2008).

There are some indicators that the state is willing to improve the ability of civil society organizations to operate. New regulations are devised to increase the ability of nongovernmental groups to participate in the environmental sector, which would create more opportunities for people to work in the environmental field. These organizations should have the right to provide information, engage in dialogue with the government, be able to conduct independent tests and suggestions as well as issue complaints about environmental problems (Government of Vietnam 2012). However, due to the authoritarian nature of the Vietnamese state with the predominance of the Vietnam Communist Party, which seeks to represent the society as a whole, the barriers for greater civil society activism are significant. Dissent is discouraged and can have serious consequences as demonstrated in the arrest of influential activists and the blocking of activist websites during the campaign against a potentially environmentally hazardous bauxite mining project in the Central Highlands between 2007 and 2010 (Marston 2012). In other words, while governance structures are slowly evolving in regard to the nongovernmental sector, the future development is heavily contingent on political changes within the state apparatus.

The Business Sector

In order for environmental governance to be truly effective, the government needs the support and cooperation of the business sector. Basically, there are three different options. The first is to use fines and other punishments to force compliance. Secondly, the business sector can be convinced that environmental protection is congruent with company goals. There are basically two approaches to achieve this. A consumer or polluter pays principle induces companies to switch to more environmental friendly technologies. Another approach relies on education and training to show companies how environmental protection can be beneficial to the company. Finally, there have even been attempts to develop complex mechanisms that include both fines and incentives to deal with local business interests.

The most common method remains the use of fines or other punishments to force compliance. In Vietnam, a wide array of fines exist for violations of environmental laws. The particular focus of these fines is the sustainable management of natural resources. The use of fines so far has not had the desired effect as there are basically two challenges that government administrators face. First of all, the fines are too low and companies rather pay them than to invest in new technologies. In this regard, the government is in the process of increasing the fines. According to Decree No. 179, as of 2014 companies are faced with fines reaching up to two billion VND (approximately USD 94,280). In general companies either ignore the fines or pay them instead of upgrading their equipment, which is in most cases much more expensive. They thus have little impact on the environment. Moreover, the government has come to rely on the payment of the fines which enhances the environmental ministry's meager budget. Secondly, policing of environmental offenders is lagging. Lack of sufficient staff at local environmental departments means that very few companies are forced to pay fines. Moreover, it is nearly impossible to bring a polluting company to court because a company cannot be sued and instead an individual needs to be found directly responsible. It is thus no surprise that there has not yet been any successful court case. The government has recognized this problem and is working on new legislation that would alleviate this problem.

While fines are often seen as the best method to deal with environmental offenses, a much more effective method obviously would be to demonstrate how environmental protection can be in the interest of businesses. This can naturally be achieved through the introduction of fees for the usage and disposition of resources, such as water, electricity, waste, etc. As a consequence, companies may be enticed to invest in more efficient technologies to save money. While in principle sound, the implementation is quite complex and often runs into conflict with economic growth interests. Lack of sufficient qualified government staff again is the main obstacle in enforcing these fees as a majority of companies simply refuse to pay (Le 2009). A much less contentious approach is the attempt to educate companies of the benefits of environmental protection in what has been called the Cleaner Production Mechanism. In many instances, companies are not aware of the long-term savings by implementing environmentally friendly methods. For instance, energy saving through more efficient machines or modern light bulbs can effectively drive down the costs of enterprises. The government has commissioned studies to show the benefit of energy saving light bulbs which can be used to convince businesses of their value. The information needed to find such a beneficial approach can be complex. Moreover, Vietnam's bureaucratic businesses are wary of change and generally reluctant to upgrade when initial investments are high (Mitchell 2006; Nguyen and Ngo 2013).

Obviously, it is impossible to always find a situation in which a mutually beneficial approach can be found. Instead of merely falling back on punishments and better policing, which of course is essential as well, the Vietnamese have also tried to develop more complex solutions that combine elements of payments and benefits. The approach which has been called Payment for Environmental Services requires those people who benefit from the clean environment to pay a fee and the money is channeled to those who would benefit from its destruction (Nguyen 2011). This system has been piloted in the forestry sector of the two provinces of Lam Dong and Son La. The areas who benefit from the tourism downstream are made to pay a tax that is channeled through an environmental fund to those people who would benefit from logging upstream. This kind of scheme, however, is very complex and difficult to implement. In the case of this project, it was achieved with the help of foreign donors (To et. al. 2012).

In summary, it is noteworthy that despite all of these approaches, Vietnam lags behind other rapidly developing countries, including China. The governance approach is the least well developed in regard to the business sector. The dominant approach still relies on fines to enforce compliance, which are either paid without making any changes or completely ignored. Legal enforcement of environmental regulations is also often ineffective. The attempt to entice and convince corporations to comply and the use of more complex mechanisms is sill rudimentary and has succeeded in only a few instances. This is reflected in the low interest in environmental technologies. In order to make significant progress, greater attention must be paid toward developing effective governance structures in regard to businesses, which involves them directly in the process.

The Role of International Actors

A main reason behind the evolving environmental governance structures rests with the significant presence of international players in the country. The growing international focus on environmental politics has been the realization that environmental problems do not stop at national borders but have an impact on the whole planet. Developing countries such as Vietnam have been able to profit from the growing international attention to environmental concerns. International organizations, which include both governmental and nongovernmental as well as national and multinational organizations, have poured great amounts of money into various different development projects in developing countries to assist them in their development. Many developed countries have created donor organizations that provide funding and low interest rate loans to poorer nations, in part out of a sense of responsibility for the disparities which are the negative outgrowth of economic globalization. In Vietnam, there are more than 30 international actors including UN organizations which play a significant role in environmental protection efforts (it is difficult to count the number as there are many different forms of organization). Many of these organizations have opened an office in Vietnam, mostly in Hanoi due to the city's political center, and some also have additional offices in other parts of the country, most notably in Ho Chi Minh City, the economic powerhouse.

International actors have a significant impact on the environmental governance in Vietnam. They provide financial resources and expert knowledge, help enhance policies and institutions, contribute to the increase in capacity of government officials for policy implementation, and finally enhance the awareness of environmental concerns as well as the need for greater involvement of more actors in the process. In essence, international organizations are promoting the idea of environmental governance and supporting the need for civil society. For instance, the promotion of "payment for eco-system services" (PES), which has sought to introduce a market in forest management, has been promoted by a wide variety of different actors from the World Bank and the United Nations Development Program (UNDP) to international NGOs dealing with biodiversity and poverty. While the project has sought to introduce market mechanisms in which certain actors pay for the protection of forests, which are valued as "ecosystem-services," the Vietnamese state has maintained strong control over the implementation and widespread notions of equity have inhibited the spread of neoliberal ideas. Nevertheless, as Pamela McElwee (2016: 205) attests "PES continues to pick up steam in Vietnam, with a multitude of new donor projects and the attention and the support of the state. These networks have been important in pushing forward new iterations of environmental rule." In the process, new governance structures are created that seek to deal with environmental problems more effectively, even if that does not always happen.

Most importantly, both governmental and nongovernmental actors have been significant sources of funding for environmental projects or for the need to include environmental concerns in developmental projects. Money often comes in the form of low interest loans but can also be donations. The role of international actors often extends beyond the primary task of providing project funding to also include active support in the form of experts. The Vietnamese government and international actors sometimes cooperate by setting up their own organizations. This close cooperation allows the international actors to actively participate in the environmental policy implementation process. For instance, the Vietnam Environmental Governance Project (VPEG), which ran from 2008 until 2013, has aided the local governments in a number of provinces by enhancing their capacity and developing mechanisms for future improvements. At certain stages, international experts were involved in assisting the implementation of the individual projects at the local level. Nevertheless, there was also significant reluctance to allow more support from foreign experts because they could get too deeply involved in political issues.

International actors are also involved in the policy-making process by providing support for the government ministry and its think tanks to improve its environmental policy and by directly giving advice. International experts are useful assets in the policy-making process as they can provide additional knowledge and expertise and thus enhance the policy recommendations. Moreover financial support can enable workshops and also provide other resources during the policy-making process.

Similar to local NGOs, international NGOs have also been linked closely to the state through the registration process. Falling under the Vietnam Union of Friendship Organisations (VUFO), all international NGOs need to regularly report to the government. While this is officially aimed at ensuring compliance with local laws, the opaque political system can lead to difficulties. Sometimes, it is even necessary to continue operating without an existing permit. The requirement to register under VUFO, however, also provides the basis for networking between international NGOs, the government, and occasionally with local NGOs. The VUFO-NGO Resource Centre in Hanoi hosts 17 active working groups, some of which meet on a regular basis. In regard to the environment, the most active group is the Climate Change Working Group, founded in 2008, which meets on a monthly basis. Most of the groups, however, do not have an emphasis on environmental concerns and many important environmental problems, such as air pollution, do not have any group.

Environmental projects which are funded with the assistance of international organizations face a great challenge when the end of the project time frame nears. Donors generally place a time-limit on the completion of a project. Even though many projects are co-funded, most conclude once international funding ends. While there are attempts to make the efforts sustainable beyond the end of the project, the departure of the foreign organization makes this obviously dependent on local interests. This raises the question whether the effects of the project have been deep enough to survive even when the additional funding and manpower is withdrawn. In a project on enhancing the role of societal players funded by the Danish donor organization DANIDA, the end of funding left the unions without important resources to continue their work (Parenteau and Nguyen 2005).

Finally, while most donor organizations still primarily deal with the state as their primary partner, many projects have stressed the need to include businesses, community-organizations, NGOs, and other relevant parties. While support for local NGOs is not a particular focus of many international players, a growing number of donors are making an effort to consider them in funding requests and to make use of their local expertise. Some donors have, for instance, begun to translate the tender procedures into Vietnamese and allowed submissions of requests in Vietnamese. This is important because many of the small NGOs lack sufficient resources such as adequate English language skills. Promoting the idea that more actors need to be included in the policy-making and implementation process has overall opened the process further and allowed greater governance structures to emerge.

Conclusion

In Vietnam, environmental politics has changed dramatically since the change from a planned to a market socialist economy initiated under the Doi Moi economic reform process in 1986, which has led to the emergence of a growing number of governance mechanisms. The government has enhanced the environmental legislation and planning. It has consolidated as well as professionalized the environmental institutions, which are now more powerful than ever before. In addition, the state has granted more space to societal organizations and has at least officially promoted communities and individuals to become more active. Networks have formed between different organizations which have allowed them to play a larger role in politics. At the same time, the government has increasingly sought to gain the support of the business sector with advanced mechanisms. In order to deal with the massive pollution, the government has attempted to force polluters to pay for their refuse. It has also cooperated with businesses to promote the idea of cleaner production, which would reduce production costs and environmental pollution at the same time thus creating a win-win situation. The government has also experimented with a more complex governance mechanism, the Payment for Ecosystem Services, especially in the forestry sector. This has created a market in which those who profit from the preservation of the forest pay for it and compensate those who are interested in making money out of the forest land. Finally, international governmental as well as non-governmental organizations have become deeply involved in the environmental politics from policy-making all the way to policy implementation. They have formed networks among themselves and with the government to become more effective.

While these examples show that environmental governance in Vietnam is evolving, there are still many shortcomings. The greatest challenge is the fact that the capacity of the environmental institutions is still very weak. Underfunded and understaffed, both central and local administrators are overwhelmed by the massive challenges. Polluters neither pay fines nor fees and even the worst offenders are not closed down. The legal system is inadequate as companies cannot be sued for pollution. Besides the problem of widespread corruption, the lack of functional independence between state and those companies it owns is clearly also problematic. Moreover, the attempt to demonstrate polluting companies the incentives of cleaner production has shown very little success because the initial investments in new technologies are very high. Finally, societal and international players still move around in a very restrictive environment. The ruling party is more worried about losing control over the process, which is still predominantly organized in a top-down fashion, than enhancing the governance structures. As such, the future of environmental governance in Vietnam depends on the government's willingness to introduce more fundamental reforms that enhance the rule of law as well as increase transparency and public accountability.

Acknowledgements I would like to thank all the people who contributed to this work, especially the many interviewees in Vietnam who have offered me their time and explained to me the intricacies of environmental politics. I would like to also extend my thanks to my assistants Hoang Ngoc Han and Vu Ngoc Anh who have helped me with the language and other aspects of daily life. This work was supported in part by an Early Career Scheme Grant (ECS) from the University Grants Committee of the Hong Kong government (Project No. 21609618).

References

An, D. 2013. Corruption? What? Where? *Thanh Nien News*, July 12. http://www.thanhniennews.com/index/pages/20130711-corruption-what-where.aspx. Online Access January 21, 2014.

Anonymous. 2013. Mở ra cơ hội làm việc trong lĩnh vực môi trường. *Vietnam Forum of Environmental Journalism*, April 24. http://www.vfej.vn/vn/

3644n/mo-ra-co-hoi-lam-viec-trong-linh-vuc-moi-truong.html. Online Access July 15, 2013.

Aschhoff, N. 2008. *What Role Can NGOs Play to Support Grass-roots Democracy? The Example of the Vietnamese NGO CRP*. Sankt Augustin: Konrad-Adenauer-Stiftung. http://www.kas.de/vietnam/en/publications/14689/. Online Access January 21, 2014.

Bach T.S. 2004. Institutional Challenges for Sustainable Development in Vietnam: The Case of the Coal Mining Sector. In *Reaching for the Dream: Challenges Of Sustainable Development in Vietnam*, ed. M. Beresford and N. A. Tran. Copenhagen: NIAS Press.

Benz, A., S. Luetz, U. Schiman, and G. Simonis. 2007. Introduction. In *Handbuch Governance: Theoretische Grundlagen und empirische Anwendungsfelder*, ed. ibid. Wiesbaden: VS Verlag.

Can, Le Thac. 2002. Environmental Capacity Building in Vietnam. In *Capacity Building in National Environmental Policy: A Comparative Study of 17 Countries*, ed. Helmut Weidner and Martin Jänicke, 393–408. Berlin: Springer.

Clausen, A., H.H. Vu, and M. Pedrono. 2011. An Evaluation of the Environmental Impact Assessment System in Vietnam: The Gap Between Theory and Practice. *Environmental Impact Assessment Review* 31: 136–143.

Duong, Le Bach, and Khuat Thu Hong. 2008. Third Sector Governance in Vietnam. In *Comparative Third Sector Governance in Asia: Structure, Process, and Political Economy*, ed. Samiul Hasan and Jenny Onyx. New York: Springer.

Economy, E. 2006. Environmental Governance: The Emerging Economic Dimension. *Environmental Politics* 15 (2): 171–189.

Gilley, B. 2011. Paradigms of Chinese Politics: Kicking Society Back Out. *Journal of Contemporary China* 20 (70): 517–533.

Gilley, B. 2012. Authoritarian Environmentalism and China's Response to Climate Change. *Environmental Politics* 21 (2): 287–307.

Government of Vietnam. 2003. *National Strategy for Environmental Protection Until 2010 and Vision Toward 2020*. Hanoi.

Government of Vietnam. 2012. *National Strategy for Environmental Protection Until 2020 and Vision Toward 2030*. Hanoi.

Hannah, J. 2007. *Local Non-Government Organizations in Vietnam–Development, Civil Society and State-Society Relations*. PhD. Thesis, http://faculty.washington.edu/jhannah/dissertation/Hannah%20-%20dissertationTOC.htm. Online Access May 26, 2014.

Howell, J. (ed.). 2004. *Governance in China*. Lanham: Rowman & Littlefield Publishers.

Jeong, J. 1997. The Rise of State Corporatism in Vietnam. *Contemporary Southeast Asia* 19: 2.

Le, H.T. 2009. Assessing the Impacts of Environmental Regulations on the Food Processing Industry In Vietnam. *Economy and Environment Program for Southeast Asia Research Report*, No. 2009-RR8.

Lemos, M.C., and A. Agrawal. 2006. Environmental Governance. *Annual Review of Environmental Resources* 31: 297–325.

Mann, M. 1986. The Autonomous Power of the State: Its Origins, Mechanisms and Results. In *States in History*, ed. J. Hall, 109–136. New York: Basil Blackwell.

Marston, H. 2012. Bauxite Mining in Vietnam's Central Highlands: An Arena for Expanding Civil Society? *Contemporary Southeast Asia: A Journal of International and Strategic Affairs* 34 (2): 73–196.

McCarty, A. 2001. Governance Institutions and Incentive Structures in Vietnam. Building Institutional Capacity in Asia conference, Jakarta, March 12.

McElwee, P.D. 2016. *Forests Are Gold: Trees, People, and Environmental Rule in Vietnam*. Seattle and London: University of Washington Press.

Ministry of Natural Resources and Environment. 2011. *National State of Environment 2011: Solid Waste*. Hanoi: Government Printer.

Mitchell, C.L. 2006. Beyond Barriers: Examining Root Causes Behind Commonly Cited Cleaner Production Barriers in Vietnam. *Journal of Cleaner Production* 14: 1576–1585.

Nguyen, M.C. 2008. *A Theoretical Framework and Principles for the Establishment and Management of Civil Society Organizations in Vietnam*. Hanoi: Institute for Social Studies.

Nguyen Q.T. 2011. Payment for Environmental Services in Vietnam: An Analysis of the Pilot Project in Lam Dong Province. *IGES Occasional Paper*, No. 5, April.

Nguyen T.D.T., and T.N. Ngo. 2013. Progress on the Viet Nam Green Growth Strategy. Presentation for the G20 Development Working Group Workshop on Inclusive Green Growth, Moscow, July.

Norlund, I. 2007. Civil Society in Vietnam. Social Organisations and Approaches to New Concepts. *Asien* 105: 68–90.

O'Rourke, D. 2004. *Community-Driven Regulation: Balancing Development and the Environment in Vietnam*. Cambridge, MA and London: MIT Press.

Ortmann, S. 2017. *Environmental Governance in Vietnam: Institutional Reforms and Failures*. Cham: Palgrave Macmillan.

Parenteau, R., and Q.T. Nguyen. 2005. The Role of Civil Society in Urban Environmental Rehabilitation: A Case Study (Thanh Xuan district, Hanoi, Vietnam). *Environment and Urbanization* 17: 237–248.

Rozzaque, J. 2013. *Environmental Governance in Europe and Asia: A Comparative Study of Institutional and Legislative Frameworks*. Abingdon: Routledge.

Shi, H., and L. Zhang. 2006. China's Environmental Governance of Rapid Industrialisation. *Environmental Politics* 15 (2): 271–292.

Sidel, M. 1995. The Emergence of a Nonprofit Sector and Philanthropy in the Socialist Republic of Vietnam. In *Emerging Civil Society in the Asia Pacific Community Nongovernmental Underpinnings of the Emerging Asia Pacific Regional Community*, ed. Tadashi Yamamoto. Institute of Southeast Asian Studies and Japan Center for International Exchange: Singapore and Tokoyo.

Sigley, G. 2006. Chinese Governmentalities: Government, Governance and the Socialist Market Economy. *Economy and Society* 35 (4): 487–508.

Stoker, G. 1998. Governance as Theory: Five Propositions. *International Social Science Journal* 50 (155): 17–28.

Stone, D. 2005. Think Tanks and Policy Advice in Countries in Transition. Paper prepared for the Asian Development Bank Institute Symposium: "How to Strengthen Policy-Oriented Research and Training in Viet Nam," Hanoi, August 31. http://www.adbi.org/files/2005.09.dp36.think.tanks.jfppt.pdf. Online Access May 20, 2012.

Taylor, W., et al. 2012. *Civil Society in Vietnam: A Comparative Study of Civil Society Organizations in Hanoi and Ho Chi Minh City*. Hanoi: The Asia Foundation.

Thayer, C.A. 2009. Vietnam and the Challenge of Political Civil Society. *Contemporary Southeast Asia* 31 (1): 1–27.

To, P.X., W.H. Dressler, S. Mahanty, T.T. Pham, and C. Zingerli. 2012. The Prospects for Payment for Ecosystem Services (PES) in Vietnam: A Look at Three Payment Schemes. *Human Ecology* 40 (2): 237–249.

Vu, N.A. 2017. Grassroots Environmental Activism in an Authoritarian Context: The Trees Movement in Vietnam. *VOLUNTAS: International Journal of Voluntary and Nonprofit Organizations* 28 (3): 1180–1208.

Vu, T. 2014. Persistence Amid Decay: The Communist Party of Vietnam at 83. In *Politics in Contemporary Vietnam*, ed. Jonathan London, 21–41. London: Palgrave Macmillan.

Wells-Dang, A. 2010. Political Space in Vietnam: A View from the 'Rice-Roots'. *The Pacific Review* 23 (1): 93–112.

Wischermann, J. 2010. Civil Society Action and Governance in Vietnam: Selected Findings from an Empirical Survey. *Journal of Current Southeast Asian Affairs* 29 (2): 3–40.

World Bank. 2013. Vietnam: Achieving Success as a Middle-Income Country. *World Bank Website*, April 12. http://www.worldbank.org/en/results/2013/04/12/vietnam-achieving-success-as-a-middle-income-country. Online Access January 21/2013.

PART III

State and Society: Inequality, Class and Conflict

CHAPTER 8

Consumer Socialism: Consumption, Development and the New Middle Classes in China and Vietnam

Arve Hansen

Introduction

Asia is already home to more than half of the 3.2 billion people considered as the 'global middle class', and the Asian middle classes keep expanding rapidly (Kharas 2017). These estimates obviously group together highly diverse groups of people (see Koo 2016), but the expansion nevertheless reflects social and economic changes that will have major impacts locally and globally. The extent and nature of these impacts, however, remain largely unknown. Middle classes are supposedly good for development. They are expected to represent a force for 'good politics' (see Birdsall 2015). Furthermore, as 'consumer classes' (World Bank 2018), they are somewhat paradoxically expected to both represent demand for more goods and services—contributing to building domestic markets, in turn fuelling economic development and lessening dependence on

A. Hansen (✉)
Centre for Development and the Environment, University of Oslo, Oslo, Norway
e-mail: arve.hansen@sum.uio.no

A. Hansen et al. (eds.), *The Socialist Market Economy in Asia*,
https://doi.org/10.1007/978-981-15-6248-8_8

exports—and take the lead in reducing resource use and overconsumption (Wiemann 2015). Although large parts of the 'new Asian middle classes' are far from rich, their increasing purchases of consumer goods do contribute to significant consumption booms. Indeed, following in the footsteps of production chains, the main consumer markets of global capitalism are moving east (Hansen and Wethal 2015). This is in large part due to the expansion of the Chinese middle class, already estimated to consist of a quarter billion people (*The Economist* 2016) and growing rapidly (Kharas 2017), in turn contributing to China by the end of 2017 surpassing the US as the world's largest retail market (Fickling 2018). But also the 'socialist' neighbours to the south, Vietnam and Laos, are home to rapidly expanding middle classes with increasing purchasing power. In other words, large parts of the new 'consumer classes' of global capitalism are found in nominally socialist countries.

In Asian development success stories of the past, South Korea and Taiwan are often used as examples of the central role played by the middle classes in development and democratisation processes. In reality, however, the relationship has been complex and conflicted, and parts of the middle classes indeed supported authoritarian rule (Koo 1991; Jones 1998). They did play crucial roles as consumers in the developmental state (Koo 1991), although 'consumerism', and particularly consumption of foreign goods, in turn became strongly contested (Nelson 2000). Similarly, the new socialist middle classes have so far not represented a force for democratisation, but they have contributed to a kind of consumer revolution that would have been unthinkable some decades ago. Focussing on China and Vietnam, this chapter recounts why the middle classes seemingly thrive in the 'socialist market economy' despite its Leninist, authoritarian framing (see Chapters 1 and 3, this volume), before focusing on their position in what I term 'consumer socialism'. I argue that the market reforms officially adopted in 1978 ('Opening up') and 1986 (*doi moi*), respectively (see Chapter 1), have indeed demanded a fundamental shift in the communist parties' positions on private consumption, in turn pushing the ideological boundaries of market socialism. A new focus on 'consumption-led growth' in both countries further consolidates this shift.

While the Chinese middle class has already attracted considerable attention (see for example Chen 2013; Li 2010; So 2003), and the Vietnamese some (Huong 2015; Bélanger et al. 2012; Earl 2014), comparative approaches are lacking, both when it comes to the political and the economic roles of the middle classes in the socialist market economy. Drawing on long-term engagement with—and research on—Vietnamese middle classes, combined with secondary data on China's middle classes,[1] this chapter compares and contrasts main trends in the two neighbouring countries. It analyses the developments that have fostered the rise of the socialist middle classes and their relationship to the party-states. Mainly, however, the chapter focuses on consumption. After briefly reviewing the dramatic consumer transformations that have taken place in both countries since market reforms, I zoom in on some defining consumption patterns of the middle classes in both countries, focusing on the consumption of foreign goods and the inclination to display wealth publicly. Proceeding from this, I discuss the creation of consumer socialism, and discuss how middle-class lifestyles have gone from representing unwelcome bourgeois excess to become a defining part of developmental success, as well as how responsibility for the 'right' kind of consumption under market socialism has shifted from the state to the morality of consumers.

As Koo (2016: 442) argues, '[t]he middle class is a notoriously heterogeneous category'. Instead of trying to define the boundaries of the middle classes through either income (Birdsall 2015) or other forms of capital (Bourdieu 1984)—or 'cash, credentials or culture' (Reeves et al. 2018)—I take the pragmatic and straightforward starting point of seeing them as the big group of people between the poor(est) and the rich(est). Due to the heterogeneity of this group, however, I do argue for the need to understand the concept in plural terms. The upper and urban middle classes are the focus of this chapter. Simply put, this means segments of the population that have considerable purchasing power and are far from poor yet do not belong to the elites.

The Fall and Rise of the Socialist Middle Classes

Before the socialist revolutions in the mid-twentieth century,[2] both China and Vietnam had—in very different ways—seen dramatic social and economic transformations through the end of imperial rule. Apart

[1] A heartfelt thank you to Henrik Nykvist and Rebekka Åsnes Sagild for excellent comments on an earlier draft of this chapter in general, and on the parts involving China in particular.

[2] 1975 in South Vietnam.

from their many devastating sides, both The Republic of China and French colonialism had made some forms of social mobility possible, and had opened some room for the emergence of classes between the elite minority and the peasant majority. While China, in the words of Fung (2000: 260) was 'essentially an agrarian society where the middle class was small, conservative, and politically unorganized', the cities, and particularly Shanghai, were also home to 'a budding bourgeois way of life' (Lee 1991: 90). Similarly, Vietnam was mainly a peasant society, but the political economy of French colonialism created business, employment and education opportunities for small sections of the Vietnamese population, in turn leading to the formation of a sort of Vietnamese urban middle class (see Bélanger et al. 2012).

The socialist projects of China and Vietnam looked quite different, but did have in common Soviet-inspired political frameworks and ideologies, as well as educated leaderships combined with a strong foundation in the peasantry (Kerkvliet et al. 1998). As is well known, they also had in common, although to different extents, violent clampdowns on anyone seen as an enemy of the socialist revolution and a strong favouring of people of 'good class background', particularly revolutionaries (Bélanger et al. 2012; Walder 2015). The urban middle classes clearly suffered under the socialist projects' aim to radically break with the past and create a new, classless society. Typical middle-class jobs disappeared and were replaced by what Chen (2013) calls a 'quasi-middle class' of salaried servants. And typical 'modern' middle-class lifestyles were judged to be in opposition to the goals of socialism (Bélanger et al. 2012).

Under socialism, consumption patterns should be homogenised in the name of equality—solved through for example rationing—and consumption should be for utilitarian purposes. For Vietnam's early communist leaders, Vann (2012: 163) argues, 'the problem with consumerism, and especially its conspicuous forms, was essentially a Marxist one, namely that it represented the pursuit of false wants and needs; people wanted more and more, and ever newer models of goods not for their practical utility, but for their value as status objects'. That said, cadres enjoyed a range of special privileges and consumption patterns were far from as harmonised in practice as they were according to ideology (Truitt 2013; Walder 2015). Making a temporal jump ahead, some decades later the market reforms involved new dramatic transformations in both countries. After decades of suppressing the anti-socialist behaviour of the suspicious middle classes, suddenly they were needed again as the communist parties started explicitly embracing the market economy and implicitly embracing capitalism.

The Socialist Market Economy and the Creation of New Middle Classes

The stories of the market reforms in China and Vietnam are well known, and are discussed throughout this volume. Apart from the obvious economic challenges, the reforms also involved difficult questions on what it meant for the socialist projects to invite the market back in. Deng Xiaoping saw no fundamental opposition between a socialist system and a market economy. He is also famous for his rather pragmatic approach towards wealth creation: 'let some people get rich first'.[3] Among political leaders in both China and Vietnam it was clear that the market economy had to be a tool used to deliver progress, not a different way of organising society. As put by Mai Huu Thuc (2001: 20), the market economy is 'an economic institution in practice, not an economic foundation of a social system'. Innumerable hours have been spent discussing exactly what this new model entails, and large quantities of text has been published in both countries justifying and explaining the combination of socialism and the market. As is well known, the result was variations around the theme 'socialist market economy', what Jonathan London (this volume) more precisely calls market-Leninism and I have previously dubbed 'state capitalism with a Leninist orientation' (Hansen 2015).

Despite considerable scepticism towards the side effects of a market economy (e.g. Elliot 2012; Dickson 2000), economic growth took off, poverty levels dropped rapidly (Banik and Hansen 2016), and living standards steadily increased following reforms. In the advent of the market and with rapidly growing economies, some got both rich and glorious, usually those with close connections to the party. But also outside the inner echelons of power, many were much better off than before, and new jobs and opportunities for education and income created a favourable political-economic environment for the emergence of new middle classes in the rapidly expanding cities. Although referring to China, Chen's (2013: 59) summary works for Vietnam as well, finding that the main overall factors contributing to the growth of the middle classes have been the expansion of college education, the reforms of enterprises, the

[3] Which in popular accounts over time has turned into 'to get rich is glorious', something he probably never said.

development of the private economy and the inflow of investments from abroad. While these are all crucial, however, I would add the associated factors of access to new consumer goods and services and the eventual embrace of consumer society.

Who Are the Middle Classes? Class Composition in the Socialist Market Economy

As stated in the introduction, I will not attempt to define the middle class in absolute terms, but rather argue for their heterogeneity and for—at least—separating between upper and lower middle classes. Simply put, the lower middle class is much better off than the poor, but they are often far from rich. Frank Trentmann (2017: 374) summarises this group well: 'For most people in China, as in India and Asia more generally, being middle class does not mean going to the mall but living on the edge in a daily struggle to pay the bills for schools and hospitals' (see also Miao 2017). By contrast, the upper middle class is relatively rich, but not part of the elite. They work in foreign companies and in international organisations, or they are running their own small companies or serving as high-ranking state employees, or both at the same time.

In the socialist market economy, above the middle class the elite is represented by what Alvin So (2003) refers to as cadre-capitalists. In his words, '[t]his hybrid state-capitalist class has monopolized political capital, economic capital, and social/network capital in the Chinese society' (So 2003: 369). Below the middle classes, a large group of peasants and blue collar workers—and many are both—make up the contemporary 'socialist' proletariat and precariat. Although living standards have increased significantly also among these less privileged classes, they have certainly also paid the cost of economic reforms through harsh working conditions and low salaries. Peasants and small-scale farming are despite their remaining vital importance frequently portrayed as outdated in the new economy, and when cheap labour is a competitive advantage and labour unions are controlled by the communist parties, the rights of workers are constantly under threat (see Nordhaug, this volume).

The party undoubtedly remains influential in every aspect of society in China and Vietnam. Outside observers have frequently predicted that the new middle class with its education from abroad and cosmopolitan lifestyles, what I refer to as the upper middle class, will challenge the authoritarian regimes (for example *Economist* 2016). So far, however, the middle class seems to be, as Gainsborough (2010: 17) has put it, 'very much of the system' (see also, for example, Dickson 2000, 2003).

The Loyal Class?

Chen (2013) argues that a politically passive middle class is to be expected during rapid reform, as the middle classes are often fragmented, worried about political stability and often benefit from the status quo. The party-states in China and Vietnam have kept delivering opportunities for the relatively well off through strong economic performance. Furthermore, the middle classes are often tied to the communist parties in a variety of ways, directly or indirectly, such as through a grandfather in an important position in the communist party or an uncle in a local committee. Particularly the upper segments of the middle classes enjoy privileges through access to private health care or the ability to skip lines in public health-care, money to buy private education or extra tutors, as well as business opportunities and access to information.

However, explanations of systemic fidelity must also factor in that the Chinese and Vietnamese party-states are highly skilled at political repression. Chinese authorities are well known for clamping down on any unrest, and even brought the army to Tiananmen square in 1989. Vietnam has not seen any event that equals Tiananmen, but Vietnamese authorities frequently suppresses dissent, particularly from urban middle classes (Kerkvliet 2014). Indeed, both countries have further intensified the crackdown on dissent and freedom of expression in recent years (Amnesty International 2018). But direct crackdowns are just the most obvious example of a whole system working against political participation. As a young, upper-middle-class interviewee told me in Vietnam, people have been trained not to care about politics and to trust that the party-state does what is best for them and the nation. Still, protests are common in both countries. However, although The Economist (2016) refers to the middle class as '225 million reasons to worry' for China's leaders, in both countries protests tend to mainly concern land issues, often in rural areas, and are driven more by labour classes and the peasantry than the middle classes (see Nordhaug, this volume). Nevertheless, protests involving middle classes do take place, such as parts of the anti-China protests in Vietnam and urban environmental protests in both countries, the latter which also involve budding middle-class environmental movements (Geertman and Boudreau 2018; Halskov Hansen and Liu 2018).

In other words, the socialist market economy has not delivered political freedoms, and the middle classes remain partly loyal to the system. It has however opened up for the freedom to consume. But in order to fully develop a consumer society, the middle classes had to start spending rather than saving their money.

From Savers to Spenders

While the *nouveau riche* tend to steal the headlines, it is worth reiterating the point that most of the new Asian middle classes are far from being wealthy. As Trentmann (2017: 374) puts it, 'most are anxious consumers on a budget'. They are also savers, particularly in China, which has one of the highest national saving rates in the world, thanks mainly to household savings and mainly due to relatively affluent households (Zhang et al. 2018). Household saving rates have increased dramatically since reforms also in Vietnam (World Bank 2012), but they are now around the global average. There are many reasons for saving money, of course. The one-child policy in China is seen as a major driver of savings since it implies fewer children to support parents during old age (Zhang et al. 2018). Apparently, the more lenient 'one-or-two-children' policy of Vietnam has not had the same effect. In general, savings are closely related to safety nets and economic security, both factors that have been strongly affected by market reforms.

Although in different ways, both China and Vietnam have seen commodification of welfare systems as they have moved from ideals of socialist universalism towards placing responsibility on households (London 2014). While Malesky et al. (2011) find that Vietnam's welfare system in general has been more redistributive than that of China, market reforms in both countries have involved dramatic increases in household spending on health and education through official and unofficial fees (London 2014). Households pay large shares of their income on welfare services, and also save money due to concerns of health security and to be able to provide children with education. Nevertheless, young people in Hanoi often talk of how their generation is breaking with their parents' generation strong focus on saving rather than spending, a tendency that is also well known in China (Xie et al. 2019). Indeed, since high saving rates means less household consumption, the communist regimes have in different ways tried to boost consumer spending.

Constructing Consumer Socialism

Although economic openness became the mantra in both China and Vietnam following reforms, many—particularly conservative forces—in the communist parties were worried about the possibly eroding impacts of embracing globalisation (Elliot 2012; Dickson 2000). As I will return to below, one of the biggest fears have concerned the degrading consequences of 'consumerism'. However, in a capitalist economy, increasing consumption is closely connected to economic growth, and increasing domestic consumption means less dependence on exports and consumption elsewhere. In the efforts to transcend its position as factory of the world, the Chinese government has been clear on the necessity to develop domestic markets. In the words of Croll (2006: 1), since the end of the 1990s

> there has been an emerging consensus in China around the importance of consumption-led growth or developing domestic demand or an internal market which has been designated variously as a "new source", the "new impetus" or the "main engine" for China's long-term economic growth.

Indeed, the imperatives of capitalist development have led to fundamental changes in the party-states' approach to consumption. In a context of high saving rates and export dependence, Gerth (2010: 9) argues, '...Chinese politicians have actually been *pushing* their population to consume more' in order to create a domestic market. Consider this statement by then premier Zhu Rongji in a report to the Ninth People's Congress in 2002:

> We need to eliminate all barriers to consumption by deepening reform and adjusting policies. We need to encourage people to spend more on housing, tourism, automobiles, telecommunications, cultural activities, sports and other services and develop new focuses of consumer spending. (in Otis 2012: 43)

More recently, the Chinese government has been seeking to boost domestic consumption in response to the US-China trade war (Tang

2019). And consumption has been boosted by the party-states in both China and Vietnam, economically through expanding access to credit and eventually through reducing tariffs on imported consumer goods. Socially through providing more leisure time and public holidays. And also culturally, through embracing middle class lifestyles as 'modern' and 'civilized', or as 'higher quality', or high-*suzhi* in China (Kipnis 2006; Miao 2017). All of these factors have paved the way for a socialist consumer revolution.

The Socialist Consumer Revolution

In addition to ideological scepticism towards consumerism, planned economies have often struggled to keep up with the demand for consumer items. With the maturing of the socialist market economy, both factors have lost importance. The increase in ownership of consumer goods in China and Vietnam the past decades has been extraordinary (see Table 8.1). While all segments of society have taken some part in this 'consumer revolution', they have so to very different extents.

Fuelled by rising incomes and—more recently—soaring household debt (Tang 2019; Nguyen et al. 2018), particularly the upper parts of the urban middle classes are adopting lifestyles and consumption patterns that are globally associated with middle class status. Young, fashionable urbanites have become emblematic of this class, with clothing styles, hairdos and eating and drinking habits to match their status. Niche stores and hip, quality-oriented cafés and coffee shops are examples of the urban spaces frequented by this segment of the middle classes. More generally, housing practices are changing towards smaller households in

Table 8.1 The socialist consumer revolution: Number of goods per 100 urban households

		Car	*Motorbike*	*Telephone*	*Refrigerator*	*TV*	*Computer*	*AC*	*Washing machine*
Vietnam	2002	0.2	56.5	32.5	33.5	81	9	4.5	14
	2016	5.5	163	233	87	119	45.5	54.5	61
China	2000	0.5	19	19.5	80	116.5	10	31	90.5
	2016	35.5	21	231	96.5	122.5	80	123.5	94.2

Source Vietnam Household Living Standard Survey (various years); China Statistical Yearbook (various years)

increasingly air-conditioned environments, the entertainment industry is booming, smart phones have become normal, shopping malls and supermarkets are popping up and so are restaurants and fast food chains, while travelling within or outside one's country for tourism purposes is becoming a normal leisure activity. The middle classes live in larger and more solid houses, often equipped with modern appliances, and spend much more on non-food items than the rest of society (see World Bank 2018). Furthermore, urban car ownership has boomed, particularly in China, where annual car sales surpassed 29 million in 2017, a more than five-fold increase compared to a decade earlier (OICA). While the Vietnamese middle classes are predominantly driving motorbikes, car sales are booming also there.

The private car is a telling example of the consumption transformations that have taken place. As I have discussed in detail elsewhere, cars convey wealth and status in public spaces better than any other goods, and is thus a central positional good (Hansen 2017). This has historically put the car in an ambivalent position in communist regimes (Siegelbaum 2008, 2011). In the new socialist market economy, however, a car—and particularly a big, expensive car—signifies success; that its owner has succeeded in the highly challenging and potentially highly economically rewarding market economy. It 'polishes one's name', according to a popular Vietnamese phrase. But a car is much more than a status symbol, it responds to new expectations of comfort and convenience. Even though the convenience of being stuck in traffic might be questioned, the possibility of moving around the city together with the family in a cool, dry and relatively safe shell are obvious appeals contributing to making the car a central possession, and even an expected possession, for the middle class (Hansen 2017). Still, the many large, expensive, and often foreign cars in the streets of Vietnamese and Chinese cities testify to some conspicuous traits of the consumption patterns of the upper parts of the new socialist middle classes: an appetite for foreign goods and a willingness to openly display wealth.

Cosmopolitanism and an Appetite for the Foreign

As the economies of China and Vietnam were opened to the outside world, the monopoly of domestic producers in most sectors came to an end in both countries. Although state-owned enterprises were either 'equitized' or otherwise geared towards the market economy (see

Knutsen and Do Ta Khanh, this volume), these processes would often prove slow and many of them would anyways struggle to compete with the dramatic inflow of foreign goods. Consumers were trusted to be patriotic and buy domestically produced goods despite the dramatic expansion in choices. China has a long history of 'consumer nationalism' (Gerth 2003), something that is still reflected in frequent consumer boycotts in the wake of international disagreements (see Fickling 2018). Vietnam has historically not seen the same extent of consumer nationalism (although see Dutton 2012), but the government has run several 'buy Vietnamese goods' campaigns to remind consumers of the importance of supporting domestic enterprises. Both countries have also employed high tariffs on imported consumer goods, particularly of the luxury kind, in order to protect domestic enterprises.

Nevertheless, a considerable appetite for foreign goods, foreign languages—predominantly English—and foreign popular culture emerged in both countries alongside the increasing economic openness (Yu 2014; Taylor 2012). China is home to the world's fastest-growing music market and soon the world's largest film market and the entertainment industry is booming also in Vietnam. While particularly China has a colossal domestic entertainment industry, Hollywood movies and K-Pop music are in vogue among young people in both countries. For the case of foreign goods, the appetite stems from curiosity and an urge to be fashionable, as well as from a deep distrust of domestically produced products, both out of concerns for quality and fear for counterfeits. These issues remain important, although the situation may be changing in China with the emergence of global brands with a Chinese origin, most famously Huawei (Shepard 2016).

Although many among the middle classes still cannot afford to travel abroad, those who can afford it increasingly go to Australia, Europe or the US to study, and international tourism is rapidly growing in popularity. Sharing pictures from trips abroad on social media is a central form of status display in both countries. Travels are also possibilities for purchasing goods, since buying goods abroad can mean considerably lower prices and secures authenticity (Yu 2014). In both countries this has led to a large, informal market for goods brought back in person by travellers, often sold online, but also in people's living rooms. In Vietnam the goods are known as *xach tay*, referring to how the goods are hand carried into the country. In China the resellers are known as *Daigou*, and the practice has been subject to recent crackdowns by the authorities (Hinsdale 2018).

More directly, and although domestic and food and dishes still dominate, a certain appetite for foreign food is developing alongside the rapidly increasing tendency to eat out (Hansen 2018; Hansen and Jakobsen 2020). Meanwhile, the popular street kitchens are increasingly facing competition from more upscale eateries, including both Western and Asian restaurants and fast food chains. The attraction of these middle-class food spaces seem to stem at least as much from matters related to social status and cultural curiosity as from the food itself (Yu 2014; Ehlerth 2016).

At more upscale food spaces, whether foreign or domestic, many of the raw materials are imported. Many restaurants will advertise for beef imported from Australia or the US. And at these upscale (upper middle class) spaces, including middle class drinking spots, imported alcohol will be served with the food. Although *baijiu* in China and *rieu* in Vietnam remain popular 'traditional' alcoholic drinks, wine and beer has increased significantly in popularity. Beer comes in a wide range of national varieties as well, but expensive imports are what matters at upscale places. At the many new and very popular steak houses, fortunes are spent on imported beef and imported wine.

It is easy to exaggerate the foreign orientation of the middle classes. Among both friends and informants in Hanoi, only the most foreign-inspired, such as those married to foreigners, would cook anything but Vietnamese food at home. But they would frequently eat both Western and other Asian food at restaurants. Importantly, going to a Western fast food restaurant does not necessarily mean a 'Westernisation' of diets. Fast food chains adapt, and rice meals are very popular at most fast food outlets. In Vietnam, most people I talk to tend to prefer Vietnamese or other Asian food, while Western food is frequently portrayed as 'too creamy' and unsuitable for Vietnamese stomachs and taste buds. The exception, it seems, are the children of the urban middle classes in both countries, who seem to fully embrace pizza, hamburgers and other foreign fast food. This fact is in turn contributing towards soaring child obesity levels (French and Crabbe 2010; Do et al. 2015).

Foreign goods, foreign popular culture and foreign food are important part of the everyday practices of middle-class consumers in the socialist market economies. Many of the foreign goods are expensive, and the use of them thus displays both purchasing power and cosmopolitanism. This puts them at the centre of practices in the socialist consumer society that radically break with past ideals of frugality: publically displaying wealth.

Displaying Wealth

Consumption is a fundamentally social phenomenon, and although most consumption is mundane and inconspicuous (Shove 2003), the display of or aspiration towards status of different kinds form a central component of consumption patterns. As Bourdieu (1984) famously argued, consumption patterns both define and are defined by social classes. In other words, the middle classes can be recognised as such based on the goods they consume and consume these goods because they belong to the middle classes. While both the status hierarchy of goods and the factors influencing consumption patterns are complex, some forms of consumption are openly aimed towards achieving certain positional ends. The car owners I interviewed in Hanoi can serve as good examples here. They bought expensive cars as a business strategy, since this would gain trust among others in the business community (Hansen 2017). Also in China cars have become central status symbols (Gerth 2016; Yu 2014), and it is clearly no coincidence that there are so many expensive cars on the roads in both countries. Nor is it a coincidence that the 'premium' segment of the motorbike market in Vietnam, where 'moto-mobility' remains dominant, is considered extraordinarily large (Hansen 2017). But in line with Bourdieu, consumption also takes place due to expectations associated with social standing. To stay with my car example, just like Gerth (2010, 2016) reports from China, I have talked to many car owners in Hanoi whose main reason for buying a car was that they felt it was expected of them and their position.

Much has been written about conspicuous consumption in China. While Trentmann (2017: 374) finds that the strict hierarchies of the Communist Party leads to a certain social immobility that actually reduces the importance of conspicuous consumption, the most common story is that Chinese consumers are infatuated with luxury goods. As Yu (2014: 64) puts it, 'owning prestige brands when it comes to fashion, accessories, autos, and technology appears to be a national obsession'. And China does have high levels of consumption of luxury products. China is vital to the global market for luxury goods, closing in on 40% of the total, driven by a generation of rich, only-child 'little emperors and empresses' (*Asia Times* 2018). In Vietnam, interestingly the North, and particularly Hanoi, is famous for a similar appetite towards positional goods (see also Fforde 2003). Also in Vietnam, the high-end market is booming. In both countries, the consumption of luxury products are not just about displaying wealth but is closely related to a culture of gift giving, related both to ways of showing respect and to 'greasing' of contacts. Under the market economy, the gifts have become more luxurious and the 'need' for and potential gains from corruption much larger. As part of anti-corruption policies, the Chinese state thus in the early 2010s started cracking down on gift giving, causing temporary slump in sales of luxury products.

Some people fully fit the stereotypes of the new, conspicuous, business-savvy and foreign-oriented middle classes. Such as the man I interviewed in Hanoi back in 2013. He ran his own small company, and most likely had family connections in the communist party. He wore an expensive-looking suit and drove a brand new X5, one of the largest and most expensive BMWs on the market. In his office, a set of golf clubs sat casually in a corner, while on his work desk he had placed a copy of Donald Trump's *How to get rich*. To an extent, this man is the result of the political economy of the socialist market economy. And, to an extent, conspicuous consumption of this kind is an integrated part of post-reform China and Vietnam. Still, however, although the communist regimes have embraced consumption, it does not mean they encourage all forms of consumption.

Conflicted Consumerism

Among communist party leaders, one of the feared negative side effects of developing a market economy and integrating with the capitalist world was the associated desire for consumer items, often imported, bringing along a consumer culture deemed incompatible with socialist values. In China, consumerism was seen as 'the defining element of cultural and moral degradation in the contemporary global era', and linked to 'materialism, hedonism, and worship of money' (Davis 2011: 339). Similar worries have been widespread in Vietnam. Taylor (2003: 139) argues that by the early 1990s there was a perceived cultural crisis brought along by opening Vietnamese society to the non-communist world, and state officials identified the main 'adverse effects' as '"a *cult* of exotic taste", the dizzying pace of borrowing, the resurgence of a cultural inferiority complex [...] and the emergence of consumerism' (italics in original). Thus, while 'openness' was the slogan, both Chinese and Vietnamese politicians started arguing for restrictions on imports, worrying particularly about the impact foreign influences had on youth (Marr and Rosen 1998). As Marr and Rosen (1998: 149) wrote in the late 1990s,

'Even Communist Party members loyal to the reform strategy sometimes wonder if Vietnam is losing its soul to Coca Cola, Madonna and Hollywood'.

Foreign influences were seen to cause a wide range of negative side effects of reforms and the following economic development, including increases in crime and violence blamed on movies from the US and other parts of Asia (Marr and Rosen 1998). But also conspicuous consumer items were treated with scepticism. Again, the private car serves as a good example. In China and Vietnam, there was little room for cars during the planned economy. In China, where the nationalist founding father Sun Yat-sen in the 1920s dreamt of a car for every man, the communists banned private cars altogether, and only high-ranking cadres and government officials had access to them (Notar 2017: 152). In Vietnam, high-ranking government officials have told me how as late as the 2000s people worried about the appropriateness of acquiring a car because people could 'get the wrong impression' (see also Hansen 2017).

This has changed significantly. Even though restrictions on car ownership still exists, particularly in China (Valler 2017), these are now due to practical issues related to transport and mobility rather than ideological reservations. The scepticism towards consumer goods has indeed become less marked as gradually, the communist parties have embraced consumer society. Indeed, as Vann (2012) argues in the case of Vietnam and Yu (2014) in the case of China, consumption is now one of the most significant forms of freedom enjoyed by citizens in these countries. Consumption is both a relatively safe 'freedom' to give to citizens, and a realm where the government can 'deliver development' to people while stimulating economic growth. In the process, in what Trentmann (2017: 394) for the case of China has called 'an extreme version of the symbiosis between consumerism and authoritarianism', consumer socialism has arguably created the ultimate capitalist consumer-citizen: unfree as citizen, free as consumer.

However, freedom comes with responsibility. Just like the New Socialist Man was expected to be selfless and always do what was good for the collective, the new socialist consumer is expected to act 'civilized' and 'modern' and in line with national culture. As Gillen (2016: 41) puts it, the state 'uses culture as a means to caution Vietnamese society against consumerism and the perils of individual wealth'. Consumption is now good, but only as long as it does not go on accord with the culture of the socialist market economy. Exactly what this means can be hard to decipher, but morality seems to be central.

As the market economy depends on middle-class consumers, prosperity has been rendered a moral issue. As put by Leshkowich (2012: 110) for the case of Vietnam, 'prosperity comes to those who embody valorized forms of selfhood and continually assess the success of their efforts to measure up to standards of culture, civilization, and modernity'. Similarly, as part of the party's embrace and promotion of high-*suzhi* lifestyles, Xi Jinping's 'Chinese Dream' involves 'an infusion of cultural values to balance materialism'. As put by *China Daily USA* (2014, n.p.):

> For the past 30 years Chinese have been manufacturing and exporting products to meet the materialistic aspirations of consumers in the West. Chinese are now ready to consume what they produce, to realize the materialistic aspect of the Chinese Dream. The only question is whether this acquisition of material goods will unfold as Western-style conspicuous consumption in China or in a more considered way, informed by a Chinese cultural appreciation for keeping life in balance.

While it seems a bit late to ask whether conspicuous consumption will come to China, it is interesting to see how the communist regimes cling to the idea of the socialist market economy as something qualitatively different from capitalist consumer society. But lofty rhetoric on socialism is a trademark of the communist parties in both China and Vietnam, and what exactly cultured and balanced consumerism entails, and the extent to which the vision of a socialist consumer culture resonates with the rapidly expanding middle classes, remains to be seen.

Conclusions

The rapid emergence of urban middle classes in the socialist market economy represents a potentially significant force for change, politically and economically. Politically, this chapter has highlighted the middle classes'—for the most part—systemic fidelity towards the authoritarian party-states. The possibility of the middle classes in the future taking to the streets in numbers and protest or in other ways demand political change cannot be excluded. Currently, however, there are few indications of any such development. If the party-states fail to continuously deliver progress and economic safety the situation could change, something that brings us to the economic dimension.

The new 'consumer classes' are vital to the economic well-being of the socialist market economy. This is already a story of immense transformation. Davis' (2011: 337) point about China is equally relevant to Vietnam: 'An economy that for three decades [...] had been defined by the ideals of ascetic socialism had become a twenty-first-century pillar of global consumer capitalism'. What consequences will the developments of consumer socialism have? Lewis H. Siegelbaum (2008) has argued that the Soviet Union struck a Faustian bargain when it introduced private automobility, as it provided freedom and also lay bare some of the shortcomings of the planned economy. Escalating levels of consumption in China and Vietnam is clearly a different case, but the point might be relevant. While at least parts of the communist regimes remain sceptical towards the culturally eroding consequences of 'consumerism', their defining power in the realm of consumption is shaky, to say the least. Their worries also appear shallow, given that the same ruling elites have been central to embedding their economies and societies in the flows of global capitalism and encouraging more consumption. An appetite for consumption has awakened, and the state is even more dependent on delivering development-as-consumption than ever before. If this stops, and the new middle classes do not see that the system has any openings for them to fulfil their aspirations, it could have significant political consequences.

Another crucial aspect of the new consumer society is that it lays bare the contradictions of the development models of China and Vietnam and unveils the capitalist nature of this rewriting of 'socialism'. According to official rhetoric, the socialist market economy is a step on the way towards constructing socialism. While this official story keeps losing credibility, the communist parties seem to embrace educated, moral and relatively affluent citizens as new forms of the 'Socialist Man'. What I term consumer socialism is of course replete with contradictions. Although developing within an official framing of socialism and equality, parts of the elites and the upper middle classes in both countries show a clear tendency towards flaunting wealth through consumption in public space. Indeed, consumer socialism reveals and thrives on the deep inequalities embedded in the political economy of the socialist market economy.

References

Amnesty International. 2018. *Amnesty International Report 2017/18: The State of the World's Human Rights*. London: Amnesty International Ltd.

Asia Times. 2018. Chinese Millennials Rule the Global Luxury Market. *Asia Times*, October 1. http://www.atimes.com/article/chinese-millennials-rule-the-global-luxury-market.

Banik, Dan, and Arve Hansen. 2016. The Frontiers of Poverty Reduction in Emerging Asia. *Forum for Development Studies*. https://doi.org/10.1080/08039410.2015.1134646.

Bélanger, Danièle, Lisa B. Welch Drummond, and Van Nguyen-Marshall. 2012. Introduction: Who Are the Urban Middle Class in Vietnam? In *The Reinvention of Distinction: Modernity and the Middle Class in Urban Vietnam*, ed. Van Nguyen-Marshall, Lisa B. Welch Drummond, and Danièle Bélanger. Dordrecht: Springer.

Birdsall, Nancy. 2015. Does the Rise of the Middle Class Lock in Good Government in the Developing World? *The European Journal of Development Research* 27 (2): 217–229.

Bourdieu, Pierre. 1984. *Distinction: A Social Critique of the Judgement of Taste*. London: Routledge & Kegan Paul.

Chen, Jie. 2013. *A Middle Class without Democracy: Economic Growth and the Prospects for Democratization in China*. Oxford: Oxford University Press.

China Daily USA. 2014. Potential of the Chinese Dream, March 26. http://usa.chinadaily.com.cn/epaper/2014-03/26/content_17380146.htm.

Croll, Elisabeth. 2006. *China's New Consumers: Social Development and Domestic Demand*. London and New York: Routledge.

Davis, Deborah S. 2011. Consumption in Postsocialist China. In *Encyclopedia of Consumer Culture*. Thousand Oaks, CA: SAGE.

Dickson, Bruce J. 2000. Cooptation and Corporatism in China: The Logic of Party Adaptation. *Political Science Quarterly* 115 (4): 517–540. https://doi.org/10.2307/2657608.

Dickson, Bruce J. 2003. *Red Capitalists in China: The Party, Private Entrepreneurs, and Prospects for Political Change*. New York: Cambridge University Press.

Do, Loan Minh, Toan Khanh Tran, Bo Eriksson, Max Petzold, Chuc T.K. Nguyen, and Henry Ascher. 2015. Preschool Overweight and Obesity in Urban and Rural Vietnam: Differences in Prevalence and Associated Factors. *Global Health Action* 8: 28615. https://doi.org/10.3402/gha.v8.28615.

Dutton, George. 2012. Advertising, Modernity, and Consumer Culture in Colonial Vietnam. In *The Reinvention of Distinction: Modernity and the Middle Class in Urban Vietnam*, ed. Van Nguyen-Marshall, Lisa B. Welch Drummond, and Danièle Bélanger. Dordrecht: Springer.

Earl, Catherine. 2014. *Vietnam's New Middle Classes: Gender, Career, City.* Copenhagen: NIAS Press.

Ehlerth, Judith. 2016. Emerging Consumerism and Eating Out in Ho Chi Minh City, Vietnam: The Social Embeddedness of Food Sharing. In *Food Consumption in the City: Practices and Patterns in Urban Asia and the Pacific*, ed. Marlyne Sahakian, Czarina Saloma, and Suren Erkman. London: Routledge.

Elliott, David W.P. 2012. *Changing Worlds: Vietnam's Transition from Cold War to Globalization.* New York: Oxford University Press.

Fforde, Adam. 2003. Vietnam—Culture and Economy: Dyed-in-the-Wool Tigers? In *Consuming Urban Culture in Contemporary Vietnam*, ed. Lisa B.W. Drummond and Mandy Thomas. London: RoutledgeCurzon.

Fickling, David 2018. Beware the Wrath of the Chinese Consumer. *Bloomberg*, July 6. https://www.bloomberg.com/opinion/articles/2018-07-06/beware-the-wrath-of-the-chinese-consumer.

French, Paul, and Matthew Crabbe. 2010. *Fat China: How Expanding Waistlines Are Changing a Nation.* London: Anthem Press.

Fung, Edmund S.K. 2000. *In Search of Chinese Democracy: Civil Opposition in Nationalist China 1929–1949.* Cambridge: Cambridge University Press.

Gainsborough, Martin. 2010. *Vietnam: Rethinking the State.* London: Zed Books.

Geertman, Stephanie, and Julie-Anne Boudreau. 2018. "Life as Art": Emerging Youth Networks in Hanoi and the Tree Hug Movement. *City & Society* 30 (2): 210–236. https://doi.org/10.1111/ciso.12162.

Gerth, Karl. 2003. *China Made: Consumer Culture and the Creation of the Nation.* Cambridge: Harvard University Asia Center.

Gerth, Karl. 2010. *As China Goes, So Goes the World: How Chinese Consumers Are Transforming Everything.* New York: Hill & Wang.

Gerth, Karl. 2016. Driven to Change: The Chinese State-Led Development of a Car Culture and Economy. In *Energy and Transport in Green Transition: Perspectives on Ecomodernity*, ed. Atle Midttun and Nina Witoszek. London: Routledge.

Gillen, J. 2016: *Entrepreneurialism and Tourism in Contemporary Vietnam.* Maryland: Lexington Books.

Halskov Hansen, M., and Z. Liu. 2018. Air Pollution and Grassroots Echoes of "Ecological Civilization" in Rural China. *The China Quarterly* 234: 320–339. https://doi.org/10.1017/s0305741017001394.

Hansen, Arve. 2015. The Best of Both Worlds? The Power and Pitfalls of Vietnam's Development Model. In *Emerging Economies and Challenges to Sustainability: Theories, Strategies, Local Realities*, ed. Arve Hansen and Ulrikke Wethal. London and New York: Routledge.

Hansen, Arve. 2017. Hanoi on Wheels: Emerging Automobility in the Land of the Motorbike. *Mobilities* 12 (5): 628–645.

Hansen, Arve. 2018. Meat Consumption and Capitalist Development: The Meatification of Food Provision and Practice in Vietnam. *Geoforum* 93: 57–68.

Hansen, Arve, and Jostein Jakobsen. 2020. Meatification and Everyday Geographies of Consumption in Vietnam and China. *Geografiska Annaler. Series B. Human Geography* 102 (1): 21–39.

Hansen, Arve, and Ulrikke Wethal. 2015. Emerging Economies and Challenges to Sustainability. In *Emerging Economies and Challenges to Sustainability: Theories, Strategies, Local Realities*, ed. Arve Hansen and Ulrikke Wethal. London and New York: Routledge.

Hinsdale, Mason. 2018. Are Luxury Stocks Overreacting to China's Daigou Crackdown? *Jing Daily*, October 16. https://jingdaily.com/crackdown-daigou-luxury/.

Huong, Le Thu. 2015. The Middle Class in Hanoi: Vulnerability and Concerns. In *ISEAS Perspective*. Singapore: ISEAS.

Jones, D.M. 1998. Democratization, Civil Society and Illiberal Middle Class Culture in Pacific Asia. *Comparative Politics* 30 (2): 147–169.

Kerkvliet, Benedict J.T. 2014. Government Repression and Toleration of Dissidents in Contemporary Vietnam. In *Politics in Contemporary Vietnam: Party, State, and Authority Relations*, ed. Jonathan London. New York: Palgrave.

Kerkvliet, B., A. Chan, and J. Unger. 1998. Comparing the Chinese and Vietnamese Reforms: An Introduction. *The China Journal* 40: 1–7.

Kharas, Homi. 2017. The Unprecedented Expansion of the Global Middle Class: An Update. In *Global Economy & Development Working Papers*. Washington, DC: Brookings Institution.

Kipnis, Andrew. 2006. *Suzhi*: A Keyword Approach. *The China Quarterly* 186: 295–313.

Koo, Hagen. 1991. Middle Classes, Democratization, and Class Formation: The Case of South Korea. *Theory and Society* 20 (4): 485–509.

Koo, Hagen. 2016. The Global Middle Class: How Is It Made, What Does It Represent? *Globalizations* 13 (4): 440–453.

Lee, Edmond. 1991. A Bourgeois Alternative? The Shanghai Arguments for a Chinese Capitalism: The 1920s and the 1980s. In *Contemporary Chinese Politics in Historical Perspective*, ed. Brantly Womack. Cambridge: Cambridge University Press.

Leshkowich, A.M. 2012. Finances, Family, Fashion, Fitness, and...Freedom? The Changing Lives of Urban Middle-Class Vietnamese Women. In *The Reinvention of Distinction: Modernity and the Middle Class in Urban Vietnam*, ed. Van Nguyen-Marshall, Lisa B. Welch Drummond, and Danièle Bélanger. Dordrecht: Springer.

Li, Cheng. 2010. Introduction: The Rise of the Middle Class in the Middle Kingdom. In *China's Emerging Middle Class: Beyond Economic Transformation*, ed. Cheng Li. Washington, DC: Brookings Institution Press.

London, Jonathan D. 2014. Welfare Regimes in China and Vietnam. *Journal of Contemporary Asia* 44 (1): 84–107. https://doi.org/10.1080/00472336.2013.822988.

Malesky, Edmund, Regina Abrami, and Yu. Zheng. 2011. Institutions and Inequality in Single-Party Regimes: A Comparative Analysis of Vietnam and China. *Comparative Politics* 43 (4): 401–419.

Marr, David, and Stanley Rosen. 1998. Chinese and Vietnamese Youth in the 1990s. *The China Journal* 40: 145–172.

Miao, Ying. 2017. Middle Class Identity in China: Subjectivity and Stratification. *Asian Studies Review* 41 (4): 629–646.

Nelson, Laura C. 2000. *Measured Excess: Status, Gender and Consumer Nationalism in South Korea*. New York: Columbia University Press.

Notar, Beth E. 2017. Car Crazy: The Rise of Car Culture in China. In *Cars, Automobility and Development in Asia: Wheels of Change*, ed. Arve Hansen and Kenneth Bo Nielsen. London: Routledge.

Otis, Eileen. 2012. *Markets and Bodies: Women, Service Work and the Making of Inequality in China*. Stanford: Stanford University Press.

Reeves, Richard V., Katherine Guyot, and Eleanor Krause. 2018. *Defining the Middle Class: Cash, Credentials or Culture?* Brookings Institution, May 7. https://www.brookings.edu/research/defining-the-middle-class-cash-credentials-or-culture/.

Shepard, Wade. 2016. How 'Made in China' Became Cool. *Forbes*, May 22. https://www.forbes.com/sites/wadeshepard/2016/05/22/how-made-in-china-became-cool/#4b47ea5577a4.

Shove, Elizabeth. 2003. *Comfort, Cleanliness and Convenience: The Social Organization of Normality*. Oxford: Berg.

Siegelbaum, Lewis H. 2008. *Cars for Comrades: The Life of the Soviet Automobile*. Ithaca: Cornell University Press.

Siegelbaum, Lewis H. 2011. *The Socialist Car: Automobility in the Eastern Bloc*. Ithaca: Cornell University Press.

So, Alvin Y. 2003. The Changing Pattern of Classes and Class Conflict in China. *Journal of Contemporary Asia* 33 (3): 363–376. https://doi.org/10.1080/00472330380000231.

Tang, Frank. 2019. China's Household Debt Has Grown So Much That Trade War Stimulus Is Largely Ineffective, Study Shows. *South China Morning Post*, August 7. https://www.scmp.com/economy/china-economy/article/3021816/chinas-household-debt-has-grown-so-much-trade-war-stimulus.

Taylor, Nora A. 2012. Exhibiting Middle Classness: The Social Status of Artists in Hanoi. In *The Reinvention of Distinction: Modernity and the Middle Class in Urban Vietnam*, ed. Van Nguyen-Marshall, Lisa B. Welch Drummond, and Danièle Bélanger. Dordrecht: Springer.

Taylor, Philip. 2003. Digesting Reform: Opera and Cultural Identity in Ho Chi Minh City. In *Consuming Urban Culture in Contemporary Vietnam*, ed. L. Drummond and Mandy Thomas, 138–154. London: RoutledgeCurzon.

The Economist. 2016. 225 m Reasons for China's Leaders to Worry. https://www.economist.com/leaders/2016/07/09/225m-reasons-for-chinas-leaders-to-worry.

Thuc, Mai Huu. 2001. Characteristics of Market Economy with Socialist Orientation in Viet Nam. *Vietnam Social Sciences* 1 (81): 20–25.

Trentmann, Frank. 2017. *Empire of Things: How We Became a World of Consumers, from the Fifteenth Century to the Twenty-First*. London: Penguin Books.

Truitt, Allison. 2013. *Dreaming of Money in Ho Chi Minh City*. Seattle and London: University of Washington Press.

Valler, Thea Marie. 2017. *Curbing Consumption in China: The Vehicle Quota System in Guangzhou*. Unpublished Masters thesis, University of Oslo.

Vann, Elisabeth F. 2012. Afterword: Consumption and Middle-Class Subjectivity in Vietnam. In *The Reinvention of Distinction: Modernity and the Middle Class in Urban Vietnam*, ed. Van Nguyen-Marshall, Lisa B. Welch Drummond, and Danièle Bélanger. Dordrecht: Springer.

Nguyen, Viet-Ha T., Hong-Kong T. Nguyen, Thu-Trang Vuong, Manh-Tung Ho, and Quan-Hoang Vuong. 2018. How Swelling Debts Give Rise to a New Type of Politics in Vietnam. CEB Working Paper No 18/026. Université Libre de Bruxelles.

Walder, Andrew G. 2015. *China Under Mao: A Revolution Derailed*. Cambridge, MA: Harvard University Press.

Wiemann, J. 2015. Sharing Global Responsibility: The Role of the Middle Classes on the Way to a Just and Sustainable Global Economy. *European Journal of Development Research* 27: 205–216. https://doi.org/10.1057/ejdr.2015.2.

World Bank. 2012. *Well Begun, Not Yet Done: Vietnam's Remarkable Progress on Poverty Reduction and the Emerging Challenges*. Hanoi: World Bank.

World Bank. 2018. *Climbing the Ladder: Poverty Reduction and Shared Prosperity in Vietnam*. Hanoi: World Bank.

Xie, S.Y., S. Li, and J. Wernau. 2019. Young Chinese Spend Like Americans—And Take on Worrisome Debt. *Wall Street Journal*, August 29. https://www.wsj.com/articles/young-chinese-spend-like-americansand-take-on-worrisome-debt-11567093953.

Yu, Lianne. 2014. *Consumption in China*. Cambridge: Polity Press.

Zhang, Longmei, Ray Brooks, Ding Ding, Haiyan Ding, Hui He, Jing Lu, and Rui Mano. 2018. China's High Savings: Drivers, Prospects, and Policies, IMF Working Paper 18/277, IMF.

CHAPTER 9

Labour Conflicts in the Socialist Market Economy: China and Vietnam

Kristen Nordhaug

Introduction

On 14 April 2014, more than 40,000 workers went on strike in the Taiwanese-invested shoe manufacturing factory Yue Yuen in Gaobu, Dongguan, Guangdong province, China. They claimed that the company had embezzled their social security payments, and bribed officials at the city government of Dongguan to ignore illegal practices. On 18 April, Yue Yuen workers in Anfu in Jiangxi province also went on strike. The city government in Dongguan supported the employer in the conflict, but President Xi Jinping's anti-corruption campaign had targeted Dongguan as a testing ground. The central government forced Yue Yuen Gaobu to repay the missing social insurance and raise wages. Police forces later detained workers who continued the strike. Yue Yuen Gaobu is owned by Hong Kong-based Yue Yuen Industrial Holdings, the world's largest branded footwear producer that is controlled by a Taiwanese business group. During the strike buyers shifted their orders to other suppliers,

K. Nordhaug (✉)
Oslo Metropolitan University, Oslo, Norway
e-mail: Kristen.Nordhaug@oslomet.no

A. Hansen et al. (eds.), *The Socialist Market Economy in Asia*,
https://doi.org/10.1007/978-981-15-6248-8_9

including Pou Yuen Vietnam, another affiliate of Yue Yuen Industrial Holdings in the Ho Chi Minh City area (Schmalz et al. 2017).

On 26 March 2015 more than 90,000 workers at Pou Yuen Vietnam went on strike against an amendment of Vietnam's social insurance law, which stipulated that workers would get pensions based on their social insurance payment at retirement age. Previously, workers were allowed to withdraw their lump sum social insurance payments before legal retirement age. They frequently needed the money to invest in farming, small businesses or to fund health emergencies. The strikers also claimed that Pou Yuen Vietnam had withheld social insurance payments. Their action triggered strikes in other industrial zones in the south, altogether over 140,000 workers participated. Pou Yuen workers marched on the National Route 1A highway thoroughfare in five days before police forces cleared the road and detained the leaders. Two days later the Prime Minister announced that Article 60 would be amended. Workers could choose between taking out lump sum social payment and saving it as a monthly pension after retirement. Soon after the strike ended (Tran 2015; Do 2017: 1065).

These two conflicts took place within foreign-owned enterprises that operated in the same line of production, and even had the same foreign owner. The strikes were extraordinarily large. Both strikes were about social security. The Yue Yuen Gaobu strike was led by veteran workers who had become line leaders. As their retirement was nearing, they discovered that the employers had defaulted their social security contributions (Lee 2017: 100–101). It is likely that the strike leaders in Pou Yuen also were older workers, who were concerned about social security. In both strikes the workers won considerable concessions, but the governments also drew a red line and used force. In Yue Yuen Gaobu the state was divided. The local government was on the employer's side, the central government forced the employer to pay the workers. The Pou Yuen workers blocked the traffic on a major highway. The Yue Yuen Gaobu workers followed the advice of an NGO advisor; "marching on public roads and other socially disruptive action not only harm public interest, they will also invite popular criticism against our legal activism" (Lee 2017: 100). Let us now take a broader look at labour conflicts and their contexts in the two countries.

China and Vietnam have undertaken relatively similar transitions from planned economies to high-growth socialist market economies, while they have retained their Leninist one-party states. From the

1990s both countries promoted export-oriented manufacturing, foreign corporations played an important role. The majority of workers in export-manufacturing are internal migrants from the countryside. Foreign enterprises are major sites of labour unrest.

The current positions of China and Vietnam in international value chains differ. Companies in the southern export centres of China in the Pearl River Delta are upgrading their production, and relocating low-end manufacturing production to areas with cheaper labour in the interior of China, and to other Asian countries. Vietnam is a major destination. According to a survey from 2016, more than 40% of the manufacturers who were on their way out of China planned to go to Vietnam (*Financial Times* 2016).[1]

In contrast, there is limited economic upgrading in Vietnam's manufacturing export sector. It is dominated by foreign enterprises that combine imported inputs with cheap local labour and land. Several scholars warn about a growing competition and wage squeeze from countries such as Cambodia, Bangladesh and Indonesia (Masina 2012; Masina and Cerimele 2018; Pincus 2015; Tran 2012).

Collective labour action in China and Vietnam takes place within party states that in theory adhere to egalitarian and anti-capitalist ideologies, but in practice rely on capitalist growth, while they suppress independent civil society organisations. The ruling communist parties of China and Vietnam control the official umbrella labour union organisations, the All-China Federation of Trade Unions (ACFTU) and the Vietnam General Confederation of Labour (VGCL). They have the official monopoly to represent workers, but they are also part of the governing apparatuses. Workers initiate collective action, such as strikes, without consulting the official unions. The task of the unions is not to support these collective actions, but rather to prevent and defuse them. Still, the unions see themselves as worker representatives and they do promote labour-friendly policies and legislation within the party states. Industrial relations

[1] Relocation to Vietnam might have been influenced by the planned Trans-Pacific Partnership Agreement (TPP), which included Vietnam and excluded China. In 2017 the Trump administration scrapped the TPP. The trade war between the United States and China since Fall 2018 also promotes relocation from China to Vietnam.

are "quadripartite", and include employers, the government, informal, non-institutionalised worker organisations and the unions (Chen 2010).[2]

There is also a division between the union hierarchy outside enterprises and local grassroots enterprise unions. The latter is weak and frequently controlled by management. A labour researcher who asked a Vietnamese worker why they went on strike before referring their grievances to the enterprise union chair received a telling answer:

> Are you kidding? He [the union chair] is a manager. If I open my mouth, the next day I am gone. And you know who would sign my dismissal decision? The union vice chair who is also the HR manager. (Do 2008: 5)

Under these circumstances, workers in Vietnam and China resort to informal single-enterprise strikes and other collective protests to promote their interests (Anner 2015: 299–300).

In spite of these similarities there are important differences between collective labour conflicts in the two countries. Anita Chan has conducted research on labour strikes within Taiwanese-owned footwear manufacturing in the Ho Chi Minh City region and the Pearl River Delta during 2006–2009. Taiwanese managers and Western buyers told Chan and her collaborator that strikes were more frequent in Vietnam than in China (Chan 2011: 213–214). I use statistical data to sustain her finding. I discuss national patterns and the patterns of the southern export centres of the two countries, provinces Ho Chi Minh City, Binh Duong and Dong Nai, in Vietnam and the province Guangdong in the south of China, home to the Pearl River Delta economic zone.

After this introduction I give a brief overview of the recent development of labour conflicts in the two countries. Then I compare the frequency of strikes in China and Vietnam, and in their southern export centres. I discuss the following possible explanations of the higher frequency of strikes in Vietnam than in China: The impact of work organisation on strike leadership, the balancing of the local state between employers and workers, legal conflict resolution as an alternative to strikes in China and the role of the housing of migrant workers in the spread of strikes.

[2] Chen discusses the ACFTU in China. In my view his analysis also applies to the VGCL in Vietnam.

The Development of Strikes in China and Vietnam

China—In the late 1990s and early 2000s, collective labour protests mounted in state enterprises that faced closure, privatisation, downsizing and layoffs. The protests normally assumed other forms than strike, such as collective petitions to the authorities, demonstrations, protest marches, road blockades and confrontational meetings with enterprise management and local authorities (Lee 2007: chs. 3–4).

Chinese authorities reported 480 strikes in China in 1992, 1870 in 1995 and 1740 in the first nine months of 1996 (Lee 2010: 65). Most of these strikes took place in the export centres along the coast. Then, "an unprecedented series of ... strikes ... and walkouts" hit factories in the Pearly River Delta in 2004 (Silver and Zhang 2009: 175). In 2003 Chinese authorities had abolished the practice of repatriating migrants from the countryside without local residence papers. They comprised most of the workforce in China's export-manufacturing industry. As conditions of migrant workers in the cities stabilised, they became more willing to take part in collective action against low and unpaid wages and harsh working conditions (Qin 2016: 8–9). The number of strikes with more than one thousand participants in the Pearl River Delta increased from zero in 2002 to 13 in 2005 (Chan 2010: 37).

Average, nominal wages doubled during 2002–2008, and real wages also increased (Banister and Cook 2011: 45). Qin Ling and Chris King-Chi Chan both claim that labour shortage from 2003 to 2004 gave workers a stronger bargaining position (Qin 2016: 9; Chan 2010: 23). However, the workers' bargaining strength varied. An investigation of a sample of unskilled and skilled workers in the Pearl River Delta found that almost all of the real wage growth from 2000 to 2009 accrued to skilled workers, while the real wages of unskilled workers stagnated (Golley and Meng 2011). Scarcity of labour may still explain the militancy of skilled workers. Chris King-Chi Chan notes that "[s]killed workers with better market positions generally took the lead in workers' collective struggles" (Chan 2010: 43).

China's labour legislation was amended in 2008. The new regulations improved employment protection and facilitated workers' position in labour arbitration cases, while a new social insurance legislation codified employer contributions to welfare benefits (China Labour Bulletin 2009: 18–19). Many companies tried to evade the consequences of the law by terminating contracts and abandoning seniority rights. Their workers responded with a wave of individual and collective protest in late 2007 (Qin 2016: 16).

The international financial crisis hit the coastal areas of China the during fall of 2008. Unemployment mounted and many migrant workers returned to their home areas. The government weathered the crisis with a gigantic "stimulus package". Minimum wages were frozen for the first time in many years. During the crisis, collective worker protests targeted factory closures, bankruptcies and fleeing bosses. Their protests calmed as local governments covered unpaid wages, and the stimulus package created jobs in the home regions of returning migrant workers (Qin 2016: 18, 19).

Economic recovery in 2010 was followed by a new surge of strikes with demands for higher wages. Wages had then remained unchanged since the onset of the financial crisis, or longer. A survey in 2010 found that 20% of the interviewed workers had not received a single wage increase for five years. At Honda Auto Parts Manufacturing Corporation in Nanhai, Guangdong some 1900 workers went on strike in May 2010. The strike lasted for 19 days. It led to the total shutdown of Honda's four vehicle assembly plants in China, and reportedly cost the company 240 million RMB a day (about US$35 million). The workers obtained sizeable wage hikes. A wave of strikes followed in the Japanese automotive producer networks with 20 strikes in the Pearl River Delta alone during the next two months (China Labour Bulletin 2011: 15–16, 24).

Table 9.1 shows strikes with more than one thousand participants within manufacturing, mining and construction in China and Guangdong Province during 2011–2015 that were registered by the China

Table 9.1 Strikes with more than 1000 participants in China and Guangdong Province reported by China Labour Bulletin: Manufacturing, mining and construction

	China	*Guangdong*
2011	12	6
2012	36	21
2013	43	28
2014[a]	52	23
2015	39	13

[a]Four strikes in 2014 had more than 10,000 participants. All of them took place in Guangdong

Source China Labour Bulletin (2019)

Labour Bulletin. In Guangdong all strikes but one took place within manufacturing.

Since the CLB only registers a fraction of all strikes in China, some strikes may be missing. Nevertheless, the numbers of strikes with more than one thousand participants had ascended markedly since the early 2000s. The 2012–2015 figures for Guangdong Province are larger than those previously quoted for 2002–2005.[3] The numbers of strikes with more than 1000 participants have ascended markedly since the early 2000s.

Vietnam—Table 9.2 shows the annual number of registered strikes in Vietnam, and in the three main provinces of export-manufacturing in the south.

The trend in the two series is relatively similar. The three southern provinces accounted for most strikes in Vietnam, but their share declined as foreign investors diversified to other provinces. There were relatively few strikes during 1995–2005. The number grew strongly during 2006–2008 and then declined in 2009. There was a new escalation from 2010, a peak in 2011 and a decline during 2012–2014.

The strike trends for 2006–2011 followed the development of real minimum wages adjusted for the food consumer index with some time lag. The wages of unskilled Vietnamese workers are close to the minimum wage. They spend a major share of their income on food. Major strike waves occur when wages lag behind food prices. The first strike wave in 2006 started after a long period of unchanged nominal minimum wages (1999–2005), and declining real minimum wages. In September 2005, the press reported a forthcoming 40% increase in the minimum wage to take effect from January 2006. However, complaints from factory managers convinced the government to delay implementation until April. Then, the government responded to labour unrest by shifting the date to February and strikes escalated amidst growing confusion.

Vietnam became a member of the WTO in 2007. Foreign investments expanded strongly from 2006, and there was growing shortage of manufacturing labour. Still, employers were reluctant to raise wages, especially within export production. In response, the number of strikes

[3] The 2002–2005 figures referred to the Pearl River Delta, while the 2011–2015 figures referred to all of Guangdong Province. However, the brief descriptions published by the CLB show that 83 of the 91 listed strikes in Guangdong during 2011–2015 took place in the Delta, four took place elsewhere in Guangdong and four had unknown locations.

Table 9.2 Number of strikes in all of Vietnam, and in provinces Ho Chi Minh City, Binh Duong and Dong Nai, 1995–2015

	Vietnam	*HCMC/BD/DN*
1995	60	46
1996	59	54
1997	59	51
1998	62	55
1999	67	64
2000	71	60
2001	89	79
2002	100	79
2003	139	113
2004	125	99
2005	147	95
2006	387	330
2007	541	449
2008	762	454
2009	342	175
2010	507	329[a]
2011	1023	596
2012	601	393
2013	384	228
2014	303	194[a]
2015	316	188

[a]The provincial figures for these years may be inaccurate
Source Figures obtained from Vice Director Vu Minh Tien, Institute for Workers and Trade Unions, Vietnam General Confederation of Labour (VGCL), Hanoi, 23 August 2016

increased in 2007–2008, and peaked at 762 (454 in the three southern provinces) in 2008. Most of this increase took place in Dong Nai and Binh Dung provinces, where labour shortages were most acute. The real minimum wage declined during 2007–2008 due to the strong rise of food prices, although nominal minimum wages were raised in 2008 (Pringle and Clarke 2011: 70–71, 75: Siu and Chan 2015: 75, 77).[4]

The number of strikes decreased in 2009 when the international financial crisis peaked. Orders from brand name corporations fell. Workers were probably less eager to strike when unemployment increased (Tran 2013: 200). Moreover, the nominal minimum wage and the real minimum wage

[4]Large rice export by the Vietnamese government, which monopolises the marketing of rice, contributed strongly to the high prices. See Siu and Chan (2015: 85–86).

adjusted for food prices both increased significantly in 2009. Real wage growth flattened during 2010 and 2011. There was a strong increase in consumer goods prices and food prices during 2011, when the strike wave peaked at 1023 strikes (574 in the three southern provinces) (Siu and Chan, 2015: 75, 85).

The declining number of strikes from 2012 can also be related to real wages. From 2012 through 2015 food price inflation was low, and even negative for several months during 2012 and 2013 (Trading Economics, Vietnam Food Inflation, n.d.). The annual increases in nominal minimum wages during 2012–2015 exceeded the annual rise of food prices (Trading Economics, Vietnam Minimum Wages, n.d.). The real minimum wage increased during this period, and the national number of strikes decreased from 1023 to a low of 303 in 2014, followed by a minor increase in 2015. In the three southern provinces, there was a continuous decline from 596 in 2011 to 188 in 2015.

Comparing the Frequency of Strikes in China and Vietnam

In this section I try to sustain the claim that there are relatively more strikes in Vietnam than in China. In both countries the data on strikes are patchy. The government of Vietnam publishes the number of strikes in manufacturing, mining and construction with supplementary information on ownership, province and sector. Chinese authorities register collective "incidents", such as strikes, demonstrations, road blockages, etc., but they do not publish the figures. However, since 2011 the Hong Kong-based NGO *China Labour Bulletin* (CLB) has published an electronic "strike map" of a sample of collective labour protests based on reports by Chinese social media. It contains relatively similar information to that published in Vietnam, as well as data on other collective actions than strikes. The CLB strike map also contains information on the number of participants, their motives and official responses to the collective action.

Foreign-invested enterprises are strongly overrepresented in strikes in both countries. In 2010 the share of these enterprises in the total number of enterprises in Vietnam was 2.5% (Siu and Chan 2015: 76). Still, between 2011 and 2015, 70.8% of strikes in Vietnam within manufacturing, mining and construction took place in foreign-invested enterprises.[5] That was 28.3 times above average, based on the 2010 share of foreign enterprises.

The CLB database distinguishes between foreign-invested enterprises and enterprises invested from Hong Kong, Macao and Taiwan.[6] Added together, they accounted for 50.3% of all registered strikes in manufacturing enterprises during 2011–2015.[7] Still, only 1.8% of all enterprises in China in 2014 belonged to these two categories (China Statistical Yearbook 2015: table 1.7). The chance of a strike in foreign and overseas Chinese enterprises was then 27.7 times above average.

Since foreign-invested enterprises on an average are larger than domestic enterprises, the foreign-domestic difference is exaggerated by this measure. For China my finding is, however, confirmed by other measures. In 2003 the Chinese government was still publishing data on labour disputes (without distinguishing the type of dispute, collective or individual, legal or non-legal, etc.). There were 271 labour disputes per 10,000 workers in foreign enterprises with an average of 3.8 workers per case. In domestic enterprises there were 124 disputes per 10,000 workers and 2.3 workers per case (Rhoo 2015: 5, table 1.1) It was then 3.6 times more likely that a worker in a foreign enterprise would be involved in a labour dispute than a worker in a domestic enterprise.

The CLB strike map gives the number of 902 strikes within manufacturing, mining and construction in 2011–2015 (China Labour Bulletin 2019). The CLB has assessed that it reports 5–10% of the total number of worker's collective action. The total number of strikes between 2011 and 2015 should then be in the range of 9020–18,040. That was 37–74 strikes per million of the 2014 industrial workforce, or 6.6–13.2 strikes per million of China's 2014 population.[8]

[5] Tabulated from figures obtained from Vice Director Vu Minh Tien, VGCL, Hanoi, 23 August 2016.

[6] Hong Kong and Macao are Chinese territories since 1997 and 1999, respectively. They are designated "special-administrative regions" with home rule. Taiwan is claimed by China, but it is a de facto independent state.

[7] "Unknown enterprise ownership" in the CLB database were left out from my tabulations, while "joint ventures" of national and foreign enterprises were categorised as "domestic".

[8] Tabulated from ILOStat Country Profiles and dataworldbank.org (industrial workforce ratio) and China Statistical Yearbook (2015: table 2.5) (population ratio).

During 2011–2015 Vietnamese authorities reported 2597 strikes within manufacturing, mining and construction.[9] That was 224 strikes per million of the 2014 industrial workforce, or 29 strikes per million of Vietnam's 2014 population.[10] Based on these figures, the strike rate as a share of the industrial workforce was 3.0–6.0 times higher, and the population strike rate was 2.2–4.4 times higher in Vietnam than in China.

The frequency of strikes was also higher in Ho Chi Minh City, Binh Duong and Dong Nai than in Guangdong Province. The CLB strike figure for manufacturing, mining and construction in Guangdong during 2011–2015 was 436 (China Labour Bulletin 2019). Based on the assumptions above, that gives a total of 4360–8720 strikes, or 41–82 strikes per million of Guangdong's 2014 population.[11] The total number of strikes in the three southern Vietnamese provinces between 2011 and 2015 was 1599, or 123 strikes per million of the 2014 populations of these provinces.[12] The proclivity to strike was then 1.5–3.0 times higher in the three Vietnamese provinces than in Guangdong. My figures show more labour unrest in Vietnam than in China.

In the following I try to explain the greater proclivity to strike in Vietnam than in China. I first relate these differences to different work organisations with an influence on the access to experienced and capable strike leadership. Furthermore, I argue that worker housing in the two countries affects their solidarity and networking differently. Then I try to demonstrate that legal conflict resolution may serve as an alternative to strike in China, but not in Vietnam. Finally, I argue that the local governments' strategies to suppress or accommodate labour demands make a difference, and that these strategies reflect the revenue sources of the local governments and the ensuing government–business relations.

[9] Figures obtained from Vu Minh Tien, VGCL, Hanoi, 23 August 2016.

[10] Tabulated from ILOStat Country Profiles and dataworldbank.org (industrial workforce ratio) and Statistical Handbook of Vietnam (2015: table 7) (population ratios).

[11] Tabulated from China Statistical Yearbook (2015: table 2.5). Strikes as proportions of the industrial workforce would have been a better measure, but reliable assessments are complicated by large-scale labour migration.

[12] Tabulated from Statistical Handbook of Vietnam (2015: table 6).

Work Organisation and Strikes

As shown above, foreign-invested enterprises are strongly overrepresented in strikes. The willingness of workers within these enterprises to carry the costs of a strike, including the risk of being fired, is affected by perceived opportunities. The foreign investors are typically suppliers for large, transnational retailers with considerable market power. They are under pressure to adjust to the buyers' shifting orders based on just-in-time production, fast changes of fashion, and seasonal change. They risk fees or permanent loss of contracts if they fail to meet the orders. This strengthens the strike weapon, especially during peak seasons. Employers might wish to let strikes go on to weaken the workers' determination, but they are under pressure from the buyers to solve the strike immediately (Anner and Liu 2016: 10).

Workers may still be reluctant to go on strike unless there is experienced strike leaders among them. But work tenure in China is becoming increasingly volatile. A 2011 national representative survey found that Chinese migrant workers born before 1980 on an average had held to their job for 4.2 years, the average was 2.68 years for those born in the 1980s and 0.93 years for those born in the 1990s (Lee 2017: 98). These figures may reflect that tenure is becoming increasingly short, or that the length of workers' tenure increases as they grow older. Other data support the former option.

Producers of IT and garment in Guangdong have responded to labour shortages with technological and organisational change that increases the demand for knowledge-intensive work within management, R&D and design, while manufacturing labour has been downsized and deskilled. The new organisation facilitates swift training of new workers who perform simple, routinised operations. The manufacturing workforce still mainly consists of unskilled migrant workers from the countryside.

In their investigation of electronics production in the Pearl River Delta Lüthje and Butollo found that competition was very strong and profit margins narrow. The basic wage was low. Workers obtained most of their income through overtime work and bonuses for personal performance. Short-term employment and relocation reduced employment security (Butollo 2015; Lüthje and Butollo 2017). In three factories in the Pearl River Delta controlled by electronics giant Foxconn the researchers found that the average employment period was one year and eleven months in the first factory and one year and two months in the second factory. In the third factory average employment was four years and four months, but this was probably because the factory management retained its old workforce as it awaited relocation of the plant (Lüthje and Butollo 2017: 225). As mentioned earlier, the strike at Yue Yuen Gabou was led by experienced workers who had become line leaders. This kind of labour leaders may be in short supply in China.

I have not found figures about the duration of employment in Vietnam, but in an interview labour researcher Quynh Chi Do gave me the following assessments of export-manufacturing: 8–10 years within footwear, seven years within garments and two years within electronics. The low figure for electronics was mainly because the major producers only had operated in the country for a short period of time.[13]

Vietnam's export-manufacturing is probably more conducive to labour unrest than the Chinese due to longer employment periods. This increases the "supply" of experienced workers who are likely to become team leaders. Quynh Chi Do argues that team leaders frequently are informal representatives of workers' interests in foreign-invested enterprises. Especially in Asian-owned foreign enterprises the differentiation of wages and status between team leaders and other workers is relatively limited, and team leaders tend to identify with their co-workers, rather than with management. Team leaders serve as informal worker representatives and maintain networks with one another that help in coordinating collective actions, including strikes (Do 2008: 6–8).[14] Vietnam's work organisation may then facilitate labour unrest to a greater extent than China's.

Worker Housing and Strikes

Most migrant workers in China's export industry live in dormitories that are owned or rented by their employers and located near the production sites. Dormitory co-habitants frequently come from the same home area. Migrant workers with common roots and home areas establish strong ties of solidarity with one another. This facilitates collective action and

[13] Personal information Quynh Chi Do, Hanoi, February 16, 2017.

[14] Some companies tried to address the problem. Cannon recruited team leaders from the outside. They became a new management stratum. Still, this did not change the situation. A new generation of sub leaders took on the role that the team leaders had performed before. Personal information Quynh Chi Do, Hanoi, 16 February 2017.

contributes to "cellular activism" within the confines of single enterprises (Lee 2007: 192).

In contrast, most Vietnamese migrant workers live in "workers' villages" in, or near, industrial parks and export-processing zones, where they rent their housing from local landlords. Like in China, workers frequently co-habit with fellow migrants from the same home areas, and help one another to find jobs in the same enterprises. Unlike the Chinese dormitories that typically are run by one single enterprise, the workers' villages serve workers from several enterprises. This gives rise to cross-cutting social networks, and the sharing of information on important issues such as wages and strikes across geographical origins, family relations, workplace and gender. A high concentration of workers results in waves of strikes that affect several enterprises. Outside of industrial zones workers rent their housing in unpopular suburb areas and live among other low-income groups. Strikes do not spread in the same way as within the industrial zones (Do 2008: 8–9). Thus, both the Chinese dormitories and Vietnamese worker villages promote solidarity among workers, but the Vietnamese housing pattern is more conducive to information, inspiration and influence across enterprises.

Family co-habitation makes Vietnamese workers stay relatively long in the worker villages. Networking across enterprises makes it easy to find new jobs when workers lose or quit their previous jobs.[15] In contrast, the networking in Chinese dormitories are interrupted by job shifts and returns to the countryside in response to job loss, or marriage (Lee 2007: 204). Thus, differing housing patterns may explain why workers strike more in Vietnam than in China. Moreover, housing in workers' villages contributes to the relatively long employment period of Vietnamese workers that increases the "supply" of experienced strike leaders.

The housing of migrant workers in the greater Shenzhen area—has changed over the past ten years. Villagers near industrial regions have constructed rental buildings for migrant workers that may resemble Vietnam's worker villages. Workers frequently prefer to live in these buildings, rather than in dormitories (Siu 2015: 25). However, worker villages are still more important in Vietnam than in China.

[15] Personal information Quynh Chi Do, Hanoi, 16 February 2017.

The Institutionalisation of Labour Conflicts and Strikes

Labour conflicts have been institutionalised in different ways in China and Vietnam. In 1982 Chinese authorities responded to a wave of strikes in state-owned enterprises by removing the right to strike from the Constitution (Lee 2010: 64). Since then, strikes in China have taken place in an unregulated, legal grey zone. A quite comprehensive labour legislation was implemented in 1995. It formally required that all employees signed labour contracts with their employers. Still, only a fraction of the migrant workers within the private and foreign sectors had a contract (Lee 2007: 42–43).

The early labour code of Vietnam made no provisions for strikes. After a series of strikes in 1992/1993, collective labour disputes and the right to strike was included in the new labour code that took effect in 1995 (Kerkvliet 2011: 181–182).

The labour codes in both countries set up a three-stage process of labour dispute settlement based on mediation, arbitration and formal court procedure. The 1995 Chinese labour code did not mention collective labour disputes or strikes, only individual disputes that involved single workers and their employers. In contrast, the Vietnamese legislation distinguished between individual and collective disputes and recognised strikes. However, strikes only became legal when they had gone through all stages of dispute settlement, followed by a majority employee vote for strike in a referendum. Moreover, strikes would have to be directed by the official enterprise union under the Vietnam General Confederation of Labour (VGCL). Vietnamese workers did not bother to go through the dispute settlement mechanisms before going on strike. No strike in Vietnam was ever legal (Chan 2011: 232–234).

Amendments took the two labour codes further in different directions. The amended Chinese labour dispute conciliation code was enacted in 2008. It still defined labour disputes as individual, although "collective consultation" was declared as labour right. The new legislation facilitated arbitration for workers by prolonging the period for filing a case, and by removing the arbitration fee. Rulings of arbitrations were made compulsory, only employees—not employers—were allowed to take the case further to court. In addition, requirements for labour contracts became stronger, and employment was better protected (Chan 2011: 238–239).

Vietnam's labour legislation was amended in 2006 amidst Vietnam's first major wave of strikes. It took effect in mid-2007, right before a new strike wave. The new legislation distinguished "rights-based" from "interest-based" collective labour conflicts and stipulated different procedures for dispute resolutions, depending on the type. Illegal strikes were defined more clearly than before. The procedure of organising legal strikes was simplified, but workers would still have to go through arbitration and vote over a strike before it became legal (Pringle and Clarke 2011: 126–127; Chan 2011: 234–237).

China has instituted an extensive legal labour dispute management regime. While relatively few conflicts are decided in formal court litigation, there is a large number of cases of arbitration and mediation. The 2008 amendments strengthened the hands of the workers in these disputes. It came right before the onset of the international economic crisis that shook the coastal export centres during fall 2008. Between 2007 and 2008 the number of cases of mediation and arbitration nearly doubled from 350,000 to 693,000, and the number of workers involved in these labour conflicts increased from 650,000 to 1.2 million (China Labour Bulletin 2009: 14).

Most mediation and arbitration cases result in in-between compromise solutions. In 2015 there was no clear winner in 53.4% of the cases settled, workers won in 35.4% of the cases and employers in 11.6% according to official statistics (China Labour Statistical Yearbook 2016: table 8-2). Workers typically receive less than they demand—and probably also less than their legal entitlements—but they are likely to obtain at least some compensation, if the employer pays. As more than one million workers are involved in legal procedures every year, the system reduces collective labour action.

Vietnam's mediation and arbitration system resembles that of China, but one important difference is that the arbitrations in Vietnam are not legally binding.[16] Vietnamese workers know about the system, but rarely bother to use it. For instance, only one or two strike cases per year are reported to the arbitration council in Ho Chi Minh City (Do 2017: 1058).

In addition, a rich flora of labour NGOs in China have been encouraged by authorities to provide free or low-cost legal services to workers,

[16] Personal information, Vu Minh Tien, VGCL, Hanoi, 1 October 2019.

thus reducing the cost of choosing the legal road. These Chinese labour NGOs have more freedom of action in supporting workers in legal conflicts than their Vietnamese counterparts.[17] As individualised, legal labour conflict solution is more effectively institutionalised in China than in Vietnam, Chinese workers are more likely to choose legal procedure in situations where Vietnamese workers rather choose the strike weapon.

States and Strikes

Anita Chan claims that Chinese authorities are more willing than the Vietnamese to suppress demonstrations, sit-ins, road blockages and other forms of labour protest that disturb public order. Local Chinese governments also allow managers to retaliate strikes with mass layoffs and blacklisting of strike leaders. In Vietnam government officials and district trade union typically intervene quickly to calm down the workers and end the strike. They will frequently hear workers' grievances and bargain with the management on behalf of the workers. The workers are confident that the officials will be attentive to their claims, and do not fear punitive government action (Chan 2011: 225–227). Still, like their Chinese counterparts, Vietnamese workers fear retaliation by their employers, including layoffs. Strike leaders are very reluctant to disclose their identity to management (Do 2008; Tran 2013).

The reports from China Labour Bulletin show that police intervention and the arrest of striking and demonstrating workers are common in China. During 2011–2016 there were police intervention and arrests in 275 out of 3455 demonstrations (8.0%) and in 125 out of 1884 strikes (6.6%) in the cases reported by the China Labour Bulletin. The frequency of police intervention and arrests during strikes increased from 4.8% in 2011–2013 to 7.8% in 2014–2016.[18]

I do not have comparable figures from Vietnam, but most accounts indicate that the situation is very different there. In the Pou Yuen Vietnam strike, discussed at the start of this article, Vietnamese police forces broke up a road blockade and detained the leaders, but the demonstrators had then disturbed the traffic on a major national highway thoroughfare for

[17] Personal information Quynh Chi Do, Hanoi, 16 February 2017.

[18] Tabulated from China Labour Bulletin (2019). Unlike my previous tabulations, the service sector is included in these figures.

five consecutive days in a demonstration that unprecedently was directed at the government. During ordinary strikes or demonstrations, the police show up to maintain order and protect property, but otherwise remains passive. In China demonstrating workers have developed strategies to restrain police violence, such as putting female workers in the front line. To my knowledge this is not common in Vietnam. Government responses to labour unrest appear to be significantly more repressive in China than in Vietnam.

Both in China and Vietnam the market reforms were accompanied by considerable decentralisation of policymaking and budget responsibility, which induced local governments to attract investors to boost revenue. Ching Kwan Lee refers to a division of labour between "legitimacy" and "accumulation" in the Chinese state. The central government develops labour laws to strengthen the state's legitimacy, local governments emphasise accumulation, establish close alliances with business, and decline to uphold the labour laws in order to support their business associates (Lee 2007: 16–21).

Anita Chan argues that local governments in Guangdong have stronger incentives to give priority to accumulation and flout labour rights than those in the three southern provinces of Vietnam. Village governments in the Pearl River Delta control land as their collective property and source of revenue. They earn large incomes from renting out land and factory buildings to foreign enterprises. Local village governments are strongly pro-business in order to protect their rentier incomes. In the south of Vietnam land remained private property during the division of the country (1954–1975), and the government's efforts to collectivise land after reunification failed. In the three southern industrial provinces land is *de jure* owned by the state, *de facto* individually owned and not a source of local government revenue. Local Vietnamese governments can then balance more even-handedly between accumulation and legitimation. As they maintain public order through relatively soft responses to labour unrest, it is easier to go on strike in Vietnam than in China (Chan 2011: 229–230).

Concluding Remarks

Changes in the international division of labour create new export-manufacturing centres and new hotspots of labour conflicts, China and Vietnam are cases in point. Their labour conflicts are fierce, but fragmented and not institutionalised. The extent of conflict in these two "most similar cases" vary. My data indicate a higher frequency of strikes in Vietnam than in China. I have tried to explain the differences as outcomes of work organisation, housing, the access to legal means of conflict resolution and more or less repressive government policies.

I first argued that China's "economic upgrading" has gone along with weakened shop floor power of labour, especially regarding the "supply" of experienced labour leaders. This contrasts with the more traditional "Taylorist" work organisation in Vietnam, with longer employment periods, where experienced workers and team leaders frequently become leaders of collective actions.

A second explanation relates to the way housing affects worker solidarity and networking. I have argued that the Vietnamese worker villages are more conducive to the spread of strikes than the Chinese dormitories, because they to a larger extent sustain networking across enterprises within industrial districts and free export zones.

My third explanation is about legal conflict resolution. I argued that the Chinese labour legislation sustained by well-developed institutions to a greater extent than the Vietnamese have induced workers to choose institutionalised, and individualised conflict procedures, rather than collective action and strike.

Finally, Chinese workers have been deterred from choosing strikes and other forms of collective action by the repression of local authorities. Local governments in Vietnam have chosen a relatively accommodating response to collective labour demands. For the southern export centres of the two countries I argued that local governments in Vietnam have more autonomy towards investor interests than those in China, because they do not obtain their revenue from renting out land to manufacturers.

Vietnam's low position within global value chains with limited economic upgrading pushes down wages to a very low level. Vietnamese authorities may face growing pressure to restrain wage growth to prevent relocation of manufacturing production to new low-wage destinations. China has a greater potential than Vietnam to weather labour unrest through economic upgrading with wage increases, but this potential has been realised through bifurcation of the workforce. Industrial upgrading is accompanied with growing inequality and precarious conditions of unskilled workers that impede collective action. Vietnamese workers may continue to strike more than their Chinese counterparts, but even "successful strikes" are merely minor battle victories in the class warfare of the socialist market economy.

References

Anner, Mark. 2015. Labor Control Regimes and Worker Resistance in Global Supply Chains. *Labor History* 56 (3): 292–307.

Anner, Mark, and Xiangmin Liu. 2016. Harmonious Unions and Rebellious Workers: A Study of Wildcat Strikes in Vietnam. *ILR Review* 69 (1): 3–28.

Banister, Judith, and George Cook. 2011. China's Employment and Compensation Costs in Manufacturing Through 2008. *Monthly Labor Review*, March: 39–52.

Butollo, Florian. 2015. Industrial Upgrading and Work: The Impact of Industrial Transformation on Labor in Guangdong's Garment and IT Industries. In *Chinese Workers in Comparative Perspective*, ed. Anita Chan, 85–104. Itacha, NY: Cornell University Press.

Chan, Anita. 2011. Strikes in Vietnam and China in Taiwanese-Owned Factories: Diverging Industrial Relations Patterns. In *Labour in Vietnam*, ed. Anita Chan, 211–251. Institute of Southeast Asian Studies: Singapore.

Chan, Chris King-Chi. 2010. *The Challenge of Labour in China: Strikes and the Changing Labour Regime in Global Factories*. London and New York: Routledge.

Chen, Feng. 2010. Trade Unions and the Quadripartite Interactions in Strike Settlement in China. *China Quarterly* 201: 104–124.

China Labour Bulletin. Hong Kong. http://www.clb.org.hk.

China Labour Bulletin. 2009. *Going It Alone: The Workers' Movement in China (2007–2008).*

China Labour Bulletin. 2011. *Unity Is Strength: The Workers' Movement in China 2009–2011.*

China Labour Bulletin. 2016. An Introduction to China Labour Bulletin's Strike Map, March 29.

China Labour Bulletin. 2019. *China Labour Bulletin Strike Map.*

China Labour Bulletin. n.d. *China's Labour Dispute Resolution System.*

China Labour Statistical Yearbook. 2016. Beijing: China Statistics Press. http://www.mohrss.gov.cn/2016/indexeh.htm.

China Statistical Yearbook. 2015. Beijing: China Statistics Press. http://www.stats.gov.cn/tjsj/ndsj/2015/indexeh.htm.

Do, Quynh Chi. 2008. The Challenge from Below: Wildcat Strikes and the Pressure for Union Reform in Vietnam. Paper Presented to Vietnam Update 2008 Conference, Labour in Vietnam, November 6–7, The Australian National University, Canberra.

Do, Quynh Chi. 2017. The Regional Coordination of Strikes and the Challenge for Union Reform in Vietnam. *Development and Change* 48 (5): 1052–1068.

Financial Times. 2016. Vietnam the Big Winner from China's Move Up the Value Chain, July 29.

Golley, Jane, and Xin Meng. 2011. Has China Run Out of Surplus Labour? *China Economic Review* 22 (4): 555–572.

Kerkvliet, Benedict J. Tria. 2011. Workers' Protest in Contemporary Vietnam. In *Labour in Vietnam*, ed. Anita Chan, 160–210. Singapore: Institute of Southeast Asian Studies.

Lee, Ching Kwan. 2007. *Against the Law: Labor Protest in China's Rustbelt and Sunbelt*. Berkeley: University of California Press.

Lee, Ching Kwan. 2010. Pathways of Labor Activism. In *Chinese Society. Change, Conflict and Resistance*, 3rd ed., ed. Elisabeth J. Perry and Mark Selden, 57–79. New York and London: Routledge.

Lee, Ching Kwan. 2017. After the Miracle: Labor Politics Under China's New Normal. *Catalyst* 1 (3): 93–115.

Lüthje, Boy, and Florian Butollo. 2017. Why the Foxconn Model Does Not Die: Production Networks and Labour Relations in the IT Industry in South China. *Globalizations* 14 (2): 216–231.

Masina, Pietro. 2012. Vietnam Between Developmental State and Neoliberalism: The Case of the Industrial Sector. In *Developmental Politics in Transition: The Neoliberal Era and Beyond*, ed. Kyung-Sup Chang, Ben Fine, and Linda Weiss, 188–210. London: Palgrave Macmillan.

Masina, Pietro, and Michela Cerimele. 2018. Patterns of Industrialisation and the State of Industrial Labour in Post-WTO Accession Vietnam. *European Journal of East Asian Studies* 17 (2): 289–323.

Pincus, Jonathan. 2015. Why Doesn't Vietnam Grow Faster? State Fragmentation and the Limits of Vent for Surplus Growth. *Journal of Southeast Asian Economies* 32 (1): 26–51.

Pringle, Tim, and Simon Clarke. 2011. *The Challenge of Transition: Trade Unions in Russia, China and Vietnam*. London: Palgrave Macmillan.

Qin, Ling. 2016. Introduction: The Survival and Collective Struggles of Workers in China's Coastal Private Enterprises since the 1990s. In *China on Strike: Narratives of Workers' Resistance*, ed. Hao Ren, 1–26. Chicago, IL: Haymarket Books.

Rhoo, Sungmin, 2015. *The Worker's Dilemma: Collective Action and Factory Workers in China*. PhD Dissertation, Political Science, Stanford University.

Schmalz, Stefan, Brandon Sommer, and Xu Hui. 2017. The Yue Yuen Strike: Industrial Transformation and Labour Unrest in the Pearl River Delta. *Globalizations* 14 (2): 285–297.

Siu, Kaxton, 2015. The Working and Living Conditions of Garment Workers in China and Vietnam: A Comparative Study. In *Chinese Workers in Comparative Perspective*, ed. Anita Chan, 105–131. Itacha, NY: Cornell University Press.

Siu, Kaxton, and Anita Chan. 2015. Strike Wave in Vietnam, 2006–2011. *Journal of Contemporary Asia* 45 (1): 71–91.

Silver, Beverly, and Lu Zhang. 2009. China as an Emerging Epicenter of World Labor Unrest. In *China and the Transformation of Global Capitalism*, ed. Ho-fung Hung, 174–187. Baltimore: John Hopkins University Press.

Statistical Handbook of Vietnam. 2015. Hanoi: General Statistics Office of Vietnam.

Trading Economics. n.d. Vietnam Food Inflation. http://www.tradingeconomics.com/vietnam/food-inflation.

Trading Economics. n.d. Vietnam Minimum Wages. http://tradingeconomics.com/vietnam/minimum-wages.

Tran, Ngọc Angie. 2012. Vietnamese Textile and Garment Industry in the Global Supply Chain: State Strategies and Workers' Responses. *Institutions and Economies* 4 (3): 123–150.

Tran, Ngoc Angie, 2013. *Ties That Bind: Cultural Identity, Class and Law in Vietnam's Labor Resistance*. Itacha, NY: Cornell University Press.

Tran, Ngoc Angie, 2015. Small Victory, Systemic Problems. *New Mandala*, April 30. http://www.newmandala.org/small-victory-systemic-problems/.

CHAPTER 10

Welfare and Social Policy in China: Building a New Welfare State

Kristin Dalen

Introduction

Social policy as an independent policy arena did not exist in China until well into the reform and opening-up period launched by Deng Xiaoping. But economic reforms and increased openness to global markets combined with major changes to society and traditional social organization, created new winners and losers. Increased inequality and uneven growth across social groups and geographical regions both in terms of economic means and access to basic goods such as health, education, housing, and pensions, combined with rapid population aging, and increasing demands on the government brought social policy and the establishment of a social welfare system on the agenda around the turn of the century. The Chinese term social policy (*sheng hui zheng ce*) appeared for the first time in a top-level document in 2006, when the Chinese Communist Party (CCP) under the leadership of Hu Jintao and Wen Jiabao introduced the notion of "harmonious society." During this period

K. Dalen (✉)
Fafo Institute for Labour and Social Research, Oslo, Norway
e-mail: Kristin.dalen@fafo.no

A. Hansen et al. (eds.), *The Socialist Market Economy in Asia*,
https://doi.org/10.1007/978-981-15-6248-8_10

of high economic growth new policies were launched, abolishing agricultural taxes, extending health insurance, securing access to basic education, pensions, and income support to both rural and urban residents. These policies and initiatives were introduced to meet a range of challenges facing the Chinese society and leadership. Growing tensions over rapidly increasing inequalities, the need to stimulated domestic consumptions, continue economic growth and responding to the global recession in 2008, together with China's integration into the global market and world order, were all significant reasons for the new focus on social policies strengthening peoples' welfare. Despite the underlying rational for introducing new policies, there is little doubt that during the first fifteen years of the twenty-first-century China saw a fundamental change toward a more universal welfare state for all Chinese citizens (Kuhnle et al. 2012).

Social policies continue to be a key instrument for the Chinese government in their efforts to maintain the balance between continued economic growth, increased well-being, and social stability also after Xi Jinping took over as leader of the CCP in 2013. The focus on social development and increased social justice has been sustained. The overall approach and goal of development for the current Chinese leadership is described as:

> The wellbeing of the people is the fundamental goal of development. We must do more to improve the lives and address the concerns of the people, and use development to strengthen areas of weakness and promote social fairness and justice. We should make steady progress in ensuring people's access to childcare, education, employment, medical services, elderly care, housing, and social assistance. We will intensify poverty alleviation, see that all our people have a greater sense of fulfillment as they contribute to and gain from development, and continue to promote well-rounded human development and common prosperity for everyone. (GOV 2017)

Understanding the developments and the rational of social policies and the establishment of a welfare system can provide us with valuable understanding of the social and political development within China. Economic growth both forced and allowed the Chinese government to develop a more comprehensive social policy. Focus on peoples "well-being" is key in the plan to secure continued economic growth, transform China to a high-income society, and sustain the legitimacy of the current regime.

The first part of this chapter will provide an historical overview of the establishment of a Chinese welfare regime and how social policies have been developed to address social and economic challenges in line with the overarching goals of Chinese leadership and economic, social, and political changes. The second half of the chapter will give an introduction to the current Chinese welfare regime, describing both gains and challenges aiming to understand the structure and the organization of welfare provision. Both the historical overview and the description of the current system will pay special attention to three policy areas of great importance to the development of a broad-based and inclusive welfare state; health care, pension, and basic education.

The Chinese Welfare State, Its History and Development

The welfare state system in China has been characterized by a dual approach since it was first established, where urban and rural policies operated rather independently from each other (Kwon et al. 2009). In the late fifties, the state created and established the *Hukou* system. A household registration system that perpetuated economic and social categories, serving to distinguish urban, rural, and migrant populations with the purpose of controlling movement of people and resources from the agricultural sector to cities (Young 2013). These state-devised "boundaries and categories," determining entitlements and life chances have persisted, and despite efforts to relax the system it has been seen by many as the most important divide in Chinese society both with regards to social status and attitudes (Wang 2008, 2018; Whyte 2010).

Iron Rice-Bowls and Barefoot Doctors—The Mao Period

Before the "reform and opening up" introduced in 1978, the Chinese welfare system was characterized by work-unit based provision of comprehensive social services in of a communist planned economy that relied on universal lifetime employment. In urban areas services were organized around state-owned enterprises (SOEs) which provided their work units (*Danweis*) with a cradle-to-grave social security system. In rural areas the services were provided by agricultural communes with a minimum of social security and the public ownership of land. Urban and rural entitlements were secured by the Hukou system.

Health, Pensions, and Basic Education

The command and control health system of the Mao-era achieved near universal access to basic health care services and made impressive strides in improving population health. The health care professionals were state employees and services were provided largely for free, meaning that nearly all urban residents enjoyed comprehensive health services (Chan et al. 2008; Saich 2006). In rural areas, the key providers of health services were often termed "barefoot-doctors" in village clinics. In 1976, nine in ten villages in rural China participated in the rural Cooperative Medical Scheme (CMS), providing nearly universal basic health care coverage to the rural population (Carrin et al. 1999). The responsibility for the provision of old-age pensions in urban areas laid exclusively with the SOEs. The system combined generous eligibility criteria with high benefit levels offering replacement rates as high as 80%. In rural areas, there was virtually no formal, state-run rural pension scheme and rural residents had to rely completely on support from the rural communes and extended family for the provision of old age security (Shi 2006). The Chinese Communist Party (CCP) promoted the ideal of access to education for all. The enrollment of children in primary education increased from very low to nearly universal already in the early 1960s (Hossain 1997). Still, basic education was often of low quality, there were no laws to protect universal access, students rarely completed nine-year education and the political focus was mostly on improving higher education.

Uneven Economic Growth and Dismantling Welfare—Reform and Opening-Up

From the introduction of economic reform and "opening-up" under Deng Xiaoping in the early 1980s until late 1990s[1] China saw economic growth and reform, but also erosion of the previous welfare arrangements and a strong focus on market-oriented flexibility, "semi-privatization," cost cuts and competitiveness. This was coupled with a decentralization of responsibilities for welfare schemes which lead to a neglect of previous considerations about social security and equity. Economic growth increased rapidly in coastal cities where "new economic zones" were established to promote production and trade in the early 1980s.

[1] During the consecutive political leadership of Deng Xiaoping, Hu Yaobang, Zhao Ziyang and Jiang Zemin.

Simultaneously, the introduction of the "household responsibility system" allowed individual household to make their own decisions about production—generating private incentives and increased production, increasingly superseding the collectivist People's Communes in rural areas (Lin 1992). These gradual steps of economic reform and liberalization had a profound impact on the existing structures of welfare and social security provision. The previously established basic welfare system organized around work units and agricultural communes proved incompatible with a competition-based, market-oriented economy. Economic growth and a strengthening of flexibility and competitiveness were main political priorities implying state withdrawal from welfare provision.

Health, Pensions, and Basic Education

The responsibility for health care provision was delegated to local authorities. A management reform transformed hospitals into profit-oriented entities with substantial autonomy, causing a dramatic decline in government health spending (Chan et al. 2008). The overall trend was characterized by state withdrawal and increased out-of-pocket payments (Saich 2004). In rural areas the Cooperative Medical Schemes collapsed, village collective funds virtually disappeared and left 900 million rural residents without health insurance coverage (Chan et al. 2008). Health care in both urban and rural areas was increasingly provided by private, profit-oriented facilities, and substantial parts of the population could not afford even basic medical treatment (Saich 2004). Escalating personal medical costs and inequitable distribution of health resources resulted in serious access problems, high rates of medical impoverishment and widening inequalities (Egglestone et al. 2008). Pension schemes dismantled, SOEs came under increased financial pressure, and pension obligations were often disregarded. The government tried to introduce new pension insurance schemes, but these only applied to the privileged group of SOE workers (Chan et al. 2008). In rural areas the solidarity of the extended family had traditionally been the most important source of support for the elderly. However, the rapid ageing of the population triggered by an increase in life expectancy and the one-child policy adopted in 1979, coupled with the exodus of young, productive migrant workers moving to the cities, profoundly undermined the viability of traditional structures of extended family support for the elderly (Shi 2006). Compulsory nine-year education became a political goal in the 1980s and led to the new education law enacted in April 1986. The new law consolidated previous initiatives and was the first law for compulsory education in China. But in line with health and pensions, the responsibility for compulsory nine-year education was decentralized leaving financing mainly up to the lowest level of government (township and village level). Despite differences between localities, the financial burden of education was too often left to parents and extended family through the introduction of various kinds of fees and expenses. This was particularly true where village authorities had little access to financial incomes. The single most important reason for children not attending school in 1995 was the lack of financial means (UNICEF 1995: 90). To remedy some of the unsustainable developments, the responsibility for compulsory education was lifted from village to country level (*the Country Centered Reform*) in 1994 aiming to reduce the unsustainable burden on farmers and poor households (Cai 2013).

After the reform and opening-up period, uneven economic growth and social contradictions became increasingly prominent. Even though many saw real improvements in their living conditions, others were disillusioned by the negative consequences of the reforms. The lack of redistributive policies led to inequality of opportunity and access to public goods such as education, health care, long-term care, pensions, employment, and social benefits. Large portions of the Chinese population were left with very limited social protections (Whyte 2010).

Toward a New Welfare Regime—The Hu-Wen Era (Social Justice and Fairness)

When Hu Jintao and Wen Jiabao took over as Party leader and Premier in 2003, growing economic and social inequality and the lack of equal access to benefits caused increasing social tensions and unrest. Social policies were put on the political agenda through the slogan of "harmonious society" (*hexie shihui*), and focus shifted from economic growth toward more redistribution (social balance). The 11th five-year plan (2006–2011) stated that "greater attention should be paid to social equity and justice" (*shehui gongping zhengyi*) a concept rarely used prior to this (Xinhua News 2006). Through the formulation of the goals of a "harmonious society" (*hexie shehui*) and inclusive growth, and the aspirations to become a "moderately well-off society" (*xiaokang shehui*) by the 100 years' anniversary of the Chinese Communist Party in 2020, the party state crafted a developmental direction that promised greater social inclusion and socio-economic leveling. "Moderate universalism" was introduced by the Ministry of Civil Affairs as the guiding welfare principle in 2007, and substantial reforms were introduced to the Chinese welfare system focusing on integration, basic rights and universality.

Facing major challenges, but at the same time experiencing large economic growth and with access to fiscal revenues, the Hu-Wen administration launched a series of social policyreforms to move China toward a more integrated and balanced social welfare system. On an overarching level, focus was put on the improvement of welfare policy management,[2] tax reforms and the design of a social insurance law.[3] Policies included establishing national social insurance programs for both health services and pensions. Particular emphasis was put on reducing the gap between urban and rural populations and a grand campaign to improve life in rural areas "Building a new and socialist countryside" (*jianshe shehuizhuyi xinnongcun*) was launched. Further, the establishment of a comprehensive social assistance system was initiated and efforts to improve labor conditions and social protection for rural-to-urban migrants were rolled out, the introduction of social services was key in these efforts. Social services were not a part of national social policies in China until the 2000s. The "new" focus on social services can be seen as a response to the unbalances social development that came about after the rapid but uneven economic growth and changes in the populations structure. Societal challenges such as aging populations, living and working conditions of the disabled, drug abuse, youth offenders, victims of domestic violence, psychological illness, left-behind children, women and elderly in the countryside, and security of migrant workers were all identified as tasks that should be targeted through social work and social services. The Hu and Wen administration introduced social work to the implementation of social policies in China. At the same time, a wide range of policies and reforms of policies related to social security, health care, elderly care and pensions, and free basiceducation for all were initiated.

Health, Pensions, and Basic Education

Throughout the 1990s political leaders in China gradually came to acknowledge that the health sector was facing severe challenges which might undermine economic growth and social stability. Evidence on the

[2] The new 'Ministry of Human Resources and Social Security' was established in 2008.

[3] 'The Social Insurance Law of the People's Republic of China' was instituted in 2010.

adverse effects of economic reforms for health care was mounting, and the World Health Report 2000 shocked many within the government by ranking China as number 188 out of 191 members on an evaluation of health fairness in financial contribution (WHO 2001). The SARS crises in 2002–2003 brought the world's attention to the weaknesses and inequities of China's health care system. Since the mid-2000s a number of measures to alleviate the challenges facing the health sector were introduced. A health insurance plan aimed at covering the entire Chinese populations (including migrants and rural populations) was put forward. The New Rural Cooperative Medical Scheme (NRCMS), an insurance system where the government pays the larger part of the premium and all rural populations should be guaranteed to participate, was initiated in 2003 and implemented nationwide in 2005. In 2006, the Urban Resident Basic Medical Insurance (URBMI) for the urban unemployed (not covered by the insurance for urban workers) was introduced, resembling the NRCMS. The new health insurances led to substantially higher health insurance coverage despite substantial differences in coverage across geographical regions (Tang 2014). Between 2004 and 2014 the coverage increased from 15 to 94% in rural areas, 51–94% in urban areas, and from 9 to 87% for rural to urban migrants (numbers taken from the Distributive Justice Survey conducted by the author and partners).

Rooted in the State Council Document No. 26, *Establishment of a Unified Pension System for Enterprise Employees*, China established a contributory pension system for urban enterprise employees in 1997, this system can be seen as the cornerstone of the Chinese pension system and is mandatory for all contracted workers.[4] At the 17th national congress of the CCP in 2007, Hu Jintao set out a goal to make the pension program national in scope—reaching full coverage by the year 2020. This should be achieved through including new groups in the pension system for worker and by introducing two new pilot pension schemes, namely, the "New Rural Social Pension Scheme" (2009) and the "Urban Resident Social Pension Scheme" (2011). Both new schemes are voluntary and have basic similarities; they are mainly financed through individual contributions paired with government subsidies. In 2014 the government

[4]Workers contribute based on their individual wage, at a rate of up to 8%, while employers contribute a percentage of the total wages paid to their workforce, usually around 20%.

merged the NRSPS and the URSPS into a new unified pension system for all residents without employment termed "Unified Urban-Rural Resident Basic Pension System". From 2004 to 2014 pension coverage increased from 8 to 47% in rural areas, from 52 to 62% in urban areas and from 7 to 32% among rural to urban migrants (China Distributive Justice Survey). Furthermore, a generous pension system for public service workers was abolished in 2015 making public sector employees contribute to their own pensions in line with other employees.

In 2001, the State Council issued "*Notification on pilot work of rural tax and fee reform*". The rural tax and fee reform was primarily designed to eliminate taxes and improve economic and social conditions for households in the Chinese countryside. The reform was implemented as a pilot in Anhui province in 2000, a reached 20 provinces and autonomous regions by 2002, finally extended to all parts of China by 2003.[5] The most important effect of the "Rural Tax and Fee Reform" on rural compulsory education, was canceling educational fees from parents. The system changed from one that mainly depended on additional educational taxes to one that depended on a system of government financial allocation (Gao 2004a, b). Still, lack of tax revenues, mismanaged of funds, unbalanced investment, and unfair public resource allocation continued to be a problem on the local level (Gao 2004a, b). As a result, a new set of reforms were introduced. In December 2005 the state council issues the "*Notification on Deepening the Reform of Fund Management of Rural Compulsory Education*". It aimed at ensuring financial security to rural education under a system of clear rules and responsibilities. In June 2006, the revised Compulsory Education Act was issued, enhancing the central government's financial responsibility of for rural compulsory education including free tuition, free textbooks and construction and maintenance of school premises over the national budget.

Summing up Chinese Welfare Reforms from 2000 to 2015

Since the turn of the century until the end of the Hu-Wen era, the Chinese state's willingness to take responsibility for peoples' welfare increased. Entitlements were to a larger extent secured by law, and a wide range of different schemes was made national and more unified,

[5] With the exception of Tibet Autonomous Region.

with the aim of covering the entire population. Social services were identified as important tools in the implantation of social policies on the way to reaching important political goal such as establishing a "moderately well-off society" (Fig. 10.1).

Based on the reforms described above, the Chinese welfare state could be seen as having moved from the selective welfare of liberalism toward a more inclusive model with a dual focus on development and enhanced social inclusiveness resembling the East Asian welfare states who belong to the so-called "first group" (Taiwan, Korea and Japan) (Kuhnle 2011, Kuhnle et al. 2012). Scholars have analyzed the significance and directions of policy reforms during the Hu-Wen era from different perspectives. They generally agree that the decade can be seen as a milestone in China's social policy development. Jane Duckett characterizes these reforms as a compromise between the party states responsibility to provide basic social goods and safety nets and the continued dominance of the market and private sector (Duckett 2019). Mark Frazier highlights the governments push for universal coverage and unified social insurance and assistance

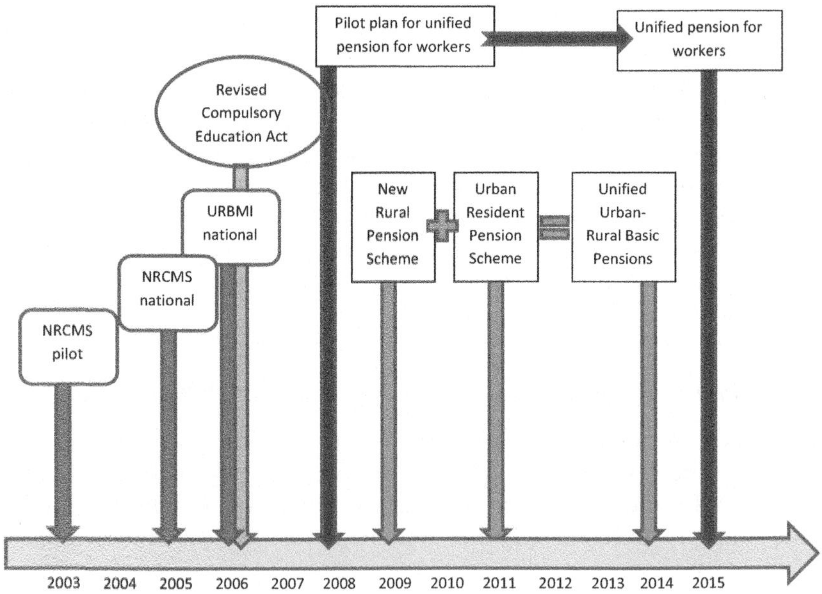

Fig. 10.1 Chinese reforms of education, health and pensions since 2003

systems across the urban–rural divide, despite the persistent large gap in benefits. He argues that the continued urbanization trend would drive greater political demands for equal access and benefits and erode the differences between urban and rural social welfare systems (Frazier 2014).

On the Way to a Moderately Well-off Society—"The Moderate Universal Welfare principle"

As Xi Jinping took over the leadership from Hu Jintao in 2013, he announced that China would enter what Deng Xiaoping described as the third phase of China's modern economic development. In this phase Chinese economy and society will reach the income and living standard levels on par with the OECD average, and eradicate all form of severe poverty. Five years later, the 19th party congress announced that China was entering into a "new era" or a "new historical state" and that the description of the principle contradiction within society has changed from between "*the ever growing material and cultural needs of the people and a backward social production*" to "*unbalanced and inadequate economic development and the ever growing needs of the people for a better life.*" Redefining the principle contradiction from the previous statement made by Deng Xiaoping in 1981, indicates a shift in the development focus from unbridled economic growth to better quality expansion and wealth distribution across geographic areas and social groups. New focus is put on quality in supply and production of services and goods and how the government could do more to improve the lives and address the concerns of people and use development to: "promote social fairness and justice, by ensuring access to childcare, education, employment, medical services, elderly care, housing and social support" (GOV 2017).

The reformulation of the principle contradiction comes in a time when the economy must complete the transition to a service-, consumption- and productivity-driven economy, in which innovation, technology, and education will be key. At the same time, China continue to face serious population challenges such as low and decreasing fertility, a rapidly growing elderly population and a shrinking labor force, coupled with slowing economic growth, growing public expectations, and a lack of trust in both non-state and state actors. New "winners and losers" will emerge from the transition and potential new social risks can arise. As his predecessors, Xi Jinping sees social policy and the further development of a Chinese welfare state as key in promoting well-being for the population and stability for the regime. Public services and social provisions have a prominent place in the first five-year plan (NDRC 2016). Health, employment, education, and pensions features high on the agenda. Previously established policies are to be continued and further developed, social services should be "equalized" and sever poverty should be eliminated.

Beyond further developing policies initiated and implemented during the Hu-Wen era, the new leadership has increased the focus on innovation, digitalization, standardization, and establishment of national reporting and registration systems both for fiscal spending and for participants in insurance and social programs. Aiming to improve not only the coverage but also the quality of insurance and social programs. Systems of reporting and auditing of fiscal budgets (Wong 2016) and new administrative procedures have been introduced. Responsibilities have been defined and sometimes reassigned, as in the new organization of ministries and departments in 2017. Strategies presented under the current government has increased focus on "innovation in the provision of social services" featuring digital solutions such as e-health and e-learning. In addition to expanding the scope and the depth of programs, the ambitions to increase the quality of the programs is indicated through the emphasis on innovation both in the design and implementation of programs and in the delivery of services. To meet the challenge of unequal access to services and benefits across the population, particularly related to migration, the Xi administration has emphasized hukoureform. In November 2013 the CCP decided to speed up the pace of the long-awaited hukou reforms and in 2014 the "New-Type Urbanization Plan (NUP)" was launched (Wang et al. 2015). The plan entails that all residents of urban areas regardless of hukou status should have access to the same benefits. Hukoureform is a slow process particularly in the largest cities, but by September 2016, even Beijing municipal government announced that distinctions between urban and rural entitlements will gradually be eased until all residents enjoy equal access to services, including health (SCMP 2016).

Health, Pensions, and Education

Under the leadership of Xi Jinping the coverage of all insurance programs (among them pensions and health) has increased. The streamlining of the insurance programs continues, and the social health insurance schemes for urban nonemployed and rural residents have been combined into one scheme, much in line with the unification of the pensions insurance scheme for urban nonemployed and rural residents in 2015. To improve migrants access to health insurance a national swap fund was established in 2018. The fund was also promoted to make pensions insurance transition between different provinces accessible, with the aim to equalize the benefit standard (GOV 2018). As a first step, 17 provinces had clarified that the civil affairs department of their local government was responsible for the administration (MOHRSS 2016).

In 2015 the CCP central committee endorsed the "Healthy China 2030" strategy. The strategy is linked to the Sustainable Development Goals for 2030 and is core both in the reform of the health services, defining the health policy for the next decade, and in the provision of care and services to the rapidly aging population in China. Improving the population's health has become a "political priority and a strategic goal in national development" (Tan et al. 2017). The strategy aims to foster innovation, use scientific development, and improve fairness and justice. The goals of the strategy are linked to better coordination and transferability (establishing health information systems, health cards), strengthening the primary health services at the local level, promoting digitalization and e-health, and strengthening the role of non-state actors in the provision of health care and services. In addition to substantial reforms of the public health care, the Chinese government has put emphasis on the role of the market in providing health care. "Social forces provide health care" (*Shehui banyi*) is the new buzzword in health reform documents (GOV 2013). The official policy is now that the government is responsible for providing basic medical services *or* purchasing certain services. Nonbasic medical services should be provided by the market, with the government assuming responsibility for the necessary evaluation, supervision, and regulation. The concept of "social forces" does not only refer to commercial actors but also to non-profit civil society organizations. In 2013 China's State Council unveiled detailed guidelines on developing a large scale industry of private health services by 2021, although the government will remain responsible for basic medical care (State Council 2013). The government has launched several key supportive policies to encourage private health provision, including expanding the state medical insurance scheme to qualified private hospitals and improved approval procedures for private hospitals. As a result, the number of private health facilities has grown rapidly. Yet, private hospitals face challenges in attracting qualified personnel due to smaller professional environments, less resources for research and development and less exposure to complicated treatment cases and advanced treatment skills. People generally trust public health facilities more than private ones.

In education, broadening of the use of digital technologies and the enhancement of e-learning has been the key focus of reforms. China has emerged as one of the global leaders in promoting information and communication technology for education (ICT4E) and has implemented ICT4E infrastructure in a majority of schools (Shulte 2018). But the competence and acceptance of digital education technology is still slowed by lack of competence among both teachers, students, parents, and administrators and social and cultural skepticism toward moving away from the traditional methods of teaching and learning. With the growing emphasis in the population on educational achievements and quality of education, the percentage of private institutions in basic education has increased steadily, according to the World Bank the percentage of private primary schools increased from 3.5 to 8 from 2006 to 2018 (World Bank 2018). Despite the success of educational reforms in providing education to all, the regional inequalities in education are still widespread.

Policy Development, Financing, and Oversight

The CCP is responsible for policymaking on the highest level, but the state council, with the help of its subordinate departments and local governments has the main responsibility to specify the outline with concrete programs, projects, and policies. Although national institutions such as the CCP central leadership, the National Peoples' Congress and the State Council are the key in China's general public policymaking process, some government departments under the state council are particularly important in the social policy process.[6] In developing national

[6] After the administrative reorganization launched in 2017 these are: The Ministry of Human Resource and Social Security (MOHRSS), in charge of policy concerning social insurance and employment. The Ministry of Civil Affairs (MOAC), mainly in charge of social assistance and poverty reduction policy. The National Health Commission (NHC), in charge of health care and population policy. The Ministry of Education (ME), in charge of educational policy. The Ministry of Housing and Urban Rural Development (MOHURD), in charge of housing and construction policy. The Ministry of Veterans Affairs, responsible for the welfare of military veterans. The National Development and

policies, China has employed extended use of pilot schemes to test how different programs work, how to tailor these programs best to local conditions and how to scale programs up to a national level. This has been a characteristic of Chinese policy development and implementation within all fields, including social policies. Ideas, goals, and targets can be launched from both central and local level, program development and implementation is tested out in selected areas, evaluated and readjusted, before eventually adapted to the national level. Social policy development and implementation varies across policy areas and is characterized by both top-down directions and decentralized implementation. One example is centralized health policies, and decentralized poverty reduction policies.

The total spending on poverty reduction, health services, pensions, and education has increased dramatically over the last decade, as government has seen increased revenues and commitment to extend public services (Wong 2016). In some instances, such as health and education, spending increased with up to 20% year over year (Wong 2016; Stephan and Duckett 2018). But despite increased availability of funds at the central level, the main responsibility for financing social policies lays with the local governments, and transfers of funds to the local level has not increased to match the increased responsibility to provide services. Without sufficient dedicated funds on the local level to implement central policies—there has been substantial variation across China—rich areas often have much better services than poor areas. One of the most important changes on the financing and oversight of social policy implementation since the third plenum of the 18th Party congress in 2013 has been the introduction of a comprehensive reform of the fiscal system. The first phase of the reform was initiated in 2014 and related to public financial management and focused on reining in extra budgetary resources and local government borrowing, strengthening accountability and transparency. The two next phases relate to tax reform and intergovernmental reform (reassignment of revenues and responsibilities). The most important driver for change was the Budget Law and associated documents introduced in 2014 and 2015 (Wong 2016). The budget law imposed a mandate for governments at all levels to compile and release to the public a comprehensive government financial report that required reporting of all fiscal resources, including public finance budgets, government funds (including

Reform Commission of the PRC (NDRC), responsible for policies for economic and social development.

land revenues), revenues from state capital operations, and social insurance funds. Through this reform, the government can be seen to have committed to building a new and more rigorous government accounting system, along with a stronger system of auditing and disclosure mechanisms for government financial reports. A national auditing system under the Ministry of Finance (Supervision Department) and the National Audit Office and its local branches is strengthened and given more power and resources, contributing to increased transparency and accountability. The reforms have strengthened the three pillars of public financial management systems: the budgeting system itself, the audit system and the information system of budget reporting. Furthermore, performance management mechanisms and institutions have become more important. If implemented according to plan, the new government financial reporting system will provide comprehensive and accurate information on government operations, providing an opportunity for evaluation of public sector performance and important improvements of the implementation of social policy and programs.

Challenges Ahead

The Chinese leadership has made impressive efforts in their stride to establish a more comprehensive welfare system, but China is changing rapidly; aging, urbanization, and changing employment patterns are key when new social service delivery strategies and social policies are developed. An ageing population and higher demands on government provision of affordable public services are among the main challenges in the future implementation of social policies and programs in China. As of today, the previous role of the work units in fulfilling public service functions has dismantled, and families are no longer able to take the main responsibility for providing the care needed by children, elderly, and disabled. Social and economic change has transformed the labor market; migration has dismantled traditional family structures; increased living standards have changed expectations and a much higher degree of information about how others live their lives have led to higher demands. Despite the fact that many of the challenges facing the development of social policy and welfare in China are similar to challenges in mature welfare states in developed countries, it is worthwhile to point to some of the most daunting ones. These challenges may be more or less interlinked, below they are presented in three main categories; challenges related to economic changes, challenges related to the organization and implementation of social policy, and challenges related to peoples' changing expectations.

New Labor Relations and Digitalization

With the transformation of the Chinese economy away from traditional industries toward service and innovation, the organization of the labor market changes. More people are employed in the so-called "grey economy" where employment more often is based on self-employment. The safety net compared to traditional labor relations (contracts and permanent positions) is less developed and social security is weaker. Since most social insurance schemes in China (health, pension, work-related injury, maternity, etc.) are linked to employment, changes to the labor market relations may be significant in the future provision and financing of welfare and social policies. The Chinese government has strategically promoted IT solutions and digitalization of employment, education and social service delivery since the turn of the century, improving management and provision of public services (Indeerjet 2016). Yet, there is still a divide between localities and population groups as to what extent they have been able to acquire skills and infrastructure to benefit from digitalization. China has committed to major public investments in IT infrastructure in both rural and urban areas (the "Internet Plus Action Plan," presented by Li Keqiang in 2015) and digitalization presents new opportunities, but to achieve equalization of social services, bridging the digital divide will be crucial. As laborers continue to be more mobile, issues related to *hukou* continues to be a challenge. Despite revisions of the system, allowing for easier transfer of registration and eligibilities to and between second and third tier cities in China, mobility to and between the biggest cities is still heavily restricted. New systems to secure equalization and transportability of benefits and entitlements are developed and implements, but the *hukou* system still represents a hurdle to securing welfare for all.

Organization and Implementation

Despite clear commitments to the extension of public services and increased revenues to the central government from economic growth and tax reforms, the willingness to channel sufficient funds to the local governments has been low. Hence, local governments who are responsible for the provision of these services, are often left with unfunded mandates and few incentives to fulfill them. The lack of earmarked funds from central government has led to substantial variation across areas, localities and regions in the implementation of social policies. The new Budget Law and increased transparency, couples with the inclusion of public service delivery in the performance indicators for local government may lead to more equality, yet the lack of willingness to finance public services directly from the central government is still a challenge to the equal implementation of policies, access to- and delivery of services. The budget law, together with the resent government reshuffle may help meet the challenge of efficient coordination of delivery of public services across government entities (ministries, departments, commissions, and leading groups). Unprecedented economic growth in China over the last 30 years has provided the Chinese government with the financial means to invest in welfare. Economic growth will most likely slow in the years to come and tax reforms will be crucial in the future financing of a Chinese ever expanding welfare state.

With the rapid growth of the welfare state and the new focus on social work as a central part of delivering services to the population, China is facing a lack of experienced and trained social workers. Realizing the importance of social care, the current welfare reform requires new tasks concerning service provision, professionalization, and the delivery system (Leung and Xu 2015). Social workers are important professional service providers in China (GOV 2013), but the education and training of social workers is a new field, and the number of professionally trained social workers is still low. The organization of social work will continue to represent a challenge for the implementation of social policies in China. Central and local governments alike have recognized their limitations in providing social services directly, and the government increasingly supports and depend on social organizations in their fulfillment of policies. In 2016 the government enacted the "Opinion on Reforming the Organization and Management of Social Organizations and Promoting the Health and Well-organized Social Organization" welcoming the development of social service organizations as well as people's associations and nonprofit organizations to provide service (MCA 2016). Sharing the task of social service provision with organizations and associations is crucial in the strategy to reach a well-off society, but increased concerns about the quality of services have arisen from the rapid expansion of social care

(Pan et al. 2017). The challenge of integrating multiple non-state actors including NGOs and private companies into the provision of welfare includes both the development of a professional system of education, supervision and a certification and quality assurance system.

Public Expectations

A final set of challenges worth mentioning are those related to peoples' changing expectations both with regards to the range of public services and their quality. Research from the "China Distributive Justice Project" shows that peoples' preferences for the government as main provider of basic education, health, and elderly care increased substantially from 2004 to 2014.[7] By 2014 a clear majority of Chinese preferred the government to be the main provider of basic public services. In addition to growing expectations on what the government should deliver, the preference of government as a main provider presents a challenge in promoting non-state actors as key in the service delivery. Building trust in non-state actors as providers is a long-term and difficult efforts. After public health scandals such as the handling of the SARS outbreak in 2002–2003, the 2008 "Baby milk formula scandal" and the "Vaccine scandal" in 2018, trust in both state and non-state service providers is low. With increased use of social media, news about scandals and mismanagement travels fast. Even though public institutions generally enjoy more trust than private ones, increasing distrust may lead the upper middle-class to opt-out of public services—contributing to the development of a large scale industry of private service delivery that may drain the public services of qualified personnel. Contributing to a new divide between those that can afford to pay for private services and those who depend on the government to provide services for them.

Conclusion

Since the turn of the century, China has made impressive achievements in their development of social policies and the establishment of a welfare system. Responding to uneven economic growth, rapidly

[7] Health 30.5–66%, basic education: 44–79%, old age care: 33–55%.

increasing inequality and social unrest, focus was shifted from unbridled economic growth to better quality expansion and wealth distribution across geographic areas and social groups. Efficient, just and fair provision of basic needs is key in meeting public demands and securing the regimes legitimacy as China enters a new historical phase where the Chinese economy and society aims to reach the income and living standard levels on par with the OECD average.

Successful in their efforts to provide basic health, pensions, and educational services, new parts of the population have gained access to rights and benefits. This is particularly true for people living in rural areas and rural to urban migrants, even though the regional differences in the quality of basic services are still wide, access to basic rights and benefits has provided a new sense of basic security for many. Twenty years into the new century, the social policies and the emerging welfare state are characterized by a focus on quality over quantity. Emphasizing technology, organization and innovation, efforts are made to establish better systems for implementation, monitoring, and evaluations. A national and regional registration systems to better secure provisions of basic needs to all, allowing for transfers of rights and benefits across geographical areas is about to be implemented. A recent government reshuffle is designed to try to meet the challenge of efficient coordination of delivery of public services across government entities (ministries, departments, commissions, and leading groups) and the new budget law contributes to more transparency in the implementation at the local level.

Developing a welfare system, the Chinese government sees inclusion of both state and non-state actors as key, particularly within health, old age care, and social services. The private welfare sector in China is growing and the government is encouraging this development through policies and initiatives facilitating the establishment of both market-based and not-for-profit organizations and strengthening the education of social workers. The government is purchasing more services from non-state actors, at the same time willingness to spend money on services such as health, education, and care is increasing among the growing middle class.

Despite substantial achievements, the new Chinese welfare system is faced with daunting challenges that needs to be met in the efforts to be just, fair, equitable, and sustainable. New technology and innovation of systems can help meet some of these challenges such as increased mobility of people, yet other challenges such as dealing with the restructuring of the labor market, aging populations, and declining fertility requires other approaches. The future financing of a Chinese welfare system is still an important challenge. The central government provides goals and strategies but the lack of earmarked funds from central government has led to substantial variation across areas, localities, and regions in the implementation of social policies. The new Budget Law and increased transparency, coupled with the inclusion of public service delivery in the performance indicators for local government may lead to more equality, yet the lack of willingness to finance public services directly from the central government is still a challenge to the equal implementation of policies, access to- and delivery of services. Willingness to pay individual tax is low in China, indirect taxes and company tax are important sources for financing welfare, but as economic growth seems to slow and as the labor force is rapidly shrinking, financing future welfare remains a challenge.

As the Chinese leadership recognizes peoples ever growing needs for a better life as closely linked to basic rights and access to services and benefits—the development of a social policies and just, fair and equitable welfare systems will continue to be a central part in the future development of the Chinese nation.

References

Cai, L.L. 2013. The Challenges and Strategies of Country Centered Management System to Rural Compulsory Education Management. *Educational Science Research* 7: 46–55.

Carrin, G., A. Ron, H. Yang, et al. 1999. The Reform of the Rural Cooperative Medical System in the People's Republic of China: Interim Experiences in 14 Pilot Counties. *Social Science and Medicine* 48: 961–972.

Chan, Chak Kwan, King Lun Ngok, and David Phillips. 2008. *Social Policy in China: Development and Well-Being*. Bristol: Policy Press.

Duckett, J. 2019. International Influences on Policymaking in China: Network Authoritarianism from Jiang Zemin to Hu Jintao. *The China Quarterly* 237: 15–37.

Eggleston, K., L. Li, Q. Meng, M. Lindelow, and A. Wagstaff. 2008. Health Service Delivery in China: A Literature Review. *Health Economics* 17 (2): 149–165.

Frazier, M. 2014. State Schemes or Safety Nets? China's Push for Universal Coverage. *Daedalus* 143 (2): 69–80.

Gao, R.F. 2004a. A Positive Analysis of Current Financial System of Rural Compulsory Education in China. *Educational Research* 5: 3–20.

Gao, R.F. 2004b. Policy Recommendations for Restructuring Financial System of Rural Compulsory Education in China. *Educational Research* 7: 18–25.

GOV. 2013. Opinions on Accelerating the Development of Social Sector Run Medical Institutions (关于加快发展社会办医的若干意见). National Health and Family Planning Commission. Accessed at http://www.nhfpc.gov.cn/tigs/s7846/201401/239ae12d249c4e38a5e2de457ee20253.shtml.

GOV. 2017. Report of the 19th National Congress of the Communist Party of China. Accessed at http://www.chinadaily.com.cn/china/19thcpcnationalcongress/2017-11/04/content_34115212.htm.

GOV. 2018. Circular of the State Council on Establishing the National Swap Fund for the Pensions Insurance Urban Employees. Accessed at http://www.gov.cn/zhengce/content/2018-06/13/content_5298277.htm.

Hossain, S.I. 1997. Making Education in China Equitable and Efficient. Policy Research Working Paper 1814. World Bank, Washington, DC.

Indeerjet, Singh Sodhi. 2016. E-Government in China: Status, Challenges and Progress. In *IGI Global Trends, Prospects and Challenges in Asian E-Governance*, 36–54.

Kuhnle, Stein. 2011. Towards a Nordic-East Asian welfare dialogue? *Journal of Asian Public Policy* 4: 254–262.

Kuhnle, Stein, Anna Sanders, and Christopher Schmitt. 2012. Towards a Chinese Welfare State? Tagging the Concept of Social Security in China. *The Perspective of the World Review* 4 (2): 9–35.

Kwon, Huck-ju, Thandika Mkandawire, and Joakim Palme. 2009. Introduction: Social Policy and Economic Development in Late Industializers. *International Journal of Social Welfare* 2009 (18): S1–S11.

Leung, J.C.B., and Y. Xu. 2015. *China's Social Welfare*. Cambridge: Policy Press.

MCA. 2016. Opinion on Reforming the Organization and Management System of Social Organizations to Promote the Healthy and Orderly Development of Social Organizations. Accessed at http://www.mca.gov.cn/article/zwgk/mzyw/201608/20160800001526.shtml.

MOHRSS. 2016. Opinion of the State Council on Integrating the Medical Insurance System for Urban and Rural Residents. Accessed at http://en.pkulaw.cn/display.aspx?cgid=dc0f8f9e30d26f93bdfb&lib=law.

NDRC. 2016. The 13th Five-Year Plan for Economic and Social Development of the Peoples' Republic of China 2016–2020. Accessed at http://en.ndrc.gov.cn/policyrelease/201612/P020161207645766966662.pdf.

Pan, Y., Y. Sui, and S. Chen. 2017. Building Comprehensive Social Service System for the Elderly in the Community with Chinese Characteristics. *Population and Society* 33 (2): 30–38 and 58.

Saich, Anthony. 2004. China's New Social Challenges and the Provision of Social Welfare. In *Diaspora Philanthropy: Comparative Analysis of China and India*, ed. L. Chen and P. Geithner, 33 pp.

Saich, Anthony. 2006. China in 2005: Hu's in Charge. *Asian Survey* 46 (1): 37–46.

Shi, Shih Jiunn. 2006. Left to Market and Family—Again? Ideas and the Development of the Rural Pension Policy in China. *Social Policy & Administration* 40 (7): 791–806.

Shulte, Barbara. 2018. Digital Technologies for Education in China: National Ambitions Meet Local Realities. In *Serve the People—Innovation and Social Development Agenda*, ed. Matthias Stepan and Jane Duckett. Metrics Papers on China, No. 6.

South China Morning Post (SCMP). 2016. Accessed at http://chinadigitaltimes.net/2016/09/beijing-scrap-urban-rural-residency-distinction/.

State Council. 2013. Opinions of the State Council on Promoting Development of Health Service Industry, State Directive [2013] Number 40 (国务院关于促进健康服务业发展的若干意见国发[2013]40号).

Stepan, Matthias, and Jane Duckett (Eds.). 2018. *Serve the People—Innovation and Social Development Agenda*. Metrics Papers on China, No. 6.

Tan, X., X. Liu, and H. Shao. 2017. Healthy China 2030: A Vision for Health Care. *Value in Health Regional Issues* 12: 112–114.

Tang, Shenlang. 2014. Developing a More Equitable and Efficient Health Insurance in China. Paulson Policy Memorandum, The Paulson Institute. Accessed at http://www.paulsoninstitute.org/wp-content/uploads/2017/01/PPM_Health-Insurance_Tang_English_R.pdf.

UNICEF. 1995. Children and Women in China: A Situation Analysis (draft). Beijing: UNICEF.

Wang, Feng. 2008. *Boundaries and Categories: Rising Inequality in Post-Socialist Urban China*. Palo Alto, CA: Stanford University Press.

Wang, Xin-Rui, Eddie Chi Man Hui, Charles Choguill, and Sheng-Hua Jia. 2015. The Urbanization Policy in China—Which Way Forward? *Habitat International* 47: 279–284.

Wang, G. 2018. Principle-Guided Policy Experimentation in China: From Rural Tax and Fee Reform to Hu and Wen's Abolition of Agricultural Tax. *China Quarterly*: 1–20.

WHO. 2001. The World Health Report 2000—Health Systems: Improving Performance. Accessed at https://www.who.int/whr/2000/en/.

Whyte, Martin King. 2010. *Myth of the Social Volcano: Perceptions of Inequality and Distributive Injustice in Contemporary China*. Palo Alto, CA: Stanford University Press.

Wong, C. 2016. Budget Reform in China: Progress and Prospects in the Xi Jinping Era. *OECD Journal on Budgeting* 15 (3): 27–36. Accessed at https://doi.org/10.1787/budget-15-5jm0zbtm3pzn.

World Bank. 2018. Accessed at https://data.worldbank.org/indicator/SE.PRM.PRIV.ZS?end=2018&locations=CN&start=2005.

Xinhua News. 2006. China Publishes Resolution on Building of Harmonious Society. Accessed 15 May 2015 at http://news.xinhuanet.com/english/2006-10/18/content_5219143.htm.
Lin, Justin Yifu. 1992. Rural Reforms and Agricultural Growth in China. *The American Economic Review* 82 (1): 34–51.
Young, Jason. 2013. *China's Hukou System: Markets, Migrants, and Institutional Change*. Basingstoke: Palgrave Macmillan.

CHAPTER 11

Capitalist Transformation and Habitus in Laos

Boike Rehbein

Introduction

Since its Tenth Congress in 2016, the Lao People's Revolutionary Party (LPRP) seems to have returned to a socialist agenda. The party has tightened its control of society, has embarked on a widely publicized struggle against corruption, declares to move toward self-sufficiency and fashions a socialist rhetoric, which champions the leadership of the party, rediscovers Marx, argues against foreign interference, claims that Laos progresses toward socialism and proclaims the values of solidarity, national unity and scientific socialism. It even includes the return of the socialist form of address, "comrade" ("sahai"). The agenda is pushed by the remaining heroes of the revolution of 1975, who dominate the central committee and have close links with the Vietnamese Communist Party. The agenda of promoting socialism against capitalism and Western imperialism looks coherent and credible (cf. Rehbein 2019).

However, the leadership of the LPRP comprizes many millionaires and social inequality has been increasing drastically over the past decade. What is more, the party refuses to talk about inequality and even discourages the use of the term. Nothing seems to be done to counter inequality

B. Rehbein (✉)
Institute for Asian and African Studies, Humboldt University, Berlin, Germany
e-mail: rehbeinb@hu-berlin.de

A. Hansen et al. (eds.), *The Socialist Market Economy in Asia*,
https://doi.org/10.1007/978-981-15-6248-8_11

apart from the struggle against corruption. Oxfam (2018: 53) has identified Laos as one of the countries least committed to reducing inequality. Against this background, the socialist agenda looks less convincing. It rather seems to serve as a pretence to strengthen the position of the LPRP against the centrifugal forces of globalization, civil society and capitalism.

In this chapter, I wish to argue that both interpretations are correct to some degree—but they have to be linked to an analysis of Lao society. The socialist rhetoric aims at the majority of the population and is welcomed by it. These are the losers of the transition to a market economy or, as I prefer to call it, the capitalist transformation: the peasants and the socialist apparatus (including the members of the LPRP and its sub-organizations as well as the bureaucracy and state employees). The socialist agenda caters to them in order for the LPRP to remain in power and to counter the forces of capitalism. Together, the peasants and the bureaucracy comprize between two thirds and three-quarters of the population. The social groups fully integrated into the market economy are a minority, even if they are growing in number and power.

The chapter analyzes this social configuration in order to argue that the return to a socialist rhetoric increases the support for the LPRP in its traditional base, namely the peasants and the socialists, while politically countering the rise of the forces of globalization, especially the new urban middle class. The argument draws on my empirical work in Laos since 1994, particularly on a study I carried out in 2015 (Rehbein 2017). This study comprizes several series of interviews, including a final set of 80 serving as the basis of the argument presented here, with representatives of all sections of Lao society. The first section briefly outlines the theoretical framework of the study and the methodology associated with it. In the following section, I trace the social changes that have resulted from the socialist and the capitalist transformations. Section three introduces the habitus types that can be found in contemporary Lao society and their relation to the transformations. The final section deals with the impact of capitalism, the socialist agenda and their connection to the habitus types in Laos.

Theoretical and Methodological Background

The theoretical framework informing the argument presented in this chapter is based on the assumptions that social structures are embodied and that fundamental patterns of acting and thinking are acquired in early childhood. This entails that aspects of a social structure can persist even after radical social change. I call the persisting structures *sociocultures* and refer to the embodied structure with Pierre Bourdieu's concept of *habitus*. In this chapter, I will argue that Laos experienced two major transformations within two decades hardly more than one generation ago. For this reason, three sociocultures coexist in contemporary Laos embodied in people's habitus, since many people are still alive who experienced both transformations.

Social structures constantly change. However, some of these changes are so radical that they produce a new type of social hierarchy. I refer to these radical changes as *transformations*. Transformations are closely related to revolutions but can also occur in connection with a war, a natural disaster or massive technological innovation. Even though these changes are radical, they are merely transformations and not creations of a new society from scratch. This is due to the fact that they build on earlier structures and institutions, which are relatively persistent. This is true for the entire system of structures, cultures and practices, which partly persist even after a transformation. I refer to these persisting systems as *sociocultures*.

Any practice has a long history which it partly incorporates. Its current form blends old elements with transformed and new elements. This is true for the entire society too. We can picture society as a mountain consisting of layers of rocks and sediments. As sociocultures persist, so do those forms of action or institutions that appear outdated, such as religious rituals or aristocratic titles. Practices within their frameworks are determined and assessed against the background of their history. Many practices and values seem to belong to another time or even another world. Actually, this is the case for a lot of our everyday practices, such as superstition, help without monetary return, or reading a book.

An important reason for the persistence of sociocultures and outdated practices is the fact that humans do not invent themselves from scratch every day but learn their patterns of action under certain conditions. These patterns persist—at least to a certain degree—even if the conditions change. This is what Bourdieu's concept of *habitus* refers to. The concept is based on the assumption that one has the tendency to act in the way in which one has learnt to act (Bourdieu 1990). A form of behaviour is learnt and then repeated. With repetition, one adopts a pattern which is put to action when a similar situation arises. Through multiple repetitions the pattern becomes habitualized. The habitus not only tends to reproduce earlier behaviour but seeks conditions which correspond to its own production—mainly because it is made for these conditions.

In his main work, Bourdieu (1984) focused on a stable European society, namely France. The structure of this society had not undergone any major transformations for decades. Therefore, it seemed convincing that Bourdieu presented the habitus as uniform, homogeneous and reproductive. Most societies, however, are less stable than France and, interestingly, Bourdieu had first developed the concept of habitus with regard to a great transformation, namely the capitalist transformation in Algeria of the 1950s. Even with regard to France, the assumption that the habitus is a uniform system without interior contradictions has been challenged (Lahire 1998). The emptiness of the concept has been criticized as well: How does it actually explain observable actions and how does it actually incorporate social structures (Rehbein and Saalmann 2009)?

Since the concept of habitus, as introduced by Bourdieu, is too broad and empty, excessively uniform and impossible to operationalize, I restrict the concept to deep-seated patterns of action that are specific for social groups and relevant in capitalist societies. This makes sense both for France and for Laos. The deep-seated patterns are those that are mostly acquired in early childhood. Therefore, they reflect the family of origin and can be changed only with great difficulty later in life. I subsume these patterns under the concept *primary habitus*. In contrast, characteristics of the secondary habitus are acquired later on in life and are easier to modify, e.g. preferences in lifestyle or a foreign language. Furthermore, I do not look at patterns that are shared by the entire society or humanity or that characterize only an individual or a subculture but at patterns that distinguish a hierarchical layer in a socioculture, i.e. at the habitus as *social distinction*. And I only study sociocultures in *capitalist societies* because the habitus is used as a resource in the competition for social positions in this type of society. In a feudal or a society defined by kinship, a change in one's habitus rarely, if at all, leads to a change in one's social position.

The methodology to research the habitus aims at the socially relevant primary habitus. For my study, I accessed it by means of life-course interviews. An interview is a social practice and reveals aspects of one's habitus. At the same time, the life-course interview delivers information about the formation of the habitus in the interviewees' childhood and later life. Karl Mannheim (1964: 108) distinguished between what-meaning and how-meaning of a narrative. Whereas the what-meaning refers to the semantic dimension of the information in the interview, the how-meaning refers to the pragmatic dimension of the way things are said—or the habitus.

Mannheim's approach was developed into a sophisticated methodology by Ralf Bohnsack (2014), which inspired the approach of my research. The documentary method aims at the construction of habitus types in an inductive way. The method comprizes four steps. In the first step, the what- and the how-meaning are identified in a sequence analysis and recorded in a descriptive way. The second step consists of the identification of important categories that characterize the types and distinguish one from the other. The third step comprizes the comparison of categories and their combinations in the interviews. Finally, types are constructed on the basis of similarities and differences in combinations of categories.

For the construction of habitus types, an additional instrument had to be applied. From Bourdieu's perspective, the habitus is always a combination of characteristics, such as self-confidence or intellectualism, that combine with certain amounts and types of capital. Only certain combinations of factors occur in reality while others are rare or even non-existent. Therefore, research has to identify the actual combinations of factors. For this purpose, I applied a statistical tool to the results of the interview interpretations, namely multiple correspondence analysis, which was also used by Bourdieu (1984). It allows to identify the joint existence of social characteristics. I generally follow Bourdieu in regarding capital and habitus as the most fundamental characteristics for social structure in a capitalist society.

Lao Sociocultures

Laos experienced two major transformations in the recent past, an independence struggle culminating in a socialist revolution in 1975 and the gradual introduction of a market economy since 1986. Like China and Vietnam, Laos retains the political system of a one-party state under the leadership of a communist party, the LPRP, while transforming the economy and many associated institutions into a capitalist society. The respective conditions under quasi-colonial rule before 1975, under quasi-Stalinist rule after 1975 and in a more liberalized environment since the mid-1990s differ very strongly from each other. It is as if 200 years of European history of the nineteenth and twentieth centuries were compressed into twenty years.

Laos presents a complex mosaic of ethnic groups, forms of life, environmental conditions and social structures. The mosaic evolved historically through migration, adaptation and integration. This complexity persists within the framework of the nation-state. A small ethnolinguistic group is usually scattered over a large territory, has neighbours from a different ethnolinguistic family and adapts to different environmental conditions in each place. Therefore, it is impossible to establish unequivocal correlations between territory, ethnicity, culture and/or social structure. It is clear, however, that the entire rural population lives in villages and most people are peasants and have grown up as peasants. In spite of the cultural, social and linguistic differences, the peasants share important elements of their habitus. Usually, most villagers are related to each other and the village's social structure is determined by kinship. This means that one's social position increases with age. In terms of gender, there are ethnolinguistic groups that are extremely patriarchal, very few tend toward matriarchal structures and many have a gender balance with a slight domination of the male. Even within an ethnolinguistic group, these relations vary.

Within most villages, a huge variation of lifestyles, mentalities and behaviours will be tolerated. However, the primary habitus is quite uniform not only within a particular village but across much of Laos. Since I propose to restrict my use of the term habitus to capitalist societies and to distinctions between social groups, the term cannot be applied to those Lao peasants, who have not been integrated into the capitalist structure to a significant degree. I would rather speak of a culture—which has become a socioculture after the recent transformations. Peasant culture is characterized by subsistence ethic, a term coined by James Scott (1976). Peasants are not geared toward competition, profit and accumulation but toward having enough until the next harvest. A large surplus of food would rot and a large surplus of other items is useless. Scott identified reciprocity, reinforcing family ties and traditionalism as characteristics of subsistence ethic. I consider this description appropriate for Lao peasant culture.

Villages of different ethnolinguistic affiliation have interacted for millennia across Southeast Asia. Pottery, metal and salt were traded over large distances. Even older are the divisions of labour between nomadic and sedentary as well as between mountain and valley peoples (Higham 1989: 59). The different environmental conditions resulted in different types of production. Groups traded their specialties for items they needed or wanted. Maybe two millennia ago, an unequal relationship emerged with the villages in the plains occupying a superior position since they were more likely to produce a surplus and to become nodes of trade (ibid.). The inequality between groups was partly ethnic in character. However, many villages were and are multi-ethnic. Which ethnic group was dominant and which was dominated, depended on the local configuration. Inequality existed between valley/sedentary and mountain/nomadic, not between ethnic groups as such. The multi-ethnic configuration only changed with the installation of nation states.

The centres of trade and communication developed into towns with an increasing division of labour and sociopolitical stratification (ibid.). Many of the surrounding villages came under the domination of these centres. However, the entire population on the territory of contemporary Laos was only fully integrated into structures of political domination around the turn of the twenty-first century. Many villages kept their political and often economic independence over time because they were too difficult to access or simply evaded domination by migrating elsewhere. The result was a mosaic of centres, dependent villages and independent villages without clear territorial demarcations. This structure has been called "mandala" with regard to Southeast Asia (Wolters 1999) and "baan-muang" (or "village-town/state") with regard to Tai polities (Raendchen and Raendchen 1998). The main character of the relation was the exchange of tribute and manpower against security. Loyalties shifted frequently depending on the ability of the centre to guarantee security and stability.

Muang structures were hierarchical. A superior tried to accumulate as many bonds of loyalty by inferiors as possible to enhance his (and, less often, her) position whereas inferiors tended to look for superiors who could guarantee security. Just as subsistence ethic characterized the culture of the village, patrimonialism was the prevalent culture of the muang. This is a term introduced by Max Weber and applied by Ernst Boesch (1970) to Thailand. It is appropriate to describe social relations in precolonial Laos as a baan-muang-structure. The structure consisted of some independent baan, various dependent baan, minor muang and a centre-muang.

Much of contemporary Laos came under the domination of the Siamese state (or muang) in 1828, while the area east of Luang Prabang was annexed by Annam. In 1893, some of the Lao-speaking muang were integrated into the French colonial empire, while others remained with Siam. The French managed to move into Siamese territory but stopped short of integrating all Lao-speaking peoples into their colonial empire. They created a new territorial entity, which they called Laos. They attempted to codify a national language on the basis of the former muang-languages, to introduce a bureaucratic administration and to integrate the independent villages (Pholsena 2006). These attempts transformed Laos but were only partly successful. After the Second World War, the French tried to re-establish their colonial empire in Southeast Asia but had to grant independence to Vietnam, Cambodia and Laos in 1954.

The United States attempted to maintain control of Indochina for fear of communism sweeping the region. The communists were important forces in the independence movements of all three states but were nowhere near taking power in Laos, where the government was formed by a coalition of neutralists, a conservative American-friendly faction and the communists. The neutralists under Prince Souvanna Phouma were the strongest faction. The United States, however, insisted on the exclusion of the communists, which eventually resulted in a military coup in 1960. The US-backed coup pushed the neutralists and the communists out of the government and provoked a civil war. The communists withdrew to the Northeast of Laos, which had been granted to them by the peace settlement of 1954. From there, they organized the revolution with help from the neighbouring North Vietnamese communists.

There is little doubt that Laos would have remained a modernizing muang-state headed by a royal household if the United States had not intervened. Instead, Laos was as heavily bombed as Germany during the Second World War, became contaminated with agent orange, lost a sizeable part of its population—and came under the rule of a communist party. The communists consisted of a small group of muang intellectuals educated in French institutions, a few workers and mostly peasants from different ethnolinguistic families. From the perspective of muang culture, they were unsophisticated and backward. They had little urban and certainly no aristocratic culture, since they had built up their base in the most remote and rural region of Laos.

The civil war had transformed the towns into centres of capitalism, while the Northeast had become socialist. After the takeover of the communist movement in 1975, up to ten percent of the population, mostly urbanites with a patrimonial or emerging capitalist habitus, left the country. One-third of the population was displaced. The overwhelming majority of people remaining in Laos were peasants and/or had been brought up as peasants. They were ruled by a small party elite, which consisted of intellectuals, workers and peasants. The socialist nation-state with less than three million inhabitants had very little infrastructure, basically no industry and a tiny urban population. It mainly reverted to a peasant economy. Attempts to build a Stalinist and even a more moderately socialist economy remained unsuccessful (Evans 1990). This is because the structure of collectives controlled by the party with the aim of producing a surplus contradicted subsistence ethic. The peasants were somewhat egalitarian and anti-capitalist but they were not proto-communists. This was quickly recognized by the party leadership (Phomvihane 1985, vol. I: 106).

Laos under socialism was dominated by the LPRP but most people continued to live in the socioculture of the baan, while the muang lost much of its relevance. In contrast to the patrimonial structure, the party apparatus allows for social mobility. With its ranks and corresponding powers, it resembles a muang but differs in its ideology and its relation to the population. Anyone can enter the party and rise through its ranks. And everybody is controlled by the party structure. Socialist Laos was part of the Soviet bloc that began to disintegrate in the mid-1980s. Along with other socialist states, the Lao leadership began to introduce a market economy in 1986 and slowly opened up for foreign capital, installed a standardized institutional framework for the market economy and abolished direct state control of business.

Currently, Laos has a market economy under the control of a socialist party. Formally, most institutions of the state resemble capitalist democracies. There is a division of powers including a parliament, whose members are elected, laws and the constitution have been modelled after Western states, Laos has signed many international agreements and tries to adhere to the standards set by international organizations. However, all institutions are—in the last instance—subordinate to the politburo. This is also true for all major political and legal decisions. The economy as well does not seem to differ from capitalist democracies. There is private property, most business is private, Laos has a stock exchange and liberal, floating exchange rates, a central bank and private banks (including foreign ones) etc. However, all business is subject to indirect state control, which means control by the LPRP.

Laos under a socialist market economy is a hybrid, which comprizes elements not only of socialism and capitalism but also of earlier structures. At least three levels of social structure coexist, baan-muang, socialism and the market comprising the sociocultures of subsistence ethic (baan), patrimonialism (muang), socialism and capitalism (see Table 11.1). The sociocultures can be detected in people's habitus today. At least half of the population clearly adheres to subsistence ethic. Around forty percent still are peasants with little contact to the market economy. A tiny minority of old urban families (some of whom had been in exile and have returned to Laos) have incorporated patrimonialism. The socialist structure comprizes around twenty percent and the remainder has arrived in capitalist structures. In our interviews, we found the strong insistence on having enough to be a clear indicator of subsistence ethic. Patrimonialism reveals itself in a preference for hierarchy. Socialists praise egalitarianism, are members of an organization associated with the LPRP and would quote slogans from the latest party agenda. The capitalist socioculture is characterized by a logic of investment and self-interest.

The socioculture is passed on to the next generation and partly persists even if the children begin to be active in the capitalist economy. Basically, the children also retain the relative social position of their parents. In Laos, there are two typical deviations, however. First, the revolution actually led to social mobility. The pattern of mobility is easily explained. The revolutionary fighters had the chance to enter the administration after 1975, irrespective of their background. Children from well-educated households and revolutionaries who received further training abroad became high officials and party leaders. The second type of social mobility was and is actual migration from peasant households. Migrants with family networks in the city had the chance to move upward and become small self-employed businesspersons, skilled labourers or employees in the private sector, while those migrants without family in the city become unskilled labourers, monks or may often remain otherwise poor. The first

Table 11.1 Sociocultures and strata in Laos

Baan-muang (50%)	*Socialism (20%)*	*Capitalism (30%)*
Patrimonial elites	Party leadership	Capitalists
Old urban population	Party cadres	Urban middle class
	Administration	Commercial farmers
Peasants	Rural party	Labourers
Minorities		Marginalized

type of mobility took place between 1975 and 1995, while the second type still persists, even though upward mobility is decreasing.

Habitus Groups

People who remain in the same environment as their parents evidently share fundamental traits of their primary habitus with them. This is clearly the case for people in Laos who are peasants today, since their parents were peasants as well. However, it is only true for a minority of those who are active in the socialist or the capitalist socioculture today. They develop a habitus, which differs from that of their parents. The emergence of capitalism also changes the habitus of those peasants, who live in close proximity to urban centres or who are being integrated into the capitalist economy (for the following, see Rehbein 2017).

On the basis of my interviews, I identified four habitus types in Laos. I analyzed the interviews in terms of their characteristics and established a list of characteristics that seem to be important in Lao society. Finally, I carried out a multiple correspondence analysis to find out which characteristics are likely to appear in certain combinations with other characteristics and thereby form clusters that can be interpreted as habitus types. The characteristics that appeared to be relevant are: autonomous vs. heteronomous (which means independent decision-making), integration vs. isolation (social network), task-orientation vs. selfishness (which means an opposition between community- and self-orientation), satisfaction vs. dissatisfaction, work vs. fun, traditional vs. experimental, collective vs. family, the type of education in the family (supportive, traditional, neglecting or negative), self-confidence, goal-orientation, power orientation, the importance of education and the view of class as a category. All characteristics were given a numerical value, either ranging between the opposites or corresponding to the estimated strength of its presence.

The multiple correspondence analysis of the characteristics identified as relevant by the interview interpretation showed four clusters, which correspond to four habitus types (see Table 11.2). One cluster combines very low levels of autonomy, self-confidence and satisfaction. Another cluster is defined by traditionalism, community-orientation, dissatisfaction and a lack of goal-orientation. The characteristics of autonomy, discipline and self-orientation are grouped close together and define the third cluster. The fourth cluster is characterized by goal-orientation, an experimental attitude to life, satisfaction, an interest in power and ambition.

Table 11.2 Habitus types in Laos

	Traditionalist	*Depressed*	*Disciplined*	*Ambitious*
Autonomy	0	–	+	+
Goal-orientation	–	–	+	+
Discipline	0	–	+	+
Satisfaction	–	–	+	+
Traditionalism	+	0	0	–
Self-confidence	0	–	0	+
Selfishness	–	0	+	+

The characteristic of autonomy and goal-orientation distinguish the upper from the lower levels in the social hierarchy, whereas traditionalism and community-orientation distinguish baan and muang from capitalism. I have called the first cluster the depressed habitus type, the second cluster traditionalist, the third disciplined and the fourth ambitious.

It is interesting that only four (primary) habitus types can be discerned in Laos, which today hosts a population of almost seven million. The main reason for the low level of differentiation is the dominance of the traditionalist habitus type, which comprizes all peasants (the baan) as well as a few families in the other sociocultures. We can speak of habitus with regard to the peasants now, since they are being integrated to varying degrees into a capitalist nation-state and actively and passively distinguish themselves from other social groups. Almost all Lao have incorporated at least an element of traditionalism, since basically everybody who was born between about 1965 and 1985 grew up as a peasant and more than half of those before and after were raised as peasants too. This entire group, certainly the majority of the population, can be reduced to one habitus type. There is little variation of the primary habitus between the ethnolinguistic groups as well. Their forms of life are very diverse, but they share subsistence ethic and some principles, all of which are incorporated in the habitus.

The other three habitus types are predominantly urban and cover both the socialist and the capitalist socioculture. There is no clear distinction because people in the socialist structure either remain peasants at heart or become capitalists in much of their everyday life. The disciplined habitus type prevails in the socialist socioculture but it extends to the labourers and the new urban middle class as well. The upper strata of the socialist and the capitalist sociocultures have mostly incorporated the ambitious habitus type. A subtler analysis would reveal a differentiation of the disciplined and the ambitious habitus types into a socialist and a capitalist version with some distinct core characteristics. However, both types share the same history to a large degree, as their roots are in the urban muang population. Once again, the habitus types only refer to the primary, social habitus and are ideal types with hybrid, overlapping and changing forms occurring frequently.

The depressed habitus type prevails in the marginalized groups of the baan and capitalism. It comprizes around ten percent of the population. This type is defined by negative attributes or by a lack of traits that are valued in society: low values in terms of goal-orientation, autonomy, discipline and self-confidence. I decided to call the type depressed, because people with this habitus have been oppressed and the habitus is linked to a feeling of exclusion, marginalization and dissatisfaction. We found a similar type in other countries (Jodhka et al. 2017). In Thailand, we also refer to it as depressed (Thongsawang et al. 2020). In Thailand and Laos, the depressed type has a similar social and historical origin, namely the transformation of the baan-muang-structure, which is based on an all-encompassing kinship in the village and a patrimonial community in the muang, into a capitalist society of social classes. The depressed type consists of the social groups that enter capitalism with a minimum of capital and little opportunity.

The core trait of this habitus type is the lack of initiative due to continuous marginalization and frustration. On account of the poor and remote state of the parental home, representatives of this habitus receive little schooling but rather have to work in and around the house from an early age. In most cases, no professional training is added to the poor educational background. As members of a marginalized family, they never accumulated any significant social and symbolic capital. The depressed social situation during the formation of the habitus results in low self-respect, which translates in the afore-mentioned lack of initiative, autonomy and goal-orientation.

This habitus type probably emerged under colonialism—just like the other two predominantly urban types—but largely disappeared in the socialist period. It comprizes a high proportion of ethnolinguistic minorities and almost exclusively descendants of poor peasants: unskilled workers, unemployed, beggars, rural labourers and marginalized peasants. Most live in urban areas but there are many in villages as well. Entire villages that have been socially constructed as poor by government or aid programmes can transform into a depressed culture. Often, families from ethnic minorities who migrate into Lao-speaking areas—urban or rural—become depressed, since they lack social networks, education, linguistic abilities and symbolic capital that is valued in the new environment. Many villages host at least one family without land or with at best a tiny stretch of rugged terrain.

An example for the depressed habitus type would be a 28-year old unskilled labourer I interviewed. In the interview, she says: "My parents are peasants in Luang Prabang province. We are very poor. I could only attend school in the village. At the age of 13, I had to leave school in order to work. I have to send money home, so that my younger siblings can attend school. I make around 80 USD a month and send 20 to 50 home [...] I hope to have a good husband in the future. So far, I haven't met anyone, I have no time [...] I belong to the poor. We are very poor. Therefore, I can only marry a poor man. My life is characterized by the facts that I have no time, am poor, unmarried and irrelevant".

The traditionalist habitus type comprizes all those, who acquired their primary habitus in the context of baan or muang and maintain it. The term traditionalism refers to this. Apart from traditionalism, it features community-orientation and a lack of goal-orientation, which are characteristic of subsistence ethic. They are also the direct opposites of the traits embodied by the new urban upper classes. Another characteristic of the traditionalist habitus type, namely dissatisfaction, places it in opposition to the upper classes and in proximity to the depressed type. This is the key to understanding the backing for the return to a socialist rhetoric since 2016. In the rhetoric, the peasant was the hero of the revolution but now, the peasant symbolizes underdevelopment and poverty. All peasants are aware of this. The classification as poor is not adopted by well-to-do-peasants and wealthy farmers who mostly belong to the disciplined habitus type. Peasants repeat the socialist discourse on the Lao peasant, namely that the peasant incorporates the ideal Lao and produces the national food, which is rice. The economically poor peasants settling in remote areas, however, have realized that they are regarded as backward. This is also the case for those peasants who live close to urban areas. They consider themselves poor, because they are integrated into the money economy and can assess their relative poverty.

The peasants support the socialist agenda to the degree that it raises their status and calls for socio-economic equality. But the urban society and international organizations demonstrate disrespect for their way of life. More than 90% of all adolescents and almost 100% of adolescents in urban areas who I interviewed declare that they do not want to work in agriculture. The majority of those peasants who regard themselves as poor would prefer a different source of income and a different way of life. Peasants learn from the village head, who disperses the party line, that development and eradication of rural poverty are associated with the MDGs and SDGs, or, more generally, with globalization and capitalism. The traditionalist habitus type associates selfishness, competition, alienation, environmental degradation, corruption and crime with the capitalist transformation. These are evils that did not seem to exist in former times, especially not during the socialist period. No interviewee of this habitus group failed to point to this.

The traditionalist habitus type scores lower on goal-orientation than the ambitious and disciplined habitus type. This has to be interpreted in relation to the structure of capitalist society. Peasants do not typically pursue goals like wealth, a career, a powerful position or fame. However, they pursue the goal of subsistence with diligence, planning and devotion. They also strive for other goals, such as having a nice garden or weaving beautiful textiles. These are possibly more meaningful goals than making money or becoming famous, but they do not lead to upward social mobility, which would be a typical goal in a capitalist society.

Finally, a core characteristic of the traditionalist habitus type is the importance that is given to the community. This has to be interpreted as a component of subsistence ethic, since it includes reciprocity, a communal sense of identity, cherishing personal relations and togetherness, a sense of duty and mutual help. Of course, the emphasis on community hooks up with socialism very well. It is revealing that the traditionalists in the LPRP as well as some individuals who I would classify as disciplined (see below) display a sense of community that is clearly rooted in subsistence ethic. This comes as no surprise since these persons were socialized as peasants. Behind closed doors, especially during lunch, village culture suddenly spreads among many urbanites, bonds them into a community and clearly reminds of village life. Interestingly, this is when people appear to be happiest during their work-day. A significant component of subsistence ethic is communal fun ("muan" or "sabai" in Lao).

An example would be a 41-year old peasant who one might consider pretty well-off. He owns two hectares of land suitable for wet-rice cultivation. He has a solid wooden house (whereas poor peasants would have a house made of bamboo and leaves) with a surrounding vegetable garden. In the interview, he still claims, "I am poor, everyone in the village is poor", since he only makes 30 USD a month and knows the official discourse on the peasant. At the same time, he acknowledges the positive aspects of his life. "I don't want to move to the city. It is beautiful here and peaceful and quiet. We have everything we need and more. There is no crime, we are all friends and family. I have no stress. No place on earth can be more beautiful. What more can you want?" He is aware of the developmentalist agenda and the criteria of capitalism but his roots in subsistence ethic are stronger.

The disciplined habitus characterizes members of the lower and intermediate middle classes who have to perform wage labour to make a living without attaching much meaning to their jobs. In Laos, this habitus type comprizes an orientation toward the self as opposed to the community and a significant degree of autonomy. It is incorporated mostly by the new middle-class and the socialist administration as well as by commercial farmers and labourers in stable employment conditions. The habitus type can be found in the socialist and the capitalist socioculture because discipline plays a key role in both (Foucault 1977). The dignity of the person is defined by wage labour—and the labourer, along with the peasant, is the epitome of a socialist revolution. The ideal of the socialist project is the fully disciplined and homogeneous society administered by technocratic party leadership. While the Lao population did not comply with this programme, the administrators themselves did. Within this framework, they incorporated a disciplined habitus that is useful in the capitalist socioculture as well.

Important characteristics of this habitus type are selfishness and goal-orientation. Selfishness means that survival depends on individual activity, not on the organization of the community. The meaning of goal-orientation is linked to this. The atomized individual in capitalism has to organize his or her own life. Those who have the means to organize their life can be classified as goal-oriented. In this sense, goal-orientation not only distinguishes the capitalist socioculture from the other sociocultures but presupposes a minimum level of capital.

The disciplined habitus type acknowledges the importance of formal education in order to accumulate cultural capital and get a good job. An example would be a 21-year-old employee, who makes as little money as the worker, who was quoted above as a representative of the depressed habitus type. In spite of the identical economic situation, the habitus differs significantly. The employee pursues a defined goal in the capitalist economy on the basis of discipline. “My parents are soldiers in Kasi. I moved to Vientiane in order to go to college, since my sister was already studying here. I have to work here to finance my studies. I study English and business at Wattana College. Tuition fees are 400 USD per year. I have to save most of my money to pay for the fees. [...] This job is good, even if I make little money, because I have a lot of contact with foreigners and I improve my English. I speak better than most classmates. [...] After my graduation, I want to work in a foreign company”.

The ambitious habitus type is the characteristic elite habitus. It incorporates the values and symbols of capitalism. This type shares goal-orientation with the disciplined type but differs from it in its means and goals. Whereas the middle classes are characterized by discipline, the upper classes strive for more. The middle classes work to survive and are content with little, but the upper classes seek positions of power, creative and influential jobs and self-fulfilment. This habitus type is set apart by ambition and self-confidence. Within the baan-muang-structure, peasants and urbanites have no possibility to be socially mobile. Within the socialist framework, mobility is possible, but the upper ranks have been reserved for the elite since the revolution. In capitalism, capital (in Bourdieu’s sense) is necessary to be upwardly mobile.

Ambition is closely connected to self-confidence. It is interesting that people in leading positions in any society consider themselves a species apart from the rest of the population. While they claim to have reached their position due to ambition and merit, their success is based on the family’s social position. This reconfirms their self-confidence. The ambitious habitus type also comprizes an experimental attitude to life, as opposed to traditionalism. Change, challenges and new problems are the norm, not the exception, and require new solutions.

An example would be a 37-year old high cadre of the LPRP. “My parents were peasants in the [North]. They are [members of an ethnic minority]. My father went to school and rose all the way to become head of district. My uncle was member of the central committee. [...] I attended school in the city and then studied at the National University. My relatives made sure that I got a position within the party. [...] I continue to study in order to improve my knowledge. I will continue to rise in the party ranks”. Like the disciplined habitus type, this interviewee pursues a clear goal but not on the basis of discipline and hardship. He does not dream of reaching his goal but he is confident to do so.

All four persons that I presented as examples were born into a rural peasant setting. The conditions, however, differed. The traditionalist remains embedded in the peasant setting, the depressed is integrated into the capitalist economy but without any relevant capital, the disciplined moves with parental support and social capital, while the ambitious is already linked to the elites of the country. Of course, those persons who were already born in an urban setting will display even more pronounced characteristics of the respective habitus types that appear in the socialist and capitalist sociocultures.

Socialism, Capitalism and Sociocultures

It is evident that the traditionalist habitus type implies a fundamental opposition to the market economy—or, more precisely, to capitalism. The depressed habitus type is rather indifferent to questions of social organization, since daily survival is more pressing. If at all, the depressed have a negative attitude toward politics in general. The disciplined and ambitious habitus types can be found in both the socialist and the capitalist sociocultures. Their support for one or the other depends on integration into the respective institutions. Only these two habitus types can become functional members of a capitalist structure and economy.

Clearly, subsistence ethic contradicts capitalism in many important aspects. I have tried to show in much detail that functional behaviour in the market economy is very difficult for Lao peasants and requires something like a "conversion" to an entirely different form of life (Rehbein 2004). Development aid workers who tried to help Lao peasants to commercially exploit their handicraft skills were deeply frustrated about the inability of their target population to understand the basic rules of the market. They produced the required goods not when there was demand but when they themselves had demand. The products were offered when the family needed money (e.g. for transportation) and offered at an excessive price when a lot of money was needed (e.g. for medical treatment). When no money was needed, no products were offered. Even though most peasants have started to understand the game of capitalism, it has not yet transformed their habitus. They maintain the culture of *subsistence ethic*.

Those people who enter the game of capitalism transform in different ways depending on their habitus and the conditions. Traditionalists act very much in the way just described. They take advantage of a situation but do not develop a market strategy. If someone buys their handicraft products, they may make this a regular business. If business works well, their neighbours copy the business model—and suddenly dozens of people are selling the same item in the same place. I have called this type of economic culture *occasionalism* (Rehbein 2004). Once people in Laos develop a business strategy, it is usually connected to social networks. Business takes place in the framework of *patrimonialism*. Of course, all those rooted in the muang have embodied patrimonialism anyway. Contemporary entrepreneurs still draw on it, since it persists as a socioculture and forms the backdrop of emerging capitalist structures. Where money comes from abroad, neither kinship nor patrimonial ties exist. The prevailing pattern of action is to simply take the money without any reciprocal obligation. I call this a *taking culture*. It is spread among those who work for international organizations.

Subsistence ethic, patrimonialism, taking culture and occasionalism contradict the concept of the capitalist market. A behaviour that complies with textbooks in economics or business only develops in the disciplined and the ambitious habitus types to the degree that they are integrated into the capitalist economy. This is a minority of the population even though it is growing constantly and rapidly. The key driver of capitalist culture in a general sense and a narrow economic meaning is the new urban middle class. This social class develops out of the former intermediate muang population, the colonial urbanites and the socialist administration. In Laos, it comprizes all professions that require formal education and are decently paid, from the clerk to the medical professor.

The growth of this social class in size and importance is of great concern to the Lao leadership. The new urban middle class (cf. Table 11.1) spreads capitalist culture including consumerism and a market ideology but it also opposes one-party rule. The return to a socialist rhetoric since 2016 has to be seen in this light (Rehbein 2019). The social class embracing capitalism is growing and criticizes the LPRP. Almost all members of the new urban middle class share negative opinions about the current state of affairs in Laos, which they can connect with their own experience.

Whereas most members of the new urban middle class oppose socialism, the traditionalist habitus type is in a position to support it if suitably framed. The traditionalist opposes the capitalist transformation, which entails almost exclusively negative consequences for him or her: a change of the way of life, loss of independence, disrespect, loss of free time and problems finding a livelihood—in addition to the moral and cultural differences between the sociocultures. The brief interview quote above illustrates most of these points. Peasants in Laos are scared of the future. Many peasants expressed fear of unemployment in the interviews, even though a peasant cannot technically become unemployed. But this could be the peasant's fate in the future. People experiencing this insecurity express a need for order. In Laos, this order, along with more respect for the peasants, is provided by the socialist agenda. The return of the socialist rhetoric is popular in this section of the population.

At the other end of the spectrum is the young urban population. Lao adolescents largely reproduce their parents' social position, but they move toward the capitalist socioculture. Since young people form the majority of the population, socialism is losing ground to consumerism and capitalist lifestyles on a large scale. The socialist rhetoric and the youth culture of the new urban middle class can be interpreted as exact opposites of the cultural spectrum. However, both of them differ greatly from traditionalism and subsistence ethic as well. If the LPRP manages to integrate the peasants, it certainly has the majority of the population behind it. This move, however, is clearly pointing backward to a form of life, which is as remote from socialism as from capitalism. This was clearly recognized by the revolutionary leadership (Phomvihane 1985, vol. I). The programme of shaping a new, socialist person, which took absurd and cruel forms in China and Cambodia, was embarked upon in Laos as well but never took such a violent turn. That the Lao leadership since 2016 is including self-sufficiency into the socialist rhetoric and no longer addresses the issue of the relation between social structure and habitus (or being and consciousness) indicates that it has no clear agenda of a progression toward socialism. We can rather interpret it as a defensive attitude toward an expanding market economy, which reminds of nationalist populism and anti-globalization in the Philippines and other parts of the world.

Conclusion

The population of contemporary Laos comprizes four habitus types, which are rooted in different sociocultures, namely baan-muang, socialism and capitalism. Two habitus types, the disciplined and the ambitious, are found in the socialist and the capitalist sociocultures, while the marginalized habitus type of the depressed results from the capitalist transformation. Whereas the majority of the population can be classified as belonging to the traditionalist habitus type, socialism has lost ground to the expanding capitalist socioculture. However, only a minority of Lao citizens are fully integrated into the capitalist economy, act accordingly and move into the urban and rural middle classes. Since the young are pushing in this direction as well, a strong movement toward capitalism, globalization and political liberalization has gained ground.

The Lao leadership has lost control of the capitalist transformation and seeks to turn the wheel backward. From a Marxist perspective, this backward turn can be interpreted as a step forward to socialism. The Lao who are integrated into the market economy, however, interpret it as an attempt to maintain power by rallying the sections of the population that are rooted in the socialist socioculture and the peasants. These groups still form the majority of the Lao population. That China and Vietnam have embarked on a similar course of policy and ideology, certainly strengthens the old revolutionaries in the LPRP who are associated with the Vietnamese leadership. But it is difficult to detect a progressive element in its policies, which supposedly characterizes socialism.

References

Boesch, Ernst E. 1970. *Zwiespältige Eliten. Eine sozialpsychologische Untersuchung über administrative Eliten in Thailand*. Bern, Stuttgart, and Wien: Huber.

Bohnsack, Ralf. 2014. *Rekonstruktive Sozialforschung*. Opladen: Budrich.

Bourdieu, Pierre. 1984. *Distinction*. London: Routledge & Kegan.

Bourdieu, Pierre. 1990. *The Logic of Practice*. Cambridge: Polity Press.

Evans, Grant. 1990. *Lao Peasants Under Socialism*. New Haven: Yale University Press.

Foucault, Michel. 1977. *Discipline and Punish*. New York: Pantheon Books.

Higham, Charles. 1989. *The Archaeology of Mainland Southeast Asia*. Cambridge: Cambridge University Press.

Jodhka, Surinder S., Boike Rehbein, and Jessé Souza. 2017. *Inequality in Capitalist Societies*. London and New York: Routledge.

Lahire, Bernard. 1998. *L'homme pluriel*. Paris: Nathan.

Mannheim, Karl. 1964. *Wissenssoziologie*. Neuwied: Luchterhand.

Oxfam. 2018. *Commitment to Reducing Inequality Index*. London: Oxfam.

Pholsena, Vatthana. 2006. *Post-war Laos: The Politics of Culture, History and Identity*. Singapore: Institute of Southeast Asian Studies.

Phomvihane, Kaysone. 1985. *Niphon Leuak Fen* (Selected Papers; 4 vols). Vientiane: State Press.

Raendchen, Jana, and Oliver Raendchen. 1998. Present State, Problems and Purpose of baan-müang Studies. *Tai Culture* III (2): 5–11.

Rehbein, Boike. 2004. *Globalisierung in Laos*. Münster: LIT.

Rehbein, Boike. 2017. *Society in Contemporary Laos: Capitalism, Habitus and Belief*. London and New York: Routledge.

Rehbein, Boike. 2019. Laos on the Path to Socialism? In *Southeast Asian Affairs 2019*, ed. Malcolm Cook and Daljit Singh, 163–176. Singapore: Institute of Southeast Asian Studies.

Rehbein, Boike, and Gernot Saalmann. 2009. Habitus. In *Bourdieu Handbuch*, ed. Gerhard Fröhlich and Boike Rehbein, 110–118. Stuttgart and Weimar: Metzler.

Scott, James C. 1976. *The Moral Economy of the Peasant*. New Haven and London: Yale University Press.

Thongsawang, Sirima, Boike Rehbein, and Supang Chantavanich. 2020. Inequality, Sociocultures and Habitus in Thailand, *Sojourn* 35 (3): 493–524.

Wolters, Oliver W. 1999 [1982]. *History, Culture, and Region in Southeast Asian Perspectives*. Singapore: Institute of Southeast Asian Studies.

PART IV

Concluding Observations

CHAPTER 12

Making Sense of the Socialist Market Economy

Jo Inge Bekkevold, Arve Hansen, and Kristen Nordhaug

This final chapter sets out to revisit the core themes of the book through engaging with the arguments made in the chapters, and attempts to frame the socialist market economy model within a larger international context. The main purpose of the authors of this book is to further our understanding of what the socialist market economy construct is, in theory and practice. Comparing the models of China, Vietnam and Laos in one volume, we are better positioned to see the main characteristics of the socialist market economy as a whole, and the similarities between the three countries, but we have also exposed the differences between them. Following the main overall themes of the book, the chapter looks at the

J. I. Bekkevold (✉)
Centre for Development and the Environment,
University of Oslo, Oslo, Norway
e-mail: jib@ifs.mil.no

A. Hansen
Norwegian Institute for Defence Studies, Oslo, Norway
e-mail: arve.hansen@sum.uio.no

K. Nordhaug
Oslo Metropolitan University, Oslo, Norway
e-mail: Kristen.Nordhaug@oslomet.no

A. Hansen et al. (eds.), *The Socialist Market Economy in Asia*,
https://doi.org/10.1007/978-981-15-6248-8_12

social market economy through discussions of ideology, the state and market relationship, environmental sustainability and state and society. We then take a closer look at the main similarities and differences of the model in China, Vietnam and Laos, as well as some main trends in the relationship between the three neighbouring countries. Finally, at the end of the chapter, we identify some themes for further research, with special attention given to the developmental state agenda, political developments and the impact of ongoing changes in international politics.

On Ideology

Examining the model of 'socialist market economy', a core theme is naturally the relationship between socialism and market, or socialism and capitalism. The contributors to this book agree that the market has gained increased prominence in all three countries, China, Vietnam and Laos. The private sector today accounts for a relatively large part of the output in their economies, many state-owned enterprises are or are being privatized (or 'equitized') and the authorities have opened up for private solutions within health and education, sectors that traditionally are the responsibility of the state, also in a number of Western market economies. The growing influence of market solutions in China, Vietnam and Laos over the last 2–3 decades is part of a larger international trend. The most notable international example of the neoliberal influence on earlier socialist left-oriented parties is the British 'New Labour' party and the early discourse about the 'Third Way'. The principal objective of the 'Third Way' was to temper free-market capitalism with social justice, while attempting to avoid an 'excessive domination of the state over social and economic life' (Giddens 2000: 13).

There has been a long-term decline in the support of social-democratic and socialist parties in Western Europe. During the 2017–2018 elections this decline accelerated strongly. The situation in the former socialist East and Central Europe is equally grim for the left (Berman and Snegovaya 2019; Rovny 2018). The weakening of the political left in Europe has been long in the making, and is largely caused by deep structural change and the decline of European manufacturing during the late twentieth century. In this process, a considerable part of the traditional electorates of left-wing parties has largely disappeared as a social group (Rovny 2018). The left's shift to the centre on economic issues and its acceptance of 'neoliberal' reforms such as privatization of parts of the public sector, cuts to taxes and the welfare state and deregulation of the business and financial sectors has been pointed to as an important explanation for the sudden recent weakening of its position (Berman and Snegovaya 2019; Mudge 2018).

When structural changes in the socio-economic landscape of Europe can have such a profound impact on European politics, it should come as no surprise that the 'socialist market economies' in China, Laos and Vietnam after three decades of high economic growth and globalization have also changed in fundamental ways. Although the communist parties are still in power in these three countries, their economic and social policies have been transformed, and the 'New Socialist Man' of contemporary China, Vietnam and Laos has changed accordingly (Chen 1969), and perhaps been replaced by an urban, middle-class 'socialist consumer', as Hansen argues in his chapter.

The communist parties in China, Vietnam and Laos are children of similar types of class-struggle that saw the birth of leftist parties in the West, although as noted by Cole and Ingalls in this volume, they to a larger extent started out as rural movements, and their strong anti-imperialist strand was different from in the West. Their roots go back to the interwar period. They were strongly influenced by anti-imperialist struggle against colonial rule in French Indochina, foreign dominance in the nominally independent China, fights against Japanese occupation during the Pacific Wars (1937–1945) and wars against the United States in Korea (1950–1953) and Indochina (1963–1975). The peasant support base was pivotal in many of these conflicts and garnered through aims and actions to end rural inequality. The socialist movement in Europe fragmented into communist and social-democratic political parties, with the latter working towards evolutionary changes within the existing system, whereas the communist regimes coercively made sure the socialist movements in China, Vietnam and Laos remained communist.[1]

[1] In fact, the socialist parties in Asia outside of the communist run countries also developed in a different direction than in Europe. A deep schism developed in the world Socialist movement in the early 1950s, led by the Asian Socialist parties. The schism was obvious already at the 1951 congress of the Socialist International in Frankfurt, and resulted in an independent Asian Socialist movement, which convened in Rangoon in January 1953. A discussion of the reasons for the schism is beyond reach in this chapter, but the legacy of imperialism and the Cold War setting in Asia were two important reasons. See for instance Saposs (1954).

In the 1990s and 2000s, in particular China and later Vietnam, became hosts of the manufacturing industries that had been the backbone of leftist parties in the West. But labour movements in globalizing Asian capitalism are mostly very weak, something that rather ironically also is the case in the socialist market economy, as Nordhaug discusses in his chapter.[2] Furthermore, the left and right wing political dichotomy with regard to state and market has been different in Asia than in Europe. The original East Asian developmental state model in Japan, South Korea and Taiwan remains one of the chief points of reference, both analytical and political, for those who reject the neoliberal global order.[3] However, the relatively strong state-driven economic reforms in Japan, South Korea and Taiwan did not take place under the rule of socialist parties, but under conservative or right-wing parties. Japan's economic miracle was largely formed under the leadership of the conservative right-wing Liberal Democratic Party (LDP),[4] and the developmental states in South Korea and Taiwan were to a large extent shaped under right-wing authoritarian rule (Cumings 1984). Hence, the role of the state versus the market in economic reforms has to be understood beyond the traditional schism of the political left versus the right, or socialism versus capitalism, as understood in Europe. Moreover, the economic models of Japan, South Korea and Taiwan have changed as well, and there is an ongoing debate about whether the classical developmental state model still is a viable option, under deep globalization in the world economy (Tian 2020; Hayashi 2010).

[2] The history and role of the labor movement is different in all three East Asian Developmental States, Japan, South Korea and Taiwan. In Japan, although the trade unions were closely linked to the Japanese Socialist Party, decades of conservative LDP government and high economic growth moderated the political role of the trade unions (Carlile 1994). In Taiwan, the industrialization created a large working class that played an important role in the democratization process in the 1980s, but its labour movement never remained a politically important force (Congiu 2011; Minns and Tierney 2003). In South Korea, labor activism became an integral part of the social movements demonstrating against authoritarian rule, and in particular during the 1970s and 1980s. Union activists in Korea continued to turn to the streets protesting also after democratization (Lee 2006, 2015).

[3] For a discussion on this, see for instance Stubbs (2009) and Radice (2008).

[4] The LDP was founded in 1955, after merging two right-wing parties in order to form a stronger united front against the threat of socialism. See Kapur (2018) and Sachsenröder and Frings (1998).

Describing the socialist market economy as 'Market-Leninism', London finds in his chapter that resource allocation in China and Vietnam mainly takes place through competitive markets while key features of the Leninist one-party state remains in place. State actors with close affiliation to the communist parties control important parts of the private economy, and the dividing line between private and public enterprise is frequently blurred. This view is echoed by Bui Hai Thiem, arguing that within a Leninist political system, a neoliberal logic influences the economic programmes. According to Bui Hai Thiem, in China and Vietnam, neoliberalism and statist socialism co-exist in a highly complex and fluid context. Despite these similarities, there are differences in the state's capacities to influence and transform their economies in our three cases. These differences are rooted in long-term patterns predating their socialist market economies. China has stronger capacities than Vietnam, which in turn has stronger capacities than Laos (e.g. Creak and Barney 2018; Vu 2010).

In the process of adjusting their socio-economic programmes to 'the socialist market economy' from the 1990s onwards, the authorities in China, Vietnam and Laos embraced large parts of the same neoliberal reforms that both the social-democratic parties in Europe as well as the East Asian developmental states all implemented into their party programmes in the 1990s and 2000s. However, in Laos, as noted by Rehbein, it is only a small part of the elite that has truly embraced capitalism while a somewhat larger share of the population still conforms with old socialist values.

The socialist market economies' embrace of elements of neoliberalism has been driven by four distinct, yet interlinked factors. First, political leaders realized that the market economy could serve as a tool used to deliver progress, not a different way of organizing society. Second, through trade and investments as means to economic growth, their economies were exposed to global capitalism, and the integration into the world economy meant they had to fulfil obligations in international treaties to facilitate for fair trade and reducing subsidies to state-owned enterprises. Third, in responding to changing expectations among the public as a result of increased living standards and the breakdown of previous socialist welfare institutions, the authorities have gradually implemented modern welfare policies (more so in China than in Vietnam, and more in Vietnam than in Laos) in order to ensure social stability, of which private solutions are important parts. Fourth, development success has led to massive structural changes in the socio-economic landscapes in these countries, like ageing, urbanization and changing employment patterns, and the authorities have been forced to respond to these changes. In Europe, the socialist left embraced neoliberalism to remain relevant for the voters, while in the one-party systems in China, Vietnam and Laos, the authorities embraced part of the neoliberal logic as a strategy for regime survival. Nevertheless, as London reminds us in his chapter, although the socialist market economies reflect elements of neoliberalism, their political economies are not usefully understood as neoliberal.

The urban middle classes, the old enemies of the socialist project of a classless society, are now a central part of the of the 'socialist market economy' project, although the term class is usually avoided. The middle classes, or middle-income groups in party rhetoric, are incorporated into the project to ensure stability, and are seen as a pillar in the transition to a more consumer-based economic model. According to Hansen, the middle classes are generally relatively satisfied with the 'socialist market economy', at least as long as it continues to deliver economic growth.

The 'socialist market economy' model shares some similarities with European democratic socialism in embracing elements of neoliberalism, and it resembles the original East Asian developmental state model in how the state continues to play a strong role governing the economy. Yet, the 'socialist market economy' model has some unique characteristics. One obvious distinction is the one-party system with elements from the old Leninist structures, and how this informs the protection of rights, and issues like transparency and accountability. The shortcomings with regard to labour rights are illustrated by Nordhaug in this volume. Another divergent characteristic of the 'socialist market economy' is the state control of land ownership. Furthermore, as discussed by Bekkevold, the 'socialist market economy' model has been moulded in the context of a world economy very different from the time of the classical East Asian developmental state.

The strongest trademark of the 'socialist market economy' model may be its pragmatism with regard to socialism and the market economy. The famous slogans associated with Deng Xiaoping—'*it doesn't matter whether a cat is black or white, as long as it catches mice*' and 'let some people get rich first', has continued to be a strong guide throughout the reform process. The socialist legacy still has a prominent position in party documents and rhetoric, but the solutions are increasingly market based. The pragmatism actually goes beyond embracing the market. As Rehbein discusses in detail, Laos under a socialist market economy is a hybrid of socialism, capitalism and earlier structures. In China and Vietnam, Confucianism, another old enemy of the communist revolutions, is now embraced, connecting the model with their pre-socialist legacy.

State and Market

Despite similarities with the East Asian developmental state in terms of the role of the state, China, Vietnam and Laos have been more open to trade and foreign investments in the early phase of their reforms, but like their developmental state predecessors they were also able to reap the benefits of globalization through labour-intensive manufacturing. The combination of one-party rule and being late developers within the context of a neoliberal global economy has made the socialist market economy into a unique development model.

The market and private enterprises are now integral parts of the socialist market economy. For example, the Vietnamese Party Congress in 2016 for the first time acknowledged the contribution of the private sector to the economy, and at the 5th Plenum of the Vietnamese Communist Party Central Committee in 2017, it was stated that the private sector shall be treated on a par with other sectors of the economy. Nevertheless, at the core of the socialist market economy is the idea that the state should retain control of key economic sectors.

One important way of retaining state control of the economy has been through state-owned enterprises, but in all three countries the state is now more selective in its ownership, with a focus on strategic sectors. SOEs should thus be restricted to sectors such as natural resources and public utilities that are not sufficiently remunerative for the private sector, and sectors that are important for national defence. In Laos, the authorities have undertaken considerable privatization even within one of the country's key economic sectors, hydropower electricity, and electricity companies still owned by the state are reformed into self-financing commercial entities (Songvilay et al. 2017).

Examining reforms of state-owned enterprises in Vietnam, Knutsen and Do Ta Khanh find that since 2016 there have been attempts to speed up equitization and privatization of the SOEs. In contrast to earlier reforms of the SOEs when Vietnamese authorities largely responded to demands from external agencies such as the World Bank, the policy agenda is now more motivated 'from within', driven by bad debt and corruption in state-owned enterprises. The plan is to accelerate equitization of the remaining SOEs that are not engaged in strategic industries, and sell a larger portion of the shares in already equitized SOEs and list them on the stock exchange. However, in their respective chapters, Knutsen and Do Ta Khanh as well as Bui Hai Thiem, discuss how bureaucratic obstacles and vested interests have contributed to slow down the reforms.

The transition from plan to market economy in China, Vietnam and Laos is slowest in the financial sector. In his chapter, Bekkevold discusses how the state largely remain in control in banking, finance and monetary policies, and that the state in all three countries willingly intervene and regulate the capital markets and their stock exchanges. China, Vietnam and Laos have tried to develop policies that both embrace the global economy and at the same time shield their political system and economy from too much exposure and pressures for reform. They were able to take advantage of being latecomers, integrating into global value chains through trade in goods and facilitating for inward FDIs, and viewed trade and incoming FDI as necessary tools for economic growth without losing too much control of their respective economic policies, whereas they have taken a more careful approach embracing capital market deregulation and foreign portfolio investments. The severe economic and political consequences of the Asian financial crisis convinced them to strengthen their banking and financial systems, but also to maintain a more careful approach towards financial globalization.

The stock markets in all three countries are comparatively new phenomena, and although foreign participation in their stock and bond markets has risen in recent years, it remains relatively low compared with international peers. Still, the Shanghai and Shenzhen stock exchanges are already among the largest in the world in terms of market capitalization. As Bekkevold notes, such a fast growth of newly established stock exchanges with immature regulatory agencies, human resources, auditing and reporting would cause growing pains in any country. As discussed by Bekkevold, the World Bank, the Asian Development Bank and the International Monetary Fund all point to vulnerabilities in the financial systems of China, Vietnam and Laos. Building institutions, regulatory agencies, laws and competence to run a market economy takes time, and is still very much an unfinished business in all three countries.

State, Market and the Environment

The 'socialist market economy' model has failed with regard to environmental sustainability, at least up to this point in history. The rapid economic development has taken a heavy toll on natural resources and the environment in China, Vietnam and Laos. The enormous scale of China's economic growth has turned it into the world's largest emitter of climate gases, contributing to environmental degradation on a global scale. Emissions are increasing rapidly also in Vietnam, although on a smaller scale. Furthermore, in all three countries, climate change and natural disasters threaten to undermine development.

Cole and Ingalls indeed note that Vietnam's and China's exploitation of land and natural resources to meet economic priorities has begun to take hold across the border in Laos, pointing to growing environmental and human impacts as intensive commercial agriculture has expanded into marginal rural spaces. While China and Vietnam have had some success in reforestation, they have exported deforestation to Laos, which has become a frontier for investments in exploitation of land and natural resources in the Mekong region. The abundant rivers of Laos are being dammed according to the government's target of becoming the 'battery of Asia', and although hydropower is a clean energy source and the policy is presented as 'green growth' it has irreversible environmental impacts, undermining the viability of fisheries in the rivers, displacing livelihoods and riverine farming and fishing communities.

In addition, Ortmann reminds us that Vietnam is one of the most affected countries when it comes to climate change, with flooding of coastal areas, salinated water destroying farming areas and extreme droughts. By 2050, almost ten per cent of Vietnam's population is expected to be affected by coastal flooding (UNDP 2019). Climate change will also seriously affect economic growth and livelihood in China as well as in Laos.

Explaining the reasons for the relatively bad environmental protection record in the socialist market economy, Ortmann in his chapter points to how economic growth has been the basis for the legitimacy of the regimes, to the detriment of environmental sustainability. Moreover, there is a lack of checks-and-balances in the system, and many within the governments have profited disproportionately from exploitation of the environment as the economic growth took off to unprecedented heights. Furthermore, authorities have had low environmental awareness, with a shortage of skilled personnel within the government to implement environmental programmes.

Nonetheless, the situation is not totally dark. China is seemingly taking the environmental challenge seriously. It is now taking leadership in international climate diplomacy, which is a huge step forward from only one decade ago. After the COP 15 meeting in Copenhagen in 2009, China was accused of 'holding the world ransom' and seen by many as a climate laggard (McCarthy 2009). Today, China is an indispensable party to all matters concerning global climate change (Kaneti 2020). China has implemented a wide set of policies in sectors like energy, mining, food, forestry and water to rectify decades of environmental neglect, and it is working towards a change in its energy mix with a larger percentage of green energy (Bekkevold and Tunsjø 2018). However, it will take a long time before China runs on green energy. For instance, coal consumption peaked in China in 2013, and government efforts to improve the energy structure saw coal use fall for a number of years. The decline halted and consumption rose again in 2018, suggesting China at times will de-prioritize energy saving and emissions reduction to keep its economy running (Hao and Baxter 2019).

Vietnam's environmental governance capacity is not as strong as in China, but as Ortmann discusses in his chapter, environmental sustainability started to climb higher on the agenda of Vietnamese policymakers after the turn on the century. According to Ortmann, Vietnam's authorities have strengthened the power and professionalism of environmental agencies, implemented a number of legal reforms, and built a stronger partnership with corporations, NGOs and foreign donors in order to benefit from their resources and skills. Similar to China, a focus on renewable energy—mainly hydro but increasingly also solar—coexists with large, state-owned coal and petroleum sectors.

In all three countries, China, Vietnam and Laos, environmental sector management is relatively inclusive sector in the sense that the public is being consulted and involved in policies to a larger extent than on other matters. Ortmann points to the rapid growth of new societal actors in Vietnam as the clearest indicator of the evolving governance structures, and these groups are starting to play an unprecedented role in policy-making and implementation. Activism outside of the state apparatus on environmental issues has been tolerated and even sometimes encouraged. In addition, there has been an increase in environmental protests in local communities, and in some cases the public have been successful in pressuring local governments and businesses to comply with environmental regulations. The emergence of social media has also helped activists to mobilize communities for environmental causes.

A similar development is observed in China. In 2013, the Xi Jinping administration fully embraced the concept of 'Ecological Civilization', which has been promoted as an ideological framework for guiding the future of Chinese politics and society. In 2014, the Chinese government revised the Environmental Protection Law for the first time since 1989. The modified law strengthened environmental protection by fining polluters. NGOs were permitted to bring public interest lawsuits against those who violated the law, while local officials were held accountable for the environmental standard in their regions (Mühlhahn 2019).

These initiatives from the political centre contribute to increased public awareness, and within this framework there is space for protests and negotiations at the local level between authorities and citizens (Hansen and Liu 2018). There is a 'mixture of authoritarian and democratic features' at the implementation stage of environmental policies in China (Ahlers and Shen 2018). That said, China's 'environmental state' is found to be strong in rhetoric and strategies yet often weak in implementation (Turiel et al. 2017).

The environmental sector in China, Vietnam and Laos is global both in terms of increasingly contributing to global climate change, as well as in how the authorities in these countries now engage with the international community to address the challenge. As Ortmann and Cole and Ingalls show in their respective chapters, a wide range of international actors, including governments, international organizations like the World Bank, the Asian Development Bank and various United Nations agencies, large multinational corporations and civil society organizations such as the World Wide Fund for Nature (WWF), participate in the policymaking process and the implementation of environmental policies.

State and Society

China has the most unequal income distribution of the three socialist market economies. This has been a source of growing social tension. During the leadership of Hu Jintao and Wen Jiabao in the early and mid-2000s, the government rolled out a series of social policy initiatives as a response to these tensions and to stimulate domestic consumption and economic growth. At the time, unfair access to basic social services was an important reason for a growing number of local protests across the country, and people saved a large part of their income to pay for basic welfare. The Chinese government abolished agricultural taxes, extended health insurance, secured access to basic education, pensions and provided income support to both rural and urban residents. Particular emphasis was put on reducing the gap between urban and rural populations and a campaign to improve life in rural areas—'Building a new and socialist countryside'—was launched.

Social policies continues to be a key instrument for the Chinese government also under Xi Jinping. As observed by Dalen in her chapter, high economic growth both forced and allowed the Chinese government to develop a more comprehensive social policy, and she argues that China has come a long way towards a universal welfare state for all Chinese citizens. In China, the official policy is now that the government is responsible for providing basic medical services or purchasing certain services, and that non-basic medical services should be provided by the market. In 2013 the Chinese government presented detailed guidelines on developing a large-scale industry of private health services, while non-profit civil society organizations are seen as an integral part of the social policy system. Moreover, China is giving increased priority to digital solutions such as e-health and e-learning. In fact, China has emerged as one of the global leaders in promoting information and communication technology for education (ICT4E).

Even though China has taken important steps to establish a more comprehensive welfare system, it still faces daunting challenges related to inequality. While income is distributed more evenly in Vietnam and Laos than China, their performances are also wanting. The elites in all three countries, including the most powerful so-called 'cadre-capitalist' class (So 2003), have accumulated significant amounts of wealth and power. China's wealthy are among the richest in the world, with a steady increase in the number of super rich. While this number saw a slump in 2019 following economic slowdown (Forbes 2019a), the wealth of the richest among them has continued increasing (Forbes 2019b). Five Vietnamese billionaires make it to Forbes' list of the richest people in the world, including Vietnam's richest person and owner of the powerful Vingroup conglomerate, Pham Nhat Vuong (Dat Nguyen 2019). The rich in Laos have not made it to the Forbes list, but the fact that former long-serving

President Khamtai Siphandone is close to being a billionaire and considered the country's wealthiest man (ProspectsASEAN 2018) serves as a reminder of the close connection between politics and economy also there. In his contribution to this volume, Hansen shows that not only the rich, but also the new socialist middle classes openly display their wealth. Yet, displaying wealth can be risky. A number of billionaires in China have been imprisoned and even executed if they cross the line in terms of crimes, corruption or have the wrong political ties (Anderlini 2017; Chao 2013).

Smallholder farmers were at the core of the early socialist revolutions. In the socialist period the farmers became rural workers in collective agriculture, although the depth and duration of collectivization varied between countries and regions. During the market reforms farming families received use rights to land, and smallholder family agriculture became the prevalent model of the socialist market economies. Rural income growth lagged behind urban growth in the market reforms. This trend has however been reversed in China and Vietnam, although the urban–rural income gap remains high. In Vietnam the average urban to rural income ratio declined from 2.3 in 2000 to 1.9 in 2016 (CEIC, n.d.) In China urban–rural income disparities peaked in 2009 and have declined since then. The average urban to rural income ratio was 2.7 in 2018 (Naughton 2018: 144; China Statistical Yearbook: Tables 6–11, 6–23). Data are more sparse when it comes to Laos, making a comparison difficult, but urban–rural inequalities in terms of consumption were growing from a relatively low starting point during the period 2007/2008–2012/2013 (World Bank 2014: 2, Table 4). There are obvious and stark inequalities between ethnic majority and minority populations, and ethnic minorities are grossly overrepresented in poverty statistics in all three countries (Banik and Hansen 2016; Pimhidzai and Houng Vu 2017).

Another challenge is the transformation of the labour market, with more people employed in the so-called 'grey economy' outside the established social safety net. Labour-intensive production with low-cost labour, mainly from rural migrants, have formed the backbone of the export-oriented industrialization models in China and Vietnam. As Nordhaug shows in his chapter, party-controlled labour unions have not allowed for the countervailing force of labour unions against employers, resulting in the economic growth taking place under often dire conditions for the workers. Interestingly, Nordhaug demonstrates that Vietnamese local authorities are more favourably inclined to the demands of workers than their Chinese counterparts. Nonetheless, labour contracts in the manufacturing industries guarantees access to basic services for an increasing number of workers, but this is changing as the economy moves away from traditional industries towards services and innovation, particularly in China.

Looking into the future, it will be increasingly challenging for the socialist market economies to fund the growing demands for welfare, as is the case for many Asian (and indeed also American and European) countries. This is the case in China, where the growth is slowing. And in all three countries increased living standards have changed expectations towards higher demands, particularly from the emerging middle classes.

China is soon home to the largest middle class in the world, and Vietnam has perhaps the most rapidly growing middle class in Southeast Asia. In his chapter, Hansen argues that to keep the middle classes satisfied, the socialist market economies are more dependent than ever on delivering development, and as Dalen reminds us, this also includes welfare services. At the same time, China continues to face serious population challenges such as low and decreasing fertility, a rapidly growing elderly population and a shrinking labour force. In the years to come, further tax reforms will be crucial in the financing of an ever expanding Chinese welfare state, but Dalen observes that as for now, the willingness to pay individual tax is low in China, meaning that indirect taxes and company tax are important sources for financing welfare. Moreover, there is a preference in China of the government as the main provider of welfare services, presenting the government with a challenge in promoting non-state actors as key in the service delivery. In the transition to an economy driven by services and consumption, where innovation, technology and education will be key, new 'winners and losers' will emerge in the socialist market economy, and new social risks can arise.

Development Models, Competition and Collaboration

China, Vietnam and Laos share the core characteristics of the 'socialist market economy' model presented earlier in this chapter. The one-party system is in place in all three countries, as is the restrictive regime with regard to land ownership. They have all embraced important elements of neoliberalism, but with the state still in control of key sectors of the economy. For instance, they have all been relatively open towards trade and incoming foreign direct investment, and share similar reservations with regard to liberalization of their bank and finance sector as well as monetary policies. China, Vietnam and Laos have all been late-developers and pursued state-led strategies in a global context of neoliberalization.

The three countries have to different extents been able to take advantage of their latecomer position, particularly in terms of attracting foreign investments. China has managed to develop a strong domestic industry sector and is moving towards high-tech, while Vietnam has faced a 'stalled transition' (Masina and Cerimele 2018) and mainly been able to develop a FDI-led labour-intensive industry sector which to a large extent depends on foreign technology. Laos is in this regard the odd one out, and has hardly seen any industrial development. Remaining a largely agrarian and resource-exporting economy, the country's development strategies and paths have diverged significantly from those of its two considerably larger and more powerful neighbours. Furthermore, unlike China, Vietnam and Laos were heavily reliant on foreign aid in the early phase of reform, and Laos to some degree still is.

The liberalization of trade and investments has facilitated for closer economic cooperation between China, Vietnam and Laos, both through bilateral channels, between Vietnam and Laos within the framework of the ASEAN Economic Community, and with China through the China–ASEAN Free Trade Area. Nonetheless, as Bekkevold elaborates on in his contribution, China, Vietnam and Laos have historically had a complex relationship, and some disagreements continue to shape and limit their level of cooperation.

One controversial issue is the damming of rivers in Laos, which takes place with strong Chinese involvement, and with mainly negative consequences for Vietnam (see RFA, 2016 for a useful overview). Due to the impact of damming on water levels in the Mekong, Vietnamese authorities have long been critical towards hydropower developments in Laos, but Vietnam is also concerned about China's increasingly strong foothold in Laos, Vietnam's historical ally. Interestingly, in 2019, the state-owned oil company PetroVietnam decided to invest in the construction of a large dam close to Luang Prabang in Laos, despite official Vietnamese statements against further damming of the Mekong. It is uncertain whether this decision was driven by commercial or geopolitical motives (Fawthrop 2019).

China has emerged as the most important economic investor and developmental partner for Laos. Although Thailand remains Laos' main trading partner, China's position in Laos is expected to be further enhanced by the Belt and Road Initiative (BRI). Laos, as well as Cambodia (Pang 2017), seems to be drifting into China's sphere of influence. The situation is different with regard to Vietnam. For historic reasons, there is still strong anti-Chinese currents among the Vietnamese population, and as both Bui Hai Thiem and Bekkevold point to, they have overlapping claims in the South China Sea that goes to the core of national security concerns in both countries. Vietnam seems to have more will and ability to resist a strong Chinese influence than Laos.

The degree of cooperation between China, Vietnam and Laos and the coherence of their model, will continue to be shaped partly by national characteristics and priorities, and partly by the international context at any given time. In the next and final part of this chapter, we will look at some potential developments and research agendas with regard to the future of the socialist market economy, at both the domestic and international level.

Future Developments and Research Agendas

An exhaustive list of future research agendas related to the development of China, Vietnam and Laos is beyond the scope of this brief summary. Yet we identify three broad clusters of issues that will be of importance; economic development strategies; political developments; and the positioning of these communist regimes within a changing international environment. Developments in these three clusters are closely connected and will influence each other. Let us first look at economic development. China is in the midst of several transitions of its economy, from export-driven to consumption-driven growth, from high growth to sustainable growth, and from labour-intensive to innovation-driven growth, and it is doing so with a mix of state and market, and eventually Vietnam may face many of the same challenges as China in their industrial upgrading.

One development to follow with particular scrutiny is the role of the state in innovation (Baark 2016). China has a very ambitious high-tech agenda, including the 'Made in China 2025' programme. This is at least so far mainly a state-led industrial policy that seeks to make China dominant in global high-tech manufacturing (McBride and Chatzky 2019). Many of the sectors in this programme are viewed as strategic industries, and the state is firmly in the grasp of it through an 'elite empire of state-owned enterprises' (Baark 2016; Naughton and Tsai 2015). As a response to harsh criticism from the United States, calling the 'Made in China 2025' a subsidy-stuffer to advance China as a global technology leader at U.S. expense, China has downplayed the policy, but not changed it (Wei 2019). To the extent that China's entry into the fourth generation industrial revolution and the introduction of artificial intelligence will be state dominated or more a mix of state and private entrepreneurs will be important for the future of its economic model. In Vietnam there has so far been much talk of developing a domestic high-tech agenda, and there have been attempts to use the state-owned corporation sector to strengthen upgrade yet industrial policies have largely been missing, or unsuccessful. One important exception to this rule appears to be Vietnam's state-owned telecommunications industry (Ngo 2020: 198).

Economic upgrading may be necessary to sustain the human development of the socialist market economies, but it is probably not sufficient. As argued by Nordhaug in his chapter, the socialist market economies face an uneasy balance between 'accumulation' and 'legitimation'. This applies not only to industrial relations, but also to welfare and sustainable development. Human development and sustainable development will be important to avoid labour conflicts, conflicts over land and environmental protests that may not only disturb economic development but also result in instability. It remains to be seen to what extent responsiveness towards popular concerns and increasing attention to environmental governance will contribute towards mitigating the so far dramatic environmental unsustainability of the socialist market economy.

The second cluster of issues that will inform the future of the socialist market economy is political developments. Due to the continued one-party system in China, Vietnam and Laos, special attention has to be given to political developments within these countries. In multiparty systems, the emphasis on state versus market solutions will move in cycles depending on whether the government is predominantly left or right wing. As alluded to in our introduction, the gradual and evolutionary introduction of market reforms in China, Vietnam and Laos have not been linear either, and each country has faced crossroads where they have halted, turned or even reversed the process. Bui Hai Thiem calls this the 'double movement of accommodating and resisting neoliberalism'. The political-economic cycles in the socialist market economies are not driven by change of government, but by internal disagreements, fractions, leadership priorities or reactions to internal or external shocks, like for instance the Asian financial crisis in the late 1990s.

In this volume, Rehbein describes how Laos since its Tenth Party Congress in 2016 seems to have returned to a more socialist agenda, and the agenda is pushed by the remaining heroes of the revolution of 1975. A growing number of reports argue that particularly China—but also Vietnam (Amnesty International 2018)—has rather become more rigidly suppressive in recent years (McGregor 2019; Economy 2018). In China, the Communist Party is seen as taking on a larger role in all aspects of society and governance (Batke 2018), and the separation of party and government initiated under Deng Xiaoping is now being reversed, driving China in the direction of neo-socialism with a fusion of party and state responsibilities (Brødsgaard 2018). China is attracting attention globally for its methods and innovative ways of policing society, including through its social credit system which is often portrayed as a dystopian nightmare resembling an Orwellian 'big brother' society (Mosher 2019; Chorzempa et al. 2018). Furthermore, there is a concern that the all-powerful leadership of Xi Jinping is weakening institutional governance (Shirk 2018), and it is even suggested that China has entered into some form of crony capitalism (Pei 2016). There is an inherent danger in top-down driven systems of suppressing development.

The future role of the expanding middle classes, as discussed by Hansen in this volume, merits further research, including on how it might influence political developments. So far, however, the middle class seems to be 'very much of the system' (Gainsborough 2010: 17). The uneasy relationship between the moral expectations in party rhetoric towards responsible consumption and the embeddedness of increasing consumption in the socialist market economy will also be important, particularly since the consumption patterns of these new middle classes will have global environmental consequences. Another topic to follow is the debate about authoritarian resilience, and the ability of the regimes to adapt to the changing environment (Fewsmith and Nathan 2019; Nathan 2003; McGregor 2010; Shambaugh 2008).

The third main cluster of issues that will shape the future of the socialist market economy is larger events and structural changes at the international level. The Asian financial crisis in the late 1990s and the global financial crisis a decade later in different ways informed developments in China, Vietnam and Laos. Even though the Asian financial crisis discredited the East Asian developmental state model at a global level, China, Vietnam and Laos interpreted the crisis differently, and in the process of strengthening their financial systems, they made sure that the state remained in control of the bank and finance sector (Wong 2004). The global financial crisis, at least as seen from Beijing, increased the confidence in their own state-driven model, but it again led to another round of debate on how to safeguard 'financial sovereignty' (Li and Zhou 2015).

The world economy is now facing another type of international challenge, in the form of the Covid-19 virus. It brings two lessons for China, and possibly for the socialist market economy as model. First, the foot-dragging management of the outbreak of the virus in China will lead to internal criticism and demands for increased transparency, similar to what happened in the aftermath of the SARS in 2003 (Chi 2003). Second, the effective manner in which the Chinese government has managed to contain the spread of the virus will certainly contribute to boost the confidence of the leadership in Beijing with regard to its own model.

Although originating in China, the virus has larger consequences outside of China. At the time of writing, it is too early to comprehend the consequences of what is unfolding, but Chinese authorities have managed to largely contain the spread of the virus to one single province, while in most other countries, and in particular in Europe and in the United States, the virus is spreading across larger parts of the countries. It means that whereas China can do with a local shutdown of activities, other countries have to implement a nationwide shutdown for an extended period, with long-term and wide-ranging economic consequences. Already, a few weeks into the crisis, it is speculated that the Covid-19 crisis will further increase the standing of China on the international scene (Campbell and Doshi 2020), and end globalization as we know it (Farrell and Newman 2020). In that case, the Covid-19 crisis will reinforce structural changes in world politics that have been unfolding for some time already, as discussed by Bekkevold in his contribution to the volume.

Developed market economies are increasingly sceptical towards China's economic model, criticizing China's use of state subsidies, unfair trade policies and manipulation of the currency. The United States has since the 1990s continuously conveyed this criticism towards China, but due to China's recent arrival as an economic competitor and rival, the United States is now more willing to follow up its criticism with actual policies, and Europe and other developed countries have turned more critical towards China. In the United States and Europe, the demand for protectionism is growing. In January 2020, the United States and China reached a Phase-1 commercial agreement that brought to close their intense trade war, but it is argued that this deal may only be a short-term solution, and that the U.S.–China relationship increasingly will be characterized by a more permanent situation of economic competition and rivalry.

At the core of the U.S.–China rivalry is China's rise as peer-competitor, and not only in economic terms, but as a military power. The United States is responding to this by moving military assets to Asia, and by decoupling parts of its economic ties to China. World politics is moving from an era of deep globalization to a world more characterized by a political and economic divide between the United States and China. If this scenario unfolds, it will have consequences for how connected China will be to the world economy, and the balance of state and market in its development model. During China's trade war with the United States a number of foreign-invested enterprises moved their operations from China to Vietnam. Nonetheless, in a more long-term outlook, a political-economic divide between China and the United States will place Vietnam as well as Laos within China's sphere of influence.

References

Ahlers, Anna L., and Yongdong Shen. 2018. Breathe Easy? Local Nuances of Authoritarian Environmentalism in China's Battle Against Air Pollution. *The China Quarterly* 234: 299–319.

Amnesty International. 2018. *Amnesty International Report 2017/18: The State of the World's Human Rights*. London: Amnesty International.

Anderlini, Jamil. 2017. China Sends Its Billionaires a Chilling Message. *Financial Times*, February 1. https://www.ft.com/content/4335d364-e7d4-11e6-893c-082c54a7f539.

Baark, Erik. 2016. The Chinese State and Its Role in Shaping China's Innovation System. In *The Asian Developmental State: Reexaminations and New Departures*, ed. Yin-wah Chu, 159–173. New York: Palgrave-Macmillan.

Banik, Dan, and Arve Hansen. 2016. The Frontiers of Poverty Reduction in Emerging Asia. *Forum for Development Studies* 43 (1): 47–68. https://doi.org/10.1080/08039410.2015.1134646.

Batke, Jessica. 2018. *Party All the Time: Governance and Society in the New Era*. Winter, Issue 55, Hoover Institution: China Leadership Monitor.

Bekkevold, Jo Inge, and Øystein Tunsjø. 2018. Sustaining Growth: Energy and Natural Resources. In *The Sage Handbook of Contemporary China*, ed. Weiping Wu and Mark Frazier, 262–280. London: Sage.

Berman, Sheri, and Maria Snegovaya. 2019. Populism and the Decline of Social Democracy. *Journal of Democracy* 30 (3): 5–19.

Brødsgaard, K. E. 2018. China's Political Order Under Xi Jinping: Concepts and Perspectives. *China: An International Journal* 16 (3): 1–17.

Campbell, Kurt M., and Rush Doshi. 2020. The Coronavirus Could Reshape Global Order: China Is Maneuvering for International Leadership as the United States Falters. *Foreign Affairs*, March 18. https://www.foreignaffairs.com/articles/china/2020-03-18/coronavirus-could-reshape-global-order.

Carlile, Lonny E. 1994. Party Politics and the Japanese Labor Movement: Rengo's 'New Political Force'. *Asian Survey* 34 (7): 606–620.

Congiu, Francesca. 2011. Taiwan: The Organized Labour Movements and Its Obstacles. *Rivista Degli Studi Orientali* 84 (1/4): 217–233.

CEIC. No date. *Vietnam Monthly Income Per Capita*. Retrieved 29 March 2020. https://www.ceicdata.com/en/vietnam/monthly-income-per-capita.

Chao, Rebecca. 2013. Why Do Chinese Billionaires Keep Ending Up in Prison? *The Atlantic*, January 29. https://www.theatlantic.com/international/archive/2013/01/why-do-chinese-billionaires-keep-ending-up-in-prison/272633/.

Chen, Theodore Hsi-en. 1969. The New Socialist Man. *Comparative Education Review* 13 (1): 88–95.

Chi, Fulin. 2003. *Alarming Bell: China, SARS Crisis and System Reform*. Transition Report 2003, China Institute for Reform and Development.

Chorzempa, Martin, Paul Triolo, and Samm Sacks. 2018. China's Social Credit System: A Mark of Progress or a Threat to Privacy? *Policy Brief*, 18–14. Washington, DC: Peterson Institute for International Economics. https://www.piie.com/system/files/documents/pb18-14.pdf.

Creak, Simon, and Keith Barney. 2018. Conceptualising Party-State Governance and Rule in Laos. *Journal of Contemporary Asia* 48 (5): 693–716.

Cumings, Bruce. 1984. The Origins and Development of the Northeast Asian Political Economy: Industrial Sectors, Product Cycles, and Political Consequences. *International Organization* 38 (1): 1–40.

Dat Nguyen, T. 2019. Vietnam Billionaire Count Rises to 5 on Forbes List. https://e.vnexpress.net/news/business/companies/vietnam-billionaire-count-rises-to-5-on-forbes-list-3890145.html. 5 March 2019.

EIA. 2016. Leaked Report Reveals Huge Scale of Laos Illegal Logging. https://eia-international.org/news/leaked-report-reveals-huge-scale-of-illegal-logging-in-laos/.

Economy, Elizabeth C. 2018. *The Third Revolution: Xi Jinping and the New Chinese State*. Oxford: Oxford University Press.

Farrell, Henry, and Abraham Newman. 2020. Will the Coronavirus End Globalization as We Know It?: The Pandemic Is Exposing Market Vulnerabilities No One Knew Existed. *Foreign Affairs*, March 16. https://www.foreignaffairs.com/articles/2020-03-16/will-coronavirus-end-globalization-we-know-it.

Fawthrop, Tom. 2019. Did Vietnam Just Doom the Mekong? *The Diplomat*, November 26. https://thediplomat.com/2019/11/did-vietnam-just-doom-the-mekong/.

Fewsmith, Joseph, and Andrew J. Nathan. 2019. Authoritarian Resilience Revisited: Joseph Fewsmith with Response from Andrew J. Nathan. *Journal of Contemporary China* 28: 116, 167–179.

Forbes. 2019a. Billionaires: The Richest People in the World, March 5. https://www.forbes.com/billionaires/#3a5adf64251c.

Forbes. 2019b. Wealth of 400 Tycoons on 2019 Forbes China Rich List Rises by More Than a Fifth Despite Slowdown and Trade Friction. https://www.forbes.com/sites/forbespr/2019/11/06/wealth-of-400-tycoons-on-2019-forbes-china-rich-list-rises-by-more-than-a-fifth-despite-slowdown-and-trade-friction/#53e3b7b11e6c.

Gainsborough, Martin. 2010. Present but not Powerful: Neoliberalism, the State, and Development in Vietnam. *Globalizations* 7 (4): 475-488.

Giddens, Anthony. 2000. *The Third Way and Its Critics*. Cambridge, UK: Polity Press.

Hansen, Mette Halskov, and Zhaohui Liu. 2018. Air Pollution and Grassroots Echoes of 'Ecological Civilization' in Rural China. *The China Quarterly* 234: 320–339.

Hao, Feng, and Tom Baxter. 2019. China's Coal Consumption on the Rise. *China Dialogue*, March 1. Retrieved 21 March 2020. https://www.chinadialogue.net/.

Hayashi, Shigeko. 2010. The Developmental State in the Era of Globalization: Beyond the Northeast Asian Model of Political Economy. *The Pacific Review* 23 (1): 45–69.

Kaneti, Marina. 2020. China's Climate Diplomacy 2.0. *The Diplomat*, January 2. https://thediplomat.com/2020/01/chinas-climate-diplomacy-2-0/.

Kapur, Nick. 2018. *Japan at the Crossroads: Conflict and Compromise After Anpo*. Cambridge: Harvard University Press.

Lee, Byoung-Hoon. 2015. Changing Cross-Movement Coalitions Between Labor Unions and Civil Society Organizations in South Korea. *Development and Society* 44 (2): 199–218.

Lee, Yoonkyung. 2006. Varieties of Labor Politics in Northeast Asian Democracies: Political Institutions and Union Activism in Korea and Taiwan. *Asian Survey* 46 (5): 721–740.

Li, Guoping, and Hong Zhou. 2015. Globalization of Financial Capitalism and Its Impact on Financial Sovereignty. *World Review of Political Economy* 6 (2): 176–191.

Masina, Pietro. 2006. *Vietnam's Development Strategies*. London and New York: Routledge.

Masina, P., and M. Cerimele. 2018. Patterns of Industrialisation and the State of Industrial Labour in Post-WTO-Accession Vietnam. *European Journal of East Asian Studies* 17 (2): 1–36.

McBride, James, and Andrew Chatzky. 2019. Is 'Made in China 2025' a Threat to Global Trade? CFR Backgrounder, Council on Foreign Relations, May 13. https://www.cfr.org/backgrounder/made-china-2025-threat-global-trade.

McCarthy, Michael. 2009. China Holds the World to Ransom. *The Independent*, December 18. Retrieved 20 March 2020 from https://www.independent.co.uk/environment/climate-change/china-holds-the-world-to-ransom-1844247.html.

McGregor, Richard. 2010. *The Party: The Secret World of China's Communist Rulers*. Allen Lane: Penguin Books.

McGregor, Richard. 2019. Party Man: Xi Jinping's Quest to Dominate China. *Foreign Affairs* September/October. https://www.foreignaffairs.

Minns, John, and Robert Tierney. 2003. The Labour Movement in Taiwan. *Labour History* 85: 103–128.

Mosher, Steven W. 2019. China's New 'Social Credit System' Is a Dystopian Nightmare. *New York Post*, May 18. https://nypost.com/2019/05/18/chinas-new-social-credit-system-turns-orwells-1984-into-reality/.

Mudge, Stephanie L. 2018. *Leftism Reinvented: Western Parties from Socialism to Neoliberalism*. Cambridge: Harvard University Press.

Mühlhahn, Klaus. 2019. *Making China Modern: From the Great Qing to Xi Jinping*. Cambridge: Harvard University Press.

Nathan, Andrew J. 2003. China's Changing of the Guard: Authoritarian Resilience. *Journal of Democracy* 14 (1): 6–17.

Naughton, Barry. 2018. *The Chinese Economy: Adaptation and Growth*. Cambridge, MA: MIT Press.

Naughton, B., and K. Tsai (eds.). 2015. *State Capitalism, Institutional Adaptation, and the Chinese Miracle (Comparative Perspectives in Business History)*. Cambridge: Cambridge University Press.

Ngo, Christine Ngoc. 2020. *Rent Seeking and Development: The Political Economy of Development in Vietnam*. New York, NY: Routledge.

Pang, Edgard. 2017. 'Same-Same But Different': Laos and Cambodia's Political Embrace of China. *ISEAS Perspective* 66, September 5.

Pei, Minxin. 2016. *China's Crony Capitalism: The Dynamics of Regime Decay*. Harvard University Press.

Pimhidzai, Obert, and Linh Houng Vu. 2017. *Lao Poverty Policy Brief: Why Are Ethnic Minorities Poor?ເປັນຫຍັງຊົນເຜົ່າ ກຸ່ມນ້ອຍຈຶ່ງ ທຸກຍາກ?*.Washington, DC: World Bank Group.

ProspectsASEAN. 2018. Meet the 10 Richest People in Southeast Asia (by Country), September 8. https://www.prospectsasean.com/meet-10-richest-people-southeast-asia-by-country/.

Radice, Hugo. 2008. The Developmental State Under Global Neoliberalism. *Third World Quarterly* 29 (6): 1153–1174.

RFA—Radio Free Asia. 2016. Laos and Its Dams: Southeast Asia's Battery, Built by China. https://www.rfa.org/english/news/special/china-build-laos-dams/.

Rovny, Jan. 2018. What Happened to Europe's Left? *Blog*. London School of Economics and Political Science, February 20. https://blogs.lse.ac.uk/europpblog/2018/02/20/what-happened-to-europes-left/.

Sachsenröder, Wolfgang, and Ulrike E. Frings (eds.). 1998. *Political Party Systems and Democratic Development in East and Southeast Asia: East Asia*, vol. 2. Aldershot: Ashgate.

Saposs, David J. 1954. The Split Between Asian and Western Socialism. *Foreign Affairs* 32 (4): 588–594.

Shambaugh, David. 2008. *China's Communist Party: Atrophy and Adaptation*. Berkeley: University of California Press.

Shirk, Susan L. 2018. China in Xi's 'New Era': The Return to Personalistic Rule. *Journal of Democracy* 29 (2): 22–36.

So, Alvin Y., 2003. The Changing Pattern of Classes and Class Conflict in China, *Journal of Contemporary Asia* 33 (3): 363–376. https://doi.org/10.1080/00472330380000231.

Songvilay, Latdavanh, Sthabandith Insisienmay, and Mark Turner. 2017. Trial and Error in State-Owned Enterprise Reform in Laos. *Asian Perspective* 42: 239–262.

Stubbs, Richard. 2009. What Ever Happened to the East Asian Developmental State? The Unfolding Debate. *The Pacific Review* 22 (1): 1–22.

Tian, He. 2020. Transforming the East Asian Developmental State: Democratic Mobilisation and the Role of the Middle Class. *Asian Journal of Comparative Politics* 18: 1–18.

Turiel, J., I. Ding, and J. Liu. 2017. *Environmental Governance in China*. Leiden: Brill.

Vu, Tuong. 2010. *Paths to Development in Asia. South Korea, Vietnam, China, and Indonesia*. Cambridge: Cambridge University Press.

Wei, Lingling. 2019. Beijing Drops Contentious 'Made in China 2025' Slogan, But Policy Remains. *The Wall Street Journal*, March 5. https://www.wsj.com/articles/china-drops-a-policy-the-u-s-dislikes-at-least-in-name-11551795370.

Wong, Joseph. 2004. The Adaptive Developmental State in East Asia. *Journal of East Asian Studies* 4 (3): 345–362.

World Bank. 2002. *Vietnam Development Report 2003: Vietnam Delivering on its Promise*. Hanoi: World Bank.

World Bank. 2014. *Poverty Profile in Lao PDR: Poverty Report for the Lao Consumption and Expenditure Survey 2002–2013*. Vientiane: World Bank.

Correction to: Reforming State-Owned Enterprises in a Global Economy: The Case of Vietnam

Hege Merete Knutsen and Do Ta Khanh

Correction to:
Chapter 5 in: A. Hansen et al. (eds.),
***The Socialist Market Economy in Asia*,**
https://doi.org/10.1007/978-981-15-6248-8_5

Chapter 5, "Reforming State-Owned Enterprises in a Global Economy: The Case of Vietnam" was previously published non-open access. It has now been converted to open access under a CC BY 4.0 license and the Copyright Holder is "The Author(s)". The book has also been updated with this change.

The updated version of this chapter can be found at
https://doi.org/10.1007/978-981-15-6248-8_5

A. Hansen et al. (eds.), *The Socialist Market Economy in Asia*,
https://doi.org/10.1007/978-981-15-6248-8_13

Index

A. Hansen et al. (eds.), *The Socialist Market Economy in Asia*,
https://doi.org/10.1007/978-981-15-6248-8

X

Y

Z

The manufacturer's authorised representative in the EU is Springer
Nature Customer Service Centre GmbH, Europaplatz 3, 69115 Heidelberg,
Germany. If you have any concerns regarding our products, please
contact ProductSafety@springernature.com

Printed and bound by CPI Group (UK) Ltd, Croydon, CR0 4YY
30/09/2026
02225286-0012